SELF-DEFEATING BEHAVIORS

EXPERIMENTAL RESEARCH, CLINICAL IMPRESSIONS, AND PRACTICAL IMPLICATIONS

THE PLENUM SERIES IN SOCIAL / CLINICAL PSYCHOLOGY

Series Editor: C. R. Snyder

University of Kansas
Lawrence, Kansas

SELF-DEFEATING BEHAVIORS
Experimental Research, Clinical Impressions, and Practical Implications
Edited by Rebecca C. Curtis

A Continuation Order Plan is available for this series. A continuation order will bring delivery of each new volume immediately upon publication. Volumes are billed only upon actual shipment. For further information please contact the publisher.

SELF-DEFEATING BEHAVIORS

EXPERIMENTAL RESEARCH, CLINICAL IMPRESSIONS, AND PRACTICAL IMPLICATIONS

EDITED BY
REBECCA C. CURTIS

Adelphi University
Garden City, New York

PLENUM PRESS • NEW YORK AND LONDON

CONTRIBUTORS

CRAIG A. ANDERSON, Department of Psychology, University of Missouri—Columbia, Columbia, Missouri

STEVEN BERGLAS, McClean Hospital/Harvard Medical School, Belmont, Massachusetts

LISA M. BOSSIO, 4707 Fairway Drive, Rohnert Park, California

DONNAH CANAVAN, Department of Psychology, Boston College, Chestnut Hill, Massachusetts

REBECCA CURTIS, Department of Psychology, Adelphi University, Garden City, New York

JOHN M. DARLEY, Department of Psychology, Princeton University, Princeton, New Jersey

NORMAN T. FEATHER, Discipline of Psychology, The Finders University of South Australia, Bedford Park, South Australia

JOHN H. FLEMING, Department of Psychology, University of Minnesota, Minneapolis, Minnesota

ALLEN J. FRANCES, Department of Psychiatry, New York Hospital, Cornell Medical Center, Payne Whitney Clinic, New York, New York

ARTHUR FRANKEL, Department of Psychology, Salve Regina—The Newport College, Newport, Rhode Island

RAYMOND L. HIGGINS, Department of Psychology, University of Kansas, Lawrence, Kansas

JAMES L. HILTON, Department of Psychology, University of Michigan, Ann Arbor, Michigan

RONNIE JANOFF-BULMAN, Department of Psychology, University of Massachusetts-Amherst, Amherst, Massachusetts

CHRISTOPHER PETERSON, Department of Psychology, University of Michigan, Ann Arbor, Michigan

MORGAN P. SLUSHER, Department of Psychology, University of Missouri—Columbia, Columbia, Missouri

C. R. SNYDER, Department of Psychology, University of Kansas, Lawrence, Kansas

MEL L. SNYDER, Department of Psychology, Rutgers University, Newark, New Jersey

TIMOTHY J. STRAUMAN, Department of Psychology, University of Wisconsin-Madison, Madison, Wisconsin

CAROL E. THOMAS, Department of Psychology, University of Massachusetts-Amherst, Amherst, Massachusetts

THOMAS A. WIDIGER, Department of Psychology, University of Kentucky, Lexington, Kentucky

PREFACE

In the desert
I saw a creature, naked, bestial,
Who, squatting upon the ground,
Held his heart in his hands,
And ate of it.
I said: "Is it good, friend?"
"It is bitter—bitter," he answered;
But I like it
Because it is bitter,
And because it is my heart."

Stephen Crane
The Black Riders and Other Lines

"It is the function of great art to purge and give meaning to human suffering," wrote Bernard Knox (1982, p. 149) in his introduction to *Oedipus Rex*. This is done by showing some causal connection between the hero's free will and his suffering, by bringing to the fore the interplay of the forces of destiny and human freedom. Knox states that Freud was wrong when he suggested that it was "the particular nature of the material" in Oedipus that makes the play so deeply moving, and not the contrast between destiny and human will. Knox believes that this play has an overpowering effect upon us, not only because we share the tendency of Oedipus to direct "our first sexual impulse towards our mother" and "our first murderous wish against our father," as Freud tells us, but also because the theological modification of the legend introduced by Sophocles calls into question the sacred beliefs of our time (Knox, 1982, pp. 133–137). It is the juxtaposition of the forces of fate and free will that creates the tension in *Oedipus* and in our most powerful dramas, as Knox points out. So it is also in the interplay of these forces that tension is created in all of our lives. It is in our behaviors emanating out of these moments of conflict that we create meaning in our lives, and that we create our identities. Feeling the pull of opposing forces, we perpetuate or transform our ways of acting and our way of being. In so doing we defeat or enhance our "self."

appropriately to a wide variety of self-defeating behaviors, including those behaviors related to academic achievement, aging, physical abuse, institutionalization, and mental retardation.

Part III examines self-defeating behaviors as they may be related to chronic personality dispositions. Berglas proposes a model for such a disorder, suggesting three different subtypes. Widiger and Frances review the arguments for and against the inclusion of a separate psychiatric classification labeled "self-defeating personality." Strauman then assesses the state of the theory of the self in social and clinical psychology and argues that two types of motivation have been emphasized in examinations of the self-system: survival-related motives and consistency-related motives.

Finally, in Part IV, Curtis presents a model of self-defeating behaviors as developing from the expectation of unpleasant outcomes and as being especially difficult to change when they involve one's fundamental self-theories and views of others. It should be pointed out that the self-defeating behaviors explored in this volume are largely those which have been studied in the laboratories of experimental social psychologists and are not intended to be all-inclusive.

Theoretically, the volume begins with the external situations leading to particular types of self-defeating behaviors and ends with speculations about the personality dispositions which precede recurring behaviors. The chapters thus tend to move from those which focus upon social-psychological theory related to the development of self-defeating behaviors in normal people to those which focus more upon clinical theories and more pathological types of behavior. Because the book is intended for both social psychologists and practitioners from clinical and counseling psychology as well as psychiatry, it is unavoidable that the ideas presented may appear overly simplistic to the individual readers in some parts, yet obtuse in other parts.

Although the self-defeating behaviors discussed in the present volume excludes those resulting primarily from psychotic distortions of reality, the behaviors considered include a wide variety ranging from depression, sabotage of success at work and in relationships, and neglect of physical health.

REFERENCES

Baumeister, R. F. (1987). How the self became a problem: A psychological review of historical research. *Journal of Personality and Social Psychology, 52*, 163–176.

Bridgman, P. W. (1927). *The logic of modern physics*. New York: Macmillan.

Bridgman, P. W. (1952). *The nature of some of our physical concepts*. New York: Philosophical Library.

Bridgman, P. W. (1959). *The way things are*. Cambridge, MA: Harvard University Press.

Doi, T. (1986). *The anatomy of self: The individual versus society* (M.A. Harbison, Trans.). Tokyo: Kodansha International Ltd.

Dostoevsky, F. (1960). *Notes from the Underground* (R. E. Matlow, Trans.). New York: E. P. Dutton. (Original work published 1864)

Festinger, L. (1957). *A theory of cognitive dissonance*. Stanford, CA: Stanford University Press.

Freud, S. (1981). The economic problem in masochism. In J. Strachey (Ed.), *The standard edition of the complete psychological works of Sigmund Freud* (Vol. 19, 159–170). London: Hogarth Press. (Original work published 1924)

Hall, E. T. (1986). [Foreword]. In T. Doi (Ed.), *The anatomy of self: The individual versus society* (p. 7–10). Tokyo: Kodansha International Ltd.

Jaynes, J. (1976). *The origin of consciousness in the breakdown of the bicameral mind*. Boston: Houghton-Mifflin.

Leary, M. R., & Maddux, J. E. (1987). Progress toward a viable interface between social and clinical-counseling psychology. *American Psychologist, 42*, 904–911.

Leary, M. R., & Miller, R. S. (1986). *Social psychology and dysfunctional behavior*. New York: Springer-Verlag.

Schlenker, B. R. (1980). *Impression management. The self-concept, social identity, and interpersonal relations*. Monterey, CA: Brooks/Cole.

Schlenker, B. R. (1982). Translating actions into attitudes: An identity analytic approach to the explanation of social conduct. In L. Berkowitz (Ed.), *Advances in experimental social psychology* (Vol. 15, pp. 193–247). New York: Academic Press.

Skinner, B. F. (1969). *Contingencies of reinforcement: A theoretical analysis*. New York: Appleton-Century-Crofts.

Stevens, S. S. (1935). The operational basis of psychology. *American Journal of Psychology, 47*, 323–330.

haviors. Most obvious among these are various beliefs about the self, ranging from beliefs about personal competence to beliefs about one's physiological functioning. For example, John is assured by the "Famous Writers" correspondence school that he has great potential as a writer, only to find that friends who have answered the same advertisement have all received the same evaluation. This should suggest to John that the original information was of little value, yet John persists in believing that the evaluation is accurate in his case and embarks on a writing career destined for failure (after Ross, Lepper, & Hubbard, 1975). If this example seems divorced from common experience, consider the effects of evaluations that occur every day within our educational system. Feedback in schools is inherently focused on the perceived competence of the individual students. Given new information to learn or a novel task to master, a student will acquire a sense of competence (or lack thereof) based on experiences of success or failure. The fact that performance may reflect the quality of instruction as much as or more than personal ability is often overlooked. Rather, students who receive substandard instruction and experience subsequent failure often persist in believing in their lack of ability. This effect is so strong that it occurs even in those rare cases where the students are fully aware that they received inadequate training (Lepper, Ross, & Lau, 1986). Consequently, these students may show a decreased sense of self-efficacy (see Bandura, 1977), demonstrate decreased motivation, and never display or utilize the true ability they possess.

People often hold irrational beliefs about themselves or about the way their activities fit into the context of the social environment (Ellis, 1977). Such beliefs have been related to psychological conditions associated with self-defeating behaviors. For example, Anderson and Arnoult (1989) found that irrational beliefs were positively correlated with negative affect and depression. A person who believes that "In order to be truly happy, I must prove that I am thoroughly adequate and achieving in most things I attempt" may find it difficult to simultaneously believe that "I am a happy person" or even that "I can become a happy person." It may become a therapist's task to change the initial belief about the conditions necessary for personal happiness. Thus, a change in self-defeating behaviors associated with depression is often predicated on first changing a persistent maladaptive belief.

Beliefs about personal competence affect behavior in many realms of activity. For example, some people have severe doubts about their social abilities. As a consequence, they may avoid interpersonal interactions and develop a variety of interpersonal problems such as loneliness, shyness, and depression (Anderson & Arnoult, 1985a, 1985b; Anderson, Horowitz, & French, 1983; Horowitz, French, & Anderson, 1982). These problems occur even in people who, when forced to interact under various laboratory conditions, show no true social inability (Anderson, 1983c; Brodt & Zimbardo, 1981). Research relating perseverant beliefs to loneliness, shyness, and depression are examined in more detail later in this chapter.

Incorrect perceptions of superior skills also may lead to maladaptive behaviors. Business managers with inflated self-assessments may fail to request or properly use needed assistance on a given problem, resulting in even larger problems. Witness the decision errors made by NASA managers leading up to the destruction of the space shuttle *Challenger* and the deaths of seven crew members. The expertise for the proper decision was available but ignored (several engineers on the project strongly recommended against a launch attempt in the abnormally cold weather).

Less dramatic but more representative examples abound. In our own experience we have witnessed medical researchers who, in their ignorance of experimental methodology and their firm belief in their own skills, have wasted countless thousands of dollars and innumerable man-hours on valueless research. One of the present authors, while working on a bridge construction crew one summer, was almost drowned in an accident caused by a crane operator who overestimated his ability to maneuver his equipment.

Perceptions of ability are not, however, the only self-relevant beliefs that can lead to maladaptive behaviors. Erroneous beliefs about physiological functioning can lead to inappropriate actions as well. For example, this has been demonstrated among insomniacs concerned with the effects of exercise prior to bedtime. Objective measures show that the stimulation of exercise delays the onset of sleep. However, many insomniacs subjectively feel that the exhaustion associated with exercise actually helps them to sleep (Freedman & Papsdorf, 1976), and they therefore continue to engage in such self-defeating activity.

In sum, erroneous beliefs about oneself can lead to self-defeating behaviors in any domain of human enterprise. The resulting mistakes often injure others as well as oneself. Factors which perpetuate such maladaptive self-beliefs thus exacerbate the problem.

Beliefs about Someone Else

All too often, incorrect beliefs about other people (social impressions) also lead to self-defeating behaviors. An example is the businessman whose stereotype of Hispanics keeps him from hiring the most qualified applicant for a job—just because the person is Hispanic. Or consider the often ill-considered actions of a would-be lover who misattributes the friendly responses of his intended to more romantic motives, even after repeated denials. The growing awareness of so-called date rape in our society points to one serious consequence of such a scenario. Clearly, the attributions we make for the behaviors of another person can affect our own behavior toward that person, and mistaken attributions can lead to inappropriate reactions.

Our beliefs about others may also affect our motivation to emulate positive behavior. For example, a friend may succeed in making many new friends at a party while our own attempts meet with less success. Was our friend born with a magnetic personality or did she just use the right strategy to meet new people at the party? The latter attribution would suggest that we could also develop a successful strategy. The former attribution, however, could lead to self-defeating behaviors (e.g., giving up), because we have decided that the route to making new friends is unattainable.

Research on the (occasionally) long-lasting effects of first impressions also demonstrates self-defeating consequences of perseverant social impressions. Initial impressions bias interactions and judgments in a wide variety of contexts, ranging from formal job interviews (Dipboye & Macan, 1987) to informal "get acquainted" sessions (Snyder & Swann, 1978; Snyder, Tanke, & Berscheid, 1977).

Kelley's (1950) classic study of students' responses to a new instructor described as "warm" or "cold" reminds us of the self-defeating behaviors of a small but visible minority of students in our introductory classes. These students start the semester with the beliefs that psychology is simple and psychologists are stupid. This first impression, based on conversations with their advisors in the "real" sciences, leads to a variety of self-defeating behaviors including failure to study, failure to pay attention to lectures, and often failure of the class.

Initial impressions of another person may be based on limited exposure to that person or on reports from a mutual acquaintance. They also can be based on stereotypes about the person's social or racial class. Such stereotypic beliefs are but one example of a third type of belief leading to unwarranted and self-defeating behavior, namely, social theories.

Social Theories

Social theories are our beliefs about the relations between variables in the social environment. They are by nature causal belief systems; that is, social theories are beliefs about how, why, and in what way the variables in question are related. Thus, stereotypes are not simple listings of features typically associated with a given group but are in fact beliefs about features that are somehow causally related to the group (see Anderson & Sedikides, 1989). Other types of social theories also causally link variables in the social domain. For instance, beliefs relating personality traits of job incumbents to job performance are social theories if the traits are seen as being causally relevant to job performance (e.g., Anderson & Sechler, 1986). Irrational beliefs (e.g., Ellis, 1977) also can take the form of social theories, as when a person believes that only highly talented individuals can get the deepest kind of satisfaction out of their work. As noted earlier, beliefs such as these have been linked with depression and negative affect (Anderson & Arnoult, 1989). Other examples of self-defeating social theories might be beliefs that nice people come in last, anyone who dates is only interested in sex, or love can only lead to heartbreak.

Many judgments are made on the basis of social theories. Nuclear arms negotiations are heavily based on beliefs about how the various sides would behave under different military scenarios. Politicians make decisions regarding a host of matters incorporating social theories about economic policy and inflation, welfare programs and poverty, or education and productivity. When these people cling to outdated theories or poorly justified beliefs, they may jeopardize not only their own careers but the welfare of society as well. Even in the purportedly impartial atmosphere of the courtroom, social theories play an important role, as when a juror develops a belief concerning the guilt or innocence of the defendant based on a social theory relating the defendant's social category (e.g., race, sex, occupation) to the type of crime under investigation. Certainly, social theories play a large role in decisions about intimate relationships. A person who believes that love can only result in pain will most likely be unwilling to take the risks associated with intimacy.

A final example may help to focus on the important relation between incorrect beliefs, the perseverance of these beliefs, and the self-defeating behaviors that may result. In the United States, early cases of Acquired Immune Deficiency Syndrome (AIDS) were found primarily among gay men, drug abusers, and Haitians. This led the government to designate these as high-risk groups, with the media encouraging a popular mislabeling of the syndrome as a gay disease. As a result,many people came to believe that they would risk their health by any association with gay men, however casual. At the same time, sexual activity among nongay individuals was considered risk-free (at least for AIDS). However, with the discovery of the viral nature of AIDS, these beliefs were discredited. Medical concern shifted away from high-risk groups to emphasize the dangers of high-risk activities, activities that could be engaged in by anyone. Yet, indications are that many nongay individuals continue to believe that they are not at risk for AIDS, and so they continue to engage in risky activities. For a significant number of these people, the self-defeat associated with this particular perseverant belief may be final.

These examples provide an indication of the ubiquity of erroneous beliefs and self-defeating behavior and hint at the important role played by belief perseverance phenomena. People's beliefs are frequently based on faulty teachings or faulty evidence (or the faulty assimilation of valid evidence), or they may be grounded in circumstances that change, making previously reasonable beliefs reasonable no longer. Such experiences have stimulated a variety of questions which researchers have attempted to answer in recent years. What processes lead to the formation of erroneous beliefs? What are the characteristics of some beliefs that make them so resistant to change? How is new information processed in light of current beliefs? What is the continuing influence of discredited information? How can educational efforts challenge deeply ingrained beliefs that lead to maladaptive behaviors? These and related questions are being addressed by social scientists in both the theoretical and applied domains. In the next section we examine some of the origins of incorrect beliefs.

THE ORIGINS OF INCORRECT BELIEFS

Formal and Informal Socialization

Beliefs can arise from two conceptually distinct sources. First, there are the beliefs that we are taught, either formally, as in a classroom, or more informally through socialization into our culture. These beliefs come to us essentially prepackaged, and account for a large portion of our knowledge about the world around us. For example, the 4-year-old son of the second author already has acquired a fairly complex set of beliefs about sex roles. He knows that boys grow into men, whereas girls grow into women. He knows that only a woman can have a baby, but that it takes both a man and a woman to make a baby. These ideas relating gender to particular features were formally taught. He also seems to be learning traditional sex-role stereotypes concerning employment work and household work. These ideas apparently have been acquired informally via peers at a day-care center. Our point here is that beliefs are simply and continuously acquired by relatively mundane socialization or learning processes. Many such beliefs will be incorrect in some way; some will be maladaptive.

Personal Experience and Observation

The Naive Psychologist

The second, and often more interesting, source for the formation of beliefs is personal experience and observation. Connecting the observation of objective facts with subjective beliefs is the fallible process of human inference (Kahneman, Slovic, & Tversky, 1982; Nisbett & Ross, 1980). This process represents the "naive psychology" (Heider, 1958) of ordinary people as they attempt to make sense of the social environment, deriving lawful relations among social variables and trying to explain the causes of events. In attempting to answer these "what" and "why" questions, the naive psychologist uses methods quite analogous to those of the professional scientist (Ross & Anderson, 1982). As with all scientists, the naive psychologist is guided by implicit assumptions about the nature of the subject at hand, in this case human nature and human behavior. For example, people are generally "dispositionists," believing that others' behaviors result from some internal motives or characteristics. This tendency can be seen in the theorizing of professional research psychologists as well (cf. Anderson & Slusher, 1986; Miller & Ross, 1975).

To test and build upon these assumptions, the naive psychologist uses data extracted from the environment, either directly from personal experience or more indirectly through communication with others or through the mass media. Then these data must be coded and stored in some way that is retrievable for use. Finally, just as the professional scientist must combine assumptions with data to produce a meaningful yet parsimonious picture of the phenomenon under study, the naive psychologist must use techniques to summarize, analyze, and interpret the data to achieve a better understanding. The rewards of this process are clear: people do not need to react to each event in their lives as wholly new and as unrelated to past experiences. Instead, people can predict events, understand the causes and meanings of events, and integrate events into consistent patterns of related incidents. When accurate, this process allows the individual to master the social environment. However, when systematic biases exist at any phase of the inferential process, serious errors may arise. Thus, inaccurate assumptions, biased data (or biased perception of data), or inappropriate summation and interpretation can ultimately result in improper inferences and beliefs. As we see later, the inferential process also contributes to the persistence of these beliefs.

Errors and Biases in the Attribution Process

The process by which people attempt to understand the causes and implications of events in their environment, and thus develop beliefs about themselves and their environment, is the attribution process (Heider, 1958; Jones & Davis, 1965; Kelly, 1967, 1973). Although the process generally works well, a number of biases have been identified that frequently give rise to inaccurate beliefs. The most frequently cited bias is referred to as the *fundamental attribution error*, which is the tendency for attributors to overestimate dispositional factors and underestimate situational factors in the control of behavior (Heider, 1958; see Ross & Anderson, 1982, for a review). This bias is evident when people draw "correspondent" personal inferences about actors who respond to obvious situational influences. For example, when Jones and Harris (1967) required speakers to voice pro-Castro remarks, observers assumed that some correspondence existed between the remarks and the speakers' private opinions, even though they were well aware that the speakers had no choice of what to say.

A second common bias in the attribution process is known as the salience, or availability, bias (see reviews by Ross & Anderson, 1982; Taylor & Fiske, 1978). Any aspect of the environment that is especially apparent to the attributor is typically given more weight in the causal attribution. For example, an actor who is distinctive within a group for some reason (race, sex, dress, lighting, etc.) will be seen as particularly responsible for any outcome to which he or she contributed. This bias also appears to account for a discrepancy often found in the attributions assigned by actors and observers (Jones & Nisbett, 1972). Actors frequently attribute events to the environment, since they are focused on the environment, whereas observers attribute the same events to dispositional features of the actor, toward whom the observer is focused.

Other attributionally relevant biases have been identified, but further discussion is beyond the scope of this chapter. Our point here is that erroneous beliefs arise from many sources, including socialization and attributional processing. Once inappropriate beliefs do arise through these and other biases in the attributional process, they often are stubbornly resistant to change. The next section reviews some of the processes responsible for belief perseverance.

THE PERSEVERANCE OF BELIEFS

Once beliefs are established, it often seems that they are inordinately resistant to change. We have all been faced with the friend who defies our best efforts at "reeducation," and even among scientists there is a tendency to defend an established theory in light of considerable discrepant evidence. Often this is completely appropriate. Well-established theories, grounded in valid evidence, deserve to be retained when challenged with evidence of uncertain validity. A pregnant teenager's disclaimer about sexual activity and a television evangelist's claims of raising the dead should not change our beliefs about birth and death, respectively. However, circumstances do arise which seem to demand at least some modifications to existing beliefs. But what modifications are appropriate?

Do people in fact make the appropriate changes? If not, what mechanisms allow a person to reconcile an old belief with new and inconsistent data?

Several major reviews have discussed a broad spectrum of research related to belief perseverance (Jelalian & Miller, 1984; Ross & Anderson, 1982; Ross & Lepper, 1980). These reviews have examined such important issues as normativeness (how much beliefs should change), the proper blend of theory-driven thought versus empiricism, and the important positive benefits of inferential processing in day-to-day thought. The current review takes a more applied approach. In keeping with our emphasis on relating belief perseverance to self-defeating behaviors, we posit a very particular situation at the outset and review the literature as it relates to this circumstance. The situation we wish to consider is one in which a maladaptive self-defeating behavior is tied to some particular belief (or perhaps to some constellation of beliefs). Strictly speaking, it is not necessarily important to know the accuracy of this belief. In this context, it may be more appropriate to talk about adaptive and maladaptive beliefs, rather than correct and incorrect beliefs. What *is* assumed is that some agent (e.g., the self, a therapist, a friend) has determined this belief to be the basis for maladaptive behavior and wishes to effect a change. We examine four types of challenges that may be introduced to produce this change and what processes affect the likelihood of success.

Challenging the Formative Evidence

The first challenge questions the validity or relevance of evidence that originally led to or helped to bolster the belief. For example, a singer may believe that her talent is inadequate and her career is hopeless after failure at an important audition. To challenge this, her teacher may point out the residual effects of a recent cold, or the immense competition in this particular audition, or the fact that this was an opera audition and the singer's training and expertise point to Broadway. Each of these arguments would tend to discredit the results of the audition as being diagnostic of the singer's future career. What are the chances that these arguments will change the singer's beliefs? Likewise, a therapist may be faced with a depressed client suffering acutely from the effects of rejection (in romance, in employment, in family relationships, etc.). If the therapist points out extenuating circumstances that suggest the rejection is not due to characteristics of the client, what are the chances that the therapist can change the client's beliefs? A considerable amount of research has addressed the issue of belief perseverance in the wake of discredited evidence. Two broad categories of beliefs have been examined in this context—specific impressions about a person (self or someone else) and more general social theories.

Self- and Social Impressions

Interestingly, the earliest research on this issue was related to maladaptive self-beliefs arising from psychological research itself. Walster, Berscheid, Abrahams, and Aronson (1967) were concerned about lasting effects of deception in psychology experiments. Of particular concern were those experiments in which fictitious feedback was employed to manipulate subjects' self-esteem or perceived abilities, often lowering self-esteem in the process or leading the subjects to feel inadequate in some way. They questioned whether the standard debriefing, in which subjects were simply informed about the fictitious nature of their feedback, was adequate to return subjects to the preexperimental state. Walster *et al.* (1967) suggested such a debriefing would not eliminate the self-impressions created by the feedback, and that this effect might arise because the false feedback would lead subjects to recall other *consistent* information from their past, but not corresponding *inconsistent* information. To test this hypothesis, Walster *et al.* provided subjects with false feedback regarding their social skills and measured the subjects' perceptions of their sociability following a debriefing in which the false nature of the feedback was disclosed. The results of their study were both clear and disturbing; the effects of the false feedback lingered after the debriefing. Subjects who were given favorable sociability feedback rated themselves significantly more sociable than subjects given the unfavorable feedback. Clearly, the complete discrediting of the initial evidence did not adequately change the beliefs associated with this evidence.

Valins (1974) found that beliefs arising from false physiological feedback could be resistant to change as well. Subjects were exposed to what they believed to be their heart-rate reactions in response to viewing photographs of nudes. The heart-rate reactions were actually manipulated experimentally and were designed to indicate increased arousal in response to particular pictures. Later in the experiment some subjects were informed of the deception in a debriefing. But the false feedback significantly influenced reported attitudes toward the various nudes, regardless of whether the subjects were debriefed or not. Valins suggested that subjects were engaging in a self-persuasion process, wherein they invested considerable cognitive activity to convince themselves that a given nude was attractive or not in accordance with their alleged physiological reaction. Once persuaded, they persisted in these attitudes regardless of the validity of the feedback.

In two experiments, Ross, Lepper, and Hubbard (1975) extended the finding that experimentally induced perceptions of ability could persevere in the aftermath of a thorough debriefing. Whereas the Walster *et al.* (1967) study had been fairly narrowly focused on the adequacy of experimental debriefing procedures, Ross *et al.* were interested in a more general question. They wanted to know whether social perceptions as well as self-perceptions would be subject to a perseverance effect when evidence supporting the initial perception was completely discredited. They utilized a novel task requiring subjects to attempt to discern authentic suicide notes from fabricated suicide notes. Feedback was manipulated to indicate that a given subject had either high or low ability on this task. In Experiment 1, subjects were given a standard debriefing, informing them of the false nature of the feedback. Nevertheless, the feedback continued to affect subjects' judgments, influencing their estimates of both past and future performance as well as their performance self-estimates relative to the average student. In Experiment 2, some subjects observed as others performed the same novel task and received the same debriefing. Perseverance effects were observed for both the actors and observers, demonstrating that the phenomenon is not restricted to self-perception alone; that is, not only did the actor subjects display self-judgments consistent with the discredited feedback, but the observer subjects showed the same distorted judgments of the actors. In another condition of this experiment, subjects were given a "process" debriefing, in which the experimenter attempted to explain that the study dealt with the perseverance of impressions, described the phenomenon, and speculated on some of the processes thought to underlie the effect. In this condition, perseverance occurred only for the observers, with the process debriefing apparently being successful in neutralizing the beliefs of the actors.

A much more recent study demonstrated perseverance of self-impressions in a setting completely removed from the psychology laboratory. Lepper, Ross, and Lau (1986) showed high school students instructional films purportedly designed to help them solve a novel class of mathematical problems. Half of the students saw a film that accomplished exactly what it was purported to do. These students were quite successful in solving the problems after viewing the film. However, the other students were shown a film that was more confusing than instructional, and as a result these students failed to solve the problems. Students naturally felt that their performance was reflective of their ability after their initial success or failure. The evidence for this belief was discredited, however, when students were allowed to see the opposite film. This experience made it clear to all the students that their performance, good or bad, was more a result of adequate or inadequate instruction than of their personal abilities. Nevertheless, students continued to believe that they possessed either high or low ability, depending on their initial experience of success or failure, even 3 weeks after the exercise. Motivation levels with regard to this particular type of problem also mirrored the self-impressions of ability.

Manipulations in which initial information is discredited do sometimes influence impression judgments. But the amount and direction of the influence varies as a function of numerous variables, such as the timing of the discrediting, type of evidence being discredited, and the type of judgment (e.g., likeability ratings versus trait ratings) being made (for examples, see Thompson, Fong, & Rosenhan, 1981; Wyer & Budesheim, 1987; Wyer & Unversagt, 1985).

Social Theories

Although specific impressions about oneself or some other person are important in the development of self-defeating behaviors, they certainly are not the only beliefs that are relevant. Consider, for example, the social theories held by many rapists. Research (e.g., Burt, 1980; Koss, Leonard, Beezley, & Oros, 1985; Malamuth, 1986; Scully & Marolla, 1984) has shown that these people tend to hold a variety of "rape myth" beliefs and attitudes which function like social theories. These beliefs may arise from a variety of sources, such as general cultural beliefs, certain films, books, and "testimony" from peers. The evidential base for these beliefs can be challenged (e.g., the films are only make-believe). Given that there is little real supportive evidence for these social theories, one might expect evidential challenges to be particularly effective. What do we know about the persistence of social theories when the evidence on which they are based is challenged? As in the case of self- and social impressions, social theories frequently persist even in the face of logically overwhelming evidence.

Anderson, Lepper, and Ross (1980) extended the study of the perseverance effect into the realm of social theories, using the same debriefing paradigm used by others in the study of self- and social impressions. In these studies, however, subjects were not led to believe something about themselves or a particular other person. Rather, they were given evidence suggestive of a particular social theory which they were unlikely to have thought about previously. They were allowed to use this evidence to formulate a belief about the relation between two variables before they were debriefed about the fictitious nature of the original evidence. Postdebriefing beliefs were evaluated for evidence of perseverance.

The particular task chosen by Anderson *et al.* (1980) was designed to be an especially stringent test of the perseverance effect. The initial evidence presented was minimal and logically inadequate, just the kind of evidence likely to lead to ill-founded beliefs often challenged in everyday experience. In particular, subjects were led to believe that either a positive or a negative relation existed between a firefighter trainee's preference for risky versus conservative choices and his later success as a firefighter. These beliefs were instilled on the minimal evidence provided by two purported case studies. In Experiment 1, half of the subjects were debriefed about the fictitious nature of the case studies, whereas the other half received no such debriefing. The results showed that subjects were surprisingly willing to draw conclusions about the general relation between risk preference and firefighter ability on the basis of the minimal evidence provided. In the nondebriefing conditions, final beliefs strongly differed in the positive and negative conditions, with beliefs in each condition consistent with the appropriate case studies. More importantly, beliefs in the debriefing conditions showed this same pattern. Indeed, subjects who were explicitly informed that the initial data were completely bogus held beliefs that were only slightly less extreme than the corresponding beliefs of subjects who never were told that the theory induction examples were fictitious.

There are other studies on the effects of challenges to formative evidence for self- and social impressions and social theories. Overall these studies confirm the picture sketched out above. Specifically, challenging the formative evidence often has little effect on people's beliefs. What other strategy might one try to change people's maladaptive beliefs?

Presenting New Evidence

Another strategy that one might use to change a maladaptive belief is to present *new* evidence to oppose the belief. In the case of self-beliefs, evidence which contradicts the self-impression should correct the mistaken belief. Social impressions and social theories as well should be responsive to contradictory data. The difficulties in producing changes in beliefs about others or about oneself have been documented in countless studies of attitude change and therapeutic interventions, and so are not discussed here. A brief summary of this work is, simply, that presenting new evidence to change such beliefs often meets with failure.

Most of that research, though, is only tangentially relevant to the question of effectiveness of new evidence in changing social theories. In the public forum, this is perhaps the most common method employed, particularly as opposing sides debate controversial issues, vying for public support. Logically, as evidence is accumulated supporting one side, the other side, or both sides of an issue, beliefs of those with initially extreme positions should converge on the position supported by the evidence. Confidence in the initial belief should be undermined by the presentation of contradictory evidence. As an example, consider beliefs about the health risks of smoking tobacco. Certainly in the view of the American Cancer Society, smoking is considered a self-defeating behavior, yet many smokers apparently believe that the risks have been exaggerated. Suppose that a smoker believes that smoking is not particularly harmful, but a friend decides to try to change that belief. To accomplish this, the friend presents the smoker with the results of studies demonstrating the various dangers that smoking may pose. In response, the smoker seeks out the latest research by the Tobacco Institute indicating that smoking is not the cause of many of these health problems. Assuming that neither of these people is sufficiently knowledgeable to actually judge the merits of these opposing studies, what is likely to be the outcome of this exchange? Will the smoker become less certain that smoking is safe? Will the friend concede that maybe smoking isn't so bad after all?

Research conducted by Lord, Ross, and Lepper (1979) suggests that parties in a dispute such as this will not only persevere in their original beliefs but may come to believe them even more strongly. In the Lord *et al.* study, subjects were presented with two purportedly authentic research reports on the deterrent efficacy of capital punishment laws. Prior to seeing these reports, each subject had indicated either a strong belief that capital punishment was an effective deterrent to potential murderers or a strong belief that it was not. For each study, subjects were presented with both the method and the results of the research. One study was presented as a design in which murder rates in particular states were compared before and after the introduction or elimination of death penalty laws. The design of the other study involved a comparison across states, contrasting states with and without death penalty laws in a given period of time. Appropriate counterbalancing produced all the various combinations of original beliefs, research methods, and purported research results either supporting or rejecting the deterrent effects of the death penalty.

The results of the Lord *et al.* study reveal the dubious wisdom of trying to win a debate or change another person's theory by pitting one study against another. First, subjects were asked to evaluate the quality of the two studies. The evaluations showed that subjects did not rate the studies on the basis of methodological considerations, but rather on whether or not their findings agreed with the subjects' original beliefs. The supportive study was regarded as more convincing and better conducted than the opposing study. Furthermore, detailed descriptions of the studies (including discussion of shortcomings) were not treated equally. The initial impact of a supportive result was not curtailed by further delving into the details of the study. However, when the results of a study opposed the original belief, the presentation of methodological details provided an opportunity to find even more flaws in the design, weakening the impact of the study even more. As a result of these perceptions, the overall impact of reading both studies was to *increase* the polarization of beliefs initially existing among the subjects.

Research in our own laboratory confirms that exposure to new evidence does not necessarily result in elimination of unwarranted beliefs. In one study (Anderson & Sechler, 1986, Experiment 3) subjects were led to believe that either a positive or a negative relation existed between a person's level of risk preference and his ability as a firefighter. The theory induction was accomplished simply by having subjects write out a hypothetical explanation for either a positive or negative relation. Later, subjects received purportedly real data which indicated that there is in fact no relation between the two variables. Logically, creating a hypothetical explanation for a particular theory should not lead to a belief in that theory. It did. Logically, such explanation-induced theories should not be able to survive presentation of new and contradictory evidence. They did. Three results of that study are particularly relevant here. First, subjects developed theories consistent with their assigned explanation task. Second, unlike the subjects of Lord *et al.* (1979), ours did not polarize when faced with new data; indeed, other measures yielded no evidence of biased evaluation of the new data. Instead, our subjects moderated their explanation-induced theories after seeing the new evidence. Third, exposure to the new evidence did not eliminate the differences in theories held by subjects who had explained opposite hypothetical relations; that is, the new data did not overcome the explanation-induced beliefs.

Consider what this might mean for a therapy client who is convinced that love must inevitably lead to heartbreak. To point out that half the marriages in our society lead to lifelong, fulfilling relationships (essentially neutral data) may not be very convincing. To the therapist, this may show that the cup is half-full, but to the client, this same cup may seem half-empty. Indeed, Lord's data suggest that the client will be suspicious of the apparently successful marriages.

Both of the studies above examined how social theories change (or fail to change) in response to exposure to new evidence that overall suggests no relation between the social variables. In a more recent study (Anderson & Kellam, 1988), we investigated the effects of exposure to new data which either clearly contradict or clearly support the person's initial theory. Subjects were randomly assigned to explain (hypothetically) either a positive or a negative relation between risk preference and firefighter ability. Later, they examined and evaluated a large set of scatterplots of risk scores and firefighter evaluation scores. The scatterplots showed either a strong positive or a strong negative relation. Subjects' social theories about the risk preference/firefighter ability relation were assessed both prior to the hypothetical explanation task and after viewing the scatterplots.

Two results are of interest. First, once again our subjects did not evaluate the new evidence in a biased way. Second, the new evidence did not completely override subjects' explanation-induced social theories; that is, creating a purely hypothetical explanation for a randomly assigned social theory led to beliefs that could not be overridden by a large and clear set of relevant data. In sum, it has been shown that presenting new evidence has some impact on erroneous beliefs in some circumstances, but that even logically compelling evidence often fails to induce appropriate levels of belief change.

Urging Open-Minded Observation

The next strategy that one might use to change a maladaptive belief is more indirect than the first two discussed. It involves encouraging a person to view the topic of belief with an open mind, on the assumption that if the person would just observe the environment more carefully, he or she would see that the initial belief is not justified. In a sense, this strategy is a subset of the previous one concerning presenting new evidence. The only important distinction is that here the person is explicitly asked to be open-minded in the observation of new evidence. For example, a person with stereotypical beliefs and prejudiced attitudes might be encouraged to take greater notice of members of the target group on the presumption that this would allow the person to see that these people are no worse than anyone else.

Will this strategy lead to a change in beliefs? A number of studies suggest that there are at least three problems with this strategy: causal interpretation of accurate observations, failure to change observation processes, and the use of judgment strategies that fail to incorporate observational data.

Causal Interpretation

First, the major problem with many maladaptive beliefs is not that they are based on faulty assessments of what can be seen, but in the causal interpretations given to what is seen. For example, it is an objective fact that blacks in this country are more likely to be unemployed than whites. If being open-minded in new observations of relative rates of employment led to accurate observations, then we still would conclude that blacks are less likely to be working than whites. The maladaptive feature of the stereotypical belief about blacks and unemployment is the further interpretation concerning the causes of unemployment, specifically the causal belief that "they could get work if they really wanted to; they simply are lazy."

Similarly, the social phobic's observation that "I frequently make a fool of myself at parties" may be entirely accurate. If so, that observation by itself may not be maladaptive. Rather, the attribution "I cannot behave in an appropriate manner at parties" is the maladaptive causal component leading to self-defeating behaviors, such as avoiding social interactions, rather than learning necessary social skills (e.g., Anderson & Arnoult, 1985a, 1985b; Anderson, Horowitz, & French, 1983).

Observation Processes

Second, people typically do not believe that they are taking a biased viewpoint, so the exhortation to "be open-minded" fails to change their approach. This allows biased evaluation of new observations to occur in several ways, including covariation detection problems, interpretation of ambiguous observations, and imaginal confirmation processes.

One of the most fundamental ways in which people extract beliefs from the environment is by use of the covariation principle (Kelly, 1973). Presumably, people detect the covariation of events and infer appropriate relations between social variables. Although people can and do detect covariations under some circumstances (e.g., Lane, Anderson, & Kellam, 1985), there is considerable evidence that people are not very good at this task (for reviews, see Crocker, 1981; Hamilton, 1981; Nisbett & Ross, 1980). This appears to be particularly true when people scan the environment for evidence to test a particular hypothesis or view the environment in light of a preexisting belief (Jennings, Amabile, & Ross, 1982).

The simplest possible covariation detection task involves the detection of a relation between two dichotomous variables. For example, one might seek to determine the relation between the presence of a particular physical symptom and the diagnosis of a particular disease. One could develop a contingency table presenting the number of cases where the symptom is either present or absent and the disease is either present or absent. The resulting four-cell table provides all of the information necessary to determine the relation between the symptom and the disease. Yet, given this information, people are quite poor at estimating this relation (Smedslund, 1963; Ward & Jenkins, 1965). To assess the relation properly, the data from all four cells are required. But the tendency is for people to assess the relation mainly on the basis of the absolute number of cases in the present–present cell; that is, the number of people with both the symptom and the disease. The implications of this tendency for the perseverance of beliefs is clear. If a socially insecure person believes that she makes more than her share of social mistakes, her covariation detection task becomes observation of frequencies of social gaffes and triumphs performed by her and others. When she unwittingly focuses on her social gaffes (the present–present cell), her attempt at open-minded observation will serve to strengthen the belief rather than diminish it, even if in fact she is not less socially competent than the comparison others. This is because the social-gaffes cell is not empty for even the most socially skilled among us.

In the more general case beyond dichotomous variables, the inappropriate perception of relations among variables is referred to as *illusory correlation* (Chapman & Chapman, 1969). Illusory correlations may arise from the inappropriate dependence on hypothesis-confirming cases as described above, from prior associations which connect the observed events, or from salience differences due to the relative infrequency of some events or to other attentional factors (Hamilton & Rose, 1980; Sanbonmatsu, Sherman, & Hamilton, 1987).

The observation of ambiguous data may also contribute to the perseverance of beliefs. Once again, stereotypes are a prime example of beliefs that influence our processing of new data (see Hamilton, 1979, for a review). For example, Duncan (1976) demonstrated that an ambiguous shove given during an observed interaction would be interpreted differently, depending on the race of the person giving the shove. Ambiguous information may also be recalled from memory in a biased manner, depending on a stereotypical belief (Rothbart, Evans, & Fulero, 1979; Snyder & Uranowitz, 1978; see Bellezza & Bower, 1981, however, for an alternative view).

Imagination processes may also cause new observations to contribute to the perseverance of stereotypical beliefs. People use their stereotypes to fill in the gaps in ambiguous or incomplete observation situations (such as imagining a criminal in response to a radio news report). Recent work shows that people often imagine stereotype-confirming instances. Furthermore, this research suggests that these imagined events are not always distinguished in memory from real events, thus inflating the apparent frequency of stereotype-confirming events by a process of imaginal confirmation (Slusher & Anderson, 1987).

Judgment Strategies

Finally, even if new observations are evaluated in a fair manner, such observational data may not be used when a judgment is later demanded. Strategies for making judgments frequently are based on cognitive processes and knowledge structures that are unaffected by recall of genuinely probative data. An example is a process based on the recall of vivid, concrete instances, without making use of more valid statistical information (Borgida & Nisbett, 1977). For instance, a person may fully understand the summary of automobile repairs provided by a consumer magazine, yet decide on the purchase of a particular car based on the experiences of a friend with that model. In this case, the new information observed in the magazine is evaluated fairly, but it simply is not used in the judgment process.

Similarly, beliefs about a particular person may actually contain several different cognitive structures, including trait summaries and evaluative summaries linked to particular behaviors. A new piece of relevant data (or for that matter, a challenge to old data) may influence some but not all cognitive structures concerning that person. Because different cognitive structures are relevant to different judgmental tasks, such new data (and challenges to old data) will have no impact on a particular judgment if that judgment is based on an unaffected cognitive structure (see Pryor, 1986; Wyer & Budesheim, 1987; Wyer & Unverzagt, 1985).

Urging Open-Minded Interaction

A final strategy that one might use to dislodge a person's maladaptive belief is to encourage the person to actually interact with the environment to gain experiences that disconfirm the belief. This is somewhat different from the previous strategy in which the person was encouraged to simply observe the environment. Here we are talking about a more interactive than passive process. For example, a person may have the belief that he is unlikeable. A therapist might encourage this person to get out and socialize some and hopefully discover that people will like him after all. Unfortunately, research once again suggests that through the interaction process this person's belief about himself may persevere rather than change. Swann and his colleagues (Swann & Ely, 1984; Swann & Hill, 1982; Swann & Predmore, 1985; Swann & Read, 1981a; 1981b) have studied in considerable detail what they call the self-verification process. Swann and Read (1981a) studied three distinct phases of social interaction and found that within each phase, people sought to verify their original self-conception. Specifically, subjects were more likely to seek social feedback when they anticipated that such feedback would confirm their self-conception; they elicited reactions from their interaction partners that tended to confirm their self-conception; and they showed preferential recall for feedback that confirmed their self-conception. Swann and Read (1981b) found that people solicit self-confirmatory feedback because they apparently regard such feedback as especially informative and diagnostic. Even significant others in a person's life apparently can contribute to the self-verification process by insulating the individual from the effects of discrepant feedback (Swann & Predmore, 1985).

Beliefs about others may also persevere through the social interaction process (Darley & Fazio, 1980). If a person enters a social interaction with a particular belief or expectation about another person, he or she may elicit behavior from that person to confirm that expectation. Such behavioral confirmation and related self-fulfilling prophecy effects have been demonstrated in a wide variety of contexts, including educational achievement (e.g., Rosenthal & Jacobson, 1968) and social interactions (e.g., Snyder, Tanke, & Berscheid, 1977; see J. Darley's Chapter 3, this volume, for an excellent treatment of these phenomena).

Furthermore, in some social interactions people test their hypotheses about others via behaviors (questions) that tend to elicit confirming data. Through this hypothesis-testing process (e.g., Snyder & Swann, 1978), a person may persevere in the belief that "Mary is an extrovert" by asking questions of her that guarantee an extroverted response (e.g., "What would you do to liven up a party?"). Although recent work shows that this biased hypothesis-testing process does not always occur (Bassok & Trope, 1983), there are situations in which it does.

Social theories may also be artifactually confirmed via social interaction processes. Stereotypes about groups may lead to interactions which confirm the stereotype. During the oil boom days of 1979–1982, many native Houstonians developed a strong stereotype about "the damn Yankees" moving in from the north. The stereotype included such features as pushy, hostile, aggressive, suspicious, and rude. Unfortunately, this stereotype led to interactions that had to confirm the stereotype; that is, maltreatment by longtime residents forced many newcomers to behave in suspicious and hostile ways. One common "trick" played on newcomers was to run them off the road; any car with out-of-state plates was fair game. For newcomers, the two possible responses were to not drive (a near impossibility in Houston) or to drive as aggressively themselves. The latter response, of course, confirmed the stereotype. Such defensive aggression similarly has been demonstrated in laboratory situations using games (Kelley & Stahelski, 1970). In short, people's expectations about others often lead to behaviors which elicit the expected behaviors whether driven by social impressions or social theories.

We now have outlined four strategies by which maladaptive beliefs may be challenged and seen a variety of processes by which beliefs may persevere in the face of these challenges. At this point one may be tempted to throw up one's hands in despair, both because of the ubiquity of perseverance effects and because of the apparent complexity of processes surrounding these effects. We agree that there are many routes to perseverance and many obstacles to belief change. However, we also have seen a pattern in many of these processes that gives us a clue to understanding the ubiquity of perseverance and a tool for reducing it.

UNDERLYING PROCESSES

As we see it, a common thread underlying many perseverance effects is that a preestablished point of view leads to biased outcomes of normally unbiased processes. This point of view may be a particular belief, a more general belief about human nature (e.g., people act a certain way because of dispositional factors), or simply a hypothesis which a person is testing. However, regardless of its exact nature, it appears that the biased point of view itself often arises from people's propensity to see the social world in causal terms. This propensity results in resistance to each of the challenges to beliefs presented above.

Causal Thinking and Open-Minded Interaction

The biased point of view in the "open-minded interaction" strategy is set up by causal beliefs of the form, "If Mary is an extrovert, she will answer this question in an extroverted way"; that is, Mary's trait of extroversion will cause her to behave in a particular way, and the subject can test her by seeing if she does indeed behave that way. Hence, it is the causal belief that Mary's actions are based on her disposition that justify the biased questioning. Without this causal connection, the social perceiver would be less likely to question Mary in a biased fashion, because he or she would be more likely to recognize other situational constraints on Mary's actions (such as the fact that Mary is answering biased questions, as posed by the perceiver). Again, Chapter 3 in this volume discusses the body of relevant research, so we do not examine it further here.

Causal Thinking and New Evidence

The biased point of view in the "open-minded observation" and the "presentation of new evidence" strategies also is based on causal thinking. For example, excessive reliance on the present–present cell in covariation detection tasks follows naturally from causal statements of the form, "If I am socially incompetent, then I must commit numerous social gaffes." Similarly, a belief in a particular social theory encourages one to evaluate new data in a biased light, particularly if those data are themselves of ambiguous quality. Thus, although the subjects in the study by Lord *et al.* (1979) were biased in their assessments of the quality of new data (i.e., the capital punishment studies) as a function of the data's support of their theory, these people were not unreasonable from their own point of view. The new data did have problems and ambiguities, and these were pointed out to the subjects in the stimulus materials. Data which contradict prior beliefs (be they social theories, self-impressions, or social impressions) invite closer examination than beliefs which are consistent with prior expectations.

Support for the contention that causal thinking contributes to perseverance in the face of new data comes from several studies on hypothetical explanation of social theories (e.g., Anderson & Kellam, 1988; Anderson & Sechler, 1986). Two general findings have emerged from this work. First, hypothetical (causal) explanation of an event typically increases one's subjective likelihood for the event. For example, explaining why people who take risks *might* make better firefighters than conservative people leads one to believe that people who take risks *are* better qualified as firefighters. Second, beliefs based on nothing more than hypothetical explanation are seldom abandoned when new and valid contradictory evidence is presented. It seems as if the reasonableness and availability of the hypothetical causal explanation is taken as evidence of its veracity, even when there is no objective evidence in its support and despite contradictory evidence. To date, there are no comparable studies on the impact of explanation-induced self- or social impressions when new data are subsequently examined.

Causal Thinking and Discredited Old Evidence

The role of causal thinking in belief perseverance has been most closely examined in the debriefing paradigm. Recall that in this paradigm the target beliefs are created via presentation of some initial evidence, which is later totally discredited. Self-impressions, social impressions, and social theories have been examined for causal-thinking effects in the debriefing paradigm.

Self-Impressions

Although Ross *et al.* (1975) did not empirically test any causal-thinking hypotheses in their initial work on belief perseverance, they argued that the generation of causal explanations could account for the perseverance effects observed in their study. Faced with evidence of either good or bad performance on the suicide note discrimination task, subjects would seek an explanation for this performance in light of their personal knowledge about past experiences (e.g., knowing someone who committed suicide). Even after the evidence indicating a certain level of performance was discredited, the generated explanation remained salient, causing subjects to remain convinced of their previously perceived level of ability.

Fleming and Arrowood (1979) tested this hypothesis by varying subjects' opportunity to engage in causal explanation. In their study, subjects once again were asked to perform the suicide note discrimination task and were assigned to one of four explanation conditions. In an interference condition, subjects were required to perform a simple mental task between the time they received their preassigned performance feedback and the time they were debriefed about the fictitious nature of this feedback. This was designed to discourage the generation of causal explanations related to the performance during this time. Other subjects were in a delay condition, in which they simply were asked to sit and wait during this time, whereas a third group of subjects, in a facilitation condition, were asked to write down all possible reasons for their performance. In each of these conditions, feedback was delivered only after all the suicide note trials had been completed. This differed from the procedure used by Ross *et al.* (1975), in which feedback occurred after each trial. Speculating that trial-by-trial feedback might itself foster the generation of causal explanations, Fleming and Arrowood included a fourth condition replicating the Ross *et al.* procedure, except that no delay was provided between the final trial and the debriefing. As the dependent measure, subjects in all conditions were asked to estimate their true performance relative to that of the average student. The results offered dramatic support for the role of explanation processes in belief perseverance. Perseverance was observed in all of the conditions except for the interference condition. Furthermore, the magnitude of the perseverance varied systematically across the conditions, with a regression analysis showing an increase in perseverance as one moved from interference through delay to the facilitation condition.

Davies (1982) also manipulated the amount of processing subjects were likely to carry out to explain current performance in relation to past experiences. Using mirrors, Davies manipulated the self-focus of subjects at various times in the suicide note discrimination task. Subjects who were self-focused prior to debriefing presumably engaged in more self-relevant information processing related to their apparent performance, and thus they were expected to show increased perseverance. Self-focus after debriefing was expected to show the opposite effect. This hypothesis was based on earlier research showing that self-focus helped individuals to perceive self-relevant information more accurately. Thus, subjects in this condition were expected to be more aware of the unfounded nature of their initial beliefs and therefore show decreased perseverance. In fact, this pattern of results did occur. Self-focus before debriefing did increase the perseverance effect, whereas postdebriefing self-focus decreased the effect.

Perseverance of self-impressions does not always increase when people are explicitly asked to explain the target event. This is because people can create a variety of explanations having quite different implications for self-beliefs. Jennings, Lepper, and Ross (1981) told subjects that they would be participating in a blood drive being conducted by the Red Cross. Their task would be to phone potential donors and persuade them to donate blood. The subjects phoned a confederate who either did or did not agree to donate. Half the subjects were asked to explain this success or failure and then received the discrediting information. All subjects completed the dependent measure, assessing their self-impressions, by predicting future performance at the telephone task. Results of this study once again demonstrated significant amounts of belief perseverance.

Self-impressions were significantly affected by the success or failure experience, but the discrediting of that experience did not significantly reduce its impact. However, the explanation manipulation did not have an effect in this study. The authors speculated that spontaneous explanations were occurring even in the absence of explicit instruction, due to the high self-relevance of this task (see also Anderson, 1983a). Examination of the written explanations (by Jennings and Anderson) yielded another possibility. Many subjects explained their apparent failure in terms of controllable or changeable errors they made. Such attributions generally lead to expectations of greater rather than lesser future success (e.g., Anderson & Jennings, 1980). Thus, some subjects' generally positive self-beliefs about their social persuasiveness led them to create explanations allowing positive self-assessments to persevere in the face of failure.

In sum, causal explanations seem to play an important role in perseverance of self-impressions. However, people can and do create a variety of types of self-explanations (attributions) that vary in their implications for future events. Thus, any attempt to use causal-thinking processes to change self-perceptions must ensure that the desired type of explanation is created. Otherwise, the self-perception will only be reinforced by the explanation.

Social Impressions

Only one major study has examined the role of causal thinking in social impressions within the debriefing paradigm. Ross, Lepper, Strack, and Steinmetz (1977) induced subjects to explain key target events in the lives of clinical patients whose case histories they had read. Subjects later were debriefed concerning the fictitious nature of the target events. Despite this discrediting, subjects continued to believe that the explained events would be highly likely to occur, relative to a no-explanation control group.

Social Theories

Our own lab has focused on the role of causal explanation in the perseverance of social theories. In our initial work (Anderson *et al.*, 1980, Experiment 1) the written explanation task was included simply to enhance the probability of perseverance. In Experiment 2, the presence of the explanation task was varied to explore the mediating role of explanation. Recall that the paradigm involved subjects examining case histories of two firefighters to discover the underlying relation (half saw a positive one, half negative) between risk preference and ability as a firefighter. Some subjects wrote causal explanations for the "discovered" relation before being debriefed. Other subjects heard no mention of explanations but were still debriefed. In a final condition, some subjects wrote no explanations and received no debriefing. As expected, subjects in the positive and negative conditions differed in their final beliefs, regardless of whether they were debriefed or not. However, debriefing was not completely ineffective. Within the no-explanation conditions, beliefs were significantly less extreme for those subjects who had been debriefed. That explanation is important to the perseverance effect was shown by an enhanced perseverance effect in explanation subjects within the debriefing conditions.

The degree of perseverance associated with a belief is likely to be affected by the type of evidence that produced the belief in the first place. In the Anderson *et al.* (1980) study, beliefs were found to be quite persistent when based on the weak evidence of two case studies. Logically, these beliefs should have been very susceptible to change, considering how little data there were to support them. In later research, Anderson (1983a) compared the amount of perseverance that would occur for beliefs originally based on weak concrete data with the perseverance of beliefs based on much more logically sound statistical data. Although the two data sets were equated for the strength of the initial beliefs they induced, significantly more perseverance occurred for beliefs based on concrete data. This difference was long lasting as well, being evident even a week after the data were discredited. A follow-up experiment (Anderson, 1983a, Experiment 2) revealed that subjects were considerably more likely to engage in spontaneous causal thinking when examining the concrete case history data, and that perseverance occurred primarily in those subjects who had engaged in causal thinking.

All of the research cited up to this point suggests that it is the availability of causal arguments supporting a belief that maintains the belief after evidence has been discredited. However, none of these studies have actually attempted to ascertain whether more supporting arguments than opposing arguments are available to a person who persists in his or her belief. Anderson, New, and Speer (1985) measured the availability of such competing arguments directly in the risk preference–firefighter ability paradigm by having subjects write out explanations for *both* possible relations, regardless of which relation they were led to believe. They found that the availability effects did indeed mirror the perseverance effect and that the availability of arguments was significantly correlated with beliefs.

However, a covariance analysis revealed that argument availability did not completely account for the perseverance effect. This leaves open the possibility that perseverance in this context may arise from other processes as well. One possibility warranting further examination concerns different ways people think about events. Most research to date has equated causal thinking with fairly verbal processes. It may be, though, that much causal thinking is in terms of scripts or scenarios having a less formal verbal structure and a more visual or imagery-based structure (see Anderson, 1983b; Anderson & Godfrey, 1987; Lord, 1980; Read, 1987; Schank & Abelson, 1977).

IMPLICATIONS FOR BELIEF CHANGE

If belief perseverance frequently arises from causal thinking and the biased viewpoints created by causal thinking, then one should be able to reduce perseverance by changing causal thoughts (and corresponding viewpoints). Researchers working in several domains have successfully tested this notion (Anderson, 1982; Anderson & Sechler, 1986; Koriat, Lichtenstein, & Fischhoff, 1980; Lord, Lepper, & Preston, 1984; Slovic & Fischhoff, 1977).

In our own lab, we have shown that having subjects create opposite causal theories (i.e., counterexplanations) either reduces or eliminates the biasing effects of initial causal thinking. This occurs both with the debriefing paradigm (Anderson, 1982) and the hypothetical explanation paradigm (Anderson & Sechler, 1986).

Similarly, Lord *et al.* (1984) had some subjects consider the opposite point of view in examining studies on the deterrent efficacy of capital punishment laws. They found that this technique reduced the biased evaluation of the "new data" and decreased the perseverance of initial beliefs.

To our knowledge, there have been no studies of similar counterexplanation procedures in the context of self- or social impressions. However, one might regard some attribution manipulations as counterexplanations, for they can provide an alternative explanation for such impressions. For example, if one knows the typical attributional style of a person for a particular type of task, one could provide the person with an alternative attribution for his or her performance at the task. If the alternative attribution is accepted as a counterexplanation for initial performance, one should observe future task performances more in line with the manipulated attribution than with the attributional style. One such study has been conducted (Anderson, 1983c; see also Dweck & Goetz, 1977). Subjects with a maladaptive attributional style performed better at an interpersonal persuasion task when given an adaptive attribution for initial failures than when no such counterexplanation was given. Conversely, subjects with an adaptive attributional style performed worse when given a maladaptive attribution than when no counterexplanation was given.

Earlier work on the role of counterattitudinal role playing and attitude change also is somewhat similar to our focus on explanation and counterexplanation. That research tradition found that role playing (counterexplanation?) frequently led to attitude change but sometimes did not (see Elms, 1967; McGuire, 1968, for reviews). In one successful paradigm, subjects played an emotional role with scenes that contradicted their attitudes, such as a smoker playing the role of one who has just been informed he or she has lung cancer (Janis & Mann, 1965).

More closely related to our own work is research on counterattitudinal essay writing. Several findings from this tradition mirror the perseverance findings discussed in this chapter quite closely. For example, when people expect to defend their own opinion, they tend to accept supporting arguments and reject opposing ones. However, they do not show this evaluation bias when they anticipate having to defend the opposing position (Greenwald, 1969). Although these studies differ from the perseverance literature in incorporating the motivational aspects of defending a position, the findings clearly are consistent with those on the biased evaluation of data in the capital punishment studies cited earlier (Lord *et al.*, 1979; Lord *et al.*, 1984). People also tend to change their opinions in the direction of assigned improvisation (consistent with explanation manipulations) and tend to remember personally improvised arguments better than experimenter provided ones (Greenwald & Albert, 1968), a finding not yet directly tested within the perseverance literature. Finally, counterattitudinal essay writing tends to produce essay-congruent attitude change (mirroring counterexplanation effects), but only if the person has not had an opportunity to consider and reject that position prior to being assigned to defend it (Greenwald, 1970).

Implications for Therapy

At this point it may be useful to examine in more detail what implications these issues have in the context of therapy. As noted earlier, we have been interested in circumstances in which some agent, such as a therapist, wishes to alter a self-defeating behavior by changing the underlying beliefs that support it. Research suggests that such circumstances may arise in dealing with the related topics of loneliness, shyness, and depression, problems in living that often affect therapy clients. Let us examine depression from a cognitive perspective to see when and how persistent maladaptive beliefs affect behaviors and therefore become targets for change.

One belief that has often been associated with depressed people is a belief that they experience failure because of their own internal and unchangeable characteristics (e.g., Abramson, Seligman, & Teasdale, 1978; Anderson *et al.*, 1983; Weiner, 1979). This style of attribution for failure events leads to little expectancy for future success and hence to little motivation to try for better performance in the future. Quite often, this will precipitate additional failure, and a cycle of self-defeating behaviors will ensue. Clearly, one avenue to breaking this cycle is to change the client's belief about the causes of failure. The research cited in this chapter suggests that the most effective means of accomplishing this change is to encourage the client to consider alternative explanations for failure events. This method should be effective because the initial belief is causal in nature. As long as that cause is the one most salient to the client, the belief will tend to persist despite a discrediting of the data that formed it and despite the presence of any contradictory evidence.

Just how to effect such causal belief change in clinical contexts is not clear; there is no empirical evidence to date. However, theory and laboratory studies suggest several techniques. Our own work suggests that engaging in a hypothetical explanation task for a particular event may be effective (e.g., Anderson & Sechler, 1986). Other work suggests that changing a person's "causal structure" for a situation may produce more adaptive behavior. Such a change may be brought about by subtle situational manipulations (e.g., Anderson, 1983c; Anderson & Jennings, 1980). Another possibility would be to have the person rehearse adaptive causal thoughts (see Ellis, 1977).

A prototype approach to the description of a depressed person has identified a number of other beliefs commonly associated with depression (Horowitz *et al.*, 1982). These include beliefs of inferiority, beliefs about personal attractiveness, and beliefs about how other people relate to the depressed person. By attempting to change these beliefs, a therapist can seek to reduce the number of characteristics the client has that are prototypic of a depressed person. Again, it appears that the most effective means of changing such beliefs is to look at their causal nature and attempt to provide alternative causal structures.

Problems of loneliness and shyness are related to depression but focus much more narrowly on beliefs that are interpersonal in nature (e.g., Horowitz *et al.*, 1982). For example, whereas depressed people may have a maladaptive attributional style with regard to achievement situations in general, lonely people may have such a style only with regard to interpersonal achievement situations, such as meeting new people at a party. The prototype approach shows that characteristics associated with loneliness are essentially just a subset of those associated with depression, the subset dealing with interpersonal relationships.

We may also speculate on how issues of belief perseverance effect other clinical problems. For instance, cases of paranoia clearly reflect the perseverance of unsubstantiated beliefs. In mild cases, it may be useful to probe into the causal structure of these beliefs and attempt to induce a change at that level. By creating alternative causal cognitions, maladaptive paranoid beliefs may be modified. On the other hand, other clinical problems may not be amenable to belief change in this manner, presumably because they are less cognitive in nature. For example, phobias that come about as a result of more primitive learning processes, such as classical conditioning, may not respond to changes in causal structures. Only where the problems are cognitive in origin are such cognitive interventions likely to be effective.

One final note with regard to belief perseverance in the therapy context is that the client may not be the only one susceptible to this bias. Chapman and Chapman (1969) effectively demonstrated that in this regard clinicians are as fallible as anyone. They showed that when clinicians believed that certain diagnostic signs should be associated with a condition, they found this relation supported in data that were, in fact, random. More recently, Arnoult and Anderson (1988) discussed a number of causal reasoning biases in clinical practice. Thus, it is useful for all of us to keep in mind how our preconceptions can alter our view of the world.

CONCLUDING REMARKS

Overall, research from a variety of perspectives suggests that inducing people to create causal explanations congruent with a desired belief change (whether involving attitudes, self-beliefs, social beliefs, or social theories) should be effective in reducing various perseverance-related biases. We believe that explanation and counterexplanation techniques are sufficiently understood to permit testing in certain applied contexts. Indeed, one such application has already proven successful. Specifically, Sherman and Anderson (1987) used an explanation manipulation to decrease the rate of premature termination by clients receiving counseling services at a community mental health clinic. This success provides an encouraging first step toward a broader application of these techniques. It is clear that much more work needs to be done to further our understanding of perseverance processes. However, as these processes become more fully understood, we expect to see the development of improved techniques for overcoming maladaptive beliefs and their resulting self-defeating behaviors.

REFERENCES

Abramson, L. Y., Seligman, M. E. P., & Teasdale, J. D. (1978). Learned helplessness in humans: Critique and reformulation. *Journal of Abnormal Psychology, 87*, 49–74.

Anderson, C. A. (1982). Inoculation and counterexplanation: Debiasing techniques in the perseverance of social theories. *Social Cognition, 1*, 126–139.

Anderson, C. A. (1983a). Abstract and concrete data in the perseverance of social theories: When weak data lead to unshakeable beliefs. *Journal of Experimental Social Psychology, 19*, 93–108.

Anderson, C. A. (1983b). Imagination and expectation: The effect of imagining behavioral scripts on personal intentions. *Journal of Personality and Social Psychology, 45*, 293–305.

Anderson, C. A. (1983c). Motivational and performance deficits in interpersonal settings: The effects of attributional style. *Journal of Personality and Society Psychology, 45*, 1136–1147.

Anderson, C. A., & Arnoult, L. H. (1985a). Attributional models of depression, loneliness, and shyness. In J. Harvey & G. Weary (Eds.), *Attribution: Basic issues and applications* (pp. 235–279). New York: Academic Press.

Anderson, C. A., & Arnoult, L. H. (1985b). Attributional style and everyday problems in living: Depression, loneliness, and shyness. *Social Cognition, 3*, 16–35.

Anderson, C. A., & Arnoult, L. H. (1989). An examination of perceived control, humor, irrational beliefs, and positive stress as moderators of the relation between negative stress and health. *Basic and Applied Social Psychology*.

Anderson, C. A., & Godfrey, S. (1987). Thoughts about actions: the effects of specificity and availability of imagined behavioral scripts on expectations about oneself and others. *Social Cognition, 5*, 238–258.

Anderson, C. A., Horowitz, L. M. & French, R. (1983). Attributional style of lonely and depressed people. *Journal of Personality and Social Psychology, 45*, 127–136.

Anderson, C. A., & Jennings, D. L. (1980). When experiences of failure promote expectations of success: The impact of attributing failure to ineffective strategies. *Journal of Personality, 48*, 393–407.

Anderson, C. A., & Kellam, K. L. (1988). *Hypothetical explanation of social theories and evaluation of new data*. Unpublished manuscript.

Anderson, C. A., Lepper, M. R., & Ross, L. (1980). Perseverance of social theories: The role of explanation in the persistence of discredited information. *Journal of Personality and Social Psychology, 39*, 1037–1049.

Anderson, C. A., New, B. L., & Speer, J. R. (1985). Argument availability as a mediator of social theory perseverance. *Social Cognition, 3*, 235–249.

Anderson, C. A., & Sechler, E. S. (1986). Effects of explanation and counterexplanation on the development and use of social theories. *Journal of Personality and Social Psychology, 50*, 24–34.

Anderson, C. A., & Sedikides, C. (1989). *Thinking about people: Contributions of a typological alternative to associationistic and dimensional models of person perception*. Unpublished manuscript.

Anderson, C. A., & Slusher, M. P. (1986). Relocating motivational effects: A synthesis of cognitive and motivational effects on attributions for success and failure. *Social Cognition, 4*, 270–292.

Arnoult, L. H., & Anderson, C. A. (1988). Identifying and reducing causal reasoning biases in clinical practice. In D. Turk & P. Salovey (Eds.), *Reasoning, inference, and judgment in clinical psychology: Theory, assessment, and treatment* (pp. 209–232). New York: The Free Press.

Bandura, A. (1977). Self-efficacy: Toward a unifying theory of behavioral change. *Psychological Review, 84*, 191–215.

Bassok, M., & Trope, Y. (1983). People's strategies for testing hypotheses about another's personality: Confirmatory of diagnostic? *Social Cognition, 2*, 199–216.

Bellezza, F. S., & Bower, G. H. (1981). Person stereotypes and memory for people. *Journal of Personality and Social Psychology, 41*, 856–865.

Borgida, E., & Nisbett, R. E. (1977). The differential impact of abstract vs. concrete information on decisions. *Journal of Applied Social Psychology, 7*, 258–271.

Brodt, S. E., & Zimbardo, P. G. (1981). Modifying shyness-related social behavior through symptom misattribution. *Journal of Personality and Social Psychology, 41*, 437–449.

Burt, M. R. (1980). Cultural myths and support for rape. *Journal of Personality and Social Psychology, 38*, 217–230.

Chapman, L. J., & Chapman, J. P. (1969). Illusory correlation as an obstacle to the use of valid psychodiagnostic signs. *Journal of Abnormal Psychology, 74*, 271–280.

Crocker, J. (1981). Judgment of covariation by social perceivers. *Psychological Bulletin, 90*, 272–292.

Darley, J. M., & Fazio, R. H. (1980). Expectancy confirmation processes arising in the social interaction sequence. *American Psychologist, 35*, 867–881.

Davies, M. F. (1982). Self-focused attention and belief perseverance. *Journal of Experimental Social Psychology, 18*, 595–605.

Dipboye, R., & Macan, T. (1988). A process view of the selection/recruitment interview. In R. Schuler, S. Youngblood, & V. Huber (Eds.), *Readings in personnel and human resource management*, (3rd ed., pp. 217–232). St. Paul, MN: West Publishing.

Duncan, B. L. (1976). Differential social perception and attribution of intergroup violence: Testing the lower limits of stereotyping of blacks. *Journal of Personality and Social Psychology, 34*, 590–598.

Dweck, C. S., & Goetz, T. E. (1977). Attributions and learned helplessness. In J. H. Harvey, W. Ickes, & R. F. Kidd (Eds.), *New directions in attribution research, Vol. 2* (pp. 157–179). New York: Erlbaum.

Ellis, A. (1977). The basic clinical theory of rational-emotive therapy. In A. Ellis & R. Grieger (Eds.), *Handbook of rational-emotive therapy* (pp. 3–34). New York: Springer.

Elms, A. C. (1967). Role playing, incentive, and dissonance. *Psychological Bulletin, 68*, 132–148.

Fleming, J., & Arrowood, A. J. (1979). Information processing and the perseverance of discredited self-perceptions. *Personality and Social Psychology Bulletin, 5*, 201–205.

Freedman, R., & Papsdorf, J. (1976). Biofeedback and progressive relaxation treatment of insomnia: A controlled all-night investigation. *Biofeedback and Self-Regulation, 1*, 253–271.

Greenwald, A. G. (1969). The open-mindedness of the counterattitudinal role player. *Journal of Experimental Social Psychology, 5*, 375–388.

Greenwald, A. G. (1970). When does role playing produce attitude change? Toward an answer. *Journal of Personality and Social Psychology, 16*, 214–219.

Greenwald, A. G., & Albert, R. D. (1968). Acceptance and recall of improvised arguments. *Journal of Personality and Social Psychology, 68*, 31–34.

Hamilton, D. L. (1979). A cognitive-attributional analysis of stereotyping. In L. Berkowitz (Ed.), *Advances in experimental social psychology: Vol. 12* (pp. 53–84). New York: Academic Press.

Hamilton, D. L. (Ed.). (1981). *Cognitive processes in stereotyping and intergroup behavior.* Hillsdale, NJ: Erlbaum.

Hamilton, D. L., & Rose, T. L. (1980). Illusory correlation and the maintenance of stereotypic beliefs. *Journal of Personality and Social Psychology, 39*, 832–845.

Heider, F. (1958). *The psychology of interpersonal relations*. New York: Wiley.
Horowitz, L. M., French, R., & Anderson, C. A. (1982). The prototype of a lonely person. In L. Peplau & D. Perlman (Eds.), *Loneliness: A sourcebook of current theory, research, and therapy* (pp. 183–205). New York: Wiley.
Janis, I. L., & Mann, L. (1965). Effectiveness of emotional role-playing in modifying smoking habits and attitudes. *Journal of Experimental Research in Personality, 1*, 84–90.
Jelalian, E., & Miller, A. G. (1984). The perseverance of beliefs: Conceptual perspectives and research developments. *Journal of Social and Clinical Psychology, 2*, 25–56.
Jennings, D. L., Amabile, T. M., & Ross, L. (1982). Informal covariation assessment: Data-based versus theory-based judgments. In D. Kahneman, P. Slovic, & A. Tversky (Eds.), *Judgment under uncertainty: Heuristics and biases* (pp. 211–230). New York: Cambridge University Press.
Jennings, D. L., Lepper, M. R., & Ross, L. (1981). Persistence of impressions of personal persuasiveness: Perseverance of erroneous self-assessments outside the debriefing paradigm. *Personality and Social Psychology Bulletin, 7*, 257–263.
Jones, E. E., & Davis, K. E. (1965). From acts to dispositions: The attribution process in person perception. In L. Berkowitz (Ed.), *Advances in experimental social psychology, Vol. 2* (pp. 219–266). New York: Academic Press.
Jones, E. E., & Harris, V. A. (1967). The attribution of attitudes. *Journal of Experimental Social Psychology, 3*, 1–24.
Jones, E. E., & Nisbett, R. E. (1972). The actor and the observer: Divergent perceptions of the causes of behavior. In E. E. Jones, D. E. Kanouse, H. H. Kelley, R. E. Nisbett, S. Valens, & B. Weiner (Eds.) *Attribution: Perceiving the causes of behavior* (pp. 79–94). Morristown, NJ: General Learning Press.
Kahneman, D., Slovic, P., & Tversky, A. (Eds.). (1982). *Judgment under uncertainty: Heuristics and biases*. New York: Cambridge University Press.
Kelley, H. H. (1950). The warm–cold variable in the first impressions of persons. *Journal of Personality, 18*, 431–439.
Kelley, H. H. (1967). Attribution theory in social psychology. In D. Levine (Ed.), *Nebraska symposium on motivation, Vol. 15* (pp. 192–238). Lincoln: University of Nebraska Press.
Kelley, H. H. (1973). The process of causal attribution. *American Psychologist, 28*, 107–128.
Kelley, H. H., & Stahelski, A. J. (1970). Social interaction basis of cooperators' and competitors' beliefs about others. *Journal of Personality and Social Psychology, 16*, 66–91.
Koriat, A., Lichtenstein, S., & Fischhoff, B. (1980). Reasons for confidence. *Journal of Experimental Psychology: Human Learning and Memory, 6*, 107–118.
Koss, M. P., Leonard, K. E., Beezley, D. A., & Oros, C. J. (1985). Nonstranger sexual aggression: A discriminant analysis of psychological characteristics of nondetected offenders. *Sex Roles, 12*, 981–992.
Lane, D. M., Anderson, C. A., & Kellam, K. L. (1985). Judging the relatedness of variables: The psychophysics of covariant detection. *Journal of Experimental Psychology: Human Perception and Performance, 11*, 640–649.
Lepper, M. R., Ross, L., & Lau, R. R. (1986). Persistence of inaccurate beliefs about the self: Perseverance effects in the classroom. *Journal of Personality and Social Psychology, 50*, 482–491.
Lord, C. G. (1980). Schemas and images as memory aids: Two modes of processing social information. *Journal of Personality and Social Psychology, 38*, 257–269.
Lord, C. G., Lepper, M. R., & Preston, E. (1984). Considering the opposite: A corrective strategy for social judgment. *Journal of Personality and Social Psychology, 47*, 1231–1243.
Lord, C. G., Ross, L., & Lepper, M. R. (1979). Biased assimilation and attitude polarization: The effects of prior theories on subsequently considered evidence. *Journal of Personality and Social Psychology, 37*, 2098–2109.

Malamuth, N. M. (1986). Predictors of naturalistic sexual aggression. *Journal of Personality and Social Psychology, 50*, 953–962.

McGuire, W. J. (1968). The nature of attitudes and attitude change. In G. Lindzey & E. Aronson (Eds.), *The handbook of social psychology, Vol. 3* (pp. 136–314). Reading, MA: Addison-Wesley.

Miller, D. T., & Ross, M. (1975). Self-serving biases in the attribution of causality: Fact or fiction? *Psychological Bulletin, 82*, 213–225.

Nisbett, R. E., & Ross, L. (1980). *Human inference: Strategies and shortcomings*. Englewood Cliffs, NJ: Prentice-Hall.

Pryor, J. B. (1986). The influence of different encoding sets upon the formation of illusory correlations and group impressions. *Personality and Social Psychology Bulletin, 12*, 216–226.

Read, S. J. (1987). Constructing causal scenarios: A knowledge structure approach to causal reasoning. *Journal of Personality and Social Psychology, 52*, 288–302.

Rosenthal, R., & Jacobson, L. (1968). *Pygmalion in the classroom*. New York: Holt, Rinehart & Winston.

Ross, L., & Anderson, C. A. (1982). Shortcomings in the attribution process: On the origins and maintenance of erroneous social assessments. In D. Kahneman, P. Slovic, & A. Tversky (Eds.), *Judgment under uncertainty: Heuristics and biases* (pp. 129–152). New York: Cambridge University Press.

Ross, L., & Lepper, M. R. (1980). The perseverance of beliefs: Empirical and normative considerations. In R. Shweder & D. Fiske (Eds.), *New directions for methodology of social and behavioral science: Fallible judgment in behavioral research, Vol. 4* (pp. 17–36). San Francisco: Jossey-Bass.

Ross, L., Lepper, M. R., & Hubbard, M. (1975). Perseverance in self-perception and social perception: Biased attributional processes in the debriefing paradigm. *Journal of Personality and Social Psychology, 32*, 880–892.

Ross, L., Lepper, M. R., Strack, F., & Steinmetz, J. (1977). Social explanation and social expectation: Effects of real and hypothetical explanations on subjective likelihood. *Journal of Personality and Social Psychology, 35*, 817–829.

Rothbart, M., Evans, M., & Fulero, S. (1979). Recall for confirming events: Memory processes and the maintenance of social stereotypes. *Journal of Experimental Social Psychology, 15*, 343–355.

Sanbonmatsu, D. M., Sherman, S. J., & Hamilton, D. L. (1987). Illusory correlation in the perception of individuals and groups. *Social Cognition, 5*, 1–25.

Schank, R. C., & Abelson, R. P. (1977). *Scripts, plans, goals, and understanding*. Hillsdale, NJ: Erlbaum.

Scully, D., & Marolla, J. (1984). Convicted rapists' vocabulary of motives: Excuses and justifications. *Social Problems, 31*, 530–544.

Sherman, R. T., & Anderson, C. A. (1987). Decreasing premature termination from psychotherapy. *Journal of Social and Clinical Psychology, 5*, 298–312.

Slovic, P., & Fischhoff, B. (1977). On the psychology of experimental surprises. *Journal of Experimental Psychology: Human Perception and Performance, 3*, 544–551.

Slusher, M. P., & Anderson, C. A. (1987). When reality monitoring fails: The role of imagination in stereotype maintenance. *Journal of Personality and Social Psychology, 52*, 653–662.

Smedslund, J. (1963). The concept of correlation in adults. *Scandinavian Journal of Psychology, 7*, 265–266.

Snyder, M., & Swann, W. B. (1978). Behavioral confirmation in social interaction: From social perception to social reality. *Journal of Experimental Social Psychology, 14*, 148–162.

Snyder, M., Tanke, E. D., & Berscheid, E. (1977). Social perception and interpersonal

behavior: On the self-fulfilling nature of social stereotypes. *Journal of Personality and Social Psychology, 35*, 656–666.
Snyder, M., & Uranowitz, S. W. (1978). Reconstructing the past: Some cognitive consequences of person perception. *Journal of Personality and Social Psychology, 36*, 941–950.
Swann, W. B., & Ely, R. J. (1984). A battle of wills: Self-verification versus behavioral confirmation. *Journal of Personality and Social Psychology, 46*, 1287–1302.
Swann, W. B., & Hill, C. A. (1982). When our identities are mistaken: Reaffirming self-conceptions through social interaction. *Journal of Personality and Social Psychology, 43*, 59–66.
Swann, W. B., & Predmore, S. C. (1985). Intimates as agents of social support: Sources of consolation or despair? *Journal of Personality and Social Psychology, 49*, 1609–1617.
Swann, W. B., & Read, S. J. (1981a). Acquiring self-knowledge: The search for feedback that fits. *Journal of Personality and Social Psychology, 41*, 1119–1128.
Swann, W. B., & Read, S. J. (1981b). Self-verification processes: How we sustain our self-concepts. *Journal of Experimental Social Psychology, 17*, 351–372.
Taylor, S. E., & Fiske, S. T. (1978). Salience, attention, and attribution: Top of the head phenomena. In L. Berkowitz (Ed.), *Advances in experimental social psychology, Vol. 11* (pp. 249–288). New York: Academic Press.
Thompson, W. C., Fong, G. T., & Rosenhan, D. L. (1981). Inadmissible evidence and juror verdicts. *Journal of Personality and Social Psychology, 40*, 453–463.
Valins, S. (1974). Persistent effects of information about internal reactions: Ineffectiveness of debriefing. In H. London & R. E. Nisbett (Eds.), *Thought and feeling: Cognitive modification of feeling states* (pp. 116–124). Chicago: Aldine.
Walster, E., Berscheid, E., Abrahams, D., & Aronson, V. (1967). Effectiveness of debriefing following deception experiments. *Journal of Personality and Social Psychology, 6*, 371–380.
Ward, W. C., & Jenkins, H. M. (1965). The display of information and the judgment of contingency. *Canadian Journal of Psychology, 19*, 231–241.
Weiner, B. (1979). A theory of motivation for some classroom experiences. *Journal of Educational Psychology, 71*, 3–25.
Wyer, R. S., & Budesheim, T. L. (1987). Person memory and judgments: The impact of information that one is told to disregard. *Journal of Personality and Social Psychology, 53*, 14–29.
Wyer, R. S., & Unverzagt, W. H. (1985). The effects of instructions to disregard information on its subsequent recall and use in making judgments. *Journal of Personality and Social Psychology, 48*, 533–549.

CHAPTER 3

SELF-FULFILLING PROPHECIES AND SELF-DEFEATING BEHAVIOR

JAMES L. HILTON, JOHN M. DARLEY, AND JOHN H. FLEMING

INTRODUCTION

One of the most theoretically important findings to emerge from the sociological and psychological literatures has been the discovery that expectations frequently create the conditions that bring about their own fulfillment—an effect that Merton termed the *self-fulfilling prophecy* (Merton, 1948). Much of the excitement in the research that has followed Merton's statement has been generated by its clear relevance to societal concerns, including the ways in which negatively stereotyped children are left behind in the educational process, to ways in which those who have sought treatment for mental difficulties are labeled by others and treated in a fashion that can sustain or increase their difficulties. In short, the idea that one individual, entrapped in the expectations and stereotypes of others, can somehow be caused to fulfill those expectations holds out the promise of understanding many social phenomena. Similarly, there is a great deal of

---

JAMES L. HILTON • Department of Psychology, University of Michigan, Ann Arbor, Michigan 48109. JOHN M. DARLEY • Department of Psychology, Princeton University, Princeton, New Jersey 08544. JOHN H. FLEMING • Department of Psychology, University of Minnesota, Minneapolis, Minnesota 55455. Any opinions, findings, and conclusions or recommendations expressed in this chapter are those of the authors and do not necessarily reflect the views of the National Science Foundation or the Graduate School of the University of Minnesota.

interest in *self-defeating behaviors*—the notion that we sometimes engage in behaviors that harm or defeat us. And, as with the self-fulfilling prophecy, a deeper understanding of self-defeating behaviors may enable us to design interventions that minimize their harmful effects.

Our task in this chapter is to connect these two important concepts. A series of powerful and elegant experiments has documented the operation of the self-fulfilling prophecy and make it possible to formulate an integrated account of its workings. At the same time a growing number of converging theoretical perspectives, often bolstered by experimental evidence, make it possible to consider a unified theoretical attack on the conditions that accompany the emergence of self-defeating behavior. Nonetheless, the integration of the two constructs is much less easy than the similarity of their names might suggest. The difficulty arises, in part, because the term *self* in the names of the two constructs refers to different things.

In the self-fulfilling prophecy, the term *self* refers to the expectation held by an individual, usually called the perceiver, about another. In the classic example, it is the expectation of a teacher, who believes that some children in her class are "late bloomers" while others are not (Rosenthal & Jacobson, 1968). The teacher then acts toward the children in ways that unwittingly make her prophecy come true—the late bloomers blossom while the others languish. The behavioral confirmation of the perceiver's expectation is the self-fulfilling aspect of the prophecy. However, the targets of her expectancy, and particularly the ones who were not identified as late bloomers, are the ones who are defeated by her expectations. Although originally quite controversial, by now numerous demonstrations of the self-fulfilling prophecy exist (Rosenthal & Rubin, 1978), and it is clear that the expectations held by one individual can have dire consequences for the target of those expectations.

In self-defeating behavior, on the other hand, the term *self* refers to the fact that the person committing the behavior and the person being harmed by the behavior are one and the same. At its broadest, the term *self-defeating behavior* can be taken as referring to any behavior that provokes a serious and consequential negative response from the behaving individual's physical or social environment. Thus a farmer who plants a crop that does not survive the rigors of winter, or a student who gives a report that does not pass the muster of the teacher's evaluation, are each engaging in self-defeating behavior. To make this definition do any useful psychological work, however, it is necessary to ask what the intentional circumstances are in which these behaviors can and do arise (see Baumeister & Scher, 1988).

One possibility is that a person will intentionally engage in behaviors that he or she knows will have solely or mainly self-defeating consequences. Although this is a phenomenon that clinicians may well realize that they observe among their clients, it is not a class of self-defeating behaviors upon which we focus in the current chapter.

A second possibility is that a person will engage in behavior that has negative consequences for the person, but he or she will be unaware of them. For example, a woman who was once a fantastically successful child movie star and who continues her childish mannerisms long past the time when she had the childish attractiveness to make them charming is engaging in self-defeating behavior. This sort of self-defeating behavior arises when a person continues to engage in a set of behaviors that others consistently find unattractive. It becomes particularly poignant when the person intends to produce one effect with the behavior, but consistently produces the opposite effect.* A boor, for example, who prides himself on his "honest and forthright speech" has incorporated into his character something that is quite counterproductive.

A third possibility is captured in Jones' work on self-handicapping (Berglas & Jones, 1978; Jones & Berglas, 1978). In this class of behaviors, certain behaviors that have negative consequences are engaged in because they protect the individual from circumstances that threaten self-esteem. In the self-handicapping case, the individual who is uncertain about his or her ability to repeat past successes chooses circumstances such that future performances will not provide an accurate measure of low ability, even though they are likely to lead to a poor performance. The uncertain student, for example, may set off on an all-night alcoholic binge the night before an important exam in order to avoid unambiguous feedback about his or her low ability. After all, if the exam goes badly the alcohol provides a ready excuse. It is worth noting that this kind of self-defeating behavior is both rational and entrapping. It is rational in the sense that an individual engages in behavior that admittedly has some negative consequences, but he or she is doing so to escape or avoid some consequence that is perceived to be even more negative. Baumeister and Scher (1988) refer to a similar class of self-defeating behaviors as *tradeoffs*.

The difficulty in connecting the self-fulfilling prophecy with self-defeating behavior, then, is that the self-fulfilling prophecy typically begins as a function of one member of the interaction and has its effect on the other, while self-defeating behavior typically begins with one member of the interaction and has its effect on that member. Nevertheless, there are at least four important ways in which the self-fulfilling prophecy can be thought of as self-defeating. First, it can lead the perceiver to draw inaccurate conclusions about another person. In other words, it can lead the perceiver to make perceptual or inferential mistakes. Second, it can lead the perceiver to behave in ways that make the interaction environment less conducive to achieving his or her goals. Third, it can sometimes lead the target of the prophecy to react in ways that contribute to his or her own defeat. In other words, it can sometimes lead the target to behave in ways that confirm another's negative expectation. Finally, the self-fulfilling prophecy can actually be initiated by the target's own unwitting behavior. High school "James Deans," for instance, who don antiestablishment garb as a social state-

*Elaine May used to do a routine in which a woman, determined to be charming to her date, smiles at many things that he says over dinner and on into the evening. The evening goes badly. At the end of the evening, looking in the mirror, she discovers that she has a piece of spinach unattractively lodged between her teeth, which must have made her "charming" smile grotesque. We are tempted to say that there are some people who go through life with spinach lodged between their teeth, but unlike the Elaine May character, they never seem to discover it.

ment, may create certain expectations that trigger the self-fulfilling prophecy and lead to their own demise.

We return later to this discussion of the ways in which the self-fulfilling prophecy can lead to self-defeating behavior. Before doing so, however, it is necessary to develop the concept of the self-fulfilling prophecy more fully. To anticipate our conclusions, however, one implication that follows from the model that we develop below is that the self-fulfilling prophecy is both less ubiquitous and less inevitable than it is sometimes portrayed—an implication that has important consequences for the analysis of self-defeating behavior.

TOWARD A THEORETICAL PERSPECTIVE ON SELF-FULFILLING PROPHECIES

Despite a burgeoning literature on the self-fulfilling prophecy and, more generally, expectancy-confirmation effects, theoretical accounts of the influence that expectations have on our social interactions have been slow to move beyond outcome-focused demonstrations of a confirmation effect. While a number of studies have looked at some of the individual processes that may serve to mediate expectancy confirmation (e.g., Snyder and his colleagues' work on hypothesis testing [Snyder, 1981; Snyder & Swann, 1978a] and Hamilton and his colleagues' work on illusory correlations [Hamilton & Gifford, 1976; Hamilton & Rose, 1980]), only recently have coherent models of the expectancy confirmation process begun to emerge (e.g., E. Jones, 1986; R. Jones, 1977; Jussim, 1986; Miller & Turnbull, 1986). In part, this slow emergence may reflect the fact that expectancy confirmation is a multiply-mediated phenomenon. But, it may also reflect the fact that explanations of confirmation have tended to rely exclusively on cognitive explanations. Although such explanations contribute considerably to our understanding of some aspects of the expectancy-confirmation process, they place little emphasis on the context provided by social interaction. More specifically, they fail to take into account the interaction goals (Jones & Thibaut, 1958) that both perceivers and targets bring to the social arena. It is important to remember, after all, that social perception rarely occurs in isolation. Instead, it occurs within the context provided by social interaction—a highly negotiated and frequently strategic endeavor. Moreover, from the perspective of expectancy confirmation, how perceivers or targets react to expectancy information would seem to depend, in large part, on their purposes underlying the interaction. Sometimes perceivers may seek and elicit confirming information, and sometimes they may not. Similarly, sometimes targets may attempt to behave in disconfirming ways, and sometimes they may not. The simple introduction of expectancy information into an interaction far from guarantees that the expectancy will be confirmed.

A thought experiment demonstrates this point. Imagine the interactions that a known former mental patient might have with two different social perceivers. The first social perceiver is an admissions officer at a university with a rigorous degree program who is attempting to discover whether or not the target is sufficiently recovered from a mental breakdown to withstand the pressures of the program. The second social perceiver is a fellow student who has inadvertently wound up sitting with the target at lunch one day. What are the two interactions going to be like? In the case of the admissions officer it is likely that the interaction will focus on the current mental state of the target. The admissions officer has what we might call an interaction goal of accurate assessment. Her goal is to determine whether the target is likely to suffer another breakdown, and she will, in all probability, spend a considerable amount of time and energy probing the former mental patient's current mental state. Notice also that if the former patient is sufficiently recovered, the admission officer's probes may uncover this fact and expectancy disconfirmation may occur. The student, on the other hand, is probably more interested in getting through lunch with as little social awkwardness as possible, and his interaction goal is probably far removed from accuracy. It is unlikely that he will ask the target about his current mental state, specifically because of the fear that he will elicit confirming information from the target. Notice here that, unlike the admissions officer, the student is unlikely to uncover any evidence of recovery.

A more formal demonstration of the interaction between expectancy information and the perceiver's interaction goals is provided by Shapiro and Hilton (1988). Shapiro and Hilton had subjects play a game patterned after Snyder and Swann (1978b). In this game, the subjects are told they are competing against another subject and that their task is to react as quickly as possible each time they hear a tone by pressing a reaction-time button. They are also told that on some trials they will have access to a noise weapon that can be used to impede their opponent's performance but that on other trials their opponent will have access to the noise weapon and can use it to impede their performance. In the Shapiro and Hilton experiment, half of the subjects were given information that indicated their opponent was hostile, while the other half received no such information. Independent of this expectancy manipulation, half of the subjects were told that their goal in the game was to win the reaction-time contest, while the other half were told that their goal was to use the game and the noise weapon as a way of finding out what kind of person their opponent was. In other words, half the subjects had the goal of winning, while the other half had the goal of accuracy. All subjects actually played against a confederate who responded in a tit-for-tat manner. After playing the game the subjects' use of the noise weapon and impressions they formed of the confederate were assessed. The results indicated that when subjects were attempting to win the game, the hostile expectancy had a strong influence. Among these subjects, the ones who held the expectancy used the noise weapon more and emerged from the game believing that their opponent was indeed hostile. Among the subjects attempting to arrive at an accurate impression, however, the expectancy had little influence on their use of the noise weapon or on their impressions of the target.

What this experiment and the informal thought experiment presented earlier demonstrate, and what is central to the analysis we propose, is that the goal-driven nature of human interaction plays a critical role in determining the course of any given expectancy. It is our belief that social perception and social interaction are much more closely interrelated than the trend of previous research has shown them to be and that the interaction-goals concept (Jones & Thibaut, 1958) provides a framework for explicating these interrelationships. Moreover, we focus on interaction goals because we believe that the psychological community has developed over time an increasing concern with, and understanding of, the roles that goals play in shaping behavior (e.g., Cohen, 1981; Kelley & Thibaut, 1978; Miller, Galanter, & Pibram, 1960; Showers & Cantor, 1985; Thibaut & Kelley, 1959), and it now seems possible to return to the theme of Jones and Thibaut (1958) and include interaction goals in models of social perception.

In the paragraphs that follow we develop the interaction-goals model more fully and attempt to show how the fate of an expectancy can be altered at various points in the interaction sequence. The main insight offered by the model is that the goals that perceivers and targets have for an interaction combine with the information that they have about the interaction situation and their fellow interactants to produce specific interaction tactics. These interaction tactics in turn determine, in large part, the fate of a perceiver's expectancy. Sometimes these interaction tactics involve the avoidance of the target altogether. At other times the interaction tactics will lead to interaction with the target. When perceivers do choose to interact, the specific interaction tactics they employ may or may not result in the solicitation of expectancy-relevant information from the target. Moreover, sometimes the elicited information will confirm a perceiver's expectations and sometimes it will not.

Before presenting the model in detail, however, we should hasten to add that we make no particular claims for the originality of the interaction-goals perspective. Instead, we propose it as representative of what would be a consensus view of many social psychological, personality psychological, and sociological theorists (the reader will note throughout the pervasive influence of symbolic interactionism [see Stryker & Gottlieb, 1981; Stryker & Statham, 1985] and of Goffman's thought, particularly as represented in his middle writings [i.e., "On face work;" *The Presentation of Self in Everyday Life*; and *Strategic Interaction*]). What we do claim, however, is that explicit formulations of the goals concept have been noticeably absent from many of the theoretical accounts of social perception, generally, and the self-fulfilling prophecy, more specifically.

Overview of Interaction-Goals Model

Briefly, we propose that interactions take place against a backdrop of the needs and life circumstances of the interactants and that these needs and life circumstances influence the goals that the interactants will have for any given interaction. However, prior to initiating interaction, interactants evaluate the goals that they have for the interaction in light of the information that they have about the situation (its norms, resources, and constraints) and the information that they have about their fellow interactants (expectancy information). In conducting this evaluation they generate scenarios concerning how the interaction is likely to unfold as a function of the tactics available to them. Based upon the subjective expected utility of these tactics, which in turn is based upon the outcomes that are likely to follow from them, interactants chose the specific interaction tactics they will employ during the interaction. They then implement these tactics and interact with the target of the expectancy. As the interaction unfolds, the interactants reassess the interaction in light of the new information they have (i.e., they update both person and situation information), and by generating new scenarios, they update their subjective expected utilities. Accordingly, they may generate new goals and new tactics or retain the old goals and generate new tactics to reach them. As can be readily seen, the process that we are proposing is an open loop—the cycle repeats until the interaction is concluded, or until one of the parties decides to terminate the exchange. Parties can join or depart from the loop at any stage in the process.

Needs and Life Circumstances

We begin with the assumption that social interaction takes place against a rich background of human needs and external circumstances, and that these needs and circumstances shape the goals and strategies of the interactants. A number of theorists, notably Freud, Maslow, McDougal, and Murray, have offered taxonomies of human needs. Many of the needs identified by these authors are of an interpersonal nature, such as needs for power or esteem from others. The consensus seems to be that there are many general needs that are very widely held, such as the needs for positive regard from significant others, interpersonal power, or affection and sexual gratification from others. However, the consensus would go on to recognize that many of these needs are held to varying degrees by different people (some would include the possibility that certain needs are not held at all by certain individuals) and that different people seek very diverse forms of gratification for what might be, at some general level, the same need. Obviously one's needs will influence one's goals in any particular interaction. The stereotypical bad executive, with high needs for power, will seek to establish dominance in an interaction with a newly hired corporate peer. Another executive, whose needs for affiliation are stronger, may instead seek to establish bonds of loyalty and affection with the other.

In addition to these ongoing needs, social interaction also occurs within the context provided by one's life circumstances, and these circumstances can influence one's current needs. At certain points during one's life, external circumstances play a heavy role in influencing one's hopes and needs. For example, as the senior year approaches, high school seniors with certain aspirations become increasingly concerned with getting into colleges. Similarly, job loss brought on by economic depression can suddenly make employment a central concern.

Interaction Goals

Against this background of needs and life circumstances, interactants formulate specific interaction goals. By *interaction goals* we mean those end states that one wishes to produce as a result of an interaction. The job seeker wants to be hired by the interviewer, or at least receive a favorable assessment. Meanwhile, the interviewer seeks to obtain an accurate assessment of the job seeker's skills. Similarly, teachers seek to change the knowledge levels or problem-solving abilities of their students, while mental health care professionals seek improvement in their patients' mental health. In all of these situations the participants seek fairly specific and consciously articulated goals, and they may or may not achieve those goals. In other, less prescribed interaction situations, the interactants' goals may revert to the more general self-presentational ones that we all carry around with us, such as appearing bright, warm, and charming, or intense, committed, and honest. In still other cases, such as the one that occurs when two strangers are thrown together for a few minutes, the goal is likely to be simply to have a pleasant, time-passing conversation. Goals, then, are more specific than what are ordinarily referred to as needs; they can be achieved with varying degrees of success, and they can be consciously articulated to varying degrees.

EXPECTANCY INFORMATION

In addition to having goals for a given interaction, participants also have some information about their interaction partner. This information may be of a very formal nature (e.g., letters of reference), may be derived from stereotypes or other category-based beliefs, or may consist of minimal information derived from one's initial impression (e.g., with that red dress she is probably extraverted).

That one's expectations about another, whether target- or category-based, are used by people to plan their specific moves within an interaction is generally obvious. If I seek to get you to like me and see in a place of pride on your desk a picture of you and Ronald Reagan in warm embrace, I "reveal to you" that I possess whatever conservative opinions that I can manage. A picture of John Kennedy causes me to generate quite a different set of opinion statements. Hamilton's (1981) book on stereotyping suggests that many kinds of expectations, ranging from stereotypes through implicit personality theories to networks of categories, lead us to infer attributes of other people, and that there are a number of possible ways that these inferences shape our subsequent actions toward the targets of our expectations.

THE SITUATION

The Interaction Setting

In addition to information about the target of an interaction, the perceiver has considerable information about the structure of the interaction. Every interaction situation contains elements that are important to the goal seekers' determinations of how to set out to achieve their goals. More concretely, the goal seekers' perceptions of the norms and rules that govern interaction in the situation, the resources available to the goal seekers, and the expectations that the seekers hold about their interactants, create both constraints and opportunities that are important determinants of the ways individuals go about seeking to fulfill their goals.

The claim that people come to specific interaction situations with an assessment of the rules and norms that prevail in them has been intensively discussed in the symbolic interaction literature and needs no great elucidation here. Some of the norms, for instance, norms against embarrassing another, exist across many situations. Others, such as the injunction to speak briefly, are induced by the particular nature of a specific situation (e.g., the exigency of being interviewed on television news). In any event, most people have a good general understanding of these norms.

Less well developed is the notion that situations create or possess resources that make certain kinds of strategic moves possible or impossible. Intuitively, we can make the statement plausible. A new boy in town has made friends with the boy next door. He discovers that the neighbor is on the high school basketball team and wants to know if he should attempt to make the team. If a basketball hoop is available, this question is much more easily and accurately answered than otherwise. Some generalizations also seem possible. Normally, a self-presentational claim of skill at some task, if it is not coupled with some offer to use resources that are present to demonstrate that claim, is viewed by others with some suspicion (Goffman, 1959). And as Snyder's work on self-monitoring attests (Snyder, 1979), some individuals are likely to be exceptionally adroit at manipulating situations and persons within those situations to best achieve their goals.

Situational Taxonomy

Situations can shape interactions in other ways as well. More specifically, Hilton & Darley (1985) have proposed the existence of three classes of social interactions and have suggested that the behavior of the target of a negative expectancy will be affected and evaluated differently in each class. In the first class of interactions, the target of a negative expectancy is unaware of the expectancy's existence. For example, it is unlikely that poorly dressed black kindergarten children are aware that their teachers have negative expectations concerning their reading ability, though Rist (1970) has shown this sometimes to be the case. Similarly, it is unlikely that the product of a fashionable preparatory school is aware that some of his or her teachers may have negative expectancies concerning his or her seriousness of purpose.

As previously noted, the majority of studies investigating the expectancy-confirmation effect have been conducted under precisely these circumstances, and expectancy confirmation has frequently been the outcome. Given that the target of the expectancy does not know that the expectancy exists, he or she cannot know to attempt interaction strategies designed to counteract the negative expectancy.

The second class of interactions consists of those situations in which the target of a negative expectancy is aware of the expectancy and may, therefore, attempt interaction strategies designed to overcome the expectancy. It is unlikely, for instance, that a would-be suitor will passively accept the information that the target of his affections thinks that he is cold and uncaring. Instead, he will probably actively engage in various interaction strategies designed to convince his would-be paramour that he is not cold. He might, for example, bring her flowers and invest in several candle-lit dinners in an attempt to convince her that he is warm and caring.

Confirming this, Hilton and Darley (1985) have demonstrated that, under certain conditions, alerting targets to the existence of a negative expectancy can result in expectancy disconfirmation rather than expectancy confirmation. Specifically, they found that expectancy confirmation occurred only when perceivers with negative expectancies interacted with naive targets. When the targets were informed of the existence of the expectancy, expectancy confirmation did not occur.

The third class of interactions is composed of situations in which the perceiver holds an expectancy and the target is aware of the expectancy but, additionally, the perceiver is aware that the target is aware of the expectancy. Given this recursive awareness, if the expectancy is a negative one, and if the presence of confirming or disconfirming information is seen to be under the volitional control of the target, then the perceiver may discount (Kelley, 1967) any disconfirming information offered by the target as attempts at impression management. Suppose, for example, that I expect someone else to be lazy, and upon meeting them I discover them working quite hard at some task. What am I to conclude from the observed behavior? If it is clear that the person is unaware of my expectancy, then I may very well conclude that my expectation was wrong. On the other hand, if I know that the person is aware of my expectancy, then I am in a quandary. The industrious behavior of the person could indicate that the person is not lazy, or it could indicate that the person does not want me to believe that he or she is lazy when, in fact, this is the case. From my perspective it is difficult to distinguish between the possible causes for the disconfirming behavior. After all, presumably most people would not want to be seen as lazy, and almost everyone, including lazy people, can engage in hard work. Thus, even though I am confronted by disconfirming behavior, I may still conclude that the expectancy was correct, or at least not entirely wrong.

While this complex awareness takes us deep into Goffman's (1959) world of strategic self-presentation and the seemingly endless world of recursive thinking, it also places us squarely in the real world and may provide a description of the dynamics which underlie the situation facing adult targets of consensually held stereotypes. Hilton (1985) has conducted a study that examined this situation. The goal of that study was to determine what would happen when targets disconfirm a negative expectancy under conditions in which it is clear to perceivers that the targets know of the existence of the negative expectancy. More specifically, would the attenuation of the expectancy-confirmation effect found by Hilton and Darley (1985) in turn be attenuated by telling perceivers that the target of the expectancy knew of its existence?

In order to examine this question, subjects were provided with interview questions and asked to interview another person and evaluate that person's suitability for a competitive game. The description of the game made it clear that what was required of participants was the ability to think quickly on their feet. Some subjects were given no expectancy information about the interviewee. Others were given information, in the form of fictitious personality test scores, indicating that the person they would be interviewing might have trouble thinking on his or her feet. In other words, they were given an anxious expectancy. These subjects were told that the interviewee was unaware that they had been given this information. Still others were told the interviewee was aware of the expectancy information and also aware that if selected, he or she would be able to compete for a monetary prize. All subjects then conducted an interview in which they heard an audiotaped confederate provide expectancy-disconfirming information. After the interview the subjects evaluated the target on a number of expectancy-relevant dimensions.

The results from the study support the notion that expectancy-confirmation effects will be greatest when the perceiver is told that the target is aware of the existence of a negative expectancy. Subjects who were given the expectancy that the target would be anxious, and who knew, additionally, that the target was aware both of the nature of the interview (i.e., a selection interview) and of the existence of the anxious expectancy, recalled more instances of nervous behavior than did subjects who received the expectancy but who believed the target to be unaware of its existence and unaware of the nature of the interview. They also tended to rate the target in more expectancy-consistent ways.

INTERACTION TACTICS

Based jointly on their interaction goals, the possibilities and constraints that they perceive to exist in the situation, and the initial information that they have about their fellow interactants, individuals generate specific interaction tactics.* A job seeker meets an influential member of the corporation at a social gathering. Given that there are relatively high constraints on showing off technical knowledge and skills at a party, and relatively few resources with which to do so, and far fewer constraints on displaying charm or sociability, the job seeker decides that his or her specific interaction purpose or strategy should be to bring the influential person to like him or her. But how do perceivers translate and integrate all of the information that is available to them about their needs and goals, the situation, and the target into a reasonable set of interaction behaviors? We

*We need to acknowledge that our choice of terminology here, like that of others who have struggled with the strategic vocabulary, is not perfect. For instance, in commenting on the state of two individuals who meet in a waiting room, presumably to pass time before an experiment begins, we will say that their goal is only to have a pleasant interaction. But in several ways this is stretching the language a bit. It is unlikely to be the case that the interactant enters the room with the thought "well now, it is time to have the goal of having a pleasant interaction." An alternate way of describing the case would be to say that the person had no particular goals in mind. (Although if the conversation began to turn unpleasant, it is likely that the goal of pleasantness or withdrawing from the field would become both more explicit and more conscious for the interactant.)

would like to suggest that a useful way to conceptualize the process by which a perceiver arrives at a set of interaction behaviors or tactics is by the use of scenarios.

SCENARIOS

For present purposes, scenarios are the numerous courses of action and potential outcomes that a perceiver imagines occurring as the interaction unfolds. It is by the generation and analysis of possible scenarios that the perceiver integrates goal, situation, and target information into a set of interaction tactics. Scenarios consist of two rather distinct parts. First, there is the stream of behaviors itself along with the culminating outcome of that particular imagined interaction. These may be more or less vivid, mundane, or compelling. Second, and a critical determinant of the interaction tactics a perceiver will ultimately choose to employ, is the subjective estimate of how likely a particular sequence is to produce a desired outcome. Imagined scenarios that produce desirable outcomes with a high degree of (imagined) certainty will obviously hold greater sway over the choice of interaction tactics than will low-likelihood scenarios. (Bandura [1986], in his work on self-efficacy, and the motivational theorists, in their work on expectancy valence [e.g., Atkinson, 1964; Fishbein, 1967; Rotter, 1954], incorporate similar concepts.)

For example, if one of us were attempting to make a 4:00 train and encountered an angry individual who sought an afternoon appointment with us, we can imagine a number of ways the interaction might proceed. If we were to say to the angry person, "Look, I'm in a hurry and don't have time to wait for people like you," we imagine that we would risk eliciting an unpleasant response from the person. On the other hand, if we were to use a different tactic and say instead, "I'm terribly sorry, but I must make a 4:00 train. Could we schedule the appointment for another time?" we imagine that the risk would be less. In other words, the resulting scenarios that we generate suggest that with this particular person (expectancy information, perhaps target-based or category-based) under these particular circumstances (situation information), this opening move would probably produce more positive results (as defined by my goals for the interaction). During the course of this imagining process, some of the imagined outcomes will be more vivid and involving or less so. Being severely rebuked by an angry person, for example, is a vivid image that fills many of us with trepidation.

From the scenarios that are imagined, the interactant chooses his or her opening moves based on those imagined opening moves that are most likely to accomplish his or her goals for the interaction. It is important to note that this scenario generation can be conceived of as having two phases: an initial phase immediately prior to interaction followed by a continuing reevaluation as the interaction proceeds. Perhaps most intriguing about the suggestion that interactants generate scenarios about the effects that specific interaction behaviors or tactics will produce is the possibility that certain outcomes (as anticipated by the generation of mental scenarios) are either so attractive or so repulsive that they obviate all other interaction possibilities. A basic dichotomy can be identified at the level of interaction tactics. The consideration of one set of scenarios may lead perceivers to adopt an interaction tactic of avoidance. For example, if the angry individual from above is sufficiently violent, we may choose never to interact with him. The consideration of other scenarios, however, may lead to the conclusion that engaging in interaction is the most reasonable tactic to employ. We return to this basic dichotomy in the final section of the chapter.

The Interaction Unfolds

In many instances the interaction tactics that arise from the perceiver's interaction goals, knowledge of the situation, and knowledge about the target (i.e., expectancies) will be explicitly directed at the discovery of information about another person. In other instances, very different tactics are generated. But what consequences will these tactics have for the perceivers' subsequent impressions of the target? We have recently conducted a study in which we examined the impact of perceivers' interaction goals on the tactics that they adopt during an interaction and on their subsequent impressions of the target of a negative expectancy (Darley, Fleming, Hilton, & Swann, 1988). Subjects were asked to participate in an experiment on interpersonal communication and perception. They were led to expect that their interaction partners might have difficulty performing well under pressure. Half the perceivers were placed in an interaction setting that made the goal of evaluating the target as a possible teammate for a future cooperative task relevant (the "potential partner" conditions), and half were placed in an interaction setting that made relevant the interaction goal of passing a few harmonious moments with the other (the "casual conversation" conditions). Orthogonal to this manipulation, half the perceivers interacted with a target who, if probed, provided evidence that was consistent with the expectancy, and half interacted with a target who, if probed, provided evidence that was inconsistent with the expectancy. The interaction between the perceiver and the target was structured so that the perceiver asked the target eight questions chosen from a longer list of preset questions.

We predicted that perceivers for whom the interaction goal of assessing the target as a potential partner was relevant would ask significantly more questions designed to test the expectancy than would perceivers for whom the goal of passing a few harmonious moments with the target was relevant. Additionally, we predicted that whether the initial expectation was confirmed or disconfirmed would be a complex interactive product of the perceiver's interaction goal and information provided about the target's disposition in response to the perceiver's probes. The results were consistent with our predictions. Only when the perceiver adopted interaction tactics designed to search for expectancy-relevant information, and the target, if probed, presented expectancy-disconfirming information, was the perceiver's initial expectancy disconfirmed. In the other three conditions, the perceivers retained impressions of the targets that were, to various degrees, consistent with their initial expectancy about them.

In addition, an interesting finding emerged about the different natures of confirming and disconfirming information in response to perceiver probes. For perceivers who received primarily confirming information in response to their probes, their evaluations of the targets on expectancy-related dimensions were unrelated to the number of expectancy-relevant questions they asked during the interaction. In contrast, for perceivers who received primarily disconfirming information in response to their probes, their evaluations of the targets were significantly affected by the number of expectancy-relevant questions they asked. Specifically, the more expectancy-relevant questions these perceivers asked, the less likely they were to rate the targets as consistent with the original expectancy. It would appear that confirming and disconfirming information are asymmetrical—confirming information simply serves to validate the original expectancy regardless of how much confirming information is received. On the other hand, disconfirming information appears to produce a stepwise revision of the expectancy; the more disconfirming information that is received, the less the target is rated as consistent with the expectancy. This finding is quite interesting, but further research is necessary to understand it more clearly.

At a more general level the experiment makes clear that the interaction tactics that perceivers adopt have important consequences for the way in which the interaction unfolds and the extent to which initial expectancy information is perceived as having been confirmed. In some instances the interaction tactics chosen by perceivers may alter the behavior of targets. Sometimes the alteration will lead the target to behaviorally confirm the perceiver's expectations. These instances represent the self-fulfilling prophecy. In other instances the alteration will lead the target to behaviorally disconfirm the perceiver's expectations. These instances represent self-disconfirming prophecies (cf. Merton, 1957). In still other instances the perceivers' tactics will not alter the behavior of the target in ways that lead the target to behaviorally confirm or disconfirm the perceivers' original expectations. Nevertheless, perceptual confirmation and disconfirmation may still take place even when the target's behavior is unchanged. (For a more complete discussion of the logical possibilities, see Miller & Turnbull, 1986). Regardless of the specific course the interaction takes, as the interaction unfolds, perceivers continually update information relevant to the situation, their fellow interactants, and their interaction goals, as they generate new scenarios and new tactics.

In summary, then, the interaction-goals model maintains that an individual enters an interaction against a background of needs and general circumstances. Various situational norms and rules set a structure for the interaction, in that they make normative certain actions while setting other kinds of actions out of bounds. The resources available in the situation make certain kinds of interactions easy, other kinds difficult or impossible. Expectations about the other create an image of the other's personality, which includes hints about the moves to which the other will respond well or badly. From a consideration of all of these factors (and the consideration is often a brief and less than completely conscious one), the individual generates his or her interaction goal and turns again to various situational cues, including ones about the other person, to generate scenarios which in turn determine his or her specific interaction tactics, which are then carried out.

IMPLICATIONS FOR SELF-DEFEATING BEHAVIOR

In the opening paragraphs of this chapter we broadly identified four ways in which the self-fulfilling prophecy could result in self-defeating behavior either on the part of the prophet or on the part of the target of the prophecy. With the interaction-goals model as background, in the remainder of the chapter we focus on these aspects of the self-fulfilling prophecy.

INACCURATE PERCEPTION

One way in which the self-fulfilling prophecy is sometimes defeating is that it can lead social perceivers to reach inaccurate conclusions about the abilities and dispositions of others. Through the workings of the self-fulfilling prophecy we may, for example, come to believe that someone who is actually of average sociability is hostile (Snyder & Swann, 1978b) or that someone who is actually sane is insane (Farina & Ring, 1965; Rosenhan, 1973). During the 1970s and 1980s, the issue of accuracy has been a central concern of the person perception literature. Typically, the assumption has been that accurate assessments allow perceivers to render the world more predictable and controllable. In other words, the assumption has been that accurate assessments are functional because they allow perceivers to gain greater mastery over their environment (Heider, 1958; Jones & Davis, 1965; Kahneman, Slovic, & Tversky, 1982; Nisbett & Ross, 1980; Tversky & Kahneman, 1974). Even a casual glance at the person perception literature, however, reveals that perceivers are frequently woefully inaccurate. A host of biases and errors have been identified. These include the tendency to overattribute behavior to dispositional causes (Heider, 1958; Jones & Harris, 1967; Ross, 1977), an insensitivity to base-rate information (Nisbett & Borgida, 1975; Tversky & Kahneman, 1974), an inability to revise beliefs and perceptions in the face of new information (see Slusher & Anderson, Chapter 2, this volume), and a tendency to test new hypotheses in a biased manner (Snyder, 1984; but see also Trope & Bassok, 1982). In short, the image of the social perceiver that emerges is one of a rather inept scientist who bases his or her conclusions on too little evidence that has been gathered in too biased a manner (Nisbett & Ross, 1980).

Swann (1984), however, has taken issue with this characterization of the social perceiver. Taking a pragmatic approach to perception, Swann has argued that perceivers usually make accurate inferences, at least at a circumscribed level; that is, Swann argues that perceivers typically are quite accurate in their predictions of the behavior of others when certain conditions are met. Specifically, he argues that perceivers will be accurate in their predictions in those instances in which the predictions call for anticipating the behavior of others when the others are in the presence of the perceiver, when the prediction covers a limited amount of time, and when the prediction is restricted to a limited number of situations. Swann argues that it is primarily when making more generalized inferences that perceivers go awry. For example, we may be able to predict quite accurately whether or not an irate student who has just flunked our course is on the verge of resorting to physical violence, but we may be quite poor at predicting how violently the student typically deals with nonacademic problems.

Swann's distinction between circumscribed and global accuracy is important because it allows us to locate more precisely the inaccuracies that result from the self-fulfilling prophecy. From the standpoint of circumscribed accuracy, the self-fulfilling prophecy creates few problems. The prophet holds an expectancy, arranges his or her behavior accordingly, and elicits confirming behavior from the target. His or her circumscribed accuracy is quite high. For example, imagine that Jane has heard through the grapevine that Rick is a painfully shy person. Upon meeting him for the first time she attempts to insulate herself from his reputed shyness by adopting an aloof persona and refraining from engaging in conversation. He, sensing her coolness, responds in kind and behaves in a distant manner. Jane now has evidence that Rick is, in fact, shy, and we would be hard pressed to say that she is inaccurate from the standpoint of circumscribed accuracy. After all, if we had a naive observer watch Rick's behavior, the observer too would conclude that Rick had behaved in a shy manner. Jane will be inaccurate, however, if she attempts to generalize from her interaction with Rick to Rick's interactions with other people in different situations. She will, for example, be unable to predict accurately how he behaves in front of an audience or how he acts with his wife. It is at this more global level of accuracy that the self-fulfilling prophecy creates problems for the perceiver. In many situations we are called to make predictions about others in contexts other than ones in which we have previously interacted, and here the self-fulfilling prophecy can lead us seriously astray.

For example, Word, Zanna, & Cooper (1974) have demonstrated how racial stereotypes can lead interviewers to behave in ways that create self-fulfilling prophecies. Specifically, Word *et al.* examined black–white dyadic interactions and found that white interviewers created a more distant interview by spending less time and engaging in less immediate behaviors (Mehrabian, 1968) with black interviewees than with white interviewees. They also found that white interviewees tended to have more successful interviews than did black interviewees. More importantly, in a second part of the experiment Word *et al.* were able to demonstrate that the performance difference between white and black interviewees could be attributed to the behavior of the interviewers rather than to any objective difference between the white and black interviewees. When confederate interviewers were trained to treat white interviewees in the manner that subject interviewers had previously treated black interviewees, the white interviewees did poorly also. Again, notice that from the standpoint of circumscribed accuracy, the negative evaluations of the black interviewees in the first part of the experiment were highly accurate. Black interviewees did worse in the interviews than did white interviewees. Because the difference was due to the behavior of the interviewer rather than the interviewee, however, from the standpoint of global accuracy the negative evaluations were highly inaccurate and, moreover, potentially maladaptive. After all, there is no reason to expect that the differences would persist once the perceiver (interviewer) was removed from the scene and interviewers who fell prey to the self-fulfilling prophecy would have passed over people who would have been well-suited for the job.

A similar point is made in a study conducted by Strickland (1958), though the study is rarely thought of as one examining the self-fulfilling prophecy. Strickland had subjects act as supervisors over two other people. He arranged it such that the subjects monitored one of the individuals more closely than the other. Despite similar performance levels, Strickland found that the supervisors placed greater trust in the person they spent less time monitoring. Apparently, the subjects came to believe that the monitored individuals required monitoring in order to keep production at the current level. Again, from the standpoint of circumscribed accuracy, the subjects could accurately predict the behavior of the monitored individuals while the individuals were being monitored. Where they were inaccurate was in their predictions about how the individuals would perform in the absence of supervision, and had they allocated resources according to their perceptions, they would have allocated them in an inefficient manner.

In both the Word *et al.* (1974) and the Strickland (1958) studies, perceivers made errors when generalizing to other situations in part because they failed to recognize correctly the nature of the impact that their own behavior and expectations had on their fellow interactants. Stated more generally, self-fulfilling prophecies can be self-defeating because they provide the perceiver with a data base that is accurate only in those instances in which the perceiver does not have to generalize to situations in which he or she will not be present. Whenever the perceiver is called upon to make a more general prediction, the data base is *systematically* biased toward the perceiver's expectations by the previous workings of the self-fulfilling prophecy process.

Consistent with the previous comments, the bulk of the expectancy literature has been concerned with the mechanisms that lead people to emerge from interactions with their beliefs about others intact. Little research has been done on the question of what impact expectancies have prior to interaction, and we would like to suggest that this is an important and crucial omission. Recall that one possible tactic that may emerge from the preinteraction scenario generation is that the perceiver will decide that the best tactic is one of avoidance; that is, in some instances the preinteraction phase of scenario generation may yield a set of potential interaction outcomes that are all contrary to the perceiver's goals. Or, the perceiver may imagine one particularly nasty outcome that seems more likely to occur than any of the other imagined scenarios. In these cases, it seems likely that the perceiver will choose not to interact with the target person and may instead opt for some other course of action. Moreover, it seems to us that this preinteraction avoidance behavior is one of the most crucial, and most overlooked, aspects of the expectancy-confirmation sequence. But how exactly might expectancy confirmation arise in this situation?

We can all imagine situations in which we heard something about someone else, but failing to interact with that person either because of our own avoidance of the person or because circumstances prevented it, we nonetheless remain convinced that the original information we had was correct. This is particularly likely to be the case, for example, with negative racial stereotypes.* One possible description of this "autistic confirmation" process might be as follows: I discover something rather nasty about you that could have severe consequences for me should we ever interact. Because of this knowledge, I choose to avoid you, rather than to interact with you face-to-face. In order to avoid you, however, I must expend a certain amount of mental and physical effort. When asked what I think you are like, I recall the effort involved in avoiding you and decide that I would not have expended so much energy unless my worst fears would have been realized, had I actually confronted you. As a result, I conclude that you must be truly nasty. Why else would a rational person have engaged in all of that avoidance?

From our earlier discussion, it is not difficult to see that the basic interaction tactics dichotomy between choosing to interact and avoiding interaction provides particularly fertile circumstances for perceivers to engage in potentially self-defeating behavior. For some individuals, the anxiety produced by imagining the outcomes of various interpersonal moves may push them toward avoiding the target, when in reality their anxieties are not justified. This self-imposed isolation may make the perceiver feel better in the short haul, but in the long run may lead to further avoidance and greater isolation. Others may choose to engage in interaction, but the expectations that they hold may lead them to adopt interaction tactics which subsequently bias their perceptions of their fellow interactants.

Goal Interference

A second way in which the self-fulfilling prophecy can be self-defeating is one that is more obviously consistent with the way the term *self-defeating* is typically used. Consider, for example, U.S.–Soviet relations at the height of the cold war. Presumably, the goal of both countries was to ensure peace. Each country, however, believed that the other country could not be trusted, and each adopted the tactic of increasing its own nuclear arsenal. Over time, each side then pointed to the nuclear stockpiles of the other country as evidence of that country's malevolent intent. Newcomb (1947) early on identified this state of affairs with his description of autistic hostility. Or, consider the case of a student who, worried about failing an exam, avoids the anxiety created by thinking of the exam by avoiding studying for it, thereby assuring the receipt of a poor

*Here we are reminded of Newcomb's (1947) autistic hostility effect—that persons who are in conflict tend to avoid one another with no possibility of resolution of their difficulties—or Jones' (1964) autistic conspiracy, in which both ingratiators and the targets of ingratiation prefer to see the other in a positive light to avoid the negative consequences of accepting each other's ingratiation roles. The theoretical framework we have advanced here, as well as some additional social-psychological theory, can shed some light on how these effects may come about.

grade. In both examples, the expectancy information (i.e., hostility and failure) combines with the perceiver's knowledge of the situation and general interaction goals to initiate a self-fulfilling prophecy which, in turn, renders the perceiver's interaction goal less attainable. In the first instance the self-fulfilling prophecy occurs interpersonally, while in the second it occurs intrapersonally. In both instances the prophet is defeated by the prophecy.

Empirical support for this type of self-defeating outcome of the self-fulfilling prophecy can be found in studies by Kelley & Stahelski (1970) and Snyder & Swann (1978b). In the Kelley & Stahelski study, for example, subjects played the prisoner's dilemma game. Some subjects (cooperators) indicated that they believed that the world was composed of both cooperators and competitors and that their strategy would be to begin by cooperating. Other subjects (competitors) indicated that they believed that the world was uniformly composed of competitors and that their strategy would be to begin by competing. Of particular interest here was the behavior of the competitors. These subjects presumably wanted to win the game (maximize their own payoff), but their expectations of competitive behavior from others led them to behave in a competitive manner. This behavior, in turn, elicited competitive behavior from their opponent, even when their opponent's original intention had been to cooperate. Moreover, we know from other studies that competitive behavior in the prisoner's dilemma game reduces payoffs to each participant, so the competitive player inflicted self-damage by playing competitively. Subjects also emerged from the study reinforced in their belief that the world is exclusively composed of competitors—an example of circumscribed accuracy and global inaccuracy.

Target Complicity

So far, we have noted the ways in which the self-fulfilling prophecy can be self-defeating from the perspective of the perceiver and have presented the interaction goals model from the perceiver's perspective. From the perspective of the interaction-goals model, however, the distinction between target and perceiver is a rather arbitrary one. In ongoing interactions each interactant is both target and perceiver. There are at least two ways, however, in which the self-fulfilling prophecy can be said to be self-defeating from the perspective of the target.

One way in which the self-fulfilling prophecy can be self-defeating from the target's perspective is that negative expectations can shape interactions in ways of which the target is unaware and against which he or she is powerless to defend; that is, because targets are frequently unaware of the existence of a negative expectancy, they fail to make disconfirmation an interaction goal and become unwitting accomplices to their own destruction. The majority of studies investigating the self-fulfilling prophecy have been conducted under precisely these circumstances and provide ample demonstration of the ways in which targets can be induced to confirm the perceiver's negative expectations (e.g., Curtis & Miller, 1986; Rist, 1970; Rosenthal & Jacobson, 1968). To return to our earlier example, Rick, because he is unaware of the cause of Jane's aloof manner, behaves in ways that fuel her beliefs about his shyness. If he had been aware of the expectancy, he might have been able to muster the resources to address it directly and overcome its deleterious effects (Hilton & Darley, 1985; Swann & Ely, 1984; Swann & Read, 1981).

Although obvious exceptions obtain (i.e., some expectancies, such as race and gender, are more obvious than others), the normative limitations on social interactions make it rare that a person is aware of the existence of negative expectations. Research by Farina (1965, 1968) and his colleagues, however, suggests a second way in which the self-fulfilling prophecy can be self-defeating from the target's perspective. Specifically, their research suggests that in some instances even knowledge of a perceiver's negative expectations won't help a target overcome the effect of the expectancy. In fact, their findings suggest that in some instances simply alerting targets to the existence of a negative expectancy is sufficient to cause the target to behave in potentially confirming ways. For example, Farina and Ring (1965) told targets that their fellow interactants had information indicating that the targets were former mental patients. Other targets were not so informed, and the fellow interactants never, in fact, had this information. The results showed that targets who were told that the perceiver had the negative expectancy actually behaved in ways that were consistent with the label of mental illness.

Along similar lines, Farina, Allen, and Saul (1968) conducted an experiment to examine the effects of a target's knowledge of a negative expectancy on others' perceptions of him or her. Subjects participated in pairs, and the target in each pair was asked to prepare a written life history describing himself or herself either as relatively normal, as an overt homosexual, or as an ex-mental patient who continued to suffer from emotional problems. The experimenter then supposedly took the written statements to the other member of the pair who in reality received a life history that portrayed the target as relatively normal. The pairs then interacted and the interactions were recorded. From the present perspective, the important result that emerged was that the interactions involving targets who thought the other member of the pair had received a stigmatized life history were relatively more distant and contained few immediate behaviors. Targets in these conditions spoke less and initiated fewer conversations than did targets in the normal life history condition. In other words, stigmatized targets apparently gave off cues that led others to curtail their interactions with them. Our own interpretation of the curious results that emerged in the Farina and Ring (1965) and Farina *et al.* (1968) studies is that targets who were informed of the labels were so disconcerted that they behaved in less competent or "normal" ways.

The circumstances described in this section so far are ones in which targets are unwitting accomplices to their own destruction. But there are also situations in which targets actively contribute to expectancy confirmation. For example, targets' attempts to disabuse the perceiver of an expectancy can sometimes backfire. The targets' protestations, or attempts to present a self-image different from that portrayed by the expectancy, may actually provide grist for the perceiver's expectancy-confirmation mill. These distancing behaviors may actually arouse suspicion on the part of the perceiver and serve further to reinforce his or her original impressions. Here we are reminded of the Queen in *Hamlet*, who upon witnessing a reenactment of the King's murder betrays her suspicion of one of the characters by remarking, "Methinks, the lady doth protest too much" (*Hamlet*, act III, scene 2).

In summary, if we recall Snyder and Swann's (1978b) demonstration of the behavioral-confirmation effect, in which unwitting targets responded to perceivers' hostile overtures with hostility, it is not hard to see that targets can be led down the garden path by the expectations of others and provide those others with evidence sufficient to confirm their prior beliefs. Farina and his colleagues' work further suggests that targets can lead themselves down the garden path. In some instances knowledge of a negative expectancy will lead the target to behave in ways that are perceived as confirming.

Creating the Conditions for Our Own Demise

A second way in which the self-fulfilling prophecy can lead to self-defeating behavior on the part of targets is that targets can actually trigger the negative expectancies that set the self-fulfilling prophecy effect into motion. For example, a junior faculty member is probably closer to the graduate students in terms of age and social status than he is to the other members of the faculty. This identification with the graduate students may make him feel more comfortable; he may dress and behave more like a graduate student than a faculty member. This behavior, in turn, may trigger expectations within the other members of the faculty that can have negative consequences for his career. They may see him as not coming along very well in his new position. Thus, what he makes up for in comfort he may lose in credibility with his colleagues.

Another obvious location for the emergence of this sort of effect is in job interview situations. Judging by the frequency with which the advice is given, apparently some individuals still do not recognize that the ways in which they dress for the interview are taken as signals of their attitudes, and particularly their attitudes toward the job. So, for instance, to arrive at an interview in running clothes may be taken by the interviewer as a sign of a too-casual approach to the job.

In general, then, behaviors that trigger negative expectations are likely to be self-defeating, particularly if they bring about any one of several events that can lead to negative outcomes for that individual (Darley and Fazio, 1980). All of this is obvious enough, but an examination of the word *behaviors* can lead to some more subtle realizations. When we say "behaviors," we first think of the set of actions that a person takes and more specifically those actions that are under that person's conscious control. Thus the therapy for these behaviors, if the behaviors are self-defeating, is simply to make the person aware of their self-defeating character and perhaps to coach him or her in alternative, non-self-defeating behaviors. Other behaviors, under less conscious control, can be dealt with by more imaginative coaching methods. Videotaping an individual who is being interviewed and then showing her the habitual and nonconscious fidgets or "feminine deference patterns" in her behavior may make her conscious of them and more open to adopting alternative forms of behavior. By and large then, what is at issue here is what behavioral therapists discuss under the rubric of skills training, with an orientation toward altering those behaviors that trigger negative expectancies in powerful interactants. However, there are other actions that trigger negative expectancies that do not readily come to mind when we think of the word *behavior*. Race is one such characteristic (Rist, 1970), as is the accent and regional intonation with which one speaks. Although these characteristics are not under the target's control, they remain terribly important in generating negative expectancies and in influencing the ways in which the target will respond to others and others will respond to the target. In the future it may be useful to broaden the examination of the self-defeating behavior syndrome to include these attributes.

GENERAL CONCLUSIONS

The notion that interaction goals are important has had one of those curious careers. It is a notion that at some level is widely accepted, yet it has not had as great an influence on research and theory as its proponents expected. From the work of Jones (1986), Swann (1984), Snyder (1984), and the theoretical work of Miller and Turnbull (1986), we sense a renewed interest in gaining for that perspective a second chance, and it is to this that we seek to contribute. In the current chapter, our goal has been to show that social perception and social interaction are much more closely interrelated than the trend of previous research has shown them to be, and that the concept of interaction goals provides a useful mechanism for explicating and ordering some of these interrelationships. Moreover, we have attempted to use the interaction-goals model as a framework within which the relationship between self-fulfilling prophecies and self-defeating behaviors could be examined. One implication that emerges from the current perspective is that, although it has generally been argued that self-fulfilling prophecies are virtually always destructive (if not always self-defeating), expectancy effects in general, and self-fulfilling prophecies in particular, need not be construed so negatively. On the contrary, it is relatively easy to imagine that such effects, in addition to their often pernicious consequences, can also produce the sorts of conditions that foster interpersonal perception (or at the very least do not impede it). It is our belief that the interaction goals framework can provide considerable guidance in specifying when and how these very different consequences will occur. Finally, we hope that the interaction-goals model will not only shed light on expectancy effects, but that it will also illuminate the relationship between expectancy effects and self-defeating behavior and help specify the conditions under which self-defeating behaviors occur.

ACKNOWLEDGMENTS

The material presented in this chapter is based upon work supported by the National Science Foundation under grants #BNS-8717784 and #BNS-8707412 to the first and second authors, respectively, and by a University of Minnesota Graduate School Grant-in-aid to the third author.

REFERENCES

Atkinson, J. W. (1964). *An introduction to motivation*. Princeton, NJ: Van Nostrand.

Bandura, A. (1986). *Social foundations of thought and action: A social cognitive theory*. Englewood Cliffs, NJ: Prentice-Hall.

Baumeister, R. F., & Scher, S. J. (1988). Self-defeating behavior patterns among normal individuals: Review and analysis of common self-destructive tendencies. *Psychological Bulletin, 104*, 3–22.

Berglas, S., & Jones, E. E. (1978). Drug choice as a self-handicapping strategy in response to noncontingent success. *Journal of Personality and Social Psychology, 36*, 405–417.

Cohen, C. E. (1981). Goals and schemata in person perception: Making sense from the stream of behavior. In N. Cantor and J. Kihlstrom (Eds.), *Personality, cognition, and social interaction* (pp. 45–68). Hillsdale, NJ: Erlbaum.

Curtis, R. C., & Miller, K. (1986). Believing another likes or dislikes you: Behaviors making the beliefs come true. *Journal of Personality and Social Psychology, 51*, 284–290.

Darley, J. M., & Fazio, R. H. (1980). Expectancy confirmation processes arising in the social interaction sequence. *American Psychologist, 35*, 867–881.

Darley, J. M., Fleming, J. H., Hilton, J. L., & Swann, W. B., Jr. (1988). Dispelling negative expectancies: The impact of interaction goals and target characteristics on the expectancy confirmation process. *Journal of Experimental Social Psychology, 24*, 19–36.

Farina, A., Allen, J. G., & Saul, B. B. (1968). The role of the stigmatized person in affecting social relationships. *Journal of Personality, 36*, 169–182.

Farina, A., & Ring, K. (1965). The influence of perceived mental illness on interpersonal relations. *Journal of Abnormal Psychology, 71*, 421–428.

Fishbein, M. (Ed.). (1967). *Readings in attitude theory and measurement*. New York: Wiley.

Goffman, E. (1955). On face-work: An analysis of ritual elements in social interaction. *Psychiatry, 18*, 213–231.

Goffman, E. (1959). *The presentation of self in everyday life*. Garden City, NY: Doubleday Anchor.

Goffman, E. (1969). *Strategic interaction*. Philadelphia: University of Pennsylvania Press.

Hamilton, D. L. (Ed.) (1981). *Cognitive processes in stereotyping and intergroup behavior*. Hillsdale, NJ: Erlbaum.

Hamilton, D. L., & Gifford, R. K. (1976). Illusory correlation in interpersonal perception: A cognitive basis of stereotype judgments. *Journal of Experimental Social Psychology, 12*, 392–407.

Hamilton, D. L., & Rose, T. L. (1980). Illusory correlation and the maintenance of stereotypic beliefs. *Journal of Personality and Social Psychology, 39*, 832–845.

Heider, F. (1958). *The psychology of interpersonal relations*. New York: Wiley.

Hilton, J. L. (1985). *Discounting and expectancy confirmation: An investigation of recursive social awareness*. Unpublished doctoral dissertation, Princeton University.

Hilton, J. L., & Darley, J. M. (1985). Constructing other persons: A limit on the effect. *Journal of Experimental Social Psychology, 21*, 1–18.

Jones, E. E. (1964). *Ingratiation: A social psychological analysis*. New York: Appleton-Century-Crofts.
Jones, E. E. (1986). Interpreting interpersonal behavior: The role of expectancies. *Science, 234*, 41–46.
Jones, E. E., & Berglas, S. (1978). Control of attributions about the self through self-handicapping strategies. The appeal of alcohol and the role of underachievement. *Personality and Social Psychology Bulletin*, 4(2), 200–206.
Jones, E. E., & Davis, K. E. (1965). From acts to dispositions: The attribution process in person perception. In L. Berkowitz (Ed.), *Advances in experimental social psychology* (Vol. 2, pp. 219–266). New York: Academic Press.
Jones, E. E., & Harris, V. A. (1967). The attribution of attitudes. *Journal of Experimental Social Psychology, 3*, 1–24.
Jones, E. E., & Thibaut, J. (1958). Interaction goals as bases of inference in interpersonal perception. In R. Tagiuri & L. Petrullo (Eds.), *Person perception and interpersonal behavior*. Stanford, CA: Stanford University Press.
Jones, R. A. (1977). *Self-fulfilling prophecies: Social, psychological, and physiological effects of expectancies*. Hillsdale, NJ: Erlbaum.
Jussim, L. (1986). Self-fulfilling prophecies. A theoretical and integrative review. *Psychological Review, 93*, 429–445.
Kahneman, D., Slovic, P., & Tversky, A. (Eds.). (1982). *Judgment under uncertainty: Heuristics and biases*. New York: Cambridge University Press.
Kelley, H. H. (1967). Attribution theory in social psychology. In D. Levine (Ed.), *Nebraska Symposium on Motivation* (Vol. 15, pp. 192–241). Lincoln: University of Nebraska Press.
Kelley, H. H., & Thibaut, J. (1978). *Interpersonal relations: A theory of interdependence*. New York: Wiley.
Kelley, H. H., & Stahelski, A. J. (1970). Social interaction basis of cooperators' and competitors' beliefs about others. *Journal of Personality and Social Psychology, 16*, 66–91.
Mehrabian, A. (1968). Inference of attitudes from the posture, orientation, and distance of a communicator. *Journal of Consulting and Clinical Psychology, 32*, 296–308.
Merton, R. K. (1948). The self-fulfilling prophecy. *Antioch Review, 8*, 193–210.
Merton, R. K. (1957). *Social theory and social structure*. New York: Free Press.
Miller, D. T., & Turnbull, W. (1986). Expectancies and interpersonal processes. In M. R. Rosenzweig & L. W. Porter (Eds.), *Annual review of psychology* (Vol. 37, pp. 233–256). Palo Alto, CA: Annual Reviews.
Miller, G. A., Galanter, E., & Pribram, K. H. (1960). *Plans and the structure of behavior*. New York: Holt, Rinehart & Winston.
Newcomb, T. M. (1947). Autistic hostility and social reality. *Human Relations, 1*, 69–86.
Nisbett, R. E., & Borgida, E. (1975). Attribution and the psychology of prediction. *Journal of Personality and Social Psychology, 32*, 932–943.
Nisbett, R. E., & Ross, L. (1980). *Human inference: Strategies and shortcomings of social judgment*. Englewood Cliffs, NJ: Prentice-Hall.
Rist, R. (1970). Student social class and teacher expectations: The self-fulfilling prophecy in ghetto education. *Harvard Educational Review, 40*, 411–451.
Rosenhan, D. L. (1973). On being sane in insane places. *Science, 179*, 250–258.
Rosenthal, R., & Jacobson, L. F. (1968). *Pygmalion in the classroom*. New York: Holt, Rinehart & Winston.
Rosenthal, R., & Rubin, D. B. (1978). Interpersonal expectancy effects: The first 345 studies. *The Behavioral and Brain Sciences, 3*, 377–415.
Ross, L. (1977). The intuitive psychologist and his shortcomings: Distortions in the attribution process. In L. Berkowitz (Ed.), *Advances in experimental social psychology* (Vol. 10, pp. 174–221). New York: Academic Press.

Rotter, J. B. (1954). *Social learning and clinical psychology*. Englewood Cliffs, NJ: Prentice-Hall.

Shapiro, J., & Hilton, J. L. (1988). *The impact of interaction goals on expectancy confirmation*. Paper presented at the Sixtieth Annual Meeting of the Midwestern Psychological Association, Chicago, IL.

Showers, C., & Cantor, N. (1985). Social cognition: A look at motivated strategies. In M. R. Rosenzweig & L. W. Porter (Eds.), *Annual review of psychology* (Vol. 36, pp. 275–306). Palo Alto, CA: Annual Reviews.

Snyder, M. (1979). Self-monitoring processes. In L. Berkowitz (Ed.), *Advances in experimental social psychology* (Vol. 12, pp. 86–131). New York: Academic Press.

Snyder, M. (1981). Seek, and ye shall find: Testing hypotheses about other people. In E. T. Higgins, C. P. Herman, & M. P. Zanna (Eds.), *Social cognitions: The Ontario symposium*. (Vol. 1, pp. 277–304). Hillsdale, NJ: Erlbaum.

Snyder, M. (1984). When belief creates reality. In L. Berkowitz (Ed.), *Advances in experimental social psychology* (Vol. 18, pp. 248–306). New York: Academic Press.

Snyder, M., & Swann, W. B., Jr. (1978a). Hypothesis-testing processes in social interaction. *Journal of Personality and Social Psychology, 36*, 1202–1212.

Snyder, M.,& Swann, W. B., Jr. (1978b). Behavioral confirmation in social interaction: From social perception to social reality. *Journal of Experimental Social Psychology, 14*, 148–162.

Strickland, L. H. (1958). Surveillance and trust. *Journal of Personality, 26*, 200–215.

Stryker, S., & Gottlieb, A. (1981). Attribution theory and symbolic interactionism: A comparison. In J. H. Harvey, W. J. Ickes, & R. F. Kidd (Eds.), *New directions in attribution research* (Vol. 3l, pp. 425–458). Hillsdale, NJ: Erlbaum.

Stryker, S., & Statham, A. (1985). Symbolic interactionism and role theory. In G. Lindzey & E. Aronson (Eds.), *Handbook of social psychology* (3rd ed., Vol. 1, pp.311–378). New York: Random House.

Swann, W. B., Jr. (1984). The quest for accuracy in person perception: A matter of pragmatics. *Psychological Review, 91*, 457–477.

Swann, W. B., Jr., & Ely, R. J. (1984). A battle of wills: Self-verification versus behavioral confirmation. *Journal of Personality and Social Psychology, 46*, 1287–1302.

Swann, W. B., Jr., & Read, S. J. (1981). Self-verification processes: How we sustain our self-conceptions. *Journal of Experimental Social Psychology, 17*, 351–372.

Thibaut, J. W., & Kelley, H. H (1959). *The social psychology of groups*. New York: Wiley.

Trope, Y., & Bassok, M. (1982). Confirmatory and diagnosing strategies in social information gathering. *Journal of Personality and Social Psychology, 43*, 22–34.

Tversky, A., & Kahneman, D. (1974). Judgment under uncertainty: Heuristics and biases. *Science, 185*, 1124–1131.

Word, C. O., Zanna, M. P., & Cooper, J. (1974). The nonverbal mediation of self-fulfilling prophecies in interracial interaction. *Journal of Experimental Social Psychology, 14*, 148–162.

CHAPTER 4

TRYING AND GIVING UP

PERSISTENCE AND LACK OF PERSISTENCE IN FAILURE SITUATIONS

NORMAN T. FEATHER

INTRODUCTION

In my 1982 book, *Expectations and Actions* (Feather, 1982b), Janoff-Bulman and Brickman (1982) discussed the question of what people learn from failure and how their behavior in failure situations can be maladaptive. They described two kinds of maladaptive response: excessive trying or persistence when expectations are high and repeated failure is experienced, and giving up too quickly in the face of failure when expectations are low. My intention in the present chapter is first to summarize the main points of their discussion and to describe subsequent research that was suggested by their analysis. I then review a sample of theoretical approaches that relate to the analysis of persistence and that have implications for the general question of when persistence or lack of persistence is self-defeating or maladaptive.

My emphasis is on situations in which people experience repeated failure, whether it be failure to succeed at a task or to achieve some other goal. One could also discuss situations in which persistence or lack of persistence occurs under conditions of repeated success, as when people cling to tasks at which they always do well or turn away from success when it continues. The intermediate situations in which both success and failure occur in varying amounts are also of

NORMAN T. FEATHER • Discipline of Psychology, The Flinders University of South Australia, Bedford Park, South Australia 5042.

interest. The theoretical approaches described later in this chapter are relevant to both of these latter situations, but my main focus is on behaviors that involve trying or giving up under conditions of repeated failure. Space does not permit an exhaustive review of the literature in all of these areas. Indeed, my discussion of undue persistence after failure and quitting too hastily after failure involves a selective sampling of the recent literature directed toward providing ideas and theoretical frameworks that might be useful in future research.

THE PATHOLOGY OF LOW AND HIGH EXPECTATIONS

Janoff-Bulman and Brickman (1982) distinguish between two "pathologies." One they call the pathology of low expectations, the other the pathology of high expectations. The former pathology is discussed primarily in relation to people with low expectations who perform poorly or show lack of persistence under conditions of failure. For example, studies that I conducted in the 1960s indicated that prior failure at task items led to lower expectations of success and to impaired performance on subsequent items when compared with prior success at task items (Feather, 1966, 1968; Feather & Saville, 1967; see Feather, 1982a, pp. 74–78, for a review). Performance levels also tended to be positively related to initial estimates of chances of success under conditions where the actual difficulty of the task was truthfully represented to subjects. A similar experimental procedure that involves initial failure has been used more recently in investigations of learned helplessness in which the emphasis has been on the debilitating effects of expectations of uncontrollability on subsequent activity (Garber & Seligman, 1980).

Janoff-Bulman and Brickman (1982) describe other studies concerned with the negative effects of low expectations and failure, and they provide a number of explanations that relate to these effects. Thus, people may perform poorly or withdraw from a task after failure because they believe that outcomes are independent of their responses; that is, they have no control over events. They may develop causal attributions that failure is due to internal and stable causes, such as lack of ability, and give up trying. They may not try hard because enhanced effort would be dissonant with their low expectations of success. They may have high test anxiety and avoid tasks on which they expect to fail. They may attend to distracting features of the situation when they fail to meet defined performance criteria, especially if they become very anxious. All of these analyses suggest to Janoff-Bulman and Brickman that people who expect to do poorly will persist less in their efforts to solve problems, especially when they experience failure, and that it is this lack of persistence that determines deficits in problem-solving behavior among those who have low expectations of success and who fail.

Why might this behavior be maladaptive? It is clearly not maladaptive when low expectations are an accurate indication of one's abilities and when the task is either impossible or well beyond one's capabilities. In these cases quitting the task is the sensible thing to do. When one's low expectations are based on inaccurate information, however, a speedy withdrawal from a task in the face of initial failure, when one could in fact succeed at it, may be at some personal cost and may also preclude future benefits. A girl who has been brought up to believe that women are less able at mathematics than are men may develop a low expectation of her abilities in mathematics and science, may disengage or not even pursue studies in these areas, and may thereby foreclose on academic areas that could excite her interest and lead to a productive career, assuming that she was able to succeed in these areas (e.g., Eccles, Adler, & Meece, 1984; Feather, 1988b). Low expectations are therefore dangerous when they are based on false or inadequate information and do not accurately reflect the realities of person and task.

How might the pathology of low expectations be reduced? Janoff-Bulman and Brickman (1982) suggest that one might develop treatments that encourage people with low expectations to persist, to attribute their failures to lack of effort (a modifiable cause), and to focus their attention more strongly on task contingencies. They refer to studies concerned with attribution retraining (e.g., Diener & Dweck, 1978, 1980; Dweck, 1975) and the positive effects of focused attention (e.g., Brockner, 1979) that are consistent with these recommendations. I would add to their list of therapies, the development of procedures that undo falsely based expectancies and that replace them with expectancies that are based on valid information. This form of intervention might not necessarily lead to higher expectancies of success, but it could have that effect if individuals are seriously underestimating their abilities on the basis of generalized and ill-founded beliefs.

The pathology of high expectations refers to those cases in which individuals with high expectations of success persist for long periods of time at tasks for which no satisfactory solution can be found. These effects have been found in research involving subjects with strong levels of need achievement and low levels of test anxiety (Feather, 1961, 1962) and also among people with a generalized expectation that outcomes are under internal control (Weiss & Sherman, 1973). Other studies have found positive relations between expectations of success and persistence (e.g., Battle, 1965), and the results of more recent research indicate similar positive relations when the expectations concern perceived self-efficacy (e.g., Brown & Inouye, 1978).

Why might this behavior be maladaptive? Janoff-Bulman and Brickman point out that, in these experimental studies, dogged persistence against failure when expectations are high means the expenditure of time and effort with no more success than would have occurred had one quit early. In many real-life cases one might have even less to show for extreme persistence, and final outcomes might be on the negative side of the ledger. For example, the cost of persistence may be especially high if one misses out on valued alternatives because of a single-minded pursuit of a goal, as when a person who has decided to buy a new car or a new house rejects excellent opportunities in the hope that something better will come along. A failure to quit and cut one's losses may also result in escalating negative outcomes that can build up into catastrophic loss. Waiting for a declining share market to improve or for the next battle to be won in some conflict may result in much larger losses than would have occurred had one disengaged earlier. The negative effects of high expectations are also evident in situations where high expectations of internal control cannot be fulfilled, as occurs to some extent when a person enters a hospital or a nursing home or suffers a serious accident or illness (e.g., Janoff-Bulman & Marshall, 1978). Negative effects may also be apparent among people who show the Type A behavior pattern, characterized by a great sense of time urgency, competitive achievement striving, hostility when thwarted, and high expectations. There is evidence that the Type A behavior pattern is correlated with heart disease, though the precise causal basis is still the subject of investigation (Booth-Kewley & Friedman, 1987; Smith & Anderson, 1986). Recently, Strube and Boland (1986) showed that Type A's persisted at a task longer when it was difficult and when it was viewed as relatively low in information value or diagnosticity (Trope, 1983; Trope & Ben-Yair, 1982).

Janoff-Bulman and Brickman (1982) propose explanations for the pathology of high expectations that parallel those they discussed for the pathology of low expectations, namely, attribution theory, dissonance theory, the theory of learned helplessness, and the effects of test anxiety; but in this case these explanations operate in reverse. Thus, people who expect to do well may blame themselves when they fail and believe that they can change the situation by their own efforts. They may work harder because not working hard would be dissonant with their high expectations and with a belief that failure can be avoided by increased effort. They may be lower in test anxiety and may therefore be less likely to avoid test situations and more likely to focus attention on the task. Janoff-Bulman and Brickman suggest that people with high expectations might also profit from attribution retraining. They found that people with high expectations could be immunized against unprofitable persistence by telling them that some tasks were insoluble (Janoff-Bulman & Brickman, 1976). These results indicate the positive effects of correcting false expectations so that they are based on accurate information about the task and about other conditions of performance.

The remainder of the Janoff-Bulman and Brickman analysis is concerned with the importance of learning to discriminate between situations, so that people can decide when they should continue with a line of activity and when they should quit. They note the fact that North American society preaches the virtues of persistence but also provides reminders that one has to "know when to walk away, know when to run." They suggest that a person has to be able to distinguish between outcomes that are controllable or uncontrollable, problems that are soluble or insoluble, tasks that are difficult or easy, events that are correlated or uncorrelated, and performances that are diagnostic of ability and those that are not. They also note the need for people to receive unambiguous and informative feedback about their success and failure in particular situations, a point that I have also drawn attention to in relation to false versus accurate expectations. Finally, Janoff-Bulman and Brickman (1982) discuss a sequential model of testing one's limits that involves an "alternation between periods of working, pushing, and concentrating and periods of regrouping, drawing back, and relaxing" (p. 226). They argue that a person has to know

> how to fail, how to recognize when control has been lost and how to reassert control. . . . Control is not merely the ability to make things happen, to make

> things start. Equally important is control of the last resort, the ability to make things stop happening. (pp. 227–228)

One has to discover one's limits and learn how to use this knowledge so as to decide when to retreat and how to operate effectively within those limits.

As noted, throughout their article Janoff-Bulman and Brickman (1982) refer to a number of research findings that are consistent with the arguments that they advance, and these findings come from many different areas of psychology (e.g., research concerned with achievement motivation, test anxiety, stress and coping, dissonance theory, helplessness theory, and attribution theory). One study by McFarlin, Baumeister, and Blascovich (1984) was specifically concerned with aspects of the Janoff-Bulman and Brickman analysis. These investigators found that subjects with high self-esteem tended to show nonproductive persistence on a task, especially after an initial failure experience. They persisted longer but performed worse than did those with low self-esteem. In a second study, these investigators found that subjects with high self-esteem who received explicit advice not to spend too much time on any one puzzle still tended to persist longer on insoluble puzzles than did subjects with low self-esteem who received the same advice. These latter results contrast with those of the Janoff-Bulman and Brickman (1976) immunization study described earlier, where subjects were told that some items were insoluble. McFarlin *et al.* (1984) note, however, that receiving advice is not the same as receiving information that items are insoluble. They suggest that taking advice or ignoring it has ramifications for self-presentation and that their subjects with high self-esteem may have been more likely to ignore advice because they wanted to take personal credit for success.

A study by Trope and Ben-Yair (1982) also provides evidence about the importance of task and outcome information in relation to persistence. Trope and Ben-Yair argue that the self-assessment of ability from performance outcomes plays an important role in achievement situations that involve success and failure. People may use information about the quality of their performance to estimate their abilities in different tasks. This assumption has implications for the analysis of task persistence. Thus, Trope and Ben-Yair assert that

> persistence can be conceptualized in terms of reduction of uncertainty regarding one's ability. Each trial attempted at a task is viewed as an informational query regarding one's ability level, and persistence is identified with the number of queries made before a decision to terminate the information search is reached. . . the number of queries should be negatively related to the rate with which uncertainty is reduced over trials. (p. 638)

According to Trope and Ben-Yair (1982), the rate at which uncertainty is reduced will depend upon the diagnosticity of task performance, "that is, the degree to which performance outcomes discriminate or vary across ability levels. . . . The greater the diagnosticity, the faster the rate with which uncertainty is reduced with successive trials" (p. 638). On this basis they hypothesize that persistence will be negatively related to the diagnostic value of the task. They note that their analysis applies to both success and failure situations because success can reduce uncertainty by diagnosing high ability, whereas failure can reduce uncertainty by diagnosing low ability. Thus, it is the information value of the outcome that is important rather than whether or not outcomes are positive and negative.

Trope and Ben-Yair (1982) report the results of a study that was based on their analysis. In their study, subjects worked at a task that varied in diagnostic value about their ability for as long as they wished, and they received either success or failure trial-by-trial feedback. Trope and Ben-Yair predicted that their subjects would persist less when task diagnosticity was high rather than low, because it would take fewer trials to assess their ability for a high diagnostic task than in a task low in diagnosticity. Their results supported this prediction for both success and failure conditions. Subjects spent less time working on a task as the diagnosticity of both success and failure increased. In fact, subjects were equally persistent when succeeding or failing at the high-diagnostic task. Trope and Ben-Yair claim that these results are consistent with the self-assessment model but not with formulations that assume that success and failure have opposite effects on task attractiveness (see Ruble & Boggiano, 1980).

Baumeister and Scher (1988) have recently reviewed studies that concern counterproductive persistence and that relate to the Janoff-Bulman and Brickman (1982) analysis. They note that some studies suggest that people with high self-esteem persist longer than do people with low self-esteem (e.g., Perez, 1973; Schalon, 1968; Schrauger & Sorman, 1977). They also indicate, however, that one can design conditions in which the persistence of subjects with high self-esteem on insoluble items results in lower overall achievement, as was the case in the McFarlin *et al.* (1984) study. Baumeister and Scher observe than an important factor that seems to be involved in some cases of nonproductive persistence is the feeling that one has already invested time, effort, money, or other valued resources in working at a task and that quitting would entail wasting these investments. Hence, people can become entrapped, and they may continue to persist with an activity, despite the fact that quitting would often be the most rational strategy.

Baumeister and Scher (1988) refer to studies by Staw (1976) and Rubin and Brockner (1975) in which procedures were developed to study entrapment. Becoming entrapped in counterproductive persistence has been shown to be related to feelings of personal responsibility for the decision to engage in the task (Staw, 1976) and to high feelings of commitment and high confidence that future investments will bring success (Bazerman, Giuliano, & Appelman, 1984). Explanations that refer to the generation of cognitive dissonance and to attempts to reduce dissonance have been advanced to account for the effects of these factors. Thus, dissonance would occur when a person feels personally responsible for and committed to a decision and when the decision results in escalating negative consequences. The person may try to reduce the dissonance by cognitive and behavioral adjustments (e.g., by overestimating one's chances of succeeding at the task or by putting more time and effort into the task in the hope that success will ultimately be achieved).

Other factors that appear to influence the tendency to become entrapped in counterproductive persistence relate to self-presentation concerns (e.g., Brockner, Rubin, & Lang, 1981; Brockner, Shaw, & Rubin, 1979; Fox & Staw, 1979;

Teger, 1980). Thus, a person who initiates an activity, in the face of controversy and advice from others not to become involved with it, may persist with the activity despite failure because to quit would be to lose face or to suffer a loss in self-esteem. Baumeister and Scher summarize studies that show that people may persist out of a kind of psychological inertia (e.g., Brockner *et al.*, 1979), that modeling can either increase or decrease counterproductive persistence (Brockner *et al.*, 1984), that educating people in advance about entrapment can help them to avoid excessive persistence (Nathanson *et al.*, 1982), that people who publicly set limits in advance about how far they will persist are less likely to become entrapped (Brockner *et al.*, 1979), and that careful attention to the calculation of probabilities and contingencies results in less likelihood of becoming entrapped in counterproductive persistence (Conlon & Wolf, 1980).

Baumeister and Scher (1988) conclude that persistence becomes self-destructive when it prevents one from "engaging in alternative, more auspicious endeavors, and [when] valuable resources are wasted in futile endeavors" (pp. 13–14). They observe that

> inflated views of one's abilities, concern about how others will evaluate one, and other factors sometimes take precedence over rational consideration of probabilities and contingencies, resulting in counterproductive persistence. Additional causal factors include personal investment and a situational structure that links persistence to a passive response. (p. 14)

PERSISTENCE AND ACHIEVEMENT MOTIVATION

In the remainder of this chapter I describe more formal models that can be applied to the analysis of persistence. These models draw attention to variables that influence trying or giving up when a person works at a task and experiences failure. I begin by describing my early research on persistence and some of the main theoretical assumptions that were involved in the conceptual analysis (Feather, 1961, 1962, 1963). This form of analysis opened up new doors in the psychology of motivation and led to theoretical developments relating to the stream of behavior and the dynamics of action (Atkinson & Birch, 1970; Kuhl & Atkinson, 1986).

I started with the basic assumption that one cannot understand a person's persistence at a task unless one also knows something about the alternatives that a person can turn to. Children are less likely to persist at their homework when their friends are outside asking them to join a game of football or cricket. So, if a person is to persist at the original task, the motivational tendency to work at the task must be greater than the motivational tendencies to perform alternative tasks. But how can one analyze these motivational tendencies? My analysis was in terms of expectancy-value theory, specifically the version used by Atkinson (1957) in his risk-taking model. Expectancy-value theory is a general approach to the analysis of behavior that relates a person's actions to the perceived attractiveness and aversiveness of expected outcomes (Feather, 1982b). What a person does is seen to bear some relation to the expectations that the person holds and to the subjective value of the outcomes that might occur following the action. The expectations encompass both beliefs about whether a particular action can be performed to some required standard that defines a successful outcome and beliefs about the various positive and negative consequences that might follow the outcome. Thus, whether or not a person has a tendency to act in a particular direction will depend on that person's expectation about whether he or she can perform the action to the required standard, on a further set of expectations about the possible consequences of the action, and on the valence (or subjective value) associated with the action outcome. Those actions will be preferred that can be coordinated to the dominant motivational tendencies that relate to a combination of these expectations and valences. The combination usually is assumed to be a multiplicative one.

Consistent with Atkinson's (1957) model, my early analysis of persistence allowed for the influence of relatively stable personality dispositions or motives. The initial theory of achievement motivation (Atkinson & Feather, 1966) included motives to achieve success and to avoid failure in the equations that were used to define approach and avoidance tendencies, and more recent theoretical statements continue to allow for individual differences in the strength of needs and motives (e.g., Brown & Veroff, 1986; Kuhl & Atkinson, 1986). I have recently incorporated human values into this theoretical approach, assuming that, like needs, values can induce valences (or subjective values) on objects and events (Feather, 1986, 1987a, 1988a).

The procedure used in these early persistence studies required subjects to work at an insoluble puzzle (a line-tracing problem) for as many trials as they liked, with the option of turning to the next puzzle in the series whenever they wanted to. I found that subjects who were classified as high in need achievement and low in test anxiety showed greater persistence at the puzzle when it was presented to them as easy (70% of students can complete it, high expectation of success) rather than as very difficult (5% of students can complete it, low expectation of success). In marked contrast, subjects who were classified as low in need achievement and high in test anxiety showed greater persistence when the puzzle was presented to them as very difficult (5% pass rate, low expectation) rather than as easy (70% pass rate, high expectation). These differences were predicted from my theoretical analysis, which included a basic assumption that repeated failure at a task would reduce expectations of success, represented in the model by subjective probabilities. Decreases in these subjective probabilities were assumed to produce changes in motivational tendencies that would ultimately lead to the condition where the motivational tendency to perform the alternative task was stronger than the motivational tendency to perform the initial task. The subject would then quit the initial task and switch to the alternative.

This form of analysis drew attention to the importance of considering a set of motivational tendencies that could wax or wane in the course of task performance. It also specified one process that could underlie changes in motivational tendencies, namely, changes in expectations of success that followed success or failure at a task. The analysis also allowed for the effects of both person variables and situation variables. In this sense the analysis was influenced by Lewin's (1935) injunction that behavior is a function of an interdependent set of influences involving both the person and the psychological environment, and it predated the subsequent rediscovery of interactionism in psychology in the 1970s. Finally, the analysis was not episodic but emphasized the complex relations between changing motivational tendencies and changes in activity within the stream of behavior. It directed attention to the importance of analyzing change in activity as a basic problem for motivational theory.

What implications does this motivational analysis have for understanding maladaptive persistence or lack of persistence? It recognized that trying and giving up could be related not only to high and low expectations and to personality variables such as need achievement and test anxiety but also to the nature of the alternative activities to which a person could turn. By bringing these variables together within an expectancy-value framework that allowed for dynamic change in motivational tendencies, it provided a completely new perspective in studying persistence and change in activity.

This early analysis of persistence was followed by other ideas about how tendencies might change. Weiner (1965, 1980) assumed that persisting, unsatisfied inertial tendencies could also lead to an increase or decrease in resultant tendencies. Here was another dynamic, in addition to change in cognitive expectations, that provided a way of understanding how tendencies change. Weiner's subsequent theorizing, however, has been much more concerned with the role of causal attributions, although he retains a basic interest in a framework in which expectancies and different kinds of affect are key variables (Weiner, 1985, 1986). I now briefly describe the form of Weiner's analysis and note its implications for the analysis of persistence.

ATTRIBUTIONS AND PERSISTENCE

Weiner (1985, 1986) sees his theory as related to the expectancy-value framework but with some differences when compared with other expectancy-value approaches. In particular, he indicates that his conception is presented as a historical or temporal sequence that takes account of prior influences and that, in his approach, value is linked to the affect that is associated with goal-directed activity and its positive or negative outcomes. My own statements have also linked valences (or subjective values) with anticipated affect (Feather, 1986), but Weiner's analysis of different types of emotion is far more differentiated than mine.

In Weiner's analysis a motivational sequence is assumed to be initiated by an outcome that is interpreted as either positive (goal attainment) or negative (nonattainment of the goal). If the outcome is unexpected, negative, or important, a causal search is initiated. The person tries to explain the outcome and draws from a limited set of possible causes (e.g., ability, task difficulty, luck, effort, and personality variables), depending upon the context. These causes are themselves linked to particular kinds of antecedent (to specific information, causal rules, hedonic biases, etc.). The causes that are offered can be located in an attributional space defined by a limited set of dimensions. Weiner argues that the three main properties of causes are locus, stability, and controllability. For example, failure at an exam may be attributed to lack of ability, which is considered to be an internal, stable, and uncontrollable cause, or to lack of effort, which is considered to be an internal, unstable, and controllable cause—although these classifications must be analyzed from the point of view of the perceiver.

These causal dimensions are assumed by Weiner to have psychological consequences. A person's expectancy of success will be influenced by the stability of a cause. For example, attributing failure to lack of ability (a stable cause) will lead to a lowered expectancy of success, with failure at that type of task being seen as more likely in the future. Had failure been attributed to lack of effort (an unstable cause), a person's expectancy of success might remain unaltered because the person might see future success as possible if he or she tried harder. Causal dimensions are also assumed to be associated with affective consequences. For example, Weiner assumes that internal ascriptions elicit greater feelings of self-esteem for success and lower feelings of self-esteem for failure than do external attributions; that lower expectancies of success following attributions to stable causes will tend to be accompanied by feelings of hopelessness; and that failure will elicit anger toward others when the failure is attributed to a cause that is controllable by these other people.

Finally, Weiner (1985, 1986) assumes that expectancy and affect together determine action. He reviews research findings that support his model and suggest that his analysis has considerable generality over a wide range of research areas (e.g., achievement behavior, helping behavior, crime and parole decisions, alcoholism, depression, deprivation, loneliness, need for help, maladaptive reactions to rape, smoking, and domestic violence). He notes that the attributional analysis of depression advanced by Abramson, Seligman, and Teasdale (1978) and Janoff-Bulman's (1979) distinction between characterological versus behavioral sources of self-blame both have their source in the attributional approach that he advocates.

This type of attributional approach can be applied to the analysis of persistence or lack of persistence against failure. People may give up trying when they attribute their failure to lack of ability or to an impossible task, when they feel hopeless, anxious or depressed, and when their expectancies of success are very low. Others may continue to persist because they attribute their failures to unstable causes such as lack of effort or bad luck. They therefore maintain high expectancies, continuing to feel optimistic. Also, the causal attributions may be linked to personality dispositions. Weiner (1986, p. 168) suggests, for example, that individuals high in anxiety may be more likely to attribute failure to lack of ability than persons low in anxiety. Such low-ability attributions for failure impede motivation because they lead to low expectancies and feelings of shame and humiliation. On the other hand, people low in anxiety may be more likely to attribute failure to lack of effort. Their motivation may even be enhanced if they feel guilty about their lack of effort and if their positive expectancies are preserved. A similar analysis can be applied to people either high or low in their level of achievement needs. Those high in achievement needs may be more likely to attribute their failure to lack of effort; those low in achievement needs may be more likely to perceive their failure as due to lack of ability. Weiner (1986) describes some research findings that are consistent with this analysis (e.g., Meyer, 1970; Weiner & Sierad, 1975). I found that subjects high in the work ethic were more likely to attribute both good and bad events to internal and behavioral causes (e.g., effort or lack of effort) when compared with subjects low in the work ethic (Feather, 1983). Thus, it is possible to link trying and quitting to personality variables via mediating attributions and their cognitive and affective consequences.

Note, however, that the more recent research using the attributional concepts in the achievement domain has tended to move away from the analysis of individual differences in achievement needs to the analysis of attributional styles (conceived as a personality characteristic) and to tests of other linkages in Weiner's (1985, 1986) model. Graham (1984), for example, found that persistence at an insoluble puzzle was positively related to perceived competence and that low perceived competence was associated with attributions to low ability. In her study, however, expectancy of success was not linked with behavior.

Because causal attributions have a pivotal status in Weiner's (1985, 1986) analysis, it follows that one should be able to treat or correct quitting too early or trying for too long by attempting to change a person's attributions for failure. Shifting a person's attributions for failure from a lack of ability attribution to an insufficient effort attribution, for example, should have the effect of protecting the person's expectancy of success and maintaining his or her positive motivation to continue with the task. Foersterling (1985) has reviewed the literature on attributional retraining. Weiner (1986, pp. 80–190) also discusses the experimental findings in this area. He notes that different theories (helplessness theory, self-efficacy theory, attribution theory) all have similar implications as far as change programs are concerned in that they all agree that ascribing failure to lack of ability can be maladaptive and ascribing failure to insufficient effort can be adaptive. Weiner (1986) indicates, however, that any performance enhancements that occur following attributional therapy may be mediated not only by expectancy of success but also by changes in affect, a variable that has been neglected in discussions of the effects of attributional retraining.

DYNAMICS OF ACTION

I noted previously that my early analysis of persistence was a key influence in the development of the dynamics of action model proposed by Atkinson and Birch (1970, 1986). It would take me too far afield to describe this approach in detail. The model is applied to the stream of behavior and allows for the effects of instigating forces which increase the strength of inclinations to act in particular ways (action tendencies), consummatory forces that reduce the strength of action tendencies, inhibitory forces that increase the strength of tendencies not to act in particular ways ("negaction" tendencies), and forces of resistance that reduce the strength of negaction tendencies. The model also includes concepts that concern consummatory values, displacement and substitution, selective attention, and consummatory lag. The action and negaction tendencies wax and wane in the course of behavior, and different resultant action tendencies may become dominant as the person encounters new temptations in the environment. For example, a student working at his desk may quit his studies when a friend calls him to play football. The friend's request can be conceptualized as giving rise to an instigating force that increases the strength of the student's tendency to play football and affiliate with his friend. The strength of this tendency may increase to such an extent that it dominates the strength of the student's tendency to persist with his homework, and at that stage he leaves his desk and changes to the new activity.

Tests of the dynamics of action model have involved both experimental studies and computer simulations (Kuhl & Atkinson, 1986). The model has also been linked with concepts from the expectancy-value approach. Thus, Atkinson and Birch (1970) now assume that expectancy-value theory defines the determinants of instigating and inhibitory forces (see also Atkinson, 1982). These forces are coordinated to the products of motives, expectancies, and incentive values. This conceptual revision has implications for the earlier theory of achievement motivation (Atkinson & Feather, 1966). What were formerly called tendencies in the context of achievement motivation now become instigating forces to achieve success and inhibitory forces to avoid failure. Similarly, one can define instigating and inhibitory forces that relate to specific activities other than those linked to achievement concerns and conceptualize these forces in terms of expectancy-value products. Thus, expectancy-value theory is assumed to provide a theory about the determinants of forces which in turn are seen as influencing the rate of arousal of action tendencies and negaction tendencies. The arousal and stabilization of these two kinds of tendencies are treated separately in the dynamics of action model. Kuhl (1985) has a more extended discussion of links between the dynamic model and the cognitive expectancy-value approach, in which he relates the dynamics of action model to Heckhausen's (1977) theory of motivation.

The dynamics of action model can be used to generate predictions about persistence. An important implication of the model is that the percentage of time spent at an activity in a constant environment will depend upon the ratio of the magnitude of the instigating force for the activity to the consummatory value of the activity relative to that of other activities in the stream of behavior. Putting it in more simplified terms, the principle states that "the proportion of time spent in a given activity depends upon the strength of the tendency to do it relative to the number and strength of tendencies for all the competing tendencies in that situation" (Atkinson & Birch, 1978, p. 145). Thus, persistence at an activity is again seen as a function of motivation to perform alternatives, but, in contrast to my earlier analysis (Feather, 1961), the emphasis is not on a resultant tendency defined by an algebraic sum of positive and negative motivational tendencies but on a *ratio* of forces together with their consummatory values. This principle of time allocation has been studied experimentally by Kuhl and Geiger (1986) and also investigated in computer simulations, but further tests are required that link it to the expectancy-value approach.

ACTION CONTROL

Further extensions of the process-oriented analysis of changing tendencies and the stream of behavior have involved a reintroduction of the concept of volition and the development of models that deal with action control and the mechanisms mediating the formation and enactment of intentions. Kuhl (1987) distinguishes between an intention and a motivational tendency. An *intention* is defined as "an activated plan to which an actor has committed himself or herself" (p. 282). Kuhl (1987) notes that

> People do not always act according to their current hierarchy of motivational tendencies. Somebody who has just decided to stop smoking might still feel a stronger urge to smoke than to chew gum, but he or she may end up enacting the initially weaker motivational tendency (i.e., chewing gum) as a result of a superordinate control process which gradually changes the relative strengths of the two competing action tendencies in favor of the intentional commitment. (pp. 80–281)

One needs to formulate models that enable one to explain how intentions are preserved and enacted despite the dynamic waxing and waning of motivational tendencies.

Kuhl (1987) presents a model of action control that is developed within an information-processing framework. He assumes that converting a motivational tendency to an intention requires an act of will and the linking of the action tendency to a plan that can be accessed from memory. The plan becomes an intention when it has been activated and when the actor is committed to its execution. Kuhl's (1987) action control model involves a motivation system and three memory systems (action memory, semantic memory, emotional memory). He assumes that if "an activated plan has activated the motivation memory, it becomes a 'dynamic plan'; that is, it gains access to the executional system and it is maintained ('energized') and protected against competing plans" (Kuhl, 1987, p. 284).

He also describes a dimension of action orientation versus state orientation along which people may vary. Action-oriented people are more likely to focus on a fully developed and realistic action plan; state-oriented people are more likely to focus on past, present, or future states (especially unrealistic goals). These orientations are assumed to define the flexibility or rigidity of the motivational maintenance system that is involved in action control. Kuhl (1987) summarizes the results of studies that have included the action-orientation versus state-orientation variable, and he also links state orientation to an excessively rigid operation of the motivational maintenance system. Thus, "state-oriented individuals stick to a goal, even when all action alternatives in their repertoire have failed to attain it. Action-oriented individuals are more likely to switch to alternative goals after repeated failures to reach the current goal" (p. 289). Kuhl (1987) notes that his theoretical interpretation does not necessarily imply that action-oriented subjects have more efficient strategies for maintaining and enacting intentions. Indeed, some highly flexible action-oriented individuals may have problems in maintaining an action plan against competing action tendencies; some less flexible state-oriented individuals may have rather efficient self-regulatory strategies. The question of the relation between action and state orientations and self-regulatory efficiency is a separate issue in need of further investigation.

These ideas and other related discussions (e.g., Heckhausen, 1986; Heckhausen & Gullwitzer, 1987; Heckhausen & Kuhl, 1985) mark important new developments in the psychology of motivation because they signal a renewed interest in the psychology of volition and suggest that volition should be distinguished from motivation. Kuhl (1987) notes that much of his research has been concerned with the personal and situational determinants of the inability to abandon unsuccessful plans. He indicates that, "this inability is often accompanied by cognitions centering around states rather than actions (e.g., a past failure or a desired future state)....Perseverating, unsuccessful plans block the system to the extent that new (potentially successful) plans cannot be carried out" (p. 284). These ideas have obvious relevance for the study of persistence against failure and the effects of individual differences in state orientation versus action orientation. One would expect, for example, that a state-oriented person with a highly rigid motivational maintenance system would show high degrees of persistence. Finally, Kuhl (1987) indicates that a high ability to maintain intentions is not always adaptive. One can conceive of people who maintain and enact their intentions but who may "frustrate their own needs by failing to notice that they have to modify their intentions to adjust to situational changes" (p. 291). To solve the adaptiveness issue one needs separate measures of self-regulatory efficiency and the flexibility–rigidity of the motivational maintenance system.

ATTENTION AND SELF-REGULATION

The book on action control by Kuhl and Beckmann (1985) contains a number of other discussions concerned with relations between intentions and actions that span a range of theoretical ideas. Some of these chapters are of special interest in regard to real-life coping situations under conditions of stress (e.g., Herrmann & Wortman, 1985). I single out the control-systems approach of Carver and Scheier (1981, 1985) because, like Kuhl's (1985) approach, it is also developed within an information-processing framework. Furthermore, it has implications for the study of persistence that have been tested empirically.

Carver and Scheier (1981, 1985) develop their model of self-regulation using the principles of cybernetic control (e.g., Miller, Galanter, & Pribram, 1960; Powers, 1973a, 1973b). More specifically, they assume that "the self-regulatory efforts of the human being reflect an ongoing comparison of present behavior against salient behavioral standards, and the attempt to bring the one into correspondence with the other" (Carver & Scheier, 1985, p. 238). These activities involve reducing discrepancies between behavior and salient standards. Thus, Carver and Scheier conceive of "an input function (awareness of one's present behavior and state), a comparison between this input and some reference value (salient behavioral standard), and an output function (adjustments in behavior, when necessary) that works to minimize discrepancies between the two" (p. 238).

They describe a hierarchy of levels of control that arise from each person's attempts to impose order on experience. These levels represent the behavioral qualities involved in overt action, and they differ in their degree of abstractness (e.g., there are levels concerned with system concepts, principles, and programs). In each case a superordinate level of control specifies reference values to be used at the next lower level, and progress toward goal attainment is monitored at each level (see Carver & Scheier, 1981, for a fuller discussion with behavioral examples). Overt action is therefore related to ongoing comparisons between behavior and standards specified by the relevant level of control, and the adjustments that occur are such as to bring behavior into conformity with reference standards.

Linked to these ideas is the assumption that self-regulation of behavior depends in part upon a person's focus of attention. Carver and Scheier (1985) suggest that

> a precondition for the operation of the comparator at the superordinate level of control is the focusing of attention inward toward the self. When a behavioral standard is salient, self-focused attention is assumed to lead to an increased tendency to compare one's present behavior or state with that standard. The result of that comparison is...the engagement of the discrepancy-reducing feedback loop. (p. 242)

Self-focus has been operationalized by manipulations that remind subjects of themselves (e.g., getting them to perform in a room with a wall mirror) or by assessing individual differences in the disposition to attend to self (e.g., by using the Self-Consciousness Scale; Fenigstein, Scheier, & Buss, 1975). A self-focused person is assumed to be more likely to conform in his or her behavior to the standard that is salient. The self-focus can be on private aspects of self, on public aspects of self, or on other aspects. It is important to know which aspect of self is focused upon when framing predictions. For example, conformity to a group would be more likely to occur when the focus is on the public self and lack of conformity when the focus is on the private self (Froming & Carver, 1981).

How does a person interrupt or disengage from behavior when that behavior is ineffective in meeting salient behavioral standards? Such situations commonly arise when there are obstacles or blocks to progress and when these impediments render further attempts useless. Carver and Scheier (1981, 1985) assume that individuals assess their expectancies and that this assessment occurs separately from the discrepancy-reduction process. If the expectancy is favorable, the person returns to the attempt to match behavior to the salient reference value; if the expectancy is unfavorable, the person experiences a tendency to withdraw or disengage from that attempt. Disengagement may be overt or mental (e.g., daydreaming, task-irrelevant thought). Unfavorable expectancies and disengagement attempts may recur in situations where the person continues to be confronted by discrepancies between actions and standards. Finally, Carver and Scheier (1985) argue that the expectancy assessment process is associated with and may determine feelings of elation and depression, depending upon whether the expectancy is favorable or unfavorable.

How can this analysis be related to the study of persistence? Carver and Scheier (1981, 1985) describe investigations that relate to their control-systems approach. For example, in a study by Carver, Blaney, and Scheier (1979), subjects were first told that they had performed poorly on a set of anagrams (failure experience). They then experienced an expectancy induction that was designed to create either a favorable expectancy or an unfavorable expectancy for a subsequent task that they then performed under conditions of self-focus (mirror present) or non-self-focus (mirror absent). The subsequent task was an insoluble geometric design (Feather, 1961). Carver *et al.* (1979) found that subjects with favorable expectancies persisted longer at the task when self-focus was high than when it was lower; subjects with unfavorable expectancies were less persistent when self-focus was high than when it was lower.

Carver and Scheier (1981, pp. 246–249) also interpret the findings from my early persistence study (Feather, 1961) in terms of their model. There is not space to consider their interpretation here except to say that it does not adequately handle my finding that subjects who had low levels of need achievement and high levels of test anxiety showed very high persistence at a task that was presented to them as very difficult and where presumably, in Carver and Scheier's (1981, 1985) terms, their expectancies were unfavorable.

SELF-HANDICAPPING STRATEGIES

Kernis, Zuckerman, Cohen, and Spadafora (1982) compared the implications of the Carver and Scheier (1981) model for the analysis of persistence with those of the egotism model developed by Snyder and his colleagues (Frankel & Snyder, 1978; Snyder, Smoller, Strenta, & Frankel, 1981; Snyder, Stephan, & Rosenfield, 1978). Frankel and Snyder (1978), for example, found that, after an initial failure experience, subjects performed worse when a second task was described as moderately difficult rather than as very difficult. They argued that failure at the second task would threaten self-esteem because it may imply that the person lacks ability. Hence the individual may not try very hard because attributing failure to lack of effort is less threatening than attributing it to lack of ability. If, however, the second task is described as difficult, the person may still try very hard because failure can then be ascribed to task difficulty rather than to lack of ability; thus, self-esteem is again protected.

Kernis *et al.* (1982) combined this form of analysis with the Carver and Scheier (1981) approach. They argued that, in task situations, it is the absence of a plausible external attribution for failure that poses a threat to an individual's self-esteem. If such an attribution is available, subjects may be motivated to try harder because they have everything to gain and little to lose. Performance differences between task situations that permit externally based attributions for failure in contrast to internally based attributions may only emerge, however, under conditions of high self-awareness, that is, when attention is focused on self. Consistent with this argument, Kernis *et al.* (1982) were able to show that, after an initial failure, subjects in a high self-awareness condition (mirror present) persisted longer at an insoluble design problem when their expectancies were based on information that the problem was very difficult (other undergraduate students had performed poorly) than when their expectancies were based on information that performance on the design problem was correlated with performance on maze tests on which they had already done badly. Presumably, attributions for failure were more likely to be external and less damaging to self-esteem in the former case than in the latter case. No significant differences in persistence were obtained between the two expectancy conditions in the low self-awareness situation (mirror absent).

This type of analysis draws attention to the self-handicapping strategies that individuals may employ to protect or enhance self-esteem and to present a positive self-image to others (Jones & Berglas, 1978; Pyszczynski & Greenberg, 1983). Arkin and Baumgardner (1985) have reviewed various studies of self-handicapping in which attributional principles are merged with ideas from self-theory and from the study of impression management.

One implication of this approach is that, in some cases, high persistence can be interpreted in terms of self-handicapping strategies, as when a highly anxious person shows high persistence against failure at a task that has been presented to the person as very difficult. Self-esteem is less likely to be under threat in this kind of situation, because failure can be attributed to the difficulty of the task rather than to lack of ability, and the person can claim that he or she is making a good impression by trying hard. Manipulations that require subjects to perform in front of a mirror (Carver & Scheier, 1981) may be associated with more pronounced effects, because these manipulations may strengthen the belief that self is being evaluated and that it is important to make a good impression.

SOCIAL-COGNITIVE THEORY

Let us return to the Carver and Scheier (1981) emphasis on discrepancy reduction and self-regulation. Bandura (1988) is critical of the principle of discrepancy reduction because he believes that, while a negative feedback control system must play a central role in any system of self-regulation, it cannot provide for a complete analysis of human action. In particular, the principle implies inertness when standards are completely matched and there are no discrepancies. How can people initiate action unless there are discrepancies between performance and standards? Somehow, discrepancies have to be fed into the system whether by a person's own behavior and its departure from standards or by other means. Bandura (1988) argues that "self-motivation relies on *discrepancy production* as well as on *discrepancy reduction*. It requires *feedforward control* as well as *feedback control*" (p. 47). The feedforward control comes into play when people initially motivate themselves by setting goals or standards that create a state of disequilibrium and that lead to a mobilization of effort. Feedback control occurs as people respond to discrepancies between their performance and the standards they are trying to meet, adjusting their effort expenditure accordingly. Once they have attained these standards, people tend to move their goals upward and adopt further challenges that create new discrepancies. According to Bandura (1988), "Self-motivation thus involves a dual cyclic process of disequilibrating discrepancy production followed by equilibrating discrepancy reduction" (p. 47).

These ideas are conveyed in the context of a wide-ranging social-cognitive theory that emphasizes such factors as past learning in social contexts, the effects of role models, the individual's ability to self-regulate and monitor behavior in relation to internal standards and social influences, the capacity for individuals to discriminate between situations and to generalize past learning, the effects of cognitive expectancies in the initiation and maintenance of action sequences, and the role of self-generated affective consequences (Bandura, 1986). Particularly relevant to the present discussion is Bandura's (1986, 1988) analysis of goal theory and cognitive regulators. He argues that the "capacity to exercise self-influence by personal challenge and evaluative reaction to one's own attainments provides a major cognitive mechanism of motivation and self-directness" (Bandura, 1988, p. 41). People react to discrepancies between the goals they set and the feedback they obtain about their performance attainments. Internal standards and knowledge about performance define these discrepancies that provide a basis for self-evaluative reactions. Self-satisfactions arise from the fulfillment of valued goals or standards; dissatisfactions arise from failure to achieve these desired goals or standards.

A person might react to self-dissatisfaction arising from performance that falls short of standards by enhanced effort; that is, negative discrepancies and their affective consequences can be motivating. In other cases, however, a large negative discrepancy can discourage further effort. What seems to be important in determining one or other of these reactions is the person's judgment of self-efficacy. Bandura (1988) indicates that, "It is partly on the basis of self-beliefs of efficacy that people choose what challenges to undertake, how much effort to expend in the endeavor, how long to persevere in the face of difficulties..." (p. 42). These self-beliefs also affect how vulnerable people are to stress and despondency when they confront difficulties and suffer failures (Bandura, 1986). Thus, people "who harbor self-doubts about their capabilities are easily dissuaded by failure. Those who are assured of their capabilities intensify their efforts when they fail to achieve what they seek and they persist until they succeed" (Bandura, 1988, p. 42).

Much of Bandura's discussion of self-regulation deals with the complex interplay between the goals that people set, the performance feedback that they receive, feelings of dissatisfaction or satisfaction that may ensue depending upon the size and direction of discrepancies between performance and goals, and the role of beliefs about self-efficacy. Bandura (1986) defines perceived self-efficacy as "people's judgments of their capabilities to organize and execute courses of action required to attain designated types of performances" (p. 391). The dynamic interaction between self-evaluation, perceived self-efficacy, and self-set standards is investigated in a series of studies in which discrepancy levels are varied systematically and the effects of self-reactive influences and self-efficacy on effort expenditure are examined (e.g., Bandura & Cervone, 1983, 1986). The results of these studies show how these different factors operate in concert. For example, dissatisfaction with a level of performance that falls short of a goal or standard combined with high perceived self-efficacy for goal attainment produces heightened effort; a low sense of self-efficacy combined with low dissatisfaction about a substandard performance produces much less effort. The results of these studies also show how perceived self-efficacy is influenced by performance relative to standards. Bandura (1988) notes that when people fail to meet a challenging goal

> some become less sure of their efficacy, others lose faith in their capabilities, but many remain unshaken in their belief that they can attain a standard. . . . Surpassing a taxing standard through sustained strenuous effort does not necessarily strengthen self-beliefs of efficacy. . . . Although, for most people, high accomplishment strengthens their self-beliefs, a sizable number who drive themselves to hard-won success are left with self-doubts that they can duplicate the feat. (p. 48)

Finally, personal goal setting is also influenced by perceived self-efficacy, with higher goals being set by people who perceive themselves to be more capable.

Bandura (1986, 1988) also considers various properties of goals (goal specificity, goal challenge, goal proximity), the question of commitment to goals, and the hierarchical structure of goal systems, as well as the relations between goal discrepancies and mood. He relates his discussion of the impact of goal systems to other analyses of goal-directed behavior (e.g., Locke, Motowildo, & Bobko, 1986; Locke, Shaw, Saari, & Latham, 1981).

The foregoing summary cannot convey the depth and detail of Bandura's (1986, 1988) various discussions. It will be evident, however, that, although his social-cognitive theory has its own unique status, there are ideas that are not dissimilar to some already mentioned in previous sections of this chapter. For example, expectancies are central concepts in both expectancy-value theory and in Bandura's social-cognitive theory, and both forms of analysis recognize the ongoing nature of behavioral events and the modifications that occur in the light of experience. Bandura's discussion of the dynamic interplay between goal-setting, feedback, performance, affective reactions to discrepancies, and perceived self-efficacy is similar in many respects to the early analysis of level of aspiration behavior by Lewin, Dembo, Festinger, and Sears (1944) and compatible with some of my own past contributions (Feather, 1982a). Bandura's emphasis on the maintenance and regulation of behavior within a structure of goals and standards is consistent with the focus on action control and control systems (Carver & Scheier, 1981, 1985; Kuhl, 1987), especially in its stress on dynamic processes and the monitoring of discrepancies. Less evident in Bandura's analysis is recognition that actions may be related to competing tendencies that wax and wane in the course of behavior (Atkinson & Birch, 1970; Kuhl, 1987), nor is there any extended analysis of the effects of individual differences in needs and values on choice, performance, and persistence. The subjective values (or valences) of outcomes and events also receive less attention in the analysis when compared with the detailed treatment of beliefs about self-efficacy. Note that Bandura (1986) does not present us with a formalized model in the style of particular varieties of expectancy-value theory, control theory, or the dynamics of action model. There is no attempt to link variables together in mathematical or quasi-mathematical form and to use such a formal model in a deductive way. The scope and richness of the ideas developed by Bandura (1986), however, relate to many different areas of psychology, and they are likely to promote a great deal of further theorizing and empirical research.

What are the implications of this approach for the study of persistence? An important implication is that judgments of efficacy will "determine how much effort people will expend and how long they will persist in the face of obstacles or aversive experiences. The stronger their perceived self-efficacy, the more vigorous and persistent are their efforts" (Bandura, 1986, p. 394). Brown and Inouye (1978) found that subjects who perceived themselves to be more competent persisted longer at tasks for which they were unable to find solutions. Other studies have shown that higher perceived self-efficacy is associated with higher levels of perseverant effort (e.g., Cervone & Peake, 1986; Jacobs, Prentice-Dunn, & Rogers, 1984; Weinberg, Gould, & Jackson, 1979). Perceived self-efficacy is also assumed to determine how productively effort is deployed. In contrast, perceived self-inefficacy may impair productive functioning. According to Bandura (1988):

> Those who judge themselves inefficacious in coping with environmental demands dwell upon their personal deficiencies and cognize potential difficulties as more formidable than they really are. Such self-referent misgivings create stress and undermine effective use of personal competencies by diverting attention from how best to proceed to concern over personal failings and possible mishaps. (pp. 44–45)

This statement reminds one of Kuhl's (1985) concept of state orientation and its assumed effects and of related discussions of stress and coping (e.g., Lazarus & Folkman, 1984).

It follows that persistence can become maladaptive or self-defeating when people overestimate their capabilities and continue to fail at tasks that are beyond their competence. However, according to Bandura (1988),

> optimistic self-appraisals of efficacy that are not unduly disparate from what is possible can be advantageous, whereas veridical judgments can be self-limiting;...If self-efficacy beliefs always reflected only what people can do routinely, they would rarely fail but they would not mount the extra effort needed to surpass their ordinary performances. (p. 48)

Those who underestimate their capabilities may quit a task too early when confronted by obstacles or difficulties and thereby lose the potential benefits of success.

GENERAL DISCUSSION

The preceding review of models does not exhaust all possible theoretical approaches that are relevant to the analysis of trying and giving up, but it does cover some of the major contributions. One could also include more extended discussion of ideas that come from dissonance theory, from the analysis of learned helplessness and perceived control, and from recent discussions that deal with self-presentation and the protection of self-esteem, but, given space limitations, one has to be selective. Not to be forgotten also are the socializing effects of one's culture in determining the value assigned to persistence (a value that is more likely to develop in achievement-oriented, individualistic societies such as the United States) and the effects of contingencies of reinforcement in shaping persistent responses. We are all familiar with the partial reinforcement effect—the tendency for individuals to take longer to extinguish a response (or persist with behavior) in the face of uniform nonreinforcement when they have been partially reinforced rather than uniformly reinforced during acquisition. I discussed both trait approaches to the study of persistence and extinction studies in an early review (Feather, 1962), concluding that what was required was a motivational analysis of persistence that took account of both personality and situational variables (see also Nygard, 1977, 1981). The present review updates some of those earlier ideas after a 25-year interval, bringing a number of the more recent relevant contributions together in the one context.

This review of theoretical approaches helps to fill out the discussion by Janoff-Bulman and Brickman (1982) concerned with the pathology of low and high expectations. What implications do these analyses have for the question of when trying and giving up are adaptive or maladaptive? A difficult issue involved in this question concerns the identification of when a particular behavior is adaptive or maladaptive. For example, an inventor might be ridiculed because he or she persists in pursuing an unusual and original idea without success. The initial failures, however, might ultimately be followed by complete success. Would we term the inventor's behavior adaptive had he or she quit early? If we had prior knowledge that the task the inventor was working on had no possible solution or that the inventor had undertaken a problem completely outside of his or her capabilities, then we would feel more confident about making a judgment about the adaptiveness or maladaptiveness of the behavior. As another example, is the behavior of a young person who persistently looks for employment in an impossible job market maladaptive when the alternatives to seeking employment are inactivity, an unfulfilled life, stress, and despair? Such persistence may ultimately have negative effects on expectations, self-esteem, and psychological well-being (e.g., Feather, 1985; Feather & O'Brien, 1986, 1987), but the alternative of not seeking a job may be psychologically more destructive. In this case the behavior may be viewed as maladaptive if it is inflexible and if there are other possible solutions to the problem (e.g., retraining, further education) that could be attempted. Yet these other solutions may not be possible because of poverty and lack of government assistance. Can we then say that the young person's job seeking is self-defeating?

Clearly, one needs to specify criteria for adaptiveness and maladaptiveness, and that is not an easy task because we do not always have complete information about alternatives to the actions that are being performed and we can never be certain of the future course of events. Moreover, the criteria also involve judgments about costs and benefits, judgments that are themselves set within an evaluational framework. What defines a cost? What defines a benefit? One might rely on evidence about psychological well-being, information about health status, and whether or not coping attempts are in touch with reality. But self-fulfillment may follow pain and sadness, and self-defeating behavior is not necessarily divorced from happiness and pleasure. Note also that the criteria employed for judging adaptiveness and maladaptiveness can be viewed as social constructions, relative to time and place. What may be adaptive in one culture or in one period of history may be maladaptive elsewhere or at another time. Finally, although beliefs that are not sufficiently grounded in reality (e.g., falsely based expectations, distorted ideas about the consequences of actions) may be associated with maladaptive behavior, accurate judgments can also be self-limiting. Some evidence suggests that fictional beliefs may be adaptive for people, provided that these beliefs are not too far removed from reality and especially when they help to preserve a positive view of self (e.g., Abramson & Martin, 1981; Feather, 1987b; Greenwald, 1980; Taylor & Brown, 1988).

These are complex but important issues. I conclude with some general statements about trying and giving up that are suggested by the various theoretical discussions that I have reviewed in this chapter. In making this summary I do not attempt any sort of theoretical integration. I noted throughout my description of the different approaches concepts that are similar across theories and concepts that are unique. The following list of variables that influence persistence and quitting simply distills some of the points made earlier. Thus, persistent behavior in the face of failure can be related to the following:

- shaping experiences that involve particular kinds of reinforcement schedules that influence extinction in chance-related and skill-related situations
- a high cultural value assigned to perseverance
- low diagnosticity of outcomes in relation to the self-assessment of ability
- variables that result in entrapment in situations
- high levels of need achievement and low levels of test anxiety when expectations of success are high
- high levels of test anxiety and low levels of need achievement when expectations of success are low
- positive views about one's self-efficacy or capabilities
- dominant action tendencies that are preserved in the course of action control
- variables such as state orientation versus action orientation that influence action control
- positive expectancies and self-directed attention
- self-handicapping strategies that protect self-esteem
- causal attributions that ascribe failure to lack of effort

Quitting a task early in the face of failure can be related to the same kinds of variables in reverse. Thus, low persistence may also be associated with:

- shaping experiences that involve particular kinds of reinforcement schedules
- a low cultural value assigned to perseverance
- high diagnosticity of outcomes in relation to the self-assessment of ability
- variables that decrease the likelihood of entrapment
- high levels of test anxiety and low levels of need achievement when expectations of success are high
- high levels of need achievement and low levels of test anxiety when expectations of success are low
- negative views about one's self-efficacy or capabilities
- alternative action tendencies that come to dominate the initial action tendency to perform the behavior
- variables such as state orientation versus action orientation that influence action control
- negative expectancies and self-directed attention
- causal attributions that ascribe failure to lack of ability.

It follows that one can influence persistence and lack of persistence by manipulating any one or more of these variables. For example, earlier in this chapter I referred to attributional retraining, in which subjects are induced to attribute their failures to controllable, variable causes as a method of therapy. But one could also attempt to develop heightened perceptions of self-efficacy in individuals. Note, however, such an intervention would be counterproductive if these perceptions departed from reality so much so that people incapable of performing an action to an accepted standard were led to believe that they could in fact succeed. As Janoff-Bulman and Brickman (1982) indicate, individuals have to test their limits so as to discover their strengths and limitations in particular contexts. Adaptive behavior requires knowledge of the realities of self and situation, though people also live by their fictions.

Taken as a whole, the theoretical approaches that I have reviewed imply that the analysis of trying and quitting needs to be grounded in a sophisticated motivational psychology that considers ongoing behavior and its consequences; personality variables involving needs, values, and other dispositions; the active role of individuals in shaping their performance and their choices; cognitive processes relating to beliefs, expectations, attributions, and the evaluation of alternatives; the changing nature of motivational tendencies as action proceeds; processes involved in commitment and action control; and, in general, the dynamic interplay between thought, affect, and action within the constraints imposed by particular situations. What is clear is that the analysis of persistence in a given line of activity must consider the alternative activities to which a person can turn and not be restricted to an exclusive focus on the ongoing activity. My own preference is for approaches that bridge the gaps between cognition, affect, and action and that take both person and situation variables into account. The various formulations that have been described in this chapter indicate that significant process has been made toward this form of analysis.

REFERENCES

Abramson, L. Y., & Martin, D. J. (1981). Depression and the causal inference process. In J. H. Harvey, W. Ickes, & R. F. Kidd (Eds.), *New directions in attribution research* (Vol. 3, pp. 117–168). Hillsdale, NJ: Erlbaum.

Abramson, L. Y., Seligman, M. E. P., & Teasdale, J. D. (1978). Learned helplessness in humans: Critique and reformulation. *Journal of Abnormal Psychology, 87*, 49–74.

Arkin, R. M., & Baumgardner, A. H. (1985). Self-handicapping. In J. H. Harvey & G. Weary (Eds.), *Attribution: Basic issues and applications* (pp. 169–202). Orlando, FL: Academic Press.

Atkinson, J. W. (1957). Motivational determinants of risk-taking behavior. *Psychological Review, 64*, 359–372.

Atkinson, J. W. (1982). Old and new conceptions of how expected consequences influence actions. In N. T. Feather (Ed.), *Expectations and actions: Expectancy-value models in psychology* (pp. 17–52). Hillsdale, NJ: Erlbaum.

Atkinson, J. W., & Birch, D. (1970). *The dynamics of action*. New York: Wiley.

Atkinson, J. W., & Birch, D. (1978). *An introduction to motivation*. New York: Van Nostrand.

Atkinson, J. W., & Birch, D. (1986). Fundamentals of the dynamics of action. In J. Kuhl & J. W. Atkinson (Eds.), *Motivation, thought, and action* (pp. 16–48). New York: Praeger.

Atkinson, J. W., & Feather, N. T. (Eds.). (1966). *A theory of achievement motivation*. New York: Wiley.

Bandura, A. (1986). *Social foundations of thought and action*. Englewood Cliffs, NJ: Prentice-Hall.

Bandura, A. (1988). Self-regulation of motivation and action through goal systems. In V. Hamilton, G. H. Bower, & N. H. Frijda (Eds.), *Cognitive perspectives on emotion and motivation* (pp. 37–61). Dordrecht: Martinus Nijhoff.

Bandura, A., & Cervone, D. (1983). Self-evaluative and self-efficacy mechanisms governing the motivational effects of goal systems. *Journal of Personality and Social Psychology, 45*, 1017–1028.

Bandura, A., & Cervone, D. (1986). Differential engagement of self-reactive influences in cognitive motivation. *Organizational Behavior and Human Decision Processes, 38*, 92–113.

Battle, E. S. (1965). Motivational determinants of academic task persistence. *Journal of Personality and Social Psychology, 2*, 209–218.

Baumeister, R. F., & Scher, S. J. (1988). Self-defeating behavior patterns among normal individuals: Review and analysis of common self-destructive tendencies. *Psychological Bulletin, 104*, 3–22.

Bazerman, M. H., Giuliano, T., & Appelman, A. (1984). Escalation of commitment in individual and group decision making. *Organizational Behavior and Human Performance, 33*, 141–152.

Booth-Kewley, S., & Friedman, H. S. (1987). Psychological predictors of heart disease: A quantitative review. *Psychological Bulletin, 101*, 343–362.

Brockner, J. (1979). Self-esteem, self-consciousness, and task performance: Replications, extensions, and possible explanations. *Journal of Personality and Social Psychology, 37*, 447–461.

Brockner, J., Nathanson, S., Friend, A., Harbeck, J., Samuelson, C., Houser, R., Bazerman, M. H., & Rubin, J. Z. (1984). The role of modeling processes in the "knee deep in the big muddy" phenomenon. *Organizational Behavior and Human Performance, 33*, 77–99.

Brockner, J., Rubin, J. Z., & Lang, E. (1981). Face-saving and entrapment. *Journal of Experimental Social Psychology, 17*, 68–79.

Brockner, J., Shaw, M.C., & Rubin, J. Z. (1979). Factors affecting withdrawal from an escalating conflict: Quitting before it's too late. *Journal of Experimental Social Psychology, 15*, 492–503.

Brown, D. R., & Veroff, J. (Eds.). (1986). *Frontiers of motivational psychology*. New York: Springer-Verlag.

Brown, I., Jr., & Inouye, D. K. (1978). Learned helplessness through modeling: The role of perceived similarity in competence. *Journal of Personality and Social Psychology, 36*, 900–908.

Carver, C. S., Blaney, P. H., & Scheier, M. F. (1979). Reassertion and giving up: The interactive role of self-directed attention and outcome expectancy. *Journal of Personality and Social Psychology, 37*, 1859–1870.

Carver, C. S., & Scheier, M. F. (1981). *Attention and self-regulation: A control-theory approach to human behavior*. New York: Springer-Verlag.

Carver, C. S., & Scheier, M. F. (1985). A control-systems approach to the self-regulation of action. In J. Kuhl & J. Beckmann (Eds.), *Action control: From cognition to behavior* (pp. 237–265). New York: Springer-Verlag.

Cervone, D., & Peake, P. K. (1986). Anchoring, efficacy, and action: The influence of judgmental heuristics on self-efficacy judgments and behavior. *Journal of Personality and Social Psychology, 50*, 492–501.

Conlon, E. J., & Wolf, G. (1980). The moderating effects of strategy, visibility, and involvement on allocation behavior: An extension of Staw's escalation paradigm. *Organizational Behavior and Human Performance, 26*, 172–192.

Diener, C. I., & Dweck, C. S. (1978). An analysis of learned helplessness: Continuous changes in performance, strategy, and achievement conditions following failure. *Journal of Personality and Social Psychology, 36*, 451–462.

Diener, C. I., & Dweck, C. S. (1980). An analysis of learned helplessness: II. The processing of success. *Journal of Personality and Social Psychology, 39*, 940–952.

Dweck, C. S. (1975). The role of expectations and attributions in the alleviation of learned helplessness. *Journal of Personality and Social Psychology, 31*, 674–685.

Eccles, J., Adler, T., & Meece, J. L. (1984). Sex differences in achievement: A test of alternate theories. *Journal of Personality and Social Psychology, 46*, 26–43.

Feather, N. T. (1961). The relationship of persistence at a task to expectation of success and achievement-related motives. *Journal of Abnormal and Social Psychology, 63*, 552–561.

Feather, N. T. (1962). The study of persistence. *Psychological Bulletin, 59*, 94–115.

Feather, N. T. (1963). Persistence at a difficult task with alternative task of intermediate difficulty. *Journal of Abnormal and Social Psychology, 66*, 604–609.

Feather, N. T. (1966). Effects of prior success and failure on expectations of success and subsequent performance. *Journal of Personality and Social Psychology, 3*, 287–298.

Feather, N. T. (1968). Change in confidence following success or failure as a predictor of subsequent performance. *Journal of Personality and Social Psychology, 9*, 38–46.

Feather, N. T. (1982a). Actions in relation to expected consequences: An overview of a research program. In N. T. Feather (Ed.), *Expectations and actions: Expectancy-value models in psychology* (pp. 53–95). Hillsdale, NJ: Erlbaum.

Feather, N. T. (Ed.). (1982b). *Expectations and actions: Expectancy-value models in psychology*. Hillsdale, NJ: Erlbaum.

Feather, N. T. (1983). Some correlates of attributional style: Depressive symptoms, self-esteem, and protestant ethic values. *Personality and Social Psychology Bulletin, 9*, 125–135.

Feather, N. T. (1985). The psychological impact of unemployment: Empirical findings and theoretical approaches. In N. T. Feather (Ed.), *Australian psychology: Review of research* (pp. 265–295). Sydney: George Allen and Unwin.

Feather, N. T. (1986). Human values, valences, expectations and affect: Theoretical issues emerging from recent applications of the expectancy-value model. In D. R. Brown & J. Veroff (Eds.), *Frontiers of motivational psychology: Essays in honor of John W. Atkinson* (pp. 146–172). New York: Springer-Verlag.

Feather, N. T. (1987a). Gender differences in values: Implications of the expectancy-value model. In F. Halisch & J. Kuhl (Eds.), *Motivation, intention, and volition* (pp. 31–45). New York: Springer-Verlag.

Feather, N. T. (1987b). The rosy glow of self-esteem: Depression, masculinity, and causal attributions. *Australian Journal of Psychology, 39*, 25–41.

Feather, N. T. (1988a). From values to actions: Recent applications of the expectancy-value model. *Australian Journal of Psychology, 40*, 105–124.

Feather, N. T. (1988b). Values, valences, and course enrollment: Testing the role of personal values within an expectancy-value framework. *Journal of Educational Psychology, 80*, 381–391.

Feather, N. T., & O'Brien, G. E. (1986). A longitudinal study of the effects of employment and unemployment on school-leavers. *Journal of Occupational Psychology, 59*, 121–144.

Feather, N. T., & O'Brien, G. E. (1987). Looking for employment: An expectancy-valence analysis of job-seeking behaviour among young people. *British Journal of Psychology, 78*, 251–272.

Feather, N. T., & Saville, M. R. (1967). Effects of amount of prior success and failure on expectations of success and subsequent task performance. *Journal of Personality and Social Psychology, 5*, 226–232.

Fenigstein, A., Scheier, M. F., & Buss, A. H. (1975). Public and private self-consciousness: Assessment and theory. *Journal of Consulting and Clinical Psychology, 43*, 522–527.

Foersterling, F. (1985). Attributional retraining: A review. *Psychological Bulletin, 98*, 495–512.

Fox, F. V., & Staw, B. M. (1979). The trapped administrator: Effects of insecurity and policy resistance upon commitment to a course of action. *Administrative Sciences Quarterly, 24*, 449–471.

Frankel, A., & Snyder, M. L. (1978). Poor performance following unsolvable problems: Learned helplessness or egotism? *Journal of Personality and Social Psychology, 36*, 1415–1423.

Froming, W. J., & Carver, C. S. (1981). Divergent influences on private and public self-consciousness in a compliance paradigm. *Journal of Research in Personality, 15*, 159–171.

Garber, J., & Seligman, M. E. P. (Eds.). (1980) *Human helplessness*. New York: Academic Press.

Graham, S. (1984). Communicated sympathy and anger to black and white children: The cognitive (attributional) consequences of affective cues. *Journal of Personality and Social Psychology, 47*, 40–54.

Greenwald, A. (1980). The totalitarian ego: Fabrication and revision of personal history. *American Psychologist, 35*, 603–618.

Heckhausen, H. (1977). Achievement motivation and its constructs: A cognitive model. *Motivation and Emotion, 4*, 283–319.

Heckhausen, H. (1986). Why some time out might benefit achievement motivation research. In J. H. L. van den Bercken, E. E. J. de Bruyn, & T. C. M. Bergen (Eds.), *Achievement and task motivation* (pp. 7–39). Lisse: Swets & Zeitlinger.

Heckhausen, H., & Gollwitzer, P. M. (1987) Thought content and cognitive functioning in motivational versus volitional states of mind. *Motivation and Emotion, 11*, 101–120.

Heckhausen, H., & Kuhl, J. (1985). From wishes to action: The dead ends and short cuts on the long way to action. In M. Frese & J. Sabini (Eds.), *Goal-directed behavior: Psychological theory and research on action* (pp. 134–160). Hillsdale, NJ: Erlbaum.

Herrman, C., & Wortman, C. B. (1985). Action control and the coping process. In J. Kuhl & J. Beckmann (Eds.), *Action control: From cognition to behavior*. New York: Springer-Verlag.

Jacobs, B., Prentice-Dunn, S., & Rogers, R. W. (1984). Understanding persistence: An interface of control theory and self-efficacy theory. *Basic and Applied Social Psychology, 5*, 333–347.

Janoff-Bulman, R. (1979). Characterological versus behavioral self-blame: Inquiries into depression and rape. *Journal of Personality and Social Psychology, 37*, 1798–1809.

Janoff-Bulman, R., & Brickman, P. (1976). *When not all problems are soluble, does it still help to expect success?* Unpublished manuscript.

Janoff-Bulman, R., & Brickman, P. (1982). Expectations and what people learn from failure. In N. T. Feather (Ed.), *Expectations and actions: Expectancy-value models in psychology* (pp. 207–237). Hillsdale, NJ: Erlbaum.

Janoff-Bulman, R., & Marshall, P. (1978). *Coping and control in a population of institutionalized elderly*. Unpublished manuscript.

Jones, E. E., & Berglas, S. (1978). Control of attributions about the self through self-handicapping strategies: The appeal of alcohol and the role of under-achievement. *Personality and Social Psychology Bulletin, 4*, 200–206.

Kernis, M. H., Zuckerman, M., Cohen, A., & Spadafora, S. (1982). Persistence following failure: The interactive role of self-awareness and the attributional basis for negative expectancies. *Journal of Personality and Social Psychology, 43*, 1184–1191.

Kuhl, J. (1985). Volitional mediators of cognition-behavior consistency: Self-regulatory processes and action versus state orientation. In J. Kuhl & J. Beckmann (Eds.), *Action control: From cognition to behavior* (pp. 101–128). New York: Springer-Verlag.

Kuhl, J. (1987). A model of self-regulation. In F. Halisch & J. Kuhl (Eds.), *Motivation, intention, and volition* (pp. 279–291). New York: Springer-Verlag.

Kuhl, J., & Atkinson, J. W. (Eds.). (1986). *Motivation, thought, and action*. New York: Praeger.

Kuhl, J., & Beckmann, J. (1985). *Action control: From cognition to behavior*. New York: Springer-Verlag.

Kuhl, J., & Geiger, E. (1986). The dynamic theory of the anxiety-behavior relationship. In J. Kuhl & J. W. Atkinson (Eds.), *Motivation, thought, and action* (pp. 76–93). New York: Praeger.

Lazarus, R. S., & Folkman, S. (1984). *Stress, appraisal, and coping*. New York: Springer-Verlag.

Lewin, K. (1935). *A dynamic theory of personality*. New York: McGraw-Hill.

Lewin, K., Dembo, T., Festinger, L., & Sears, P. S. (1944). Level of aspiration. In J. McV. Hunt (Ed.), *Personality and the behavior disorders* (Vol. 1, pp. 333–378). New York: Ronald Press.

Locke, E. A., Motowidlo, S. J., & Bobko, P. (1986). Using self-efficacy theory to resolve the conflict between goal-setting theory and expectancy theory in organizational behavior and industrial/organizational psychology. *Journal of Social and Clinical Psychology, 4*, 328–338.

Locke, E. A., Shaw, K. N., Saari, L. M., & Latham, G. P. (1981). Goal setting and task performance: 1969–1980. *Psychological Bulletin, 90*, 125–152.

McFarlin, D. B., Baumeister, R. F., & Blascovich, J. (1984). On knowing when to quit: Task failure, self-esteem, advice, and non-productive persistence. *Journal of Personality, 52*, 138–155.

Meyer, W. H. (1970). *Self-concept and achievement motivation*. Unpublished doctoral dissertation, Ruhr Universitat, Bochum, Federal Republic of Germany.

Miller, G. A., Galanter, E., & Pribram, K. H. (1960). *Plans and the structure of behavior*. New York: Holt, Rinehart & Winston.

Nathanson, S., Brockner, J., Brenner, D., Samuelson, C., Countryman, M., Lloyd, M., & Rubin, J. Z. (1982). Toward the reduction of entrapment. *Journal of Applied Social Psychology, 12*, 193–208.

Nygard, R. (1977). *Personality, situation, and persistence*. Oslo: Universitetsforlaget.

Nygard, R. (1981). Toward an interactional psychology: Models from achievement motivation research. *Journal of Personality, 49*, 361–387.

Perez, R. C. (1973). The effect of experimentally induced failure, self-esteem, and sex on cognitive differentiation. *Journal of Abnormal Psychology, 81*, 74–79.

Powers, W. T. (1973a). *Behavior: The control of perception*. Chicago: Aldine.

Powers, W. T. (1973b). Feedback: Beyond behaviorism. *Science, 179*, 351–356.

Pyszczynski, T., & Greenberg, J. (1983). Determinants of reduction in intended effort as a strategy for coping with anticipated failure. *Journal of Research in Personality, 17*, 412–422.

Rubin, J. Z., & Brockner, J. (1975). Factors affecting entrapment in waiting situations: The Rosenkrantz and Guildenstern effect. *Journal of Personality and Social Psychology, 31*, 1054–1063.

Ruble, D. N., & Boggiano, A. K. (1980). Optimizing motivation in an achievement context. In B. Keogh (Ed.), *Advances in special education*. Greenwich, CT: JAI Press.

Schalon, C. L. (1968). Effect of self-esteem upon performance following failure stress. *Journal of Consulting and Clinical Psychology, 32*, 497.

Schrauger, J. S., & Sorman, P. B. (1977). Self-evaluations, initial success and failure, and improvement as determinants of persistance. *Journal of Consulting and Clinical Psychology, 45*, 784–795.

Smith, T. W., & Anderson, N. B. (1986). Models of personality and disease: An interactional approach to Type A behavior and cardiovascular risk. *Journal of Personality and Social Psychology, 50*, 1166–1173.

Snyder, M. L., Smoller, B., Strenta, A., & Frankel, A. (1981). A comparison of egotism, negativity, and learned helplessness as explanations for poor performance after unsolvable problems. *Journal of Personality and Social Psychology, 40*, 24–30.

Snyder, M. L., Stephan, W. G., & Rosenfield, D. (1978). Attributional egotism. In J. H. Harvey, W. Ickes, & R. F. Kidd (Eds.), *New directions in attribution research* (Vol. 2, pp. 91–117). Hillsdale, NJ: Erlbaum.

Staw, B. M. (1976). Knee-deep in the big muddy: A study of escalating commitment to a chosen course of action. *Organizational Behavior and Human Performance, 16*, 27–44.

Strube, M. J., & Boland, S. M. (1986). Postperformance attributions and task persistence among Type A and B individuals: A clarification. *Journal of Personality and Social Psychology, 50*, 413–420.

Taylor, S. E., & Brown, J. D. (1988). Illusion and well-being: A social psychological perspective on mental health. *Psychological Bulletin, 103*, 193–210.

Teger, A. I. (1980). *Too much invested to quit*. New York: Pergamon Press.

Trope, Y. (1983). Self-assessment in achievement behavior. In J. M. Suls & A. G. Greenwald (Eds.), *Psychological perspectives on the self* (Vol. 2, pp. 92–121). Hillsdale, NJ: Erlbaum.

Trope, Y., & Ben-Yair, E. (1982). Task construction and persistence as a means for self-assessment of abilities. *Journal of Personality and Social Psychology, 42*, 637–645.

Weinberg, R. S., Gould, D., & Jackson, A. (1979). Expectations and performance: An empirical test of Bandura's self-efficacy theory. *Journal of Sport Psychology, 1*, 320–331.

Weiner, B. (1965). The effects of unsatisfied achievement motivation on persistence and subsequent performance. *Journal of Personality, 33*, 428–442.

Weiner, B. (1980). *Human motivation*. New York: Holt, Rinehart & Winston.

Weiner, B. (1985). An attributional theory of achievement motivation and emotion. *Psychological Review, 92*, 548–573.
Weiner, B. (1986). *An attributional theory of motivation and emotion*. New York: Springer-Verlag.
Weiner, B., & Sierad, J. (1975). Misattribution for failure and enhancement of achievement strivings. *Journal of Personality and Social Psychology, 31*, 415–421.
Weiss, H., & Sherman, J. (1973). Internal–external control as a predictor of task effort and satisfaction subsequent to failure. *Journal of Applied Psychology, 57*, 132–136.

Part II

SELF-DEFEATING RESPONSES TO THE THREAT OF UNPLEASANT OUTCOMES

CHAPTER 5

EXCUSES GONE AWRY

AN ANALYSIS OF SELF-DEFEATING EXCUSES

RAYMOND L. HIGGINS AND C. R. SNYDER

INTRODUCTION

Bob faced a dilemma. His oft-stated ambition was to be a social worker. In fact, he had been one briefly but lost his job because he was unable to overcome his obsessive fears about things that might happen to him when he went to work. Over the course of several months he skipped twice as many days of work as he attended, and he ultimately agreed to "resign" his position. Now he needed only to complete a correspondence course to regain his certification.

As he thought about this situation, Bob realized that, if he were to become recertified, he might actually get a professional position. The prospect frightened him—he felt he couldn't stand it if he were to try and fail again. As things happened, Bob just couldn't find the time to work on his correspondence course. He had too many commitments and was making more all the time. Besides, every time he tried to read the course text, he fell asleep. Of all the available courses, why had he chosen this one? Something else would have been much better.

Bob's case illustrates a process of self-defeating excuse-making. Instead of assisting him through some hard times and enabling him to get on with achiev-

RAYMOND L. HIGGINS AND C. R. SNYDER • Department of Psychology, University of Kansas, Lawrence, Kansas 66045. This paper was presented in part at the 95th Annual Convention of the American Psychological Association, August 28–September 1, 1987, New York City. The order of authors was reversed for the convention paper.

ing his goals, Bob's excuses seemed to insure his failure. In this chapter, we focus on this counterproductive side of excuses. After defining what we mean by excuse making and discussing the nature of self-defeating excuses, we turn our attention to a consideration of how excuses work at both the intra- and interpersonal levels. Next, we examine the conditions under which excuses may become self-defeating. Finally, we discuss the processes underlying repetitive (e.g., dispositional) patterns of self-defeating excuse-making.

Excuse-Making Defined

In this chapter, we rely on a definition of excuse-making that we have previously articulated: excuse-making is

> the motivated process of shifting causal attributions for negative personal outcomes from sources that are relatively more central to the person's sense of self to sources that are relatively less central, thereby resulting in perceived benefits to the person's image and sense of control. (Snyder & Higgins, 1988a, p. 23)

This definition contains several concepts that are central to an understanding of self-defeating excuses. First, the definition identifies the process of excuse-making as one of "shifting" the locus of causal attributions "from sources that are relatively more central to the person's sense of self to sources that are relatively less central." In effect, an excuse does not necessarily sever the individual's causal relationship to a negative outcome. Rather, an excuse may merely serve to deflect the search for causal explanations from one source within the person (e.g., lack of ability) to another (e.g., lack of effort). To the extent that the attributional locus remains within the person, he or she is still vulnerable to some adverse repercussions from negative acts. A second key concept within the definition is the idea that some causal sources within the individual are more "central" to the person's sense of self than others. For example, an attribution to lack of interest may be far less esteem threatening than an attribution to lack of aptitude to learn.

Perhaps *the* central concept within the definition of excuse-making when it comes to understanding self-defeating excuses is that the process results in *perceived* benefits to the excuse-maker. Importantly, the individual perceiving these benefits is the excuse-maker himself or herself. Although an impartial (or not so impartial) audience may feel that an excuse has resulted in a net loss to the excuse-maker, such judgments do not warrant a conclusion that the excuse resulted in a net loss from the perspective of the excuse-maker. For example, a ball player who, after playing miserably in a losing game, confesses that he broke last night's curfew and was drinking will very likely experience some repercussions from his lax discipline. However, *he* may feel that deflecting attributions from his lack of competitive drive to his lack of rest was well worth the price.

WHAT, THEN, IS A SELF-DEFEATING EXCUSE?

In our view, self-defeating excuses are characterized by one or more of the following: (1) they undermine the maintenance of or interfere with the attainment of important external rewards (e.g., jobs, social approval), (2) they undermine or interfere with the actualization of the individual's potential (i.e., his or her attainment of "telic" goals), and/or (3) they result in the long-range undermining of the individual's self-esteem or personal control. In effect, we view self-defeating excuses as excuses whose costs, either short- or long-term, outweigh their benefits. In extreme cases, excuses may even cut off an individual's subsequent access to alternative and more functional causal (excuse) attributions. For example, an individual who blames unacceptable behavior on an "alcoholism" problem may well find that future transgressions are automatically attributed to the alcoholism by others (and perhaps by the individual).

Although it would appear reasonable to assume that all excuses that fail to accomplish their intended goal (i.e., the shifting of causal attributions to less ego-threatening sources) are self-defeating, we would argue otherwise. Closer consideration suggests that even "failed" excuses may be truly self-defeating only if they place the individual in a more compromised position than before. Moreover, we would argue that excuses that work (i.e., that successfully shift causal attributions to less central aspects of the self) may be self-defeating in some larger context. In fact, we develop the thesis later in this chapter that it is successful excuse-making of a particular type that is involved in the most clinically interesting self-defeatism. The case of Bob (see opening paragraphs) can be used to illustrate this point.

Bob excused his excessive absences from work by telling his supervisor and coworkers that he was suffering from a chronic heart ailment (he *did* have a murmur). Although this successfully concealed the true reason for his truancy (i.e., his obsessive fears) from his peers and avoided his being labeled a "mental case," we would regard the excuse as self-defeating at another level because its success abetted his chronic pattern of avoiding dealing with the fears that were increasingly delimiting his life and freedom.

Bob's "successful" excuse tactic could also be regarded as self-defeating because of its corrosive effect on his self-regard. Although his immediate feeling upon having his explanation accepted was relief that his professional acquaintances didn't know the real truth about him, the deceit inherent in the excuse was transparent to him. Subsequently, then, he suffered from personal recriminations in the form of condemnatory self-statements and a growing sense of hopelessness about ever regaining control over his life.

As detailed above, Bob's successful excuse of having a heart ailment can be regarded as meeting two of the definitional requirements for a self-defeating excuse: It undermined his attainment of telic goals (i.e., his development of adult autonomy), and it undermined his self-regard in the long run (i.e., he felt like a "fake" and a "cheat"), once he emerged from the relief of "getting away with it." Bob's case also illustrates the third type of self-defeatism. Specifically, his use of a self-handicapping strategy (i.e., taking on too many commitments in order to soften the perceived negativity of failing to complete his correspondence course) directly interfered with his ability to attain important external rewards. Interestingly, Bob's use of being "too busy" did not immediately undermine his self-regard, because he busied himself with things that were excellent and commendable things to do. He was not aware (at least initially) of the avoidance inherent in his behavior.

In this section, we have discussed what we believe to be the defining characteristics of self-defeating excuses. In order to establish a context for understanding the conditions under which excuses may become self-defeating, we now turn our attention to a brief review of how excuses work.

HOW EXCUSES WORK

Given that we have taken the position that the effect of excuses is to shift causal attributions for negative outcomes from relatively internal to relatively external sources, asking the supplementary question "How do excuses work?" invites a circular rejoinder: "They work by shifting causal attributions," and so on. A closer look, however, reveals that there must be other processes at work. Indeed, there is reason to suspect that these processes neither begin nor end with the excuse. We do not propose to offer a comprehensive or exhaustive discussion of these processes in this chapter. We do attempt to outline a general framework for thinking about excuses and their effectiveness.

EXCUSES AT THE INDIVIDUAL LEVEL

Central to our thinking about how excuses work at the individual level is the idea that there is an image–control–image cycle in which an individual's self-image influences his or her ability to exercise functional control over important events which, in turn, influences his or her self-image. This cycle is set in motion by our earliest self-experiences and continues throughout life. Discrete excuse events may influence only one iteration of the cycle, although more dispositional excuse-related attributional patterns (e.g., as measured by the Attributional Style Questionnaire; Peterson *et al.*, 1982) may have pervasive and far-reaching influences.

Excuses are only one manifestation of a far broader pattern of self-serving bias in people. Taylor and Brown (1988), for example, have concluded that mentally healthy individuals are characterized by unrealistically positive views of themselves, by exaggerated beliefs of their personal control, and by unrealistic optimism about their futures. Most excuses, then, must be seen as emerging from this background of illusory specialness. The consequences of this are twofold. First, people are almost reflexively inclined to honor their own excuses because they are consistent with their prevailing self-theories. Second, when we are not obliged to fully articulate our excuse attributions (e.g., in order to forestall more threatening attributions by an external audience), the excuses are likely to arise unconsciously and automatically. We may frequently be unaware of the self-serving nature of our excuses, or that they might be anything other than the truth.

Our ability to self-deceive during the excuse-making process is very helpful (Snyder, 1985). By being unaware of our excuses, we avoid having to excuse ourselves for making them. Our acute awareness of the social unacceptability of excuses can be readily observed in the frequent occurrence of individuals (e.g., Colonel Oliver North) preceding their excuses with pointed disclaimers (e.g., "I'm *not* making excuses, but. . ."). There is, indeed, some evidence that people are more likely to engage in excuse-making when the opportunity for self-deception is maximized. For example, self-handicapping through the reporting of test-anxiety symptoms has been shown to be reduced when the excuse value of reporting such symptoms was made explicit (Smith, Snyder, & Handelsman, 1982). Similarly, the probability of self-handicapping has been reported to increase when the adoption of the handicap can be justified on grounds that have nothing to do with excuse-making (Handelsman, Kraiger, & King, 1985). In this case, subjects were given a choice of two tests, only one of which was described as being able to indicate their true level of ability (i.e., it was "diagnostic"). The subjects were more likely to choose the nondiagnostic test if the two tests were also described as differing in format (i.e, one was true–false and the other was multiple-choice). When the tests differed in format, there was ambiguity regarding the basis for the selection of the nondiagnostic test.

The primary importance of self-deception in the making of excuses derives from the fact that it enables the individual to maintain his or her focus on external task concerns rather than being caught up in conscious self-contemplation regarding a negative performance (including the excuse, itself). Self-focused awareness has been shown to have a variety of adverse effects, including lowering self-esteem (e.g., Duval & Wicklund, 1972), intensifying dysphoric affect (e.g., Gibbons, Smith, Brehm, & Schroeder, 1981), and reducing persistence on failed tasks (e.g., Carver, Blaney, & Scheier, 1979). In contrast, the self-deceptive engagement of excuse attributions would be expected to result in the kinds of affective, self-esteem,and performance benefits detailed by Snyder and Higgins (1988a, 1988b) in their review of the effects of excuses.

Recalling our hypothesized image–control–image cycle, we would like to suggest that, beyond being facilitated and potentiated by preexisting self-serving biases, successful excuse events feed back into the cycle by further enhancing perceptions of control (through improved performance, for example). Additional benefits may accrue for the cycle as enhanced mood associated with successful excuses results in greater perceived probability of success (e.g., Brown, 1984), greater self-reward (e.g., Wright & Mischel, 1982), and improved task persistence. Extrapolating beyond the relatively circumscribed effects associated with single-excuse events, we propose that longer-range benefits (i.e., health and longevity) are associated with excuses (or excuse-related attributional styles) as a consequence of the enhanced coping described above and a consequent relative "immunity" to stress (see Snyder & Higgins, 1988a, 1988b for review).

Excuses at the Interpersonal Level

In contrast to the state of affairs with intrapersonal excuses, where the conditions for self-deception are optimal, opportunities for self-deception are minimized in interpersonal excuse arenas. Unless the desired excuse attribution is "self-evident" to the external audience (e.g., there are known situational factors that compel the audience to form an externalizing attribution), the excuse-maker may be forced to articulate (via words or gestures) his or her excuse. Moreover, the need to "announce" the excuse may be based on more than a simple desire to insure that the audience considers a more favorable attribution. The literature on apologies, for example, has shown that failing to offer apologies for transgressions may result in social disapproval (e.g., Darby & Schlenker, 1982). As with most activities that involve social interaction, it appears likely that there are cultural expectations regarding the protocol to be followed in making excuses. Excuses that violate social protocol can be expected to reap adverse consequences *that may be independent from the attributional effects of the excuse* (e.g., the excuse may successfully shift attributions but simultaneously lead to social sanctions).

As the preceding remarks imply, excuse-making in interpersonal arenas (i.e., in the presence of an external audience) necessarily involves an active process of *negotiation* between the excuse-maker and the audience concerning the outcome of the exchange. The presence of an audience can impose important constraints on the nature of the excuses that may be proffered. Effective excuse-making in such an arena requires the individual to be concerned with articulating excuses that not only work but that also conform to accepted (and expected) social conventions. Indeed, there is empirical evidence that excuse-makers actively construct their excuses to fit the social demands of the situations they encounter (e.g., Tetlock, 1981). As reported by Weiner, Amirkhan, Folkes, and Verette (1987), there is also evidence that people formulate excuses that maximize the involvement of elements (e.g., lack of intentionality, lack of controllability, and lack of foreseeability) that lead to positive audience reactions. Both types of evidence indicate that effective excuse-makers are sensitive to their social environments and adjust their behavior accordingly. Such findings also suggest that people have a relatively sophisticated understanding of the "rules" of effective excuse-making in social contexts.

Having characterized excuse-making in interpersonal contexts as involving negotiation, we have gone on to indicate at least two aspects of the negotiation process that the excuse-maker must contend with—observing social conventions and tailoring excuses to be maximally effective under the circumstances. From the point of view of the excuse audience, the negotiation process includes passing judgment on the excuse-maker's offerings and providing feedback regarding the judgment. Fortunately for the excuse-maker, there is evidence that social audiences are positively biased in their perceptions of others (e.g., Schneider, Hastorf, & Ellsworth, 1979; Sears, 1983). Moreover, this positive bias is likely to be maximized when the audience perceives itself to be similar to the transgressor (e.g., Burger, 1981).

Another asset of the excuse-maker within interpersonal contexts involves the reluctance of people to provide unambiguously negative feedback to others. When feedback is given, it is likely to be positive (Tesser & Rosen, 1975) or somewhat inscrutable (Goffman, 1955), if delivered at all (Darley & Fazio, 1980). Given that people tend to interpret ambiguous feedback as positive feedback (e.g., Jacobs, Berscheid, & Walster, 1971), it appears that excuse-makers and their audiences may, in effect, collaborate in the excuse-negotiation process to maximize the probabilities that the excuse-maker will emerge from the dialogue with his or her image and sense of control intact.

Excuses and the Negotiation of Reality

Thus far in our discussion of how excuses work, we have described them as playing a role in helping the individual maintain an equilibrium of sorts via their involvement in an image–control–image cycle. In doing so, we have advanced a number of admittedly speculative ideas about the factors that may underlie the effectiveness (or lack thereof) of excuses in both individual and interpersonal contexts. These ideas, obviously, await investigation. We have concluded, however, that there is a strong need to conceptualize excuse-making as a *process*, as an ever-evolving set of negotiations within the individual and between the individual and his or her world. Snyder and Higgins (1988a, 1988b) have called this process "reality negotiation."

The idea that excuses are involved in our efforts to negotiate our personal realities is grounded in our view that all people have beliefs and/or assumptions about themselves and their worlds (see Epstein, 1984). In part, these beliefs and assumptions (theories) are shaped by our life experiences. We are, however, more than passive processors of the things that happen to us. The significance our life experiences have for our self- and world-theories is largely a function of a motivated and purposeful process designed to reconcile inconsistencies between new information and old beliefs about ourselves. In this scheme of things, the motivation and purpose of our attempts to resolve inconsistencies derives from our underlying need to maintain a positive self-image and sense of control over our lives. Any revised self-view that results from reacting to and/or accommodating to new, discrepant personal information is a *negotiated reality*. The regnant negotiated reality is constantly evolving in reaction to the flow of events across the life span.

There are three important aspects of this reality negotiation process. First, due to the fact that it is motivated by the individual's need to maintain a positive image and sense of control, the individual's perceptions of events which challenge his or her current self-theory will be distorted to favor the preservation and furthering of these motives (see Taylor & Brown, 1988). Second, the reality negotiation process is somewhat constrained by consensual reality. In other words, a negotiated reality reflects a biased compromise between the individual's need-driven view of reality and a view of reality that outsiders would endorse. In this vein, the negotiated reality is viable so long as outside sources (e.g., impartial observers) would not seriously question it, should the individual verbalize it.

Finally, we regard reality negotiation as a coping process. Negotiating reality allows the person to slow down or manage the rate of personal change associated with reacting to threatening events. Excuse-making, as discussed in this chapter, exemplifies one possible reality-negotiating strategy. Other ego-defensive mechanisms (e.g., denial; Janoff-Bulman & Timko, 1987) may also reflect reality-negotiating processes.

WHEN EXCUSES BECOME SELF-DEFEATING

There is a substantial body of evidence indicating that excuse attributions are frequently successful in terms of beneficial effects on such things as self-esteem (e.g., McFarland & Ross, 1982), affect (e.g., Burish & Houston, 1979), depression (e.g., Rothwell & Williams, 1983), health (e.g., Elder, Bettes, & Seligman, 1982), and task performance (e.g., Rhodewalt & Davison, 1986). (See Snyder & Higgins, 1988a, 1988b for reviews.) The topic of when excuses fail to work, however, is difficult to address. First, findings related to the failure of excuses are usually null findings (i.e., investigators fail to find benefits associated with excuse attributions) that are inherently open to several interpretations. Furthermore, very few studies have illuminated the conditions under which excuses may have negative consequences.

Second, the inherent complexity of the dialogue between an excuser and his or her audience has yet to be approximated in experimental investigations. Studies have typically focused on either the excuse-maker or the audience, but not both. Such one-sided and stop-frame research ignores the ongoing excuse–feedback process. Consequently, findings may be misleading and incomplete.

With the above limitations in mind, there is evidence that some types of excuses may entail substantial costs, even though it may not be possible to definitively conclude that any particular excuse tactic is ineffective (especially from the perspective of the excuse-maker) or that the benefits are outweighed by the costs. In other instances, direct evidence is lacking, but a theoretical case can be made to suggest that certain kinds of excuses should be counterproductive.

As can be seen in Figure 1, an excuse sequence can be broken down into five relatively discrete steps. At step 1, the individual perceives a linkage to a negative outcome that threatens his or her self-image and/or self-theory. At step 2, the individual proffers an excuse attribution. This may be directed solely at the internal audience of the self (in which case it is likely to be relatively reflexive and unconscious), or it may also be directed at an external audience (thereby increasing, though not insuring, the likelihood that the excuse is consciously strategic).

At step 3, successful and unsuccessful excuses diverge. In the case of successful excuses, the externalizing attribution minimizes the individual's need to continue focusing on self and allows him or her to focus on other tasks. Unsuccessful excuses, however, maintain (and perhaps even increase) the individual's self-focus and decrease his or her ability to concentrate on external tasks. At this step, the individual (either through insight or through audience feedback) may become explicitly aware of his or her excuse tactic and its consequences for the

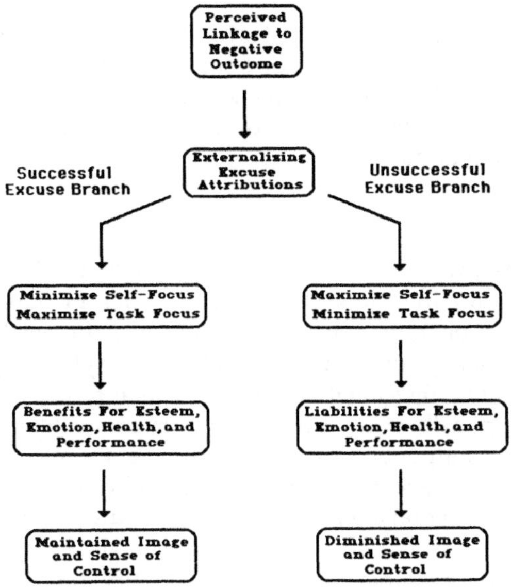

FIGURE 1: The successful and unsuccessful excuse sequences.

first time. Receiving negative feedback about an excuse prompts the individual to invest energy in salvaging the situation and detracts from his or her ability to get on with business.

At step 4, excuse attributions either result in esteem and performance benefits (in the case of successful excuses) or decrements (in the case of failed excuses). Finally, step 5 represents the culmination of the excuse sequence, with the individual's experiencing of either a maintained or a diminished image and sense of control.

In terms of the difference between successful and unsuccessful excuses, the events immediately following step 2 in the excuse sequence are critical. Once an excuse has been advanced, the response of the audience (including the excuse-maker himself or herself) determines whether it facilitates the resumption of normal activities (e.g., task focus) or leads to a continued self-focus and its consequences (e.g., task disruption, dysphoria, etc.), not to mention the possible social costs.

In the following portions of this section, we suggest certain "principles" of good excuse-making and argue that excuses that violate these principles are likely candidates to follow the path for unsuccessful excuses as diagrammed in Figure 1. We restrict our list of excuse-making principles to ones for which there is either supportive or strongly suggestive empirical evidence.

Principle 1: Be Mindful of Social Conventions

Predictable is comfortable. By necessity, our society tolerates a range of variability in the observance of social amenities. By the same token, however, there is a range of acceptability. Just as it is hard to imagine spilling red wine on a friend's new Persian rug without making some apology, it is difficult to fathom blaming the friend for having used lousy judgment in choosing a white rug. Excuses that conform to familiar and/or acceptable forms are more likely to succeed than those that do not.

Blaming

Blaming is an extremely familiar type of excuse that is designed to break (or at least share) the apparent link to a negative action or outcome. Despite its familiarity, however, blaming appears to entail some appreciable costs.

In the context of a group "survival exercise," Forsyth, Berger, and Mitchell (1981) gave groups of subjects either success or failure feedback. The subjects then rated how responsible they were for their group's outcome and were given copies of what were supposedly the other group members' ratings. These bogus ratings indicated that the respondent had taken either a high, a moderate, or a low level of personal responsibility for the group's outcome. Of particular interest here are the subjects' reactions to the "blamer," the bogus respondent who accepted a low level of responsibility. Following failure, the blamer was liked less than either the high or moderate responsibility claimers.

Dollinger, Staley, and McGuire (1981) also reported a study of blaming. These authors described a losing softball team to fifth- and sixth-grade children. Four of the team members' reactions to the loss were depicted, and the subjects were asked to rate them. The player who offered no excuse was judged to be the smartest, the most good, and the most likeable, whereas, the player who accused the other team of cheating was rated lowest on these qualities. Similar results were obtained by Dollinger and McGuire (1981). They found that 4- to 12-year-old children showed more attraction to story characters who self-blamed and somatosized than to characters who used projection and displacement.

Although the body of evidence on social reactions to blaming is small, it appears that blaming may be a high-risk excuse strategy in terms of its exacting significant social costs. The study by Dollinger *et al.* (1981), for example, suggests that children quickly learn our culture's tendency to ostracize sore losers. Along these same thematic lines, in this day of instant video replays, it would be interesting to examine the possibility that reactions to blaming may vary depending on the availability of observable evidence to prop up the accusing finger.

Foreseeability, Intentionality, Controllability

The research on blaming is not the only empirical support for the existence of culturally transmitted rules regarding the types of excuse attributions that are maximally (and minimally) effective. In particular, we would like to comment on the apparent importance of attending to the elements of foreseeability, intentionality, and controllability in the formulation of excuse attributions.

The social basis for the excuse value of "accounts" that appeal to the lack of the above three elements resides in the theoretical proposition that observers make attributions to the dispositional characteristics of an actor only if they believe the actor behaved intentionally (Jones & Davis, 1965). Indeed, a sizeable body of literature attests to the validity of this proposition. Even young children weigh the element of intentionality when rendering moral judgments (see Grueneich, 1982; Keasey, 1978, for reviews). Rotenberg (1980) found that children judged a boy to be less friendly and more aggressive when he was described as intentionally hurting another child with a ball relative to when the act was described as an accident. In the adult world, crimes that are purposefully committed are seen as especially negative (Darley & Zanna, 1982). Negative outcomes that are seen as unforeseeable are regarded more charitably (e.g., Shaw, 1968; Shaw & Reitan, 1969; Shaw & Sulzer, 1964; Sulzer & Burglass, 1968).

Weiner *et al.* (1987) have described a revealing series of four studies in which the critical dimensions of excuses are successively elaborated. In Study 1, subjects were asked to recount excuses they had offered to others as well as the real reasons they had withheld. Relative to the reasons that were withheld, the excuses (whether true or false) elicited causal attributions that were more external, uncontrollable, and unintentional. In Study 2, subjects imagined instances of social faux pas (e.g., coming late to an appointment) and rated their reactions to a series of potential excuses that had been elicited in Study 1. Subjects' ratings of the degree to which they would be angered by the various excuses were the most extreme for those that represented the most internal, controllable, and intentional causes (i.e., preference and negligence).

In Study 3, an experimental methodology was employed. Subjects arrived for an experiment that presumably involved working with another subject (a confederate), who arrived 15 minutes later. Upon arriving, the confederate offered either no excuse, a "bad" (controllable) excuse, or a "good" (uncontrollable) excuse. The uncontrollable excuses provoked less anger, resentment, irritation, unforgiveness, and dislike than either no excuse or a controllable excuse. The "good" excusers also were seen as more dependable, responsible, considerate, sensitive, and interesting than the "bad" or nonexcusing confederate. Moreover, the subjects expressed a greater willingness to interact with the good excuser.

In Study 4, the later-arriving subject of a scheduled pair was detained and instructed to devise a "good," "bad," or "any" excuse for their subsequent late arrival in the experimental room. An additional control group was told to make no excuse. Analysis of the excuses revealed that those offered in the "good" or "any" excuse conditions involved less intentionality and controllability than those offered in the "bad" excuse condition. The affective responses elicited closely resembled those obtained in Study 3, with the "good" and "any" excuse conditions yielding more positive responses and fewer negative responses (e.g., anger, irritation, dislike, unforgiveness). Interestingly, when given free rein to devise "any" excuse, subjects understood and elected to employ the elements of "good" ones.

A study by Tedeschi, Riordan, Gaes, and Kane (1984) also provides evidence for the importance of foreseeability, controllability, and intentionality. They examined the effects of a confederate's explanations for the use of threats toward his or her partner in a prisoner's dilemma game. The confederate either made no effort to explain his or her behavior or offered one of three explanations: he or she was shortchanged in a previous experiment and was trying to make up lost points; he or she was using the threats to signal opportunities for mutual cooperation; or, he or she did not clearly understand the instructions for the game. The subjects subsequently were asked to predict how the confederate would behave in five different situations.

Analysis of the predictions indicated that the excuses involving lack of intentionality and/or foreseeability (i.e., that the confederate was merely attempting to cooperate or misunderstood the instructions) resulted in reduced ratings of selfishness and aggressiveness. The excuse involving clear intentionality (i.e., the confederate was trying to make up for lost points), however, led to perceptions of deceitfulness.

Finally, we describe a study reported by Riordan (1981). Subjects read bogus newspaper reports of a U.S. Senator who had either taken a bribe or hired a prostitute and was facing charges. The senator offered one of two "justifications" (defined as admissions and attempts to reframe: he was conducting an investigation or he was only doing what everyone else was doing); or he offered one of two "excuses" (defined as denials of responsibility: he was drunk or he was so angry he didn't know what he was doing). Consistent with the theoretical difference sometimes posited between accounts and excuses (see Snyder & Higgins, 1987), the excuses reduced perceptions of responsibility, whereas the justifications reduced ratings of wrongfulness. Subjects exposed to the excuses (which minimized intentionality, controllability, and foreseeability) were least likely to believe the senator would repeat his offense, whereas those exposed to the justifications were most likely to believe he was aware of the possible consequences of his actions *and* intended to produce them.

Taken together, the above studies strongly suggest that the causal dimensions of intentionality, controllability, and foreseeability are of particular importance in determining social responses to excuses. The studies reported by Weiner *et al.* (1987) provide convincing demonstrations that ordinary people have a sophisticated understanding of the value of appeals to uncontrollability and lack of intention and are capable of skillfully using them to engineer favorable outcomes. This view of "naive" subjects as accomplished social engineers is supported by research reported by Tetlock (1981).

Tetlock asked subjects to identify events from their lives in which they behaved in either desirable or undesirable ways. He then asked them to generate explanations for their behaviors that would favorably impress others. Not only did the subjects devise explanations that mollified subsequent raters, but they also targeted them to address the specific image threats that were inherent in their negative performances.

Summary

Given the demonstrated value of appeals to lack of intentionality, foreseeability, and controllability, excuse attributions that incorporate their opposites are likely to generate adverse consequences. By the same token, we have reviewed evidence that blaming, at least in certain contexts, may entail penalties.

Our focusing on these two general areas as exemplars of the existence of social conventions that guide the creative efforts of "wise" excuse-makers should in no way be construed as suggesting that there are not other important norms or widely held values governing the use of excuses.

For example, there is evidence that teachers avoid making externalizing attributions when their role expectations clearly dictate that they take responsibility (e.g., Ames, 1975; Beckman, 1973; Ross, Bierbrauer, & Polly, 1974). Moreover, teachers who take public responsibility for their students' failures are viewed more positively than those who do not (Tetlock, 1980). Such findings may indicate that teachers "intuitively" know that accepting blame for such failures elicits greater audience support than not doing so. It is not known, however, whether teachers' private and public attributions coincide.

Principle 2: Keep Excuse-Making Ambiguous

Earlier, in our discussion of how excuses work, we noted the value of self-deception. As we pointed out, not knowing one is making an excuse considerably streamlines the process of getting on with business. We argue here that keeping an external audience in the dark about whether or not an excuse has been made is also beneficial. The mere fact that we so strenuously avoid admitting our excuses (we prefer "apologies," "justifications," and, most of all, "reasons") indicates our collective discomfort with them. It also raises the question of what happens when the excuse motive behind an externalizing attribution is (or threatens to be) apparent to those around us.

We have previously reviewed evidence that excuse-making is constrained by conditions that increase the salience of the excuse-making motive (i.e., Handelsman *et al.*, 1985; Smith *et al.*, 1982), and there are other studies that show similar effects (e.g., Arkin, Appelman, & Burger, 1980; Arkin, Gabrenya, Appelman, & Cochran, 1979; Wells, Petty, Harkins, Kakgehiro, & Harvey, 1977). In the following sections, we review evidence that unambiguous excuse-making has adverse consequences.

Excuses before "Invalidating" Sources

As we noted previously, a number of studies have indicated that people are less likely to engage in excuse-making when there is a good chance that the excuse will be recognized for what it is. An interesting study reported by Mehlman and Snyder (1985) indicates that making excuses despite a clear risk of their being detected leads to dysphoric consequences for the excuse-maker.

Mehlman and Snyder (1985) examined the consequences of subjects' making retrospective excuses for a test-taking failure while they were attached to a "lie detector." First, they gave their subjects either success or failure feedback following a test of analogies. Next, half of the subjects completed an "excuse-facilitation" questionnaire, some while attached to a lie detector and some while not attached. When not attached, subjects in the excuse-facilitation condition evidenced lessened negative affect relative to their failure-condition counterparts, whose excuse making was not facilitated. When attached to the lie detector, however, excuse-facilitated subjects experienced *more negative affect* than unfacilitated subjects.

The above result may be interpreted as indicating that people are negatively aroused when they believe others may know that they are making excuses (recall that we previously reviewed evidence that people moderate their excuse-making under similar circumstances; e.g., Arkin *et al.*, 1979). However, an equally plausible (and, in our view, complementary) possibility is that the dysphoria identified by Mehlman and Snyder derives from the increased self-scrutiny associated with being attached to a lie detector while completing a self-serving questionnaire.

The study by Mehlman and Snyder (1985) is the only one we know of to have examined the affective consequences to the excuse-maker of making potentially transparent excuses. Clearly, though, the lie detector scenario is not the only one in which an audience may be in a position to detect or invalidate an excuse attribution. Many excuses, for example, include assertions of "fact" that may be disputed by others who have specialized knowledge. A protestation that "I didn't do it" carries little weight for an audience that witnessed "it." Similarly, audiences may have knowledge of the performance arenas within which excuses are made and may, therefore, be able to invalidate certain types of excuses. An illustration of this type of invalidation and its possible consequences can be seen in two studies reported by Carlston and Shovar (1983).

Carlston and Shovar reported two studies designed to assess audience reactions to various attributions for task performance. In study 1, subjects reacted to individuals who had either succeeded or failed on a problem-solving task and who offered either internal (i.e., effort and ability) or external (i.e., luck and task difficulty) attributions for their performances. Of particular interest here were the subjects' reactions to the performer who did poorly on the task. This person was rated as more modest and honest when the attributions were internal as opposed to external. Subjects also reported being more similar to and liking the unsuccessful performer better when the attributions were to internal factors. Ratings of the performer's ability were not affected by the attributions.

Observing that the so-called self-serving attributions (i.e., luck and task difficulty) for failure elicited negative rather than positive reactions, Carlston and Shovar speculated that the raters may have regarded outcomes on the intellectual performance task as so clearly ability dependent that claims to the contrary rang hollow and led to perceptions of dishonesty.

In Study 2, the authors examined audience reactions to performance attributions on tasks that were presented as either very specific (delimited) or overall (general) measures of the ability in question and as either highly reliable and clearly ability related or of questionable reliability and subject to various non-ability factors. The results indicated that raters judged performance to be more ability dependent if the stimulus person made an internal rather than an external attribution. Also, unsuccessful performers who made external attributions were judged to have more ability than those who made internal attributions. As in the first study, unsuccessful performers who made internal attributions were judged to be more modest, more honest, and more likeable.

The findings reported by Carlston and Shovar (1983) suggest that, depending on the specific task at issue, attributions to nonability factors may or may not succeed in serving a useful impression-management function. Where the task is clearly ability dependent, self-serving attributions may actually backfire. However, even in the context of tasks that are seen as less ability dependent, self-serving attributions may afford gains in some areas (i.e., limiting nonability attributions) only at the risk of sustaining losses in others (i.e., perceptions of modesty and honesty).

Before leaving this discussion of the importance of ambiguous excuse-making, we review one final body of evidence. Our previous comments have dealt with the excuse-maker's reactions to making excuses that are at risk for being detected (i.e., Mehlman & Snyder, 1985) and with audience reactions to self-serving attributions that don't fit with the facts (i.e., Carlston & Shovar, 1983). We now consider a study that deals with audience reactions to having certain knowledge than an individual deliberately self-handicapped prior to an evaluated performance.

Obvious Self-Handicapping

There is a substantial body of literature attesting to the fact that, under appropriate circumstances, people adopt self-handicaps prior to evaluation experiences (e.g., Berglas & Jones, 1978; Harris & Snyder, 1986; Higgins & Harris, 1988; Smith *et al.*, 1982; Tucker, Vuchinich, & Sobell, 1981). These studies, however, have paid little attention to either the intra- or interpersonal consequences of self-handicapping. To our knowledge, only one study to date has shed light on the question of when self-handicapping may result in negative consequences.

Arkin and Baumgardner (1985, reported in Baumgardner & Arkin, 1987) gave subjects descriptions of an individual who, prior to an important examination, either willfully self-handicapped, was involuntarily handicapped by circumstances, or was handicap free. The person's performance was, in turn, characterized as poor, average, or good. Regardless of whether the handicap was willfully adopted, subjects made ability attributions for successful performance and nonability attributions for poor performance. However, subjects rated the person as less competent in general when the person deliberately self-handicapped.

Given the analogue nature of this study (i.e., the raters neither witnessed nor interacted with the self-handicapper), caution is warranted in drawing conclusions. However, two points seem worth making. First, the results are consistent with the theoretical proposition that handicaps should lead to favorable ability attributions on the part of observers. Second, the results suggest that handicaps may work best when they are not regarded as purposefully adopted.

Handicaps that are known (or suspected) to be deliberately adopted may generate justifiable doubts about the handicapping individual's confidence in his or her own ability. As indicated by the Arkin and Baumgardner (1985) study, however, they may still frustrate definitive nonability attributions for a *specific* performance (recall also our discussion of the findings by Carlston & Shovar,

1983). This interesting complication again raises the possibility that excuse-makers may often be willing to suffer some costs in return for limited but highly valued gains (Tetlock, 1983).

When we consider the possibility that the benefits of excuse-making are not reducible to a simple all-or-none formula, the problem of determining whether or not they are self-defeating becomes complicated indeed. To ultimately resolve this question, we may need to enter the phenomenological world of the excuse-maker. Nevertheless, it now appears very likely that excuses are most functional and adaptive when the underlying excuse motive remains obscure and the excuse is formulated in a manner that precludes its being debunked. That well-functioning individuals appear to have an intuitive or experience-based understanding of the importance of these principles is indicated by the 1987 U.S. House and Senate "Iranscam" hearings, in which witness after witness detailed the extraordinary lengths to which they went to preserve "plausible deniability" regarding their actions.

Principle 3: Don't Become a Label

Many psychotherapy clients whose behavior has earned them a psychopathological label (e.g., shy, depressed, obsessive–compulsive, alcoholic) come to regard their particular disability as beyond their control. Indeed, our society has actively promoted this trend by advocating a disease model of such conditions as alcoholism, obesity, drug addiction, depression, and mental illness in general. Our goal here is not to enrich the ongoing dialogue concerning the applicability of the disease model to the fields of psychiatry and psychology but rather to outline our thoughts regarding the liabilities associated with using "symptoms" or consistent behavior patterns as excuses.

Clinical theory is rich in tradition when it comes to the idea that psychiatric symptoms may serve as excuses for failures in life (e.g., Ansbacher & Ansbacher, 1967; Horney, 1950; Yalom, 1980). We have also seen the growth of an impressive body of empirical evidence indicating that symptoms serve excuse purposes. In anticipation of threatening evaluations, people engage in the strategic (excuse) reporting of such diverse symptoms as test anxiety (Smith *et al.*, 1982), shyness (Snyder, Smith, Augelli, & Ingram, 1985), hypochondriasis (Smith, Snyder, & Perkins, 1983), and life trauma (DeGree & Snyder, 1985). People have also been shown to adopt self-handicaps that, when engaged in repetitively and excessively, could be regarded as symptomatic (e.g., drinking alcohol: Tucker *et al.*, 1981; drug use: Berglas & Jones, 1978; Kolditz & Arkin, 1982).

The occasional use of symptom-based excuses is exceedingly common and probably benign. Most of us, for example, have feigned (or reported) one malady or another in order to get out of something. When, for whatever reasons, a person repeatedly and frequently employs a given symptom-based ploy, however, a label is likely to be attached. By the same token, a man who commonly explains away crude behavior at social gatherings by saying he was drunk and didn't know what he was doing will quickly be recognized as a probable alcoholic. Once such a label is attached, the person's subsequent behavior is at risk of being understood in light of the label.

Snyder, Higgins, and Stucky (1983) suggested that excuses that entail the acquisition of relatively enduring labels may be inherently counterproductive. Berglas (1985) subsequently argued that, while alcohol intoxication may serve as an effective self-handicapping strategy in the short run, the strategy may backfire if the drinking becomes too pervasive. One of the purposes of excuse strategies is to avoid dispositional attributions for negative outcomes. Once a label (e.g., alcoholic) has been affixed, Berglas argues, the individual invites the very dispositional attributions that intoxication is designed to avoid. Indeed, this seductive pathway has been called a "Faustian bargain," in that the short-term benefits of the alcohol excuse are reversed when the person is labeled "alcoholic" (Snyder, 1984). With this bit of background in mind, we turn to a review of research that has examined the effects of such labels within an excuse context.

Alcoholism

Critchlow (1985) reported a study in which college-student judges responded to a series of eight scenarios in which two examples from each of four categories (crimes, mild indiscretions, neutral actions, and socially desirable acts) were described as being enacted by individuals who were either characterized as drunk or sober and as either chronic alcoholics or social drinkers. Drunken protagonists were rated lower on measures of responsibility, blameworthiness, and causality than their sober counterparts. In addition, actors described as alcoholics were judged to be less responsible and to have played a less causal role than social drinkers. Although this study failed to identify liabilities associated with an "alcoholic" label, two other studies have obtained different outcomes.

In the first study, Sobell and Sobell (1975) reported a telephone survey in which respondents were asked to indicate their beliefs regarding the sentencing of an intoxicated person who perpetrated a violent crime. When the offender was described as a first offender or as a social drinker, more than 33% of the subjects recommended reduced punishment. However, when the offender was described as an alcoholic, 40% of the subjects recommended severe punishment.

A second study was conducted by Schlosberg (1985). Subjects were presented a description of an instance of child abuse. The alcohol intoxication of the abusive father was manipulated in a factorial design by having him avow (or not) that he was drunk and by presenting physical evidence (or not) that he was legally intoxicated. In addition, for half of the subjects, the offending father was described as an alcoholic. Female subjects (but not male subjects) rated the alcoholic-labeled abuser more negatively and recommended more punitive sanctions than for the nonlabeled abuser. Furthermore, for the alcoholic-labeled abuser, subjects who were presented with physical evidence of the father's legal intoxication felt there were fewer extenuating circumstances than when there was no physical evidence.

Depression

Only one excuse-related study uncovered in our literature search examined subjects' reactions to a dispositional label other than "alcoholism." Schouten and Handelsman (1987) conducted an investigation designed to examine the validity of theoretical speculations that depressive symptoms may have strategic excuse value in the sense that they avoid attributions of responsibility (e.g., Snyder *et al.*, 1983) or serve to minimize performance expectations (Hill, Weary, & Williams, 1986). Undergraduate psychology students reacted to hypothetical case studies in which male or female protagonists were portrayed as either perpetrating spousal abuse or as being confronted with losing their jobs due to poor work performance. In addition, the protagonists were described as having current depressive symptoms, current depressive symptoms and a history of psychiatric involvement, or no depressive symptoms or psychiatric history (no mention of either). Subjects rated the protagonists in both depression conditions as being less the cause of their behavior, less responsible for the consequences of their actions, and less blameworthy than the protagonist with no symptoms. Subjects were less likely to recommend that the protagonist in the work scenario be fired if he or she was depressed (with or without a psychiatric history). The depressed protagonist in the work scenario was also expected to assume fewer job-related duties, but only if he or she also had a history of psychiatric involvement.

Summary

Overall, studies on the use of alcohol intoxication as an excuse indicate that it is frequently effective in reducing judgments of responsibility and blame (e.g., Carducci & McNeely, 1981; Critchlow, 1985; Richardson & Campbell, 1980, 1982). The effects of alcoholic labels, however, appear to be more mixed, and there are indications that there may be important audience and perpetrator characteristics that influence the effectiveness of alcohol excuses. In several studies, for example (i.e., Carducci & McNeely, 1981; Richardson & Campbell, 1980, 1982), the female victims of antisocial acts were judged to be more responsible for their victimizations if they were presented as intoxicated. This may indicate that alcohol excuses would be particularly ineffective for female perpetrators, although this issue has yet to be investigated.

With regard to audience characteristics, Carducci and McNeely (1981) reported that recovering alcoholics, in contrast to college students, judged an intoxicated wife beater to be *more* responsible for his behavior. It seems likely that recovering alcoholics, due to their involvement in treatment programs, would be particularly sensitive to the responsibility avoidance associated with drinking problems. They may also be more inclined to assume the existence of a drinking problem in an individual who engages in spouse abuse while intoxicated.

At one level, the depression study by Schouten and Handelsman (1987) merely demonstrates what we already know: cultural concepts of mental illness are closely intertwined with the idea that mental patients are victims and are not responsible for the symptoms that cause them suffering. In this regard, Schouten and Handelsman have given us one view of how social reactions to depression may lead to and reinforce the use of depressive symptoms as excuse strategies. At another level, however, it is clear that there were some liabilities associated with a psychiatric history of depression. Specifically, subjects regarded the depressed person with a history of psychiatric involvement as less capable of handling job responsibilities. Such perceptions could have distinctly adverse consequences in terms of job advancement, hiring, and the like.

It seems likely that the consequences of a dispositional label depend on the specific implications of the label. One important dimension may be the extent to which people regard the individual as in control of the behavior that led to the label. Alcoholics may be regarded as having more control over their pathological behavior than depressives. If so, they are probably also more likely to be held accountable for their deviant behaviors while intoxicated (and, perhaps, while sober). Being regarded as "out of control," may have different, though not necessarily less problematic, consequences for people with other kinds of "label conditions" (e.g., depression). The case of Bob, the client whose case history initiated this paper, illustrates this latter point.

Bob's freedom of movement was severely restricted by his obsessive fears. His compensating rituals metastasized into virtually every sphere of his life. Bob's family came to view almost all of his actions as being related to his "illness." As they saw it, even apparently positive acts often had pathological motivations and were, consequently, offenses of a sort themselves. Spending time with his son, for example, was regarded as a form of emotional blackmail in the sense that, if Bob curried his favor, the son would be obligated to gratify Bob's insatiable dependency needs. (The thought *did* cross Bob's mind.) If he went shopping with his wife, she attributed it to his fear of being alone. (In part, it was true.) It came to be impossible for Bob to be credited with having any legitimate affection for his family. In family decisions, he had less power than his preadolescent son. Not only did his condition explain most of his behavior, it came to be used as a weapon against him. His exercising any disciplinary authority over his son, for example, was totally out of the question, even though he had better parental judgment than his wife.

PRINCIPLE 4: MATCH EXCUSES TO "OFFENSES"

At the beginning of this chapter, we provided a definition of excuse-making that focused on the role of excuses in shifting causal attributions for negative self-relevant outcomes from more central to less central aspects of the self. One important aspect of excuse-making that is not explicitly emphasized in that definition is the idea that some excuses are designed to reduce the perceived negativity of self-relevant outcomes. Indeed, Snyder and Higgins (1987) have suggested that excuse-making involves a two-dimensional framework of situational appraisal. The framework consists of the orthogonal factors of linkage-to-act (all to none) and valence-of-act (positive to negative; see Figure 2). Theoretically, the formulation of an effective excuse entails a consideration of where the "act" to be excused fits on both dimensions. Obviously, positive acts to which the individual is linked and negative outcomes to which the individual is not linked present no occasion for excuse-making.

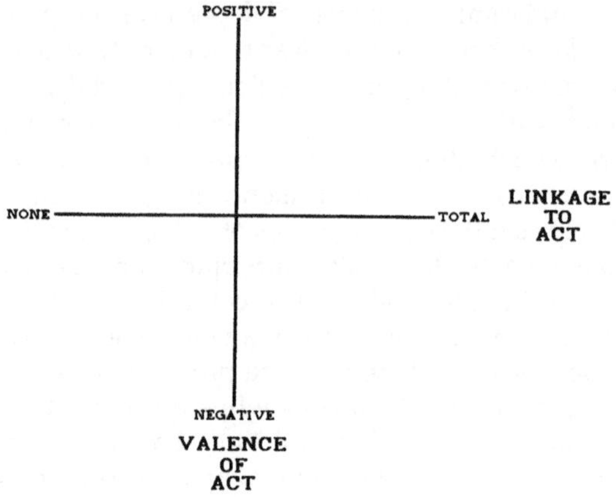

FIGURE 2: The linkage-to-act and valence-of-act appraisal dimensions.

We argue here, however, that when acts are "bad" and linkages exist, prudent excuse-making involves tailoring excuses to affect the appraisal dimension that is most amenable to being "massaged."

When young children are first learning the fine art of "slipping off the hook," they often deny doing things they obviously did. Under such circumstances (Mom and Dad didn't scribble crayons on the bedroom wall), the child's attempt to sever his or her linkage to the act falls flat. A bit more disarming in such situations are excuses that target the valence-of-act appraisal dimension. If, for example, the child pleads confusion about the performance standard in question (e.g., "But Tommy's Mom lets *him* draw on *his* wall!"), some leverage may be gained (especially if Mom and Dad don't know what Tommy *is* allowed to do). By advancing a consensus-raising excuse (i.e., other people do it) and simultaneously implying that there was no *intention* of doing anything wrong, the appraised negativity of the artwork may be softened. Although the mental gymnastics involved in selecting the best appraisal dimension to target may be too sophisticated for very young children, we expect older children and adults to function adaptively.

Lest there be any misunderstanding, we would like to point out that some situations may demand excuses aimed at the linkage-to-act appraisal dimension. For example, some acts may be so patently bad (e.g., sexual abuse of an infant) that efforts to diminish their negativity are doomed to fail. Here, the linkage-to-act dimension may be the only "game" in town. Indeed, clinicians who work with sexual abuse perpetrators are only too familiar with their extraordinary persistence in denying their behavior (apparently such acts are so esteem threatening that any linkage to them is intolerable). As denial sags under the weight of time and evidence, however, one is likely to see other linkage-to-act excuses emerge. Common occurrences are attempts to share the blame (e.g., "*she* seduced me") and claims to have been out of control (e.g., "I was drunk and didn't know what I was doing"; see McCaghy, 1968). It may be at such times (i.e., when a link is apparent and the act is particularly "bad") that people are willing to use the ultimate "psychological" linkage-to-act excuse: "I did it, but it wasn't really me. It was my alcoholism" (or some other condition that implies that the bad act was "ego alien"). It is to be expected that people will be reluctant to willingly assume the burden of a labeled condition unless the price for not doing so is high.

In some instances, when denial fails and no other acceptable linkage-breaking maneuver is available, valence-of-act excuses ultimately emerge despite their unpalatability (i.e., a person will acknowledge *some* accountability). For example, one individual who frequently exposed himself to his daughter finally acknowledged that it certainly looked like he was exposing himself to her, but he swore that it wasn't his intention to do so: it was only an unfortunate side effect of his aversion to wearing underwear under his cut-off shorts. His penis sometimes just sort of "flopped out." His only error, he insisted, was in using poor judgment in his choice of clothes (not) to wear.

Our view that effective excuses target the appraisal dimension that is most "vulnerable" makes logical sense. However, we are unaware of any studies that have directly examined this proposition. We, however, cite research (previously reviewed in other sections) that appears to lend indirect support to our thesis. First, Carlston and Shovar (1983, study 1) reported being surprised that externalizing attributions (i.e., luck and task difficulty) for poor problem-solving performance met with more negative audience reactions than internal attributions (i.e., ability and effort). They speculated that their subjects regarded the task outcomes as clearly ability dependent and, consequently, experienced the externalizing attributions as dishonest. Within our two-dimensional appraisal framework, attributions to luck and task difficulty would be regarded as targeting the linkage-to-act dimension (e.g., it wasn't me, it was the task), while attributions to ability and lack of effort focus on the valence-of-act dimension (e.g., it wasn't really so bad because I didn't try). If Carlston and Shovar (1983) are correct in believing their subjects saw performances as ability dependent, our model would predict that the externalizing attributions would be less than maximally effective.

Second, Riordan (1981) compared the effects of "justifications" and "excuses" on judges who were asked to consider the case of a U.S. Senator who had either taken a bribe or hired a prostitute. Within our framework, justifications (defined here as admissions with attempts to reframe) are inherently targeted at the valence-of-act appraisal dimension, while excuses (defined here as denials of responsibility) are inherently targeted at the linkage-to-act appraisal dimension. The aspect of this study that is of interest here is the fact that the excuses and justifications appear to have had effects that were distinctly different *and* consistent with our theoretical contrast between the appraisal dimensions: the excuses reduced perceptions of responsibility, and the justifications reduced perceptions of wrongfulness. An intriguing implication of this finding is that, in many instances, the prudent excuse-maker may be faced with a need to decide which type of effect is in his or her best interests (assuming that an excuse that simultaneously "attacks" both dimensions is not feasible).

Finally, we would like to comment briefly on the research we have reviewed above on the effects of blaming (i.e., Dollinger *et al.*, 1981; Forsyth *et al.*, 1981). We concluded that blaming is a high-risk excuse strategy in that it frequently leads to social censure. It is worth considering that negative reactions to blaming (a linkage-to-act excuse tactic) may often derive from the audience's lingering belief that the blaming individual was at least partly responsible for the disputed outcome. In this vein, recall that we raised the possibility that evidence indicating that blaming is warranted may temper (and perhaps eliminate) the negative consequences of the strategy. Indeed, in 1987 we witnessed a national struggle over this issue, as President Ronald Reagan's claim that his subordinates didn't tell him about their Iran–Contra dealings set off a monumental search for evidence that would support or refute his assertion. Even in the face of evidence that President Reagan didn't know what was going on, however, many people persisted in believing he was responsible, because they felt that, in his role as President, he should have known (cf. Tetlock, 1980).

WHY SELF-DEFEATING EXCUSES?

In the preceding section we described four principles of good excuse-making. The list is neither definitive nor exhaustive. In the absence of supporting (or suggestive) literature, for example, we omitted discussion of such possible topics as the importance of timing in excuse making (recall the difficulty Senator Edward M. Kennedy created for himself when he waited for an unseemly number of hours before telling his version of the tragic Chappaquiddick accident) or the hazards of adopting self-handicaps that are truly debilitating. In this section, we turn our attention to a brief consideration of *why* people engage in excuse-making that has a high ratio of costs to benefits.

The "whys" underlying self-defeating excuse-making probably run the gamut from mundane to sublime. Here, we discuss two general (and probably interrelated) categories of reasons: deficient excuse-making skills and characterological "sensitivities."

DEFICIENT EXCUSE-MAKING SKILLS

Growing up requires continuous enrollment in the school of hard knocks. Included among those things that must be learned are the various skills involved in coping with life's many challenges. We have argued previously (see especially our discussion of reality negotiation) that excuse-making is an important component of the adaptable individual's coping repertoire. We have also indicated that effective excuse-making can be a sophisticated process involving, among other things, accurate social perception, knowledge of cultural folkways, and awareness of an array of potential excuse strategies. Despite the rigorous training we give our children in the art of excuse-making (Snyder *et al.*, 1983), the level of skill attained varies across individuals, depending on their aptitudes and circumstances.

In most instances, we believe, the root cause of self-defeating excuse-making lies not in the fact that excuses are made but rather in the fact that they are poorly made. This can be illustrated through a consideration of studies aimed at teaching adaptive excuse-making. Zoeller, Mahoney, and Weiner (1983), for example, trained mentally retarded adults to make lack-of-effort attributions for failures on a motor coordination task. These subjects, who were predisposed to making ability attributions for failures, suffered from general motivational problems, especially following failures. The results indicated that the attribution training led to improved task performance. Lanoue and Curtis (1985) found that women given effort attributions showed improved performance in the presence of men. In a similar vein, Medway and Venino (1982) found that training elementary school students to make lack-of-effort (rather than ability) attributions for failure led to improved persistence on a visual discrimination task.

In another study involving school children, Chapin and Dyck (1976) taught children who were reading below their grade level to make effort (rather than ability) attributions for both their successes and failures. The children subsequently showed greater persistence at reading difficult sentences. Finally, Dweck (1975) taught children with poor arithmetic skills to attribute their failures to lack of effort. Following training, their math performance improved.

The above studies illustrate the adaptive benefits associated with excuse-making. However, we introduced the attribution-retraining studies under the guise of illustrating that it is *poor* excuse-making (rather than excuse-making *per se*) that is counterproductive. Without closer consideration, it appears that the subjects in the retraining studies were *failing* to make excuses (rather than making poor ones) prior to their training. In this vein, it is important to remember that the subjects in the retraining studies represented special populations that were known to have (and knew they had) particular difficulties (e.g., mental retardation, reading problems). We would like to take the liberty of suggesting that it is just such populations that are likely to use their identified (labeled) disabilities as excuse attributions. For a child with reading difficulties, for example, making the attributional statement "I can't do it—I have a reading problem" may be an effective excuse strategy for declining to begin or continue with reading exercises that expose him or her to failure. Although the attribution is to lack of ability (a relatively internal causal source), it implicates a circumscribed ability arena. That such an ability (excuse) attribution is self-defeating is apparent from the types of dependent measures employed in the attribution retraining studies (e.g., task persistence). An excuse that abets the avoidance of important skill acquisition (or increases task-disruptive cognitions due to heightened negative self-awareness) can't be all good.

Ignorance can be a crippling thing, especially when it is in the area of how to effectively manage one's life. We have indicated that not knowing how to appropriately invoke efficacy-enhancing attributional strategies can impede educational progress. There are innumerable other areas in which "not knowing how" is a hindrance. In many instances, different areas of skill deficiency converge. In the attribution retraining studies, for example, the children had educational difficulties that elicited and exposed their deficient attributional excuse-making skills. In our view this is typical of truly self-defeating excuse-making. Although empirical support for this assertion is absent, clinical examples abound.

Our familiar client, "Bob," serves us well again here. Bob had been married to his wife approximately 2 years, and they were engaged in constant battles over a range of family management issues. When he realized that she was becoming increasingly detached from him, he developed an acute fear that she might want a divorce. It was during this time that he had his first "panic attack." Subsequently, he developed an agoraphobic pattern of fears that made it intolerable for him to be alone. Either his wife or his son (who was almost symbiotically attached to his mother) *had* to be with him. If this was impossible, he would do the next best thing (e.g., hovering around outside his wife's place of employment all day long—often in subzero weather). He became so convinced of his inability to survive without his wife that he relinquished his position as a coequal marriage partner in an effort to reduce the level of conflict. Although he regarded it as a wimpy and cowardly thing to do, he felt he had no choice. Fifteen years later, in a therapy session, Bob commented that, if it hadn't been for his illness, his marriage wouldn't have lasted all these years. If it hadn't been for his fear of being alone, he mused, he would have left her years ago.

Bob's case illustrates the notion that inabilities in one area often bring forth our inabilities in other areas. For Bob, the eliciting problem was his inability to constructively resolve his marital conflicts. The only solution he found was to unconditionally "surrender," and the only way he could tolerate doing this *was to have no choice*. His unwilling dependency (i.e., his "illness"), then, became his excuse for his inability to leave a destructive marriage. Bob's case leads us to our discussion of the second general category of reasons why people engage in self-defeating excuse-making: characterological "sensitivities."

CHARACTEROLOGICAL "SENSITIVITIES"

Given the vast number of little and big excuses we make in our day-to-day lives, it is inevitable that we all suffer the consequences of the maladaptive or self-defeating excuse at some time. However, these ordinary excuse-making errors tell us little about dispositional self-defeatism. Nor do those occasional big mistakes illuminate the issue. In our experience, people for whom excuse-making is clinically significant have fallen into repetitive and rigid patterns.

It is beyond the scope of this chapter to discuss why people develop or focus on specific fears, limitations, or vulnerabilities to the extent that all (or most) arenas where their flaws may surface are instigations to hide behind characteristic excuse attributions. We also omit discussing the factors (constitutional or experiential) that may guide the individual's selection of a characteristic excuse-making style. (The interested reader, however, is referred to Berglas, 1985, for a discussion of the genesis of problematic self-handicapping.) Our emphasis here is on a general elaboration of some of the factors that may be involved in the transition to dispositional (label-based) excuse-making.

In a series of studies on the strategic reporting of "symptoms," Snyder and his colleagues preselected subjects on the basis of their reporting such symptoms as test anxiety (Smith *et al.*, 1982), hypochondriasis (Smith *et al.*, 1983), and shyness (Snyder *et al.*, 1985). In each of these studies, subjects were selected to represent either the high or low end of the college student continuum for reporting such symptoms. Also, in each of these studies, those subjects who were initially high reporters were those who subsequently enhanced their reporting of symptoms under conditions designed to elicit preemptive excuse-making. Initial low reporters did not embellish their symptom reports. These findings demonstrate that people with particular felt weaknesses or vulnerabilities can come to rely on those weaknesses as causal attributions in situations that may expose or diagnose other, more secret weaknesses. We would argue that a labeling process (either explicit or implicit) is operative in such cases.

It is a common experience that people freely volunteer that they are "shy" in anticipation of social situations that may reveal their interpersonal awkwardness. By the same token, experienced teachers are only too familiar with having students explain their poor exam performances with a statement to the effect that they suffer from "test anxiety." Students seeking admission into graduate training programs in psychology occasionally volunteer that they have "math anxiety," when asked about mediocre scores on the quantitative section of the Graduate Record Exam.

Each of these label-based attributional statements is offered in lieu of other, more impersonal and situation-bound attributions (e.g., "I had the flu when I took the GRE"). We believe that the transition from situational to dispositional attributions in such situations usually takes place because the eliciting circumstances recur with sufficient regularity and intensity that an encompassing (and uncomplicating) attribution becomes necessary. Under these circumstances, a dispositional attribution may be quite attractive, because it "explains" so much while simultaneously delimiting the scope of the search for causal attributions.

Perhaps equally important in many instances is the fact that dispositional attributions frequently provide the individual with grounds for avoiding at least some threatening arenas in the future. Besides, many label-based attributions carry with them the (probably comforting) implication that the individual suffers from the condition in question and would most certainly want it to be otherwise *if it were in his or her power to change it*. Nicely imbedded within the typical label-based excuse attribution, then, is a "higher-order" denial of responsibility. After all, one's responsibility extends only as far as one's control. A subtle, but intriguing, aspect of this higher-order responsibility evasion is the possibility that the role of self-deception in the excuse-making process shifts from one of obscuring the essential fact of excuse-making to one of obscuring the individual's accountability for his or her handicapping condition.

Earlier in this chapter, we talked about the existence of an image–control–image cycle in which an individual's self-image influences his or her ability to exercise effective control and vise versa. For the typical person, the thrust of this cycle is in the direction of enhancing the mastery of life's challenges. For problematic label-based excuse-makers, however, it is as if they have incorporated into their self images (or self-theories) suspicions, beliefs, or outright convictions that they are tragically flawed in some way that is destined to frustrate their strivings for positive efficacy. For these persons, the thrust of the image–control–image cycle becomes one of damage containment rather than one of active mastery.

We are suggesting, in effect, that to understand clinically significant dispositional excuse-making is to appreciate that the individual has probably experienced a collapse of courage (or faith) in one or more important life arenas. (We can't fail to pay homage to Alfred Adler in this context; see Ansbacher & Ansbacher, 1967.) Despite the social costs associated with label-based dispositional attributions, clinical experience indicates that the leverage they give people in concealing their presumed unacceptable flaw(s) sometimes leads them to become good, though damnable, "friends." From the individual's perspective, their conditions are damnable because they cause them suffering. From an outsider's perspective, the conditions are damnable because they abet peoples' avoidance of experiences that might help them develop positive coping skills and enable them to eschew their "tragic flaw" mentality. They seem to function like self-fulfilling prophesies in their tendency to sustain and promote the individual's discouragement.

The individual who offers up dispositional excuses is attempting to strike a bargain—with himself or herself as well as with others. Earlier, for example, we wrote of the fundamental role reality negotiation plays in our self-regulation. We described a negotiated reality as a biased compromise between the individual's need-driven view of things and externally imposed views. Dispositional excuses invite the world to understand at least certain behaviors from within a particular, restricting perspective. This perspective frequently carries the implication that the excuse-maker labors under the burden of an unwanted and uncontrollable condition. For a world that is enamored with "medical models" of worrisome things that are poorly understood (e.g., American Psychiatric Association, 1987), the excuse-maker must seem like an excellent negotiator indeed. The excuse-maker's part of the bargain, however, is a velvet trap. If a dispositional excuse attribution is to be effective, over the long run, its "hold" on the excuse-maker must be substantiated. At best, the price of an ongoing dispositional excuse is that the individual does nothing that would lead to emancipation. It is more likely, however, that the individual will need to occasionally give positive evidence of his or her continuing disability.

It is almost certain that secondary gains play an important role in facilitating the adoption of many dispositional excuse attributions. The seductive lure of adopting a "sick role" has frequently been commented upon in clinical literature (e.g., Ullman & Krasner, 1969). Not only may the dispositional attribution discount more personally threatening interpretations of substandard behavior or performances, it may also mobilize others in the individual's environment to run interference in potentially threatening arenas. The spouses of problem drinkers, for example, are commonly admonished against being "enablers" of their partners' pathology by trying to protect them or by taking on their responsibilities.

Earlier in this chapter, in our discussion of how excuses work, we placed special emphasis on the key role that the excuse-maker's perceptions play in determining whether a particular excuse has a favorable cost–benefit ratio. When we enter into the realm of label-based attributions, this point comes home forcefully. Despite the benefits we have detailed (and there are surely others), taking on a label exacts a price that objective observers frequently judge to be extreme and irrational. We would guess, however, that the dispositional excuse-maker only rarely, if ever, encounters a truly objective (or at least forthright) audience when it comes to receiving unlaundered feedback about his or her behavior. We previously cited evidence that people are poor communicators when it comes to delivering critical feedback (i.e., Goffman, 1955; Schneider *et al.*, 1979; Sears, 1983; Tesser & Rosen, 1975). There is additional evidence (Strack & Coyne, 1983) that people who form negative impressions of depressed persons are unlikely to honestly share those impressions. The evidence clearly suggests that our external audiences collude with us in our efforts to remain unaware of our faults. The dispositional excuse-maker's problem isn't in getting others to "cut some slack," it is in not getting so far out on the rope that the social contract changes and those "others" begin to restrict his or her freedom even further.

We end this chapter as we began it—with an illustration from the life of "Bob." The focus of our illustration is on some of the experiential factors in Bob's life that preceded, and we believe fostered, his transition to a "committed" agoraphobic.

Bob was raised by his mother and his abusive, alcoholic father. His dominant childhood memories were of his family's chronic poverty, of his dad's drinking, and of the obscene beatings inflicted upon his mother and sister. Being physically small, he had no hope of matching his father's drunken strength, and he recalled cowering impotently in his room while listening to his mother's screams. He was overwhelmed by feelings of shame and guilt when he thought of the pain and humiliation inflicted on his mother and sister. He despised his "cowardice" in not taking steps to stop his father. He despised his father for depriving him of his efficacy.

Being an excellent student, Bob eventually went on to college, where he precipitously married the first girl he had ever seriously dated. He was happy for the first time in his life. He believed that marriage was "forever," and he felt secure. Following graduation, Bob went out of state to look for a job. When he found one, he sent for his wife, only to learn that she had left him. There had been no warning, and he was devastated. Bob spent the next several months on a drunken binge, in and out of detoxification programs on at least three separate occasions. He was, it seemed, totally out of control of his life, totally helpless to bring back what he had lost.

Bob blamed his wife, but mostly he blamed his father. He blamed him for making him what he was, for ruining his life. He even devised a plan to kill (exorcise) his father, but got too drunk to carry it out. This and other experiences confirmed Bob's growing conviction that his life was cursed, that its course was in the hands of those "betrayers" whose memories haunted him. He feared that he was uniquely incapable of making his own way as an adult. If he were to be happy, it could only be in a committed relationship. He also, however, had become deeply distrustful, and angry. He felt he had been permanently cheated out of the life he could have had, and he became obsessively concerned with never allowing himself to be victimized again. It was in this context that he met his second wife and married her within 3 months.

Sufficient details about the course of Bob's second marriage have been given in earlier sections for the reader to appreciate that his difficulties didn't end with remarriage. Hopefully, the reader is also able at this point to understand that Bob's subsequent psychiatric illness was an understandable (and in many ways effective) response to his problems, as he perceived them. Not only did his agoraphobic fears bind his family to him spatially, it also bound them to him emotionally (they, too, believed he would be unable to function without them). Not only did his fears of being alone extricate him from marital power struggles that he couldn't win (his wife could always kick him out if he pushed things too far), they also placed him in a unique position to control the lives of his family members (they almost always acceded to his demand that one of them be with him). Not only did his illness give him a ready explanation for his repeated failures to hold steady employment, it also gave him a sense of pride and accomplishment when he made some progress against its hold on him (e.g., resisting the urge to engage in one of his many rituals). Not only did his condition give him a reason to avoid doing things that might expose him to more failure, it also gave him the reassuring feeling that, in the final analysis, it wasn't his fault (it was his father's). From Bob's unique perspective, it all must have made perfect sense.

REFERENCES

American Psychiatric Association (1987). *Diagnostic and statistical manual of mental disorders* (DSM-III-R). Washington, DC: Author.

Ames, R. (1975). Teacher's attributions of responsibility: Some unexpected counterdefensive effects. *Journal of Educational Psychology, 67*, 668–676.

Ansbacher, H. L., & Ansbacher, R. R. (1967). *The individual psychology of Alfred Adler*. New York: Harper & Row. (Originally published by Basic Books, New York, 1956)

Arkin, R. M., Appelman, A. J., & Burger, J. M. (1980). Social anxiety, self-presentation, and the self-serving bias in causal attributions. *Journal of Personality and Social Psychology, 38*, 23–35.

Arkin, R. M., & Baumgardner, A. H. (1985). *When self-handicapping fails to serve a purpose: Impressions of the strategic procrastinator*. Unpublished manuscript, University of Missouri, Columbia and Virginia Polytechnic Institute, and State University, Blacksburg. Reported in Baumgardner, A. H., & Arkin, R. M. (1987). Coping with the prospect of social disapproval: Strategies and sequelae. In C. R. Snyder & C. E. Ford (Eds.), *Coping with negative life events: Clinical and social psychological perspectives* (pp. 323–346). New York: Plenum.

Arkin, R. M., Gabrenya, W. K., Jr., Appelman, A. S., & Cochran, S. T. (1979). Self-presentation, self-monitoring, and self-serving bias in causal attribution. *Personality and Social Psychology Bulletin, 5*, 73–76.

Baumgardner, A. H., & Arkin, R. M. (1987). Coping with the prospect of social disapproval: Strategies and sequelae. In C. R. Snyder & C. E. Ford (Eds.), *Coping with negative life events: Clinical and social psychological perspectives* (pp. 323–346). New York: Plenum.

Beckman, L. (1973). Teachers' and observers' perceptions of causality for a child's performance. *Journal of Educational Psychology, 65*, 198–204.
Berglas, S. (1985). Self-handicapping and self-handicappers: A cognitive/attributional model of interpersonal self-protective behavior. In R. Hogan (Ed.), *Perspectives in personality* (Vol. 1, pp. 235–270). Greenwich, CT: JAI.
Berglas, S., & Jones, E. E. (1978). Drug choice as a self-handicapping strategy in response to noncontingent success. *Journal of Personality and Social Psychology, 36*, 405–417.
Brown, J. D. (1984). Effects of induced mood on causal attributions for success and failure. *Motivation and Emotion, 8*, 343–353.
Burger, J. M. (1981). Motivational biases in the attribution of responsibility for an accident: A meta-analysis of the defensive-attribution hypothesis. *Psychological Bulletin, 90*, 496–512.
Burish, T. G., & Houston, B. K. (1979). Causal projection, similarity projection, and coping with threat to self-esteem. *Journal of Personality, 47*, 57–70.
Carducci, B. J., & McNeely, J. A. (1981, August). *Alcohol and attributions don't mix: The effect of alcohol on alcoholics' and nonalcoholics' attributions of blame for wife abuse*. Paper presented at the meeting of the American Psychological Association, Los Angeles, CA.
Carlston, D. E., & Shovar, N. (1983). Effects of performance attributions on others' perceptions of the attributor. *Journal of Personality and Social Psychology, 44*, 515–525.
Carver, C. S., Blaney, P. H., & Scheier, M. F. (1979). Reassertion and giving up: The interactive role of self-directed attention and outcome expectancy. *Journal of Personality and Social Psychology, 37*, 1859–1870.
Chapin, M., & Dyck, D. G. (1976). Persistence in children's reading behavior as a function of N length and attribution retraining. *Journal of Abnormal Psychology, 85*, 511–515.
Critchlow, B. (1985). The blame in the bottle: Attributions about drunken behavior. *Personality and Social Psychology Bulletin, 11*, 258–274.
Darby, B. W., & Schlenker, B. R. (1982). Children's reactions to apologies. *Journal of Personality and Social Psychology, 43*, 742–753.
Darley, J. M., & Fazio, R. H. (1980). Expectancy confirmation processes arising in the social interaction sequence. *American Psychologist, 35*, 867–881.
Darley, J. M., & Zanna, M. P. (1982). Making moral judgments. *American Scientist, 70*, 515–521.
DeGree, C. E., & Snyder, C. R. (1985). Adler's psychology (of use) today: Personal history of traumatic life events as a self-handicapping strategy. *Journal of Personality and Social Psychology, 48*, 1512–1519.
Dollinger, S. J., & McGuire, B. (1981). The development of psychological-mindedness: Children's understanding of defense mechanisms. *Journal of Clinical Child Psychology, 10*, 117–121.
Dollinger, S. J., Staley, H., & McGuire, B. (1981). The child as psychologist: Attributions and evaluations of defensive strategies. *Child Development, 52*, 1084–1086.
Duval, S., & Wicklund, R. (1972). *A theory of objective self-awareness*. New York: Academic Press.
Dweck, C. S. (1975). The role of expectations and attributions in the alleviation of learned helplessness. *Journal of Personality and Social Psychology, 31*, 674–685.
Elder, G., Bettes, B. A., & Seligman, M. E. P. (1982). [Women's explanations for negative events during and prior to 1943 were found to predict overall psychological health in 1970.] Unpublished data, Cornell University. Cited on p. 368 of Peterson, C., & Seligman, M. E. P. (1984). Causal explanations as a risk factor for depression: Theory and evidence. *Psychological Review, 91*, 347–374.
Epstein, S. (1984). Controversial issues in emotion theory. In P. Shaver (Ed.), *Review of*

personality and social psychology: Emotions, relationships, and health (pp. 64–88). Beverly Hills, CA: Sage.

Forsyth, D. R., Berger, R. E., & Mitchell, T. (1981). The effects of self-serving vs. other-serving claims of responsibility on attraction and attribution in groups. *Social Psychology Quarterly, 44*, 59–64.

Gibbons, F., Smith, T. W., Brehm, S. S., & Schroeder, D. (1981). *Self-awareness and self-confrontation: The role of focus of attention in the process of psychotherapy*. Unpublished manuscript, University of Kansas, Lawrence.

Goffman, E. (1955). On face-work: An analysis of the ritual elements in social interaction. *Psychiatry: Journal for the Study of Interpersonal Processes, 18*, 213–231.

Grueneich, R. (1982). Issues in the developmental study of how children use intention and consequence information to make moral evaluations. *Child Development, 53*, 29–43.

Handelsman, M. M., Kraiger, K., & King, C. S. (1985, April). *Self-handicapping by task choice: An attribute ambiguity analysis*. Paper presented at the meeting of the Rocky Mountain Psychological Association, Tucson.

Harris, R. N., & Snyder, C. R. (1986). The role of uncertain self-esteem in self-handicapping. *Journal of Personality and Social Psychology, 51*, 451–458.

Higgins, R. L., & Harris, R. N. (1988). Strategic "alcohol" use: Drinking to self-handicap. *Journal of Social and Clinical Psychology, 6*, 191–202.

Hill, M. G., Weary, G., & Williams, J. (1986). Depression: A self-presentation formulation. In R. F. Baumeister (Ed.), *Public self and private self* (pp. 213–239). New York: Springer-Verlag.

Horney, K. (1950). *Neurosis and human growth*. New York: Norton.

Jacobs, L., Berscheid, E., & Walster, E. (1971). Self-esteem and attraction. *Journal of Personality and Social Psychology, 17*, 84–91.

Janoff-Bulman, R., & Timko, C. (1987). Coping with traumatic events: The role of denial in light of people's assumptive worlds. In C. R. Snyder & C. E. Ford (Eds.), *Coping with negative life events: Clinical and social psychological perspectives* (pp. 135–159). New York: Plenum.

Jones, E. E., & Davis, K. E. (1965). From acts to dispositions: The attribution process in person perception. In L. Berkowitz (Ed.), *Advances in experimental social psychology* (Vol. 2, pp. 219–266). New York: Academic Press.

Keasey, C. B. (1978). Children's developing awareness and usage of intentionality and motives. In C. B. Keasey (Ed.), *Nebraska Symposium on Motivation* (Vol. 25, pp. 219–260). Lincoln: University of Nebraska Press.

Kolditz, T. A., & Arkin, R. M. (1982). An impression management interpretation of the self-handicapping strategy. *Journal of Personality and Social Psychology, 43*, 492–502.

LaNoue, J. B. & Curtis, R. C. (1985). Improving women's performance in mixed-set situations by effort attributions. *Psychology of Women Quarterly, 9*, 337–356.

McCaghy, C. H. (1968). Drinking and deviance disavowal: The case of child molesters. *Social Problems, 16*, 43–49.

McFarland, C., & Ross, M. (1982). Impact of causal attributions on affective reactions to success and failure. *Journal of Personality and Social Psychology, 43*, 937–946.

Medway, F. J., & Venino, G. R. (1982). The effects of effort feedback and performance patterns on children's attributions and task persistence. *Contemporary Educational Psychology, 7*, 26–34.

Mehlman, R. C., & Snyder, C. R. (1985). Excuse theory: A test of the self-protective role of attributions. *Journal of Personality and Social Psychology, 49*, 994–1001.

Peterson, C., Semmel, A., von Baeyer, C., Abramson, L. Y., Metalsky, G. I., & Seligman, M. E. P. (1982). The Attributional Style Questionnaire. *Cognitive Therapy and Research, 6*, 287–299.

Rhodewalt, F., & Davison, J. (1986). Self-handicapping and subsequent performance: Role of outcome valence and attributional certainty. *Basic and Applied Social Psychology, 7*, 307–323.

Richardson, D., & Campbell, J. (1980). Alcohol and wife abuse: The effect of alcohol on attributions of blame for wife abuse. *Personality and Social Psychology Bulletin, 6*, 51–56.

Richardson, D., & Campbell, J. (1982). Alcohol and rape: The effect of alcohol on attributions of blame for rape. *Personality and Social Psychology Bulletin, 8*, 468–476.

Riordan, C. (1981, August). *The effectiveness of post-transgression accounts*. Paper presented at the meeting of the American Psychological Association, Los Angeles, CA.

Ross, L., Bierbrauer, G., & Polly, S. (1974). Attribution of educational outcomes by professional and nonprofessional instructors. *Journal of Personality and Social Psychology, 29*, 609–618.

Rotenberg, K. (1980). Children's use of intentionality in judgments of character and disposition. *Child Development, 51*, 282–284.

Rothwell, N., & Williams, J. M. G. (1983). Attributional style and life events. *British Journal of Clinical Psychology, 22*, 139–140.

Schlosberg, M. (1985). *Audience evaluation of alcohol intoxication as a retrospective excuse for child abuse*. Unpublished master's thesis, University of Kansas, Lawrence.

Schneider, D. J., Hastorf, A. H., & Ellsworth, P. C. (1979). *Person perception*. Reading, MA: Addison-Wesley.

Schouten, P. G. W., & Handelsman, M. M. (1987). Social basis of self-handicapping: The case of depression. *Personality and Social Psychological Bulletin, 13*, 103–110.

Sears, D. O. (1983). The person-positivity bias. *Journal of Personality and Social Psychology, 44*, 233–250.

Shaw, M. E. (1968). Attribution of responsibility by adolescents in two cultures. *Adolescence, 3*, 23–32.

Shaw, M. E., & Reitan, H. T. (1969). Attribution of responsibility as a basis for sanctioning behavior. *British Journal of Social and Clinical Psychology, 8*, 217–226.

Shaw, M. E., & Sulzer, J. L. (1964). An empirical test of Heider's levels in attribution of responsibility. *Journal of Abnormal and Social Psychology, 69*, 39–46.

Smith, T. W., Snyder, C. R., & Handelsman, M. M. (1982). On the self-serving function of an academic wooden leg: Test anxiety as a self-handicapping strategy. *Journal of Personality and Social Psychology, 42*, 314–321.

Smith, T. W., Snyder, C. R., & Perkins, S. C. (1983). The self-serving function of hypochondriacal complaints: Physical symptoms as self-handicapping strategies. *Journal of Personality and Social Psychology, 44*, 787–797.

Snyder, C. R. (1984). Excuses. *Psychology Today, 18*, 50–55.

Snyder, C. R. (1985). Collaborative companions: The relationship of self-deception and excuse-making. In M. W. Martin (Ed.), *Self-deception and self-understanding* (pp. 35–51). Lawrence, KS: Regents Press of Kansas.

Snyder, C. R., & Higgins, R. L. (1987, July). *Reality negotiation and excuse-making: President Reagan's March 4, 1987, Iran arms scandal speech and other literature*. Paper presented at the Third International Conference on Social Psychology and Language, Bristol, England.

Snyder, C. R., & Higgins, R. L. (1988a). Excuses: Their effective role in the negotiation of reality. *Psychological Bulletin, 104*, 23–35.

Snyder, C. R., & Higgins, R. L. (1988b). Excuse attributions: Do they work for the excuse-giver? In S. L. Zelen (Ed.), *Self-representation: The second attribution-personality theory conference, CSPP-LA 1986* (pp. 52–132). New York: Springer-Verlag.

Snyder, C. R., Higgins, R. L., & Stucky, R. J. (1983). *Excuses: Masquerades in search of grace*. New York: Wiley/Interscience.

Snyder, C. R., Smith, T. W., Augelli, R. W., & Ingram, R. E. (1985). On the self-serving function of social anxiety: Shyness as a self-handicapping strategy. *Journal of Personality and Social Psychology, 48*, 970–980.

Sobell, L. C., & Sobell, M. B. (1985). Drunkenness, a "special circumstance" in crimes of violence: Sometimes. *International Journal of Addictions, 10*, 869–882.

Strack, S. & Coyne, J. C. (1983). Social confirmation of dysphoria: Shared and private reactions to depression. *Journal of Personality and Social Psychology, 44*, 798–806.

Sulzer, J. L., & Burglass, R. K. (1968). Responsibility attribution, empathy and punitiveness. *Journal of Personality, 36*, 272–282.

Taylor, S. E., & Brown, J. D. (1988). Illusion and well-being: A social psychological perspective on mental health. *Psychological Bulletin, 103*, 193–210.

Tedeschi, J. T., Riordan, C. A., Gaes, G. G., & Kane, T. (1984). *Verbal accounts and attributions of social motives*. Unpublished manuscript, State University of New York, Albany, and University of Missouri, Rolla.

Tesser, A., & Rosen, S. (1975). The reluctance to transmit bad news. In L. Berkowitz (Ed.), *Advances in experimental social psychology* (Vol. 8, pp. 193–232). New York: Academic Press.

Tetlock, P. E. (1980). Explaining teacher explanations of pupil performance: A self-presentation interpretation. *Social Psychology Quarterly, 43*, 283–290.

Tetlock, P. E. (1981). The influence of self-presentation goals in attributional reports. *Social Psychology Quarterly, 44*, 300–311.

Tetlock, P. E. (1983). Accountability and complexity of thought. *Journal of Personality and Social Psychology, 45*, 74–83.

Tucker, J. A., Vuchinich, R. E., & Sobell, M. (1981). Alcohol consumption as a self-handicapping strategy. *Journal of Abnormal Psychology, 90*, 220–230.

Ullman, L. P., & Krasner, L. (1969). *A psychological approach to abnormal behavior*. Englewood Cliffs, NJ: Prentice-Hall.

Weiner, B., Amirkhan, J., Folkes, V. S., & Verette, J. A. (1987). An attributional analysis of excuse giving: Studies of a naive theory of emotion. *Journal of Personality and Social Psychology, 52*, (2), 316–324.

Wells, G. L., Petty, R. E., Harkins, S. G., Kagehiro, D., & Harvey, J. H. (1977). Anticipated discussion of interpretation eliminates actor-observer differences in the attribution of causality. *Sociometry, 40*, 247–253.

Wright, J., & Mischel, W. (1982). Influence of affect on cognitive social learning person variables. *Journal of Personality and Social Psychology, 43*, 901–914.

Yalom, I. D. (1980). *Existential psychotherapy*. New York: Basic Books.

Zoeller, C. J., Mahoney, G., & Weiner, B. (1983). Effects of attribution training on the assembly task performance of mentally retarded adults. *American Journal of Mental Deficiency, 88*, 109–112.

CHAPTER 6

MAKING THINGS HARDER FOR YOURSELF

PRIDE AND JOY

MEL L. SNYDER AND ARTHUR FRANKEL

THE PARADOX

Making things harder for yourself incorporates a paradox. Why would people apparently seeking success do things that would detract from performance and increase the chances for failure? Why do students so often procrastinate, putting term papers off to the last possible moment? Why would a high school senior stay up late the night before taking the SAT exam? In anticipation of an important job interview, why might an unemployed executive get drunk the night before? Why do the depressed so often withdraw rather than trying for the success that might improve their mood? Why do so many people take drugs that impair their abilities?

We consider two sorts of answers to the question of why people often make things harder for themselves. One answer has an emerging body of research in support of it. Indeed, other authors in this volume (Berglas, Feather, Higgins, & C. R. Snyder) have contributed to it. This first answer to the paradox is that seemingly self-defeating behavior may often be a strategy to protect self-esteem. Our own recent efforts have focused on extending this idea to understanding depression. We do not believe, however, that self-protection is the whole story. Besides pride, there is a second reason—joy. Making things harder may often

MEL L. SNYDER • Department of Psychology, Rutgers University, Newark, New Jersey 07102. ARTHUR FRANKEL • Department of Psychology, Salve Regina—The Newport College, Newport, Rhode Island 02840.

lead to having more fun. Later we argue that pride and joy commonly involve different cognitive capacities and that these emotions have different contours.

MAKING THINGS HARDER FOR YOURSELF—PRIDE

But first, let us consider how might it be that making things harder for yourself is really in the service of self-esteem protection? Consider, for example, procrastination. The student who puts off writing the term paper until the last moment does seem to be engaging in self-defeating behavior. He or she probably would have done better with an earlier start. But what if our procrastinator should fail?

There is a ready explanation for such failure. The student can point to the lack of time invested in the project and, hence, the little effort that he or she put into it. As an explanation for failure, low effort is usually preferable to lack of ability. One need not relinquish a conception of oneself as an able person as long as blame can be placed on low effort. While low effort is therefore self-protecting, it is at the same time self-defeating. The immediate effect is a reduced probability of success at the particular task. The longer range effect may be less development of the person's potential than would otherwise occur.

EGOTISM AND LOW EFFORT AFTER UNSOLVABLE PROBLEMS

Frankel and M. L. Snyder (1978) provided an experimental demonstration of the idea that low effort is used as an excuse for failure. Basing our study on the procedures used by Hiroto and Seligman (1975), we varied whether an initial set of concept formation problems were solvable or unsolvable. We assumed that working on problems with no solutions would constitute an experience of failure and would create anxiety about additional failure on a subsequent task. The subsequent task we gave subjects was a set of anagrams. We sometimes said the anagrams were moderately difficult and other times stated that the very same anagrams were highly difficult.

In the moderate difficulty condition, subjects previously given unsolvable problems did worse on the anagrams than did subjects given solvable problems. We interpret this poorer performance as the consequence of a strategy to protect self-esteem by withholding effort. In that way the subjects can attribute poor performance to lack of effort rather than make the more devastating conclusion that they lack ability. In support of this interpretation are the results when subjects previously given unsolvable problems are told the anagrams are highly difficult: they improve. This we presume is because high task difficulty provides an excuse should the subject fail, enabling the subject to try hard without worrying that failure will force an attribution of low ability.

A corollary is that subjects in the unsolvable condition who believe the task is of moderate difficulty engaged in a form of self-defeating behavior—the withholding of effort—for the purpose of protecting self-esteem. We subsumed this process under the heading of egotism, using the label that M. L. Snyder, Stephan, and Rosenfield (1978) have applied to the human tendency to take credit for success and deny blame for failure.

The Frankel and M. L. Snyder (1978) study was replicated by M. L. Snyder, Smoller, Strenta, and Frankel (1981) using the familiar manipulation of problem solvability but replacing the variation of alleged difficulty of the test task with a manipulation of the presence of music that was claimed to be distracting. From the perspective of egotism, the music provides an excuse for poor performance, allowing people to try without fear of an attribution of low ability. And once again, the results were as predicted. Those given unsolvable problems responded to the allegedly distracting music by performing better than those without music. Leary (1986) reports conceptually similar results in the realm of interpersonal abilities. Noise alleged to be distracting reduced subjects' level of physiological arousal and washed out the tendency of the chronically socially anxious to present themselves less positively than the nonanxious.

We note in passing that the M. L. Snyder *et al.* (1981) results and those of Frankel and M. L. Snyder (1978) run directly contrary to the predictions made by learned helplessness theory (Abramson, Garber, & Seligman, 1980; Abramson, Seligman, & Teasdale, 1978; Seligman, 1975; cf. Peterson & Bossio, Chapter 10, this volume). In that theory, expectancy of control is the key variable controlling motivation. Thus, working in the presence of allegedly distracting noise or on a task described as highly difficult should have lowered expectancy of control, thereby reducing effort and worsening performance. Instead these conditions had the opposite effect.

Rather, these results are reminiscent of and indeed were inspired by a phenomenon reported in the achievement motivation literature. The failure anxious respond to tasks described as highly difficult by performing better (Feather, 1961, 1963; Karabenick & Youssef, 1968; Sarason, 1961).

DEVELOPMENT AND EGOTISM: THE DIFFERENTIATION OF EFFORT AND ABILITY

Miller (1985) examined the paradigm used by Frankel and M. L. Snyder (1978) from a developmental point of view. Adults and young children have different conceptions of the relation between ability and effort. Adults understand that there may be a trade-off between ability and effort so that a modest performance might result when a person of low ability tries very hard or, alternatively, when a person of high ability gives a relatively meager effort. Ability and effort are seen as distinct factors that combine in a particular way to yield performance. It is as if we think in terms of an equation: ability times effort yields performance.

Young children, on the other hand, fail to distinguish between effort and ability and, in fact, equate the two (Nicholls & Miller, 1984). They regard effort as a sign of ability. Given such a conception of ability, it would not make sense for a child to withhold effort to protect a belief in his or her ability. To the contrary, a child concerned about demonstrating high ability would manifest high effort.

Miller (1985) noted the findings of Rholes, Blackwell, Jordan, and Walters

(1980) that young children—unlike college students (e.g., Hiroto & Seligman, 1975)—do not show a performance deficit after they work on unsolvable problems. She hypothesized that such a deficit would emerge as children learned to differentiate effort and ability and appreciate the trade-off between them in producing performance. She explored these ideas using second-grade and sixth-grade children.

All subjects were evaluated to assess their conceptions of the relation between ability and effort. Nearly all the second graders had immature conceptions. Moreover, their rankings of their own effort and ability in spelling were positively correlated. In contrast, a majority of the sixth graders had a mature conception, and their self-rankings of ability and effort were uncorrelated. Thus, we would expect most sixth graders—those with a mature conception of ability—to use low effort as an excuse, whereas those who equate ability and effort—the second graders and some of the sixth graders—would not be expected to use low effort in that way.

Miller (1985) adapted the Frankel and M. L. Snyder (1978) procedures for use with these age groups. Initially, she gave subjects a figure-matching task on which they received either success or failure feedback. Subsequently, she gave subjects anagrams with the actual difficulty level appropriate to their grade level. Sometimes the anagrams were alleged to be very difficult, other times only moderately so. The performance of second graders was unaffected by the manipulation. As the egotism hypothesis would predict, they failed to show a performance deficit after failure.

The sixth graders did show such a performance deficit. Moreover, just as in Frankel and M. L. Snyder's study, the deficit evaporated when the anagrams were described as highly difficult. There were a minority of sixth graders who lacked a mature conception of the ability–effort relationship. Like the second graders, they failed to show a significant performance deficit.

That the increasing intellectual sophistication common among sixth graders—the awareness of self as distinct from behavior, of ability as distinct from effort—could introduce a susceptibility to self-defeating behavior is ironic. The innocent seem to be protected by their own simplicity. Maturity renders one vulnerable. Preserving a belief in one's ability can lead one to make things needlessly hard for oneself. The immediate impact of reduced effort is poorer performance. The longer-term impact is less development of one's capacities than would otherwise occur. The intellectual accomplishment of the distinction between ability and effort could actually impair further development. As one grows, it becomes possible to trip over one's own self-concept.

The Role of Self-Consciousness

Besides a mature conception of the ability–effort trade-off, another factor probably necessary for egotism is some degree of attention to the self (Duval & Wicklund, 1972; Wicklund, 1975). Federoff and Harvey (1976) found that a manipulation of self-awareness mobilized subjects to deny responsibility for failure. Both Hormuth (1986) and Kernis, Zuckerman, Cohen, and Spadafora (1982) have linked the low-effort strategy for defending self-esteem to circumstances in which the person is the most plausible case for an effortful failure, and in which the person's attention is focused on the self.

Egotism and Depression

Frankel & M. L. Snyder (1987) have examined egotism as an explanation for poor performance on the part of the depressed. In a paper subtitled "Sadder but Wiser," Alloy and Abramson (1979) reported that the depressed seem to be quite accurate in perceiving contingencies between their responses and their behavior. In fact, it is the nondepressed who are inaccurate. They exaggerate their degree of control when outcomes are positive and underestimate their control when outcomes are negative. Alloy and Abramson (1982) replicated this pattern and interpreted it in terms of egotism on the part of the nondepressed. The depressed fail to show this form of egotism, perhaps because depression induces a higher need for attributional accuracy (see M. L. Snyder *et al.*, 1978).

Egotism can take many forms, and we wondered whether the depressed would follow the egotistic pattern we had found for those given unsolvable problems (Frankel & M. L. Snyder, 1978; M. L. Snyder *et al.*, 1981). Could the poor performance often shown by the depressed be a manifestation of egotism, a strategy of low effort designed to protect the fragile sense of self-esteem from a clear attribution of low ability? Returning to our main theme, do the depressed make things harder for themselves? To test this idea we used the now familiar manipulation of alleged task difficulty.

Subjects were given the Beck Depression Inventory (Beck, 1967), and the distribution of scores was divided at the median. Those with scores of 9 or higher constituted the high-depression group, 8 or lower the low-depression group. In the first of two very similar studies, Frankel and M. L. Snyder (1987) employed the same two experimental variables they used in their 1978 experiment: whether an initial task—a set of concept formation problems like those discussed earlier—was solvable or unsolvable and whether a subsequent task was described as moderately or highly difficult. Instead of using anagrams for the second task, Frankel and M. L. Snyder used an extremely difficult puzzle. The dependent variable was the number of minutes subjects worked on the puzzle—they were stopped if they reached 15 minutes.

The pattern of results was quite consistent with the egotism account of poor performance by the depressed. The depressed tended to persist longer when the task was described as highly difficult—7.65 minutes versus 5.69 minutes for the moderate difficulty group. The pattern was similar for the success and failure conditions. However, this effect fell short of conventional levels of significance ($t(68) = 1.59$, $p = .11$). We decided to conduct a replication, with the modification that we eliminated the variable of solvability of the initial task. We did so on the basis that a state of depression could be viewed as a substitute for the experience of working on unsolvable problems. So subjects began the experiment by working on the puzzle. Once again, we found that telling the depressed a task was extremely difficult led to greater persistence—11.20 minutes versus 7.93 minutes in the moderate difficulty condition ($t(44) = 2.01$, $p = .05$).

It makes no sense for someone who firmly believes in his or her inadequacy to exert greater effort the harder the task. It is as if the depressed are clinging to the belief that they are competent and seizing an opportunity to demonstrate it when the threat to self-esteem otherwise posed by high effort is removed by describing the task as difficult. In the absence of the excuse of difficulty level, depression may be perpetuated by the strategy of withholding effort to protect self-esteem. This strategy is ultimately self-defeating in that, by withdrawing, the depressed have a lower probability of immediate success and the pleasure it brings, and, over the long run, less of an opportunity to develop their potential and acquire skills that will increase their rate of success.

We regard the depressed as capable of one form of egotism—low effort to provide an excuse for possible failure. Gibbons (1986) also provides evidence that the depressed are capable of defending themselves. In a study of social comparison tendencies, he found that the depressed preferred information about those experiencing negative affect. A second study showed that exposing the depressed to others who were experiencing negative affect was a mood-elevating experience. The studies together showed that the depressed make choices that make them feel better. Gibbons' results offer a perspective on the finding that college students who room with the depressed tend to become depressed themselves (Howes, Hokanson, & Loewenstein, 1985). We wonder whether the depressed not only welcome such changes but also manage to engineer them.

The view that the depressed are capable of acting in their own interest contrasts with the more traditional perspective on the depressed as lacking in defenses. We already noted their failure to show the illusion of control (Alloy & Abramson, 1979, 1982; but cf. Vasquez, 1987). Pyszczynski and Greenberg (1985) include that failure in a list of defensive lapses shown by the depressed. The depressed compared to the nondepressed make attributions that are less egotistical (Klein, Fencil-Morse, & Seligman, 1976; Kuiper, 1978; Rizley, 1978; Seligman, Abramson, Semmel, & von Baeyer, 1979; Tennen & Herzberger, 1987). They fail to show an exaggerated evaluation of skills and abilities (Lewinsohn, Mischel, Chaplin, & Barton, 1980). And they fail to exhibit an ego defensive bias in recall of positive and negative feedback (Nelson & Craighead, 1977).

Coyne and Gotlib (1983) note that when the depressed and nondepressed respond differently on these various cognitive measures, it is difficult to specify whether and where bias or distortion occurs. More direct and convincing evidence for weaker defense of self-esteem on the part of the depressed is reported by Pyszczynski and Greenberg (1985). They found that failure produced a loss of self-esteem among the depressed, a loss not manifested by the nondepressed. Moreover, the depressed were less pleased with their performance than the nondepressed, regardless of success or failure.

Pyszczynski and Greenberg (1987) subsequently developed a theory of depression to make sense of these various phenomena, a theory centered on the concept of self-awareness (Duval & Wicklund, 1972; Wicklund, 1975). The depressed, it turns out, not only score higher on a measure of private self-consciousness (e.g., Ingram & Smith, 1984; Smith & Greenberg, 1981) but also tend to wallow in self-consciousness after failure though not after success

(Pyszczynski & Greenberg, 1985). This is opposite to the pattern shown by the nondepressed.

Pyszczynski and Greenberg's (1987) theory assumes that people function as self-regulators (Carver & Scheier, 1981; Miller, Galanter & Pribram, 1960). (The reader may wish to examine the conceptually similar theory of Hyland, 1987, published at the same time.) This is to say that people have goals, the ability to measure how far they are from achieving their goals, and a repertoire of means to use in attempting to reach the goals. If the person perceives a discrepancy between the goal and where the self actually stands, an operation to reduce the discrepancy will be selected and executed. Then the person evaluates again.

Ordinarily, once the person stops making progress toward the goal and exhausts the repertoire, the person abandons that goal and goes on to another one. Like many other theorists, Pyszczynski and Greenberg (1987) hypothesized that depression results when the person cannot regain a significant lost source of identity or self-esteem. But they went on to assert that, rather than the loss *per se*, it is the refusal of the person to abandon the goal that produces the depression. Heeding Coyne and Gotlib's (1983) call to attend more to the environment in which the depressed person finds himself or herself, we speculate that the refusal to abandon the goal might result from the paucity of other comparably attractive and plausibly attainable alternatives (cf. Brehm & Brehm, 1981, on reactance as a function of the proportion of freedom threatened).

Given the refusal to abandon the goal and lacking any promising means to attain it, what would ordinarily be a brief pause in the ongoing stream of action in order to self-evaluate and select the next direction for behavior becomes a chronic state of self-focus. Other goals thereby suffer, and under the circumstances, the ongoing excessive self-focus produces chronic effects parallel to those temporary effects known to result from acute manipulations of self-awareness in the laboratory: self-criticism, lowered self-esteem, performance deficits (resulting perhaps from lack of effort and lack of attention to the task—e.g., Brockner & Hulton, 1978), internal attributions for these negative outcomes, and intensified negative affect.

These psychological events point toward a conclusion which becomes not only increasingly plausible, perhaps especially so for those possessing a relatively simple self-concept or one with highly interdependent components (Linville, 1987), but also increasingly palatable—that one is fundamentally and thoroughly a bad person. Being a bad person explains why bad things should happen (see Lerner, Miller, & Holmes, 1976). Further, it minimizes demands for performance and the potential for further disappointment. The belief that one is good not only clashes with one's experience but also threatens to raise both the demands of others and one's own expectations. In order to sustain the conclusion that one is a bad person, there takes place an about-face in the usual pattern of self-focus. Failure is embraced and leads to enhanced self-focus, and success is rejected by avoiding self-focus.

Wicklund's (1986) concepts of dynamic and static orientation (cf. a related distinction made by Kuhl, 1986) help to illuminate this transformation. A dynamic orientation (cf. Csikszentmihalyi's 1978 concept of flow) occurs when the person possesses the perceptual and behavioral readiness to meet the demands of the situation. Lacking that—and the depressed person surely does—the person shifts to a static orientation—a tendency to think in terms of traits. The historical or evolutionary purpose of such an orientation is to identify someone who does possess the perceptual and behavioral readiness to attain the goal. Given the failure of such a search, turning the static orientation toward a feckless self may exacerbate attributions of inadequacy.

How can we reconcile with this theory our finding that depressed college students show one form of egotism—low effort as an excuse—which we infer from their persisting more when an alternate excuse for failure is provided by a description of a task as highly difficult? At the core of the Pyszczynski and Greenberg (1987) theory, in the person's refusal to abandon the goal, there is implied a nub of hope. The clinging to the goal and the chronic self-focus of the depressed suggest a kind of vigilance for opportunities to redeem oneself. A highly difficult task presents just such an opportunity without the potential for disappointment and threat to self-esteem posed by a more ordinary situation.

We have yet to examine whether this form of egotism occurs in a clinically depressed population. Finding it there would suggest that even those diagnosed as depressed are capable of certain defenses. Alternatively, its absence in a clinical population combined with its presence among college students might indicate a difference in degree of hope. The absence of hope in the clinically depressed would make all the more remarkable their hypothesized refusal to abandon the goal.

Egotism and Self-Defeat

At this juncture we need to sort out the idea of self-defeat from egotism. A decade ago most people—certainly most social psychologists—would have construed being defensive as undesirable and perceiving oneself and the world in an accurate, objective manner as desirable. The finding that the depressed are accurate—sadder but wiser—has given objectivity a bad name.

It appears that the normal if not healthy state of affairs is to perceive the world in a self-aggrandizing and self-defending manner. It is, for example, those high in self-esteem who, when their self-esteem is threatened, show a bias in favor of the ingroup (Crocker, Thompson, McGraw, & Ingerman, 1987). And earlier we noted that the nondepressed took more credit for success, accepted less blame for failure, showed an illusion of control, showed an exaggerated evaluation of skills and competencies, and manifested a biased recall of positive and negative feedback.

Could not a case be made that it is the normal, nondepressed people with high self-esteem who are risking self-defeat in the long run by their inaccurate perception of the world? M. L. Snyder *et al.* (1978) noted a number of constraints on egotistic distortion. People seem to be sensitive to the possibility of having their claims contradicted by another (Wells, 1977), or by knowledge about a prior performance (Baumgardner, Lake, & Arkin, 1985), or by a subsequent one (Wortman, Costanzo, & Witt, 1973). Moreover, egotistic motivation may be held in check by the need for accuracy (M. L. Snyder *et al.*, 1978) and might even be reversed by the need to present oneself in a modest way (Weary, 1978). To a considerable extent what we refer to as reality constrains egotism. Indeed, in an extensive and impressive program of research reported by Pittman and D'Agostino (1985), there is even evidence that deprivation of control—what we might call a failure experience—heightens sensitivity to information and reduces observer bias (Jones & Nisbett, 1971).

The factors that heighten accuracy and temper egotism among normals may be chronically present for the depressed. For example, McCaul (1983), basing his procedures on Pittman and Pittman (1980), found that the depressed were more sensitive to information about the motivational state of another. Increased accuracy may be one way the depressed cope.

In the mid-1960s, Jones and Gerard (1967) made the case that the need for accuracy is higher before a decision than afterwards. Recently, Gollwitzer, Heckhausen, and their colleagues have included pre- and postdecisional processes in their investigations of various states of mind (e.g., Heckhausen & Gollwitzer, 1987). For instance, Gollwitzer and Kinney (1987) have found that the illusion of control (Langer, 1975) occurs when people are in a postdecisional state but vanishes when people are in a predecisional state. The depressed may be more accurate because they are in a chronic predecisional state. Certainly, the depressed have been characterized as indecisive, perhaps because they are concerned about making the wrong decision (Beck, 1976).

Consideration of the Pyszczynski and Greenberg (1987) theory at first suggests the depressed—far from being indecisive—are overly committed to an impossible goal. However, such a commitment and no obvious means of fulfilling it leaves the person to ponder the means by which to do so. The depressed may be unsure about how to recover the loss and thus undecided about what to do. This chronic predecisional, contemplative state leaves the depressed person open to new information and thus more likely to draw accurate conclusions from experience. This may explain why the depressed do not show the illusion of control (Alloy & Abramson, 1979, 1982). P. M. Gollwitzer (personal communication, October 30, 1987) plans to put the depressed into a postdecisional frame of mind to see whether such a state produces the illusion.

Besides predecisional accuracy, another factor tempering egotism is the anticipation of being contradicted either by another or by one's performance (M. L. Snyder *et al.*, 1978). The loss of a relationship with a significant other, which often seems to precipitate depression, may increase fear that one's egotistic claims will be challenged, or at least go unsupported (see Cohen & Wills, 1985). And especially when it is a threat to competence that instigates depression, depleted confidence about future success may inhibit egotism for current outcomes.

However, as we saw earlier, the depressed do not seem to be entirely devoid of manifestations of egotism. Frankel and M. L. Snyder (1987) present evidence that they use a low-effort strategy. And Gibbons' (1986) research on the social comparison choices of the depressed could be viewed as evidence for downward social comparison to promote self-esteem. Moreover, C. R. Snyder, Higgins, and Stucky (1983) (see also Higgins and C. R. Snyder, Chapter 5, this volume) regard depression as a form of self-handicapping. Schouten and Handelsman (1987) document that depression can have interpersonal excuse value. At least on a paper and pencil test, a target's being depressed during a failure or a transgression reduced the inclination of others to punish.

Incidentally, C. R. Snyder and his colleagues view not only depression as a form of self-handicapping but also shyness and social anxiety. For example, those who report themselves as shy in a pretesting session score lower on a subsequent shyness test when it is made clear to them that their shyness cannot serve as an excuse for a poor performance on a test of social intelligence (C. R. Snyder, Smith, Augelli, & Ingram, 1985). Another study suggested the substitutability of excuses: When the test anxious are told that anxiety will not account for poor performance, they report exerting lower effort (Smith, C. R. Snyder, & Handelsman, 1982). To elaborate on the C. R. Snyder *et al.* (1983) view of depression: The depressed use their symptoms to lower expectations, to preempt criticism, and to elicit sympathy and reassurance (Coyne, 1976a, 1976b).

The depressed are not alone in coping by thinking about, presenting, or viewing the self in a negative way. Norem and Cantor (1986) described a strategy of defensive pessimism in which anxiety is harnessed as motivation. Similarly, Showers (1987) argued that negative thinking can be the starting point of an adaptive strategy. And Goodhart (1986) has identified conditions under which instructing subjects to engage in negative thinking (vs. positive instructions) improved performance. In a somewhat different vein, Baumgardner and Brownlee (1987) have shown that in the face of high expectations that will demand high effort to fulfill, the socially anxious will engage in strategic failure, apparently designed to lower those expectations.

Baumeister and Scher (1988) provided an important perspective on seemingly self-defeating behavior. Although they focus on normal rather than clinical populations, their distinctions nevertheless seem useful here. They note that, among normals, there is very little evidence for primary self-defeat, that is, an unalloyed intention to harm oneself. They can conceive of such a thing. For example, just as we may wish to harm another we do not like, we might harm ourselves out of self-dislike. However, they argue that instances of self-harm are nearly always interpretable as the result of either counterproductive strategies—ignorance of the consequences of a course of action or inaction—or tradeoffs in which the harm is foreseen and not desired but, rather, suffered in order to attain some other desirable outcome, often relief from anxiety.

In this regard, Cozzarelli and Major (1987) have raised an important question: How well do these defensive strategies work on the emotions of the individual who uses them? Although their correlational methodology limits the conclusions that can be drawn, their results are nevertheless provocative. They found that the use of various strategies with respect to dealing with failure on a midterm exam failed to show any buffering effect, and, indeed, defensive pessimists were more upset after doing poorly on an exam than those low in defensive pessimism. Baumeister and Scher (1988) do us the service of reminding us that strategies that turn out to be ineffective, or even counterproductive, were not necessarily intended to be so.

And sometimes excuses do serve, at least in the short term, to reduce negative emotions. Mehlman and C. R. Snyder (1985) gave some subjects an opportunity to make excuses for a failure by filling out an attributional questionnaire asking them to estimate consensus, distinctiveness, and consistency information. Compared to those without this opportunity, these subjects reported less negative affect.

The work described thus far combined with that of another contributor to this volume, Berglas's (Berglas & Jones, 1978, Jones & Berglas, 1978) work on self-handicapping, makes it clear that the defense of the self can underlie behavior that is self-defeating. Through drugs, through alcohol, by means of adopting a depressed, an anxious, or shy pattern of behavior, people may create excuses for themselves. These forms of self-defeat in the service of pride may become less mysterious if we appreciate another function that making things harder can serve.

MAKING THINGS HARDER FOR YOURSELF—JOY

M. L. Snyder (Snyder, 1985; Snyder, Hansen, & Redler, 1988; Snyder & Karl, 1986) has begun to explore the idea that there is pleasure in acquiring and exercising perceptual and cognitive competence. Inspired by White's (1959) classic paper on competence motivation, he has borrowed from the achievement motivation theorists the notion that there is an optimal level of challenge that provides the most pleasure (McClelland, Atkinson, Clark, & Lowell, 1953/1976).

An important consideration is that with experience the level of competence ordinarily increases, and consequently, so does the objective level of difficulty that is optimally challenging. In an intial study designed to make this point, Snyder (1985) asked subjects to indicate preferences between slides that varied in difficulty of discrimination. He measured preferences after subjects had either a lot or a little experience with slides of moderate difficulty. With only a little experience, subjects preferred slides that were easier than the moderate ones. With more extensive experience, subjects preferred slides that were harder than the moderate ones. It is of interest to note that contrary to what one would expect on the basis of the mere exposure hypothesis (Zajonc, 1968), subjects preferred the stimuli to which they had not been exposed—the easier slides early on and the harder ones later—to those which had been shown repeatedly—the moderate slides.

In a conceptual replication of this study, Snyder & Karl (1986) used the procedure developed by Walk (1967) and Tighe (1968) to teach subjects to identify novel instances of a painter's work. Snyder and Karl found that subjects rated more highly paintings they could accurately identify than those they could not or those they had seen several times during the training session. Once again, liking is less a function of exposure *per se* than of proximity to the optimal level of challenge. The optimal level is the greatest level of difficulty that still permits success.

The authors of achievement motivation theory were aware of this phenomenon (McClelland *et al.*, 1953/1976). They distinguished achievement motivation, however, from intrinsic motivation by noting that the former involved externally defined standards of excellence. Our position is that the emphasis on external standards places achievement motivation in the realm of extrinsic motivation. We believe that rules of behavior and the contours of emotion—pride and joy—differ between these two realms.

The distinction we wish to develop is closely related to one made by Nicholls (1984) in an insightful integration of the literature on achievement motivation. He noted that in situations where ego involvement is high—when people feel tested, competitive, under scrutiny—they will tend to use a conception of ability as capacity that is high or low in relation to others. In contrast, when the person is involved in the task, ability is viewed relative to one's past—what Higgins, Strauman, and Klein (1986) called an autobiographical reference point—rather than in comparison to others. The question is "Am I getting better?" rather than "Am I doing better or worse than others?"

At the same time Nicholls made this distinction, he also astutely blurred some others. He argued that the active ingredient in scales measuring self-esteem, achievement motivation, and test anxiety is for the most part perceived ability (cf. Kuhl, 1982). (We note that Alloy and Ahrens, 1987, found the depressed reported lower SAT scores than the nondepressed.)

Nicholls predicted that under task involvement, people of both high and low perceived ability will prefer intermediate probabilities of success. But under ego involvement those with high ability will prefer moderate or high levels of difficulty, while those with low ability will avoid moderate levels of difficulty because of their threatening qualities as described above (e.g., Frankel & M. L. Snyder, 1978). If still committed to demonstrating high ability, they will prefer high difficulty (cf. Strube & Roemmele, 1985). If oriented to avoid showing low ability, they will choose easy tasks and try hard so as to assure success. If resigned to low ability, through apathy they will choose easy tasks. Nicholls found the evidence generally supportive in that low and high perceived ability groups differ in difficulty preferences more under ego involvement than under task involvement, with the low perceived ability people choosing more extreme levels of difficulty—and avoiding moderate ones—under ego involvement.

We basically agree with Nicholls' (1984) characterization of ego involvement—the issue is pride. And what he called task involvement comes very close to our concept of intrinsic motivation. Nicholls, however, maintained that both task and ego involvement are oriented toward demonstrating ability—it is just that the conceptions of ability used differ under the two types of involvement. In contrast, our concept of intrinsic motivation emphasizes the pleasure inherent in involvement with the task. No doubt improvement in one's ability and appreciation of one's improvement can be important by-products of intrinsic motivation. And from an adaptive or even an evolutionary point of view, they may be the reasons behind intrinsic motivation. But with respect to the intentions of the individual, the most immediate force driving intrinsic motivation is, almost by definition, involvement with the task.

Our concept of intrinsic motivation may differ from Nicholls' task involvement in another way. He argued that under task involvement intermediate levels of difficulty are preferred. If by intermediate levels he means the magic .50 probability of success of achievement motivation theory, we think that this does not hold for intrinsic motivation.

The formula for achievement motivation is the product of the probability of success times the incentive value of success, which is defined as one minus the probability of success. It is a simple task to prove that—if the formula is correct—achievement motivation is maximal when the probability of success is .50. The evidence bearing on this point generally supports this prediction, though it may be that subjects actually prefer a slightly lower probability of success, namely, .40 (Hamilton, 1974).

Here, it is useful to consider the preferences for levels of difficulty found by M. L. Snyder *et al.* (1988) in a situation designed to emphasize intrinsic motivation over achievement motivation in which there were no external standards of excellence, not even the opportunity for competition. They gave subjects a game to play programmed on a calculator. The calculator presented in a brief flash a series of five digits. It was up to the subject to reproduce the series. This was harder to do the shorter the duration of the flash. For each trial the subject chose the duration of the flash. The subject played the game until he or she decided to terminate it. Most seemed to find it at least somewhat involving.

To analyze the data, they divided each subject's trials as equally as possible into three blocks. They then calculated for each subject the median speed chosen and the percentage correct for each of the three blocks.

On the first block, subjects averaged around 75% of the trials correct, far above the 50% level expected if achievement motivation were the operative force. On the second block, the level of performance was essentially sustained with the percentage correct declining nonsignificantly to 72%. Median speed, however, was dramatically faster, indicating that subjects were improving. As subjects got better, they made things harder for themselves by choosing faster speeds. By the third block, median speeds were yet a bit faster. Performance, however, fell off to 54%.

With actual performance around the magic 50% mark, achievement motivation should have been ascending. Why then did subjects terminate the game at that point?

We believe that they sensed they were nearing the limit of their capacity. Improvement came harder and slower and with greater effort. With the limit in sight the game became, or promised to become, repetitive—a perception that we argue later is incompatible with intrinsic motivation.

An alternate answer is that the subjects all suffered from high fear of failure (or, in Nicholls' (1984) view, low perceived ability). Achievement motivation theory makes it clear that when fear of failure exceeds the need to achieve, there will be aversion to achievement tasks that will be maximal when the probability of success is 50%. There are several arguments against this interpretation. First of all, by this view, subjects would be indifferent to whether success was very likely or very unlikely, as long as they could avoid an intermediate probability. This simply did not happen. The speed selected resulted in a success rate clearly above rather than merely distant from 50%.

On this same point, in the M. L. Snyder *et al.* study, the various conditions under which the subjects played the game and the results that ensued are illuminating. In two conditions, the experimenter sat face to face with the subject. In one, the subject was asked to report his or her speed choices and whether he or she got the problem correct. In the other, subjects not only reported speed choices and whether they were correct but also were asked to comment on their thinking as they played. In contrast to both of these conditions, a third group played the game under more private circumstances. The experimenter kept her back to the subject while the subject recorded his or her own speed and correctness data.

Under these more private conditions, we assume that fear of failure would be diminished. In Nicholls' (1984) terms, there would be less ego involvement and, in our terms, more pure intrinsic motivation. Yet the percentage correct was no lower in this group for the first two blocks. Moreover, while the other two groups showed significant declines in percentage correct from the first block to the third, the privacy group did not. Indeed, the privacy group's 65% correct on the third block was significantly greater than 50%. This more private group also manifested two other phenomena. They were more likely to be correct at the fastest speed they chose: 58% of the time compared to 17% in the other two conditions; that is, they judiciously chose speeds so as not to exceed their capacity, attempting nothing they could not accomplish. And they did so while attaining fastest correct speeds that nearly significantly exceeded the other two groups.

A second phenomenon exhibited by this group, which M. L. Snyder *et al.* (1988) called the making-your-last-shot effect, was a tendency to be correct on the last trial they played: 83% of the time, a figure significantly greater than 50% and greater than the values of the other two groups, both of which were under 50%. Again, an examination of the speeds they chose shows that this result does not occur because of choices of unduly slow speeds. These two findings suggest a playful self-indulgence rather than the more grim and serious business of achievement that involves trying to push oneself past others (Nicholls, 1984) and beyond one's own limits.

Attention and Satiation

Whereas the domain of achievement motivation is dominated by the logic of avoiding and approaching a probability of success of .50, in the domain of intrinsic motivation the optimal level of challenge is determined by different rules. A reading of Csikszentmihalyi (1978) suggests that the crucial factor that determines the optimal level is that which invites the full use of one's attention. He described the pleasurable experience of "flow," which derives from the intense, voluntary concentration of one's attention. There is nothing in this description that refers to probability of success, nor to success as even a salient issue.

Attention, we would argue in the case of intrinsic motivation, is not in the service of reaching some superordinate goal, for example, demonstrating one's ability or superiority, but rather is focused on the task of the moment and shifts to another when bored. Karsten's (1927/1976) research on repetition and satiation is useful here. She found that unless subjects were extrinsically motivated, to obtain money or to test their capacity to endure, they found it very difficult to repeat a task indefinitely. Their initial reaction, when asked to repeat a task, was to create variations on the original assignment. Attention is engaged not only in reaching goals but also in reformulating goals as prior goals are attained. This is what Bandura (in press)—cited in this volume by Feather—means by feedforward control, the point being that the human is not only engaged in discrepancy reduction (Carver & Scheier, 1981) but also in discrepancy production. In Karsten's study, when subjects could no longer generate variations—in Bandura's terms, produce and reduce new discrepancies—they manifested the effects of mental satiation; that is, they found the task odious and, at the same time, their performance deteriorated.

The current discussion offers a perspective on the Pyszczynski and Greenberg (1987) theory of depression. These authors emphasized the difficulty that the depressed have in abandoning the goal. Perhaps the difficulty resides not so much in abandoning an old goal but in formulating new ones—either because of an impoverished environment (Coyne & Gotlib, 1983) or for some more personal reason, such as lack of imagination.

The voluntary variation of experience—the formulation and attainment of new goals is, in our opinion, the hallmark of intrinsic motivation. A capacity for repetition, on the other hand, suggests that extrinsic motivation is operating. Indeed, we question the wisdom of using continued interest in the same task to index intrinsic motivation.

To examine preferred probabilities of success under intrinsic motivation, we deliberately chose a situation in which ability could improve and in which termination was in the hands of the subjects. In contrast, Hamilton (1974) specifically ruled out examining choices made during a stage of skill acquisition and focused instead on preferred probabilities after subjects had reached a performance plateau. Under the rules of intrinsic motivation, we would expect subjects to desire to quit, given that performing the task had become repetitious.

However, as Karsten (1927/1976) concluded, it is much easier to repeat when motivation comes from outside the task, that is, is extrinsic. Thus it made sense for Hamilton (1974) to measure an extrinsic motive—achievement—after a plateau had been reached.

Making Things Harder by Lowering One's Capacities

Ordinarily, when confronted with a novel task, people become better at it with experience. It follows that in the natural course of events, with the improved capabilities that result from experience, people will come to prefer increasingly more complex stimuli.

However, what happens if the person has little choice in the stimuli to which he or she is exposed and his or her capacities exceed the challenge of the stimulus? To move toward a better match between capacities and challenge one might increase the challenge of the stimulus by, for instance, limiting the time that one allows oneself to deal with it. Thus, procrastination on a term paper, instead of serving to protect self-esteem, could function to add some excitement to an otherwise routine event by reducing the odds of success and requiring full concentration to tackle the project.

But there may be an even more perverse way in which self-handicapping might work to enhance pleasure. One could directly reduce one's capacities in order to match them to a limited level of challenge. We all know that the consumption of alcohol makes many people feel good. Commonly, we believe that alcohol disinhibits pleasurable thoughts and actions. But there are other ways that alcohol's hedonic effects can be understood. Alcohol in all but very modest doses detracts not only from motor but also from cognitive performance (e.g., Carpenter, Moore, Snyder, & Lisansky, 1961; Carpenter & Ross, 1965; Hull & Bond, 1986).

The consequence of drinking, therefore, is that encounters with the routine, such as familiar objects or conventional social exchanges, should move closer to the optimal level of challenge and thereby become more interesting, more pleasurable. Imbibing, however, loses its charm when one can no longer deal adequately with even these mundane matters.

This analysis suggests that the affective consequences of alcohol consumption may depend on the context. Needed are stimuli at an appropriate level of challenge, below the usual optimum. Although it will not obviate the necessity for careful and systematic research, the following thought experiment might be illuminating. You come home from work, mix yourself a martini, and sit with eyes closed and ears plugged, listening to and looking at nothing. Is drinking fun under those circumstances. We think not. Nor would it be enjoyable if you were about to listen to some highly complex and unfamiliar music. In contrast, stimuli that are simpler and more familiar may gain greater appreciation after a drink or two.

A commonly heard analysis of alcoholism is that it is the result of an oral fixation, that it is a regression to infancy. The idea that alcohol impairs competence suggests how the route backwards is traversed. The ordinary course of development from infancy to adulthood is marked by gains in competence. Alcohol reverses ontogeny. It returns the drinker to an earlier level of functioning.

Several possible avenues of investigation come to mind. Consuming alcohol should shift the optimal level of stimulus complexity or task difficulty lower, the more so the more alcohol consumed. A corollary is that in anticipation of situations with little challenge, people may increase their alcohol consumption to lower their capacities so as to match the context.

Fatigue is a heretofore neglected strategy for making things harder that might entail both consequences. Being tired accomplishes several things. It may directly reduce anxiety by reducing energy level. It can provide an excuse should one make a mistake. And it may make boring tasks somewhat interesting in the same way that alcohol might, that is, by producing a better match between the capacity of the person and the person's environment.

Making things harder for yourself, whether for the purpose of pride or for joy, can be accomplished in two ways. One is by altering the features of the task—the difficulty level, the time allotted for it, the effort invested in it, and so forth. A second way is to impair one's abilities, preferably temporarily, by ingesting alcohol or other drugs or even by allowing oneself to become fatigued.

PRIDE AND JOY

We have distinguished two reasons why people might make things harder for themselves; egotism—to preserve pride—and intrinsic motivation—to move the level of challenge closer to the optimum for producing pleasure. We now turn our attention to considering the relationship between the two.

Just as Nicholls and Miller (1984) have shown that ability and effort are initially undifferentiated, so it may be with pride and pleasure. Young children may derive pride from effort which they equate with ability. And to the extent that effort entails the voluntary concentration of attention, it is also a source of pleasure (Csikszentmihalyi, 1978). Later on in life, self-esteem depends on an assessment of ability independent of effort.

TEMPORAL PERSPECTIVE

With development comes the ability to work for increasingly longer-term goals. This may happen for a variety of reasons. With age the subjective experience of the passage of time is more rapid. It is also well known that older children are better able to delay gratification—to forgo—immediate pleasure (Mischel & Metzner, 1962). We argue that temporal maturity is important in egotism, less so in intrinsic motivation.

The very young child can no doubt feel pride or, conversely, shame. Even a 3-year-old wants to act "like the big kids" and doesn't want to be treated like a baby. But at that stage, pride as well as pleasure may be more a matter of the immediate and the superficial than it becomes later. Young children readily take to blatant self-symbols, such as uniforms, hats, insignia, that we suspect would embarrass the adolescent. Moreover, pride is a transient thing. To remove the uniform is to lose the power. Identity lacks constancy. Perhaps around the time a youngster acquires the more mature conception of the ability–effort relation (Miller, 1985; Nicholls & Miller, 1984)—when ability is conceived as an enduring capacity—identity and esteem acquire a more enduring quality.

In adolescence and onward, the strategies used to preserve self-esteem have a subtlety and an ambiguity of purpose (M. L. Snyder & Wicklund, 1981), with a temporal rhythm far different from that of pleasure. Now an identity is being acquired, and the person is oriented toward developing a relatively stable and long-term image of the self. Consider, then, the preservation of pride through a strategy of low effort. A threat to self-esteem has been blunted, but there may be no acute moment of intense pride. Rather, the benefits of the strategy are to preserve a certain belief about self, which can continue long after the instigating situation is over and forgotten.

In contrast, the pattern of intrinsic motivation is distinct. Activity is permeated with involvement in the task and punctuated with moments of accomplishment. In lieu of a single-minded goal, there is a constantly changing focus as the person makes things harder and creates variety. Gratification from any particular act is immediate but of brief duration, and pleasure requires a continuing stream of new challenges to sustain itself.

Outcome-Dependent versus Attribution-Dependent Emotion

Some emotions, Weiner (1986) informs us, depend only on the outcomes that occur, whereas others depend on the attributions made for those outcomes. Happiness is based on outcomes—what happens rather than why it happens. All of us would be very happy to win the New York State lottery, but it is doubtful we would experience pride. Pride is felt when one attributes a success to internal causes. Given that we attribute winning the lottery to luck, unless we believe luck is an internal factor, we would feel happy but not proud.

It is our contention that attribution-based emotions—such as pride—will have a relatively long, flat, and enduring time course. And outcome-dependent emotions, such as happiness, will have a sharper rise and fall. In this regard the joy of winning the lottery seems to dissipate even before the money does (Brickman, Coates, & Janoff-Bulman, 1978). We find Weiner's distinction useful for differentiating the two sorts of reasons why people make things harder for themselves. Not only does pride last longer than joy but it also takes the extra cognitive step of making attributions for outcomes to process pride. In Weiner's view, pride is an inference, whereas joy is a more immediate experience.

With respect not only to the temporal perspective, but also to the cognitive sophistication required, the processes underlying pride can be more developmentally sophisticated and cognitively demanding than those behind joy.

Pleasure and the Present

We social psychologists sometimes hear our clinical brethren talking about such a phenomenon as "being in the moment," "being with the client," "experiencing" rather than merely knowing. The point seems to be that emotion depends on an immediacy of response. There is a direct connection between what one is doing or thinking and how one feels. In this sense even negative emotions are acts of consummation, as opposed to being instrumental to reach some other goal. Indeed, emotions that serve such a purpose are regarded as ingenuine. Pleasure has a dynamic focus on events, on things that happen and on things that the person does (cf. Csikszentmihalyi, 1978; Wicklund, 1986). Pride, on the other hand, has a more static orientation toward a distillation of events into a self-concept that then persists.

The capacity for experiencing joy then may depend on the ability to live in the moment rather than to ruminate on the past or plan for the future. LaRoche and Frankel (1986) have scaled temporal orientation. They measured whether people tended to be oriented toward the past, the present, or the future. Although very few people indicated they focused on the past, many could be classified as either present or future oriented. Laroche and Frankel (1986) explored the connections between temporal orientation and both depression and anxiety. They found that future-oriented people tended to score higher on both depression and anxiety than did those more oriented toward the present.

The results for anxiety make sense in terms of Hunt, Cole, and Reis's (1958) findings. They provided subjects with descriptions of frustrating situations set in the past, present, or future and inquired as to which emotions were believed to ensue. They found that fear results from apprehension that something frustrating might happen in the future. However, they also found that sorrow, an emotion we assume to be closely allied with depression, resulted from frustrating events of the past (e.g., irretrievable losses).

Why then a connection between depression and future orientation? As we saw earlier, the depressed do seem to be concerned about protecting their self-image from an impending failure, and thus in that instance they clearly are future-oriented. Their previously discussed indecisiveness and propensity for the predecisional state also suggests a future orientation. Moreover, Beck (1976), writing about clinical depression said that, "the depressed have a special penchant for expecting future adversities and experiencing them as though they were happening in the present or had already occurred (p. 117)." One of the features distinguishing depression from mere sadness may be the extent to which the person regards a loss as having implications for the future (cf. Brehm & Brehm, 1981).

Our view of the temporal perspective of the depressed is seemingly at odds with the view of Baumeister and Scher (1988). They account for self-defeating behavior as the result of a trade-off to obtain short-term benefits despite long-term costs. Higgins and C. R. Snyder have made a similar point (see Chapter 5, this volume). Although we agree that the depressed may act to relieve current emotional distress in ways that lead to long-term disadvantage, it would be a mistake to assume that the depressed person is focused on the present.

To illuminate this point we invoke Lewin's (1936) principle of contemporaneity. Lewin's idea is that in order for the past or the future to influence the person's current psychological state, the temporally distant must be represented in the person's life space. It is the vividly present threat of future loss (Beck, 1976) of self-esteem from failure that leads the depressed to withhold effort. The advantages of engaging in the task—the pleasure of accomplishment, the development of one's potential, the esteem of self and others—are psychologically absent. Or if present but weak, these advantages may be low in salience (Tversky & Kahneman, 1974). Even if salient, they may be judged as improbable (Fishbein & Ajzen, 1975). Simply getting the depressed person to think about the future rather than the present may not help and could exacerbate concern about future losses over which the person may feel he or she has little control.

One common feature of depression is called anhedonia—the inability to experience pleasure. Might it be that an inability of the depressed to live in the present underlies their difficulty in experiencing pleasure? Their defense of low effort may leave them with pride but is unlikely to produce joy.

Other currently prominent afflictions seem to share with the depressed a difficulty in feeling and expressing emotions in the present. The coronary prone have been characterized as having difficulty expressing emotion. Wolf (1969) spoke of their striving without joy. And more recently, MacDougal, Dembroski, Dimsdale, and Hackett (1985) have correlated suppressed feelings of anger with the extent of coronary artery disease.

Some of the same dynamics may underlie anorexia. Anorexics have been characterized as compulsive, depressed, impaired in experiencing pleasure, oriented toward control, concerned about their physical self-image, and denying gratification toward that end (Bruch, 1978; Eckert, 1985; Eckert & Labeck, 1985; Kinoy, 1984).

The depressed, the Type A, and the anorexic may all suffer from an excess of maturity. They are, perhaps, too concerned about controlling their long-term image—pride—and too little able to enter the child's world of immediate gratification—even when it is not harmful. These afflictions then may be diseases of civilization, the products of excessive socialization.

Part of being socialized is acquiring the ability to put off immediate gratification, to work for long-term goals. Accomplishing such goals might require the denial of certain feelings that naturally arise. For instance, Walster and Aronson (1967) found that people in the middle of a task report less fatigue than those who have worked just as long but think the task is about to end. Knowing one has substantial work to do leads one to suppress fatigue. M. L. Snyder and Glass (1974, cited in Carver, Coleman, & Glass, 1976) linked the phenomenon of fatigue suppression to the coronary-prone behavior pattern.

More recently, Walsh and M. L. Snyder (1988) discovered another instance of the suppression of negative affect. They had subjects rate the likability of each of a long list of words. Scattered through the list were words of high difficulty (e.g., dilettante, devoid, expedite). In analyzing the ratings, Walsh and M. L. Snyder grouped subjects according to their preference for various media as sources of news. They assumed that those preferring television would collectively be less verbally competent than the others. These "television" people rated the highly difficult words marginally more negatively than did those preferring other news media. A more striking effect was that they rated the last few words (crane, scatter, orchard) quite negatively, even though they were of no particular difficulty.

Walsh and M. L. Snyder (1988) interpreted this to mean that during the task the television people suppressed with partial success their feelings of frustration. They suppressed perhaps either to make the task less unpleasant or to avoid interference with performance. But then, as the end of the task neared, the frustration they felt at dealing with difficult words finally poured out, resulting in negative ratings of the last few words.

Feelings of frustration are not the only ones that get suppressed on the job. It is no secret that subordinates often feel compelled to suppress negative feelings toward their superiors. In sum, to attain many of the goals commonly adopted by adults often leads people to suppress feelings. We even suspect that the expression of positive feeling is often inhibited in the work place. Feeling good about the downfall of an internal competitor, or even feeling good about one's own promotion or raise, can be dangerous on the job, because it can provoke hostility or envy. Part of being an adult in our culture is to control emotions, which in practice often means to suppress them.

SELF-FOCUS AND THE CAPACITY FOR PLEASURE

Earlier we found Weiner's (1986) distinction between outcome-based and attribution-based emotion useful in distinguishing between pride and joy. Happiness, he said, depended on the outcome rather than on the attributions for it. Happiness, however, does not depend only on the outcome. If that were so, then in the M. L. Snyder *et al.* (1988) study, subjects would choose slow speeds and experience only successful outcomes. They seem to need, however, increasingly faster speeds to sustain their interest in the game. Csikszentmihalyi (1978) argued that for the case of intrinsic motivation, pleasure depends on the intensity of concentration.

The role of attention in the experience of pleasure suggests how anxiety and depression might be linked to anhedonia. Both anxiety (Sarason, 1975) and depression (Pyszczynski & Greenberg, 1985) have been characterized as entailing a high degree of self-focus. To the extent that attention is toward the self, less is available to focus on the task with which one is ostensibly engaged. If Csikszentmihalyi (1978) is correct, the less attention available for the task, the less pleasure it can provide.

SUMMING UP

Long before people learn to make things harder for themselves in the service of a joyless pride, they make things harder for themselves simply to make life more interesting. In other words, intrinsic motivation precedes achievement motivation. Somewhere around early adolescence, people learn that making things harder can also serve to protect self-esteem. The time also comes, perhaps typically in late adolescence, when people learn to make things harder for themselves for either purpose by lowering their own capacities. This may happen when they learn to drink or to use other drugs. Or it may happen when the pressure of a work overload forces them to work despite fatigue. Part of the rush derived from working under pressure may result from the increased challenge of the mundane when people are tired.

On the whole, making things harder in the service of joy is probably valuable, especially when it is accomplished by varying the task and increasing its difficulty, as opposed to lowering one's capacity. Making things harder for oneself to protect self-esteem poses greater danger. It renders immediate success unlikely and also reduces the likelihood of developing one's talent through practice. The person elects to forgo the possibility of immediate gratification from the task itself in favor of a longer-term goal of the preservation of pride.

This strategy would seem to be most effective and least harmful when used in a circumscribed way, that is, infrequently and in spheres of activity of little relevance to one's future (M. L. Snyder *et al.*, 1978). But to the extent that this strategy is used in the more central spheres of a person's life for an extended period of time, and to the extent that attention is focused on self rather than on the task, the person will have diminished opportunities for developing important abilities and will be deprived of the pleasurable experience of intrinsic motivation.

REFERENCES

Abramson, L. Y., Garber, J., & Seligman, M. E. P. (1980). Learned helplessness in humans: An attributional analysis. In J. Garber & M. E. P. Seligman (Eds.), *Human helplessness: Theory and Applications* (pp. 3–34). New York: Academic Press.

Abramson, L. Y., Seligman, M. E. P., & Teasdale, J. D. (1978). Learned helplessness in humans: Critique and reformulation. *Journal of Abnormal Psychology, 87*, 49–74.

Alloy, L. B., & Abramson, L. Y. (1979). Judgement of contingency in depressed and non-depressed students: Sadder but wiser? *Journal of Experimental Psychology: General, 108*, 441–485.

Alloy, L. B., & Abramson, L. Y. (1982). Learned helplessness, depression, and the illusion of control. *Journal of Personality and Social Psychology, 42*, 1114–1126.

Alloy, L. B., & Ahrens, A. H. (1987). Depression and pessimism for the future: Biased use of statistically relevant information in predictions for self versus others. *Journal of Personality and Social Psychology, 52*, 366–378.

Bandura, A. (in press). Self-regulation of motivation and action through goal systems. In G. Hamilton, B. H. Bower, & N. H. Fryda (Eds.), *Cognition, motivation, and affect: A cognitive science view* (pp. 1–25). Dordrecht: Martinus Nyholl.

Baumeister, R. F., & Scher, S. J. (1988). Self-defeating behavior patterns among normal individuals: Review and analysis of common self-destructive tendencies. *Psychological Bulletin, 104*, 3–22.

Baumgardner, A. H., & Brownlee, E. A. (1987). Strategic failure in social interaction: Evidence for expectancy disconfirmation processes. *Journal of Personality and Social Psychology, 52*, 525–535.

Baumgardner, A. H., Lake, E., & Arkin, R. M. (1985). Claiming mood as a self-handicap: The influence of spoiled and unspoiled public identity. *Personality and Social Psychology Bulletin, 11*, 349–357.

Beck, A. T. (1967). *Depression: Clinical, experimental, and theoretical aspects*. New York: Harper & Row.

Beck, A. T. (1976). *Cognitive therapy and the emotional disorders*. New York: International Universities Press.

Berglas, S., & Jones, E. E. (1978). Drug choice as a self-handicapping strategy in response to noncontingent success. *Journal of Personality and Social Psychology, 36*, 405–417.

Brehm, S. S., & Brehm, J. W. (1981). *Psychological reactance: A theory of freedom and control*. New York: Academic Press.

Brickman, P., Coates, D., & Janoff-Bulman, R. (1978). Lottery winners and accident victims: Is happiness relative? *Journal of Personality and Social Psychology, 36*, 917–927.

Brockner, J., & Hulton, A. J. B. (1978). How to reverse the vicious cycle of low self-esteem: The importance of attentional focus. *Journal of Experimental Social Psychology, 14*, 564–578.

Bruch, H. (1978). *The golden cage: The enigma of anorexia nervosa*. Cambridge, MA: Harvard University Press.

Carpenter, J. A., Moore, O. K., Snyder, C. R., & Lisansky, E. S. (1961). Alcohol and higher-order problem solving. *Quarterly Journal of Alcohol Studies, 22*, 183–222.

Carpenter, J. A., & Ross, B. M. (1965). Effect of alcohol on short term memory. *Quarterly Journal of Alcohol Studies, 26*, 561–579.

Carver, C. S., Coleman, A. E., & Glass, D. C. (1976). The coronary-prone behavior pattern and the suppression of fatigue on a treadmill test. *Journal of Personality and Social Psychology, 33*, 460–466.

Carver, C. S., & Scheier, M. F. (1981). *Attention and self-regulation*. New York: Springer-Verlag.

Cohen, S., & Wills, T. A. (1985). Stress, social support, and the buffering hypothesis. *Psychological Bulletin, 98*, 310–357.

Coyne, J. C. (1976a). Depression and the response of others. *Journal of Abnormal Psychology, 85*, 186–193.

Coyne, J. C. (1976b). Toward an interactional description of depression. *Psychiatry, 39*, 28–40.

Coyne, J. C., & Gotlib, I. H. (1983). The role of cognition in depression: A critical appraisal. *Psychological Bulletin, 94*, 472–505.

Cozzarelli, C., & Major B. (1987, August). *Chronic and situation-specific defense strategies as buffers against threatening events*. Paper presented at the convention of the American Psychological Association, New York.

Crocker, J., Thompson, L. L., McGraw, K. M., & Ingerman, C. (1987). Downward comparison, prejudice, and evaluations of others: Effects of self-esteem and threat. *Journal of Personality and Social Psychology, 52*, 907–916.

Csikszentmihalyi, M. (1978). Attention and the holistic approach to behavior. In K. S. Pope & J. L. Singer (Eds.), *The stream of consciousness* (pp. 335–378). New York: Plenum.

Duval, S., & Wicklund, R. A. (1972). *A theory of objective self-awareness*. New York: Academic Press.

Eckert, E. D. (1985). Characteristics of anorexia nervosa. In J. E. Mitchell (Ed.), *Anorexia nervosa and bulimia*. Minneapolis: University of Minnesota Press.

Eckert, E. D., & Labeck, L. (1985). Integrated treatment program for anorexia nervosa. In J. E. Mitchell (Ed.), *Anorexia nervosa and bulimia*. Minneapolis: University of Minnesota Press.

Feather, N. T. (1961). The relationship of persistence at a task to expectation of success and achievement-related motives. *Journal of Abnormal and Social Psychology, 63*, 552–561.

Feather, N. T. (1963). Persistence at a difficult task with an alternative task of intermediate difficulty. *Journal of Abnormal and Social Psychology, 66*, 604–609.

Federoff, N. A., & Harvey, J. H. (1976). Focus of attention, self-esteem and the attribution of causality. *Journal of Research in Personality, 10*, 336–345.

Fishbein, M., & Ajzen, I. (1975). *Belief, attitudes, intentions and behavior: An introduction to theory and research*. Reading, MA: Addison-Wesley.

Frankel, A., & Snyder, M. L. (1978). Poor performance following unsolvable problems: Learned helplessness or egotism? *Journal of Personality and Social Psychology, 36*, 1415–1423.

Frankel, A., & Snyder, M. L. (1987, September). Egotism among the depressed: When self-protection becomes self-handicapping. In R. Curtis (Chair), *Self-defeating behaviors:*

Situational and dispositional factors. Symposium conducted at the 95th Annual Convention of the American Psychological Association, New York.

Gibbons, F. X. (1986). Social comparison and depression: Company's effect on misery. *Journal of Personality and Social Psychology, 51*, 140–148.

Gollwitzer, P. M., & Kinney, R. F. (1987). *Effects of deliberative and implemental mindsets on illusion of control*. Manuscript submitted for publication.

Goodhart, D. E. (1986). The effects of positive and negative thinking on performance in an achievement situation. *Journal of Personality and Social Psychology, 51*, 117–124.

Hamilton, J. O. (1974). Motivation and risk taking behavior: A test of Atkinson's theory. *Journal of Personality and Social Psychology, 29*, 856–864.

Heckhausen, H., & Gollwitzer, P. M. (1987). Thought contents and cognitive functioning in motivational versus volitional states of mind. *Motivation and Emotion, 11*, 101–120.

Higgins, E. T., Strauman, T., & Klein, R. (1986). Standards and the process of self-evaluation: Multiple affects from multiple stages. In R. M. Sorrentino & E. T. Higgins (Eds.), *Handbook of Motivation and Cognition*. New York: Guilford Press.

Hiroto, D. S., & Seligman, M. E. P. (1975). Generality of learned helplessness in man. *Journal of Personality and Social Psychology, 31*, 311–327.

Hormuth, S. E. (1986). Lack of effort as a result of self-focused attention: An attributional ambiguity analysis. *European Journal of Social Psychology, 16*, 181–192.

Howes, M. J., Hokanson, J. E., & Loewenstein, D. A. (1985). Induction of depressive affect after prolonged exposure to a mildly depressed individual. *Journal of Personality and Social Psychology, 49*, 1110–1113.

Hull, J. G., & Bond, C. F. (1986). Social and behavioral consequences of alcohol consumption and expectancy: A meta-analysis. *Psychological Bulletin, 99*, 347–360.

Hunt, J. McV., Cole, M. L. W., & Reis, E. E. S. (1958). Situational cues distinguishing anger, fear and sorrow. *American Journal of Psychology, 71*, 136–151.

Hyland, M. E. (1987). Control theory interpretation of psychological mechanisms of depression: Comparison and integration of several theories. *Psychological Bulletin, 102*, 109–121.

Ingram, R. E., & Smith, T. W. (1984). Depression and internal versus external focus of attention. *Cognitive Therapy and Research 8*, 139–151.

Jones, E. E., & Berglas, S. (1976). Control of attributions about the self through self-handicapping strategies: The appeal of alcohol and the role of underachievement. *Personality and Social Psychology Bulletin, 4*, 200–206.

Jones, E. E., & Gerard, H. B. (1967). *Foundations of Social Psychology*. New York: Wiley.

Jones, E. E., & Nisbett, R. E. (1971). The actor and the observer: Divergent perceptions of the causes of behavior. In E. E. Jones, D. Kanouse, H. H. Kelley, R. E. Nisbett, S. Valins, & B. Weiner (Eds.), *Attribution: Perceiving the causes of behavior* (pp. 79–94). Morristown, NJ: General Learning Press.

Karabenick, S. S., & Youssef, Z. I. (1968). Performance as a function of achievement motive level and perceived difficulty. *Journal of Personality and Social Psychology, 10*, 414–419.

Karsten, A. (1976). Mental satiation. In J. DeRivera (Ed.). *Field theory as human science* (pp. 151–207). New York: Gardner. (Original work published 1927)

Kernis, M. H., Zuckerman, M., Cohen, A., & Spadafora, S. (1982). Persistence following failure: The interactive role of self-awareness and the attributional basis for negative expectancies. *Journal of Personality and Social Psychology, 43*, 1184–1191.

Kinoy, B. P. (1984). *When will we laugh again? Living and dealing with anorexia and bulimia*. New York: Columbia University Press.

Klein, D. C., Fencil-Morse, E., & Seligman, M. E. P. (1976). Depression, learned helplessness and attribution of failure. *Journal of Personality and Social Psychology, 33*, 508–516.

Kuhl, J. (1982). The expectancy-value approach in the theory of social motivation: Elaborations, extensions, critique. In N. T. Feather (Ed.), *Expectations and actions: Expectancy-value models in psychology* (pp. 125–160). Hillsdale, NJ: Erlbaum.

Kuhl, J. (1986). Motivation and information processing: A new look at decision making, dynamic change, and action control. In R. M. Sorrentino & E. T. Higgins (Eds.), *Handbook of motivation and cognition* (pp. 404–434). New York: Guilford Press.

Kuiper, N. (1978). Depression and causal attributions for success and failure. *Journal of Personality and Social Psychology, 36,* 236–246.

Langer, E. (1975). The illusion of control. *Journal of Personality and Social Psychology, 32,* 311–328.

LaRoche, A. N., & Frankel, A. (1986). Time perspective and health. *Health Education Research, 1,* 139–142.

Leary, M. R. (1986). The impact of interactional impediments on social anxiety and self-presentation. *Journal of Experimental Social Psychology, 22,* 122–135.

Lerner, M. J., Miller, D. T., & Holmes, J. G. (1976). Deserving and the emergence of forms of justice. In L. Berkowitz & E. Walster (Eds.), *Advances in experimental social psychology* (Vol. 9, pp. 133–162). New York: Academic Press.

Lewin, K. (1936). *Principles of topological psychology*. New York: McGraw-Hill.

Lewinsohn, P., Mischel, W., Chaplin, W., Barton, R. (1980). Social competence and depression: The role of illusory self-perceptions. *Journal of Abnormal Psychology, 89,* 203–212.

Linville, P. W. (1987). Self-complexity as a cognitive buffer against stress-related illness and depression. *Journal of Personality and Social Psychology, 52,* 663–676.

MacDougall, J. M., Dembroski, T. M., Dimsdale, J. E., & Hackett, T. P. (1985). Components of Type A, hostility, and anger-in: Further relationships to angiographic findings. *Health Psychology, 4,* 137–152.

McCaul, K. D. (1983). Observer attributions of depressed students. *Personality and Social Psychology Bulletin, 9,* 74–82.

McClelland, D. C., Atkinson, J. W., Clark, R. A., & Lowell, E. L. (1976). *The achievement motive*. New York: Irvington. (Original work published 1953)

Mehlman, G. A., & Snyder, C. R. (1985). Excuse theory: A test of the self-protective role of attributions. *Journal of Personality and Social Psychology, 49,* 994–1001.

Miller, A. (1985). A developmental study of the cognitive basis of performance impairment after failure. *Journal of Personality and Social Psychology, 49,* 529–538.

Miller, G. A., Galanter, E., & Pribram, K. H. (1960). *Plans and the structure of behavior*. New York: Holt, Rinehart & Winston.

Mischel, W., & Metzner, R. (1962). Preference for delayed reward as a function of age, intelligence, and length of delay interval. *Journal of Abnormal and Social Psychology, 64,* 425–431.

Nelson, R. E., & Craighead, W. E. (1977). Selective recall of positive and negative feedback, self-control behaviors and depression. *Journal of Abnormal Psychology, 86,* 379–388.

Nicholls, J. G. (1984). Achievement motivation: Conceptions of ability, subjective experience, task choice and performance. *Psychological Review, 91,* 328–346.

Nicholls, J. G., & Miller, A. (1984). Reasoning about the ability of self and others: A developmental study. *Child Development, 55,* 1990–1999.

Norem, J. K., & Cantor, N. (1986). Defensive pessimism: Harnessing anxiety as motivation. *Journal of Personality and Social Psychology, 51,* 1208–1217.

Pittman, T. S., & D'Agostino, P. (1985). Motivation and attribution: The effects of control deprivation on subsequent information processing. In J. H. Harvey & G. Weary (Eds.), *Attribution: Basic issues and applications*. New York: Academic Press.

Pittman, T. S., & Pittman, N. L. (1980). Deprivation of control and the attribution process. *Journal of Personality and Social Psychology, 39,* 377–389.

Pyszczynski, T., & Greenberg, J. (1985). Depression and preference for self-focusing stimuli after success and failure. *Journal of Personality and Social Psychology, 49*, 1066–1075.

Pyszczynski, T., & Greenberg, J. (1987). Self-regulatory perseveration and the depressive self-focusing style: A self-awareness theory of reactive depression. *Psychological Bulletin, 102*, 122–138.

Rholes, W. S., Blackwell, J., Jordan, C., & Walters, C. (1980). A developmental study of learned helplessness. *Developmental Psychology, 16*, 616–624.

Rizley, R. (1978). Depression and distortion in the attribution of causality. *Journal of Abnormal Psychology, 87*, 32–48.

Sarason, I. G. (1961). The effects of anxiety and threat on the solution of a difficult task. *Journal of Abnormal and Social Psychology, 62*, 165–168.

Sarason, I. G. (1975). Anxiety and self-preoccupation. In I. G. Sarason & C. D. Spielberger (Eds.), *Stress and anxiety* (Vol. 2, pp. 27–44). Washington: Hemisphere.

Schouten, P. G. W., & Handelsman, M. M. (1987). Social basis of self-handicapping: The case of depression. *Personality and Social Psychology Bulletin 13*, 103–110.

Seligman, M. E. P. (1975). *Helplessness*. San Francisco: Freeman.

Seligman, M. E. P., Abramson, L., Semmel, A., & von Baeyer, C. (1979). Depressive attributional style. *Journal of Abnormal Psychology, 88*, 242–248.

Showers, C. (1987). *The motivational consequences of negative thinking: Those who imagine the worst try harder*. Unpublished manuscript, Barnard College, Psychology Department, New York.

Smith, T. W., & Greenberg, J. (1981). Depression and self-focused attention. *Motivation and Emotion, 5*, 323–331.

Smith, T. W., Snyder, C. R., & Handelsman, M. M. (1982). On the self-serving function of an academic wooden leg: Test anxiety as a self-handicapping strategy. *Journal of Personality and Social Psychology, 42*, 314–321.

Snyder, C. R., Higgins, R. L., & Stucky, R. J. (1983). *Excuses: Masquerades in search of grace*. New York: Wiley.

Snyder, C. R., Smith, T. W., Augelli, R. W., & Ingram, R. E. (1985). On the self-serving function of social anxiety: Shyness as a self-handicapping strategy. *Journal of Personality and Social Psychology, 48*, 970–980.

Snyder, M. L. (1985, March). *In search of a preferendum: Perceptual competence as an explanation for the mere exposure effect*. Paper presented at the convention of the Eastern Psychological Association, Boston.

Snyder, M. L., Hansen, E., & Redler, D. (1988). *Preferred level of difficulty under intrinsic motivation: Evidence against p = .50*. Unpublished manuscript, Rutgers University, Psychology Department, Newark, New Jersey.

Snyder, M. L., & Karl, S. (1986, August). *The preferendum in aesthetics: perceptual competence*. Paper presented at the annual meeting of the American Psychological Association, Washington, D.C.

Snyder, M. L., Smoller, B., Strenta, A., & Frankel, A. (1981). A comparison of egotism, negativity and learned helplessness as explanations for poor performance after unsolvable problems. *Journal of Personality and Social Psychology, 40*, 24–30.

Snyder, M. L., Stephan, W. G., & Rosenfield, D. (1978). Attributional egotism. In J. H. Harvey, W. J. Ickes, & R. F. Kidd (Eds.), *New directions in attribution research* (Vol. 2, pp. 91–117). Hillsdale, NJ: Erlbaum.

Snyder, M. L., & Wicklund, R. A. (1981). Attribute ambiguity. In J. H. Harvey, W. Ickes, & R. F. Kidd (Eds.), *New Directions in Attribution Research* (Vol. 3, pp. 197–221). Hillsdale, NJ: Erlbaum.

Strube, M. J., & Roemmele, L. A. (1985). Self-enhancement, self-assessment and self-evaluative task choice. *Journal of Personality and Social Psychology, 49*, 981–993.

Tennen, H., & Herzberger, S. (1987). Depression, self-esteem, and the absence of self-protective attributional biases. *Journal of Personality and Social Psychology, 52*, 72–80.

Tighe, T. J. (1968). Concept formation and art: Further evidence on the applicability of Walk's technique. *Psychonomic Science, 12*, 363–364.

Tversky, A., & Kahneman, D. (1974). Judgment under uncertainty: Heuristics and biases. *Science, 185*, 1124–1131.

Vazquez, C. (1987). Judgment of contingency: Cognitive biases in depressed and non-depressed subjects. *Journal of Personality and Social Psychology, 52*, 419–431.

Walk, R. D. (1967). Concept formation and art: Basic experiment and controls. *Psychonomic Science, 9*, 237–238.

Walsh, K., & Snyder, M. L. (1988, April). *Suppression of negative affect to words.* Paper presented at the convention of the Eastern Psychological Association, Buffalo, New York.

Walster, B., & Aronson, E. (1967). Effect of expectancy of task duration on the experience of fatigue. *Journal of Experimental Social Psychology, 3*, 41–46.

Weary, G. (1978). Self-serving biases in the attribution process: A re-examination of the fact or fiction question. *Journal of Personality and Social Psychology, 36*, 56–71.

Weiner, B. (1986). Attribution, emotion, and action. In R. M. Sorrentino & E. T. Higgins (Eds.), *Handbook of motivation and cognition* (pp. 281–312). New York: Guilford Press.

Wells, G. (1977). *Anticipated discussion of interpretation eliminates actor–observer differences in the attribution of causality.* Unpublished manuscript, Ohio State University, Columbus.

White, R. W. (1959). Motivation reconsidered: The concept of competence. *Psychological Review, 66*, 297–333.

Wicklund, R. A. (1975). Objective self-awareness. In L. Berkowitz (Ed.), *Advances in experimental social psychology* (Vol. 8, pp. 233–275). New York: Academic Press.

Wicklund, R. A. (1986). Orientation to the environment versus preoccupation with human potential. In R. M. Sorrentino & E. T. Higgins (Eds.), *Handbook of Motivation and Cognition*. New York: Guilford Press.

Wolf, S. (1969). Psychosocial forces in myocardial infarction and sudden death. In S. Bondurant (Ed.), *Research on acute myocardial infarction* (pp. iv-74–iv-81). New York: American Heart Association.

Wortman, C. B., Costanzo, P. R., & Witt, T. R. (1973). Effect of anticipated performance on the attributions of causality to self and others. *Journal of Personality and Social Psychology, 27*, 372–381.

Zajonc, R. (1968). The attitudinal effects of mere exposure. *Journal of Personality and Social Psychology, 9* (2, Pt. 2), 1–27.

CHAPTER 7

FEAR OF SUCCESS

DONNAH CANAVAN

The apparent paradox that some people fear or avoid success has been the focus of a good deal of interest and research in the last two decades. Two discernable lines of thinking appear in the literature on fear of success. One, which for purposes of differentiation will be called neurotic fear of success, was first chronicled in the psychoanalytic literature by Freud (1915/1959) and later by Horney (1937), Menninger (1938), and others. The distinguishing factor in the neurotic fear of success is that the anchor of the syndrome is unconscious and irrational, although as the research demonstrates, powerful and quite predictable in its consequences. After Pappo's (1972) ground-breaking work produced a questionnaire to identify success fearers, there followed a resurgence of interest in the 1970s and 1980s with the empirical investigations of Cohen (1974) and Canavan-Gumpert, Garner, and Gumpert (1978a).

The second discernable line of research, frequently called the feminine fear of success, will simply be termed fear of success. It was initiated in the field of social psychology when Horner (1968) attempted to explain why the McClelland–Atkinson model of achievement motivation (Atkinson, 1957; Atkinson & Feather, 1966; McClelland, Atkinson, Clark, & Lowell, 1976) was not able to predict the behavior of women. Horner postulated that in addition to the motives to avoid failure and to achieve success, a third motive, to avoid success, was required to understand the conduct of many women. Her notions were particularly timely at their appearance in the late 1960s and generated a good deal of research, controversy (Tresemer, 1974, 1976, 1977; Zuckerman & Wheeler, 1975) and revision (Horner, Tresemer, Berens, & Watson, 1973; Zuckerman & Allison, 1976).

It is the purpose of this chapter to report the current status of research and

DONNAH CANAVAN • Department of Psychology, Boston College, Chestnut Hill, Massachusetts 02167.

thinking on both the clinical and the social-psychological notions of fear of success. It is useful at the outset to outline how the two lines of thinking and research are different, perhaps more unrelated than related. The clinical notion, as will be seen, relates the trio of motives to succeed, to avoid success, and to avoid failure into an integrated syndrome of symptoms and behaviors. The social-psychological conception attempts to separate these same three motives. The instruments used to identify individuals with the two kinds of fear of success are in fact uncorrelated. The notions about neurotic fear of success trade on the importance of unconscious motivation, anxiety, and unresolved conflict. In contrast, the social-psychological notions veer more toward conscious motives and conscious resolution or choice between competing contemporary motives. Essentially, these success fearers emphasize the costs and devalue the rewards of success. The neurotic fear of success is seen as arising from early childhood development, while in the social-psychological perspective learning, and perhaps experience, account primarily for the origin of fear of success. Finally, the range of sabotagable successes for the neurotic success fearer is extensive, though fairly conventional, while the social-psychological approach has not specifically targeted interest in successes beyond the academic.

The two lines of thinking are similar in that they both utilize a person–situation model to predict the conditions under which individuals who fear success (by either definition) will engage in success-avoidant behavior as compared to individuals who do not fear success. And, of course, they are unfortunately called by the same name, fear of success.

The chapter begins with a brief review of the theoretical background for fear of success in the psychoanalytic and self-psychology literatures. A description of neurotic success fearers, and how they are identified for research purposes, precedes a review of the research on the neurotic fear of success. Some of the research is experimental, dealing primarily with the issues of the behavioral consequences of fear of success, the differentiation between fear of success and fear of failure, and the conditions under which success fearers can succeed. The field research reports on the characteristics and conduct of success fearers in everyday settings and on potential factors in the development of fear of success. The second part of the chapter is devoted to the work on the social-psychological perspective on fear of success. It begins with a description of the seminal work of Horner and then reviews the controversy and criticism generated by that work. There follows a review of the work of Zuckerman and his colleagues (Zuckerman & Allison, 1976; Zuckerman, Larrance, Porac, & Blanck, 1980), which represents a coherent new approach related to the underlying theoretical notions in Horner's work, but modified so considerably as to warrant a separate review. Finally the chapter concludes with a summary of the state of the field and the most pressing problems for future research.

THE NEUROTIC FEAR OF SUCCESS

From Lucifer to Moses to Leonardo DaVinci to Beethoven, on down to current celebrity figures, real and potential success fearers are ubiquitous.

Though poets and novelists have puzzled over and described the dilemma, it was Freud (1915/1959), in "Those Wrecked By Success," who first laid bare the problem. In his particularly apposite clinical illustrations he described his initial bewilderment when two people came to him for treatment because they had "fallen apart" at precisely the moment when their most cherished dreams were about to come true. In the first instance he described a professor who after 30 years of diligent work in the hope of succeeding his mentor to a desired chair, upon being offered the chair, became unable to do his work and fell into immobilized confusion. Freud went on to describe a woman who cohabitated with her lover for 10 years, her happiness marred only by his refusal to marry her. When the lover finally proposed, she became disorganized and unruly in their previously harmonious domestic life. Freud's explanation lay in the Oedipus complex. He reasoned that an unconscious symbolic conflict lay behind the observable elements in these patients' current life situations; the success, be it taking the valued chair or marriage, represented the Oedipal victory, the usurpation of the cherished romantic position of the same-sex parent with the opposite-sex parent. The sabotage of the contemporary success represented the recoil from the fantasied retaliation by the same-sex parent. This is classical Freud: things aren't what we think they are, and in the end the compulsion to repeat past conflicts and make them come out the same way gains a lead over the pleasure principle.

Since the human psyche is a devious calculator, it is interesting to note here, assuming ambivalence about success, that the maximum gratification is gained in precisely the situations Freud describes: when people have, but don't totally have, what they want—the "if only" situations. The notion that the sweetest time is near but not too near the fulfillment of their strivings has led some people to make strategic use of Browning's observation, "A man's need should exceed his grasp or what's a heaven for?" Freud has always been masterful at showing us, through illustration as well as explanation, that when we understand the givens of peoples' unconscious assumptions, their conduct not only makes sense but frequently is the best bit of pleasure they can muster given these assumptions. Freud and, more recently, Miller (1981) have also argued compellingly that the core of human tragedy lies less with fate than with people's inability to give up and mourn the loss of these unconscious desires, despite the concommitant pain, in order that they may consciously take charge of their lives.

In *The Neurotic Personality of Our Time*, Horney (1937) addressed fear of success from both the point of view of American culture and early childhood experience. She described the modal American personality as suffering from the neurotic fear of competition, which was underlain by three potent assumptions:

1. People can be divided into two categories: winners and losers. The winners are seen as good, virtuous, and possessed of desirable characteristics like attractiveness, intelligence, and the motivation to work hard. The losers, on the other hand, are less able, less hard working, and more likely to be jealous of and vindictive toward the winners.
2. In a spirit of individualism and self-determination, people must compete to find out where they fall on the winner–loser continuum.
3. People should be humble, self-denying, and kind to others.

According to Horney, individuals tend to resolve this neurotic competitiveness by developing either a fear of failure (of being humiliated as a loser) or a fear of success (the fear of being seen as a selfish, not humble person coupled with a fear of jealous attack by the losers). Further, the cultural conflict was seen as being intensified by early family experiences involving hostile competitiveness among siblings as well as between parents and children (Oedipal conflicts). At the heart of Horney's work is an individual struggling to find a socially esteemed concept of self which she claims, in American society, is much dependent on riding out the vicissitudes of competitive achievement. At both the cultural and family level, failure is unequivocally eschewed as the domain of the losers. At a distance, success is believed to bring love and a sense of personal and interpersonal well-being. Up close, however, it turns out to be a mixed blessing. In addition to the positive aspects of success, the success fearer must deal not only with being too prideful and selfish, but also with feared rejection and guilt. As a result, some turn back; others approach with caution.

The final clinical theoretical position that underlies fear of success comes from the work of Sullivan (1953) and from the group of researchers and theoreticians, most notably Mahler (Mahler, Pine, & Bergman, 1975), working on self-psychology and the separation–individuation conflict. In Sullivan's formulation, fear of success originates in the way that the mother responds to the earliest strivings for independence in her young child. The first childhood conflict is between maintaining security as represented by a harmonious psychological connection with the mother, on the one hand, and the young child's gradually increasing strivings for power, mastery, and independence, on the other. If the mother responds to the child's early strivings for self-mastery with anger, withdrawal, or anxiety, then the child's security is threatened by fear of abandonment. His or her emerging independence is fraught with ambivalence, which leads to a tendency to sabotage the independence and thus restore security.

Sullivan's conception is similar to Freud's in that the conflict is repressed and reenacted. A major difference is that success represents independence, and the sabotage has as its goal the forfeit of independence in the interests of averting abandonment and restoring security. Thus, depending on the mother's reaction to the child's attempts at independence, the child experiences independence either as the joy of mastery (if the mother is supportive) or as abandonment (if the mother is not supportive). The overriding difference from Freud is the location of the origin of the problem in the mother–child relationship in the more formative pre-Oedipal period. One of Sullivan's major contributions is his stress on the extremity of the terror the child experiences when the security of the mother–child relationship is disrupted.

More recently Mahler and her colleagues (Mahler *et al.*, 1975), based on their intensive observational research of mothers and young children, have postulated that at roughly 18 months the young child achieves sufficient maturation to undergo a "psychological birth." This spells the beginnings of a perception of the self as a separate individual, no longer one with the mother and thus capable of being left or abandoned. As is all too familiar in the child's use of the word "no" in the terrible two's, the child's growing into his or her own separateness is partly expressed as opposition or conflict with the parent(s). In addition it is critical that the child learn to acknowledge and express his or her own feelings and desires. It is necessary at this time that the child have a secure and loving interaction with a "good enough" (Winnicott, 1965) mother. The good enough mother engages in a sensitive mirroring process, wherein she takes cues *from* the child and then reflects the child's emotional state back to him or her. This mirroring process assists the child in developing a sense of self which is constant and independent. These mother–child interactions become internalized in the form of a positive introject and form the basis both for a stable sense of self and for the capacity to have self-acceptance and to earn positive self-esteem. Similar to Sullivan's notions, if the mothering one at this crucial period is angry, cruel, too critical, or neglectful, then the child, though aware of his or her separateness, experiences it as abandonment and as fraught with a sense of fundamental insecurity and anxiety. Though the child may develop competently intellectually, he or she will feel inadequate and dependent on outside sources for support, acceptance, and esteem. This contrasts with the children who have internalized a good enough mother and consequently a sense of themselves as good enough children.

The research on the neurotic fear of success has developed in an interplay between the clinical ideas presented above and the data from a long series of experiments and field studies. In *The Success Fearing Personality*, Canavan-Gumpert, Garner, and Gumpert (1978a) report a program of research which began with the work of Pappo (1972) and Cohen (1974). This review of research on neurotic fear of success draws on research reported in that book as well as subsequent research.

THE EARLY RESEARCH

The empirical work on fear of success began when Pappo, thinking in a Sullivanian perspective, constructed an 83-item, yes–no questionnaire to measure fear of success. In conceptualizing her notions about success fearers, Pappo postulated that they had the following characteristics: (1) low self-esteem (self-doubt), (2) a preoccupation with evaluation, (3) a preoccupation with competition, (4) a repudiation of competency, and (5) a tendency to sabotage success. The scale she constructed, the Neurotic Fear of Success (NFOS) Scale, was made up of self-referent statements derived from these defining characteristics of success fearers. She found concurrent validation for her scale in its negative correlation with both a measure of self-esteem and a locus of control measure and in its positive correlation with a measure of test anxiety. Thus, the low self-esteem, preoccupation with evaluation and competition (test anxiety), and repudiation of competence (external locus of control) were confirmed to correlate in the expected direction with the NFOS Scale.

To validate the instrument she conducted an experiment in which male and female students either high or low on her measure of fear of success were randomly assigned to either a manipulated success or average feedback condition.

The task she used was a reading comprehension task in which a pretest performance followed by the success or average feedback was used as a reliable basis for predicting an official posttest score. In fact, a decrement in performance from pretest to posttest was predicted and found for those individuals who had scored high on the NFOS Scale under success, but not average, feedback. The results of her experiment clearly indicated that even in a fairly trivial academic testing situation, men and women who were high in the neurotic fear of success sabotaged an experimentally manipulated success.

Thus began a fledgling theory about individuals who fear success, coupled with a reliable and valid instrument to identify them. It was Pappo's belief, and the focus of her instrument, that independent personal accomplishment was the object of the fear of success.

Stimulated by Pappo's work, Cohen, whose persuasion was Freudian, tested her disagreements with Pappo by constructing a modified scale and conducting another experiment. In her work on fear of success, Cohen asserted three interrelated propositions. First, the origin of the problem was the Oedipal complex as set forth by Freud. Second, consistent with the Oedipal complex, competition was the central instigator of fear of success, making fear of retaliation the underlying stimulus to the success fearer's sabotage of success. Finally, the pertinent successes were not simply independent accomplishments but virtually any competitive success.

Cohen's Fear of Success Scale differed from Pappo's primarily in the extension of success to interpersonal situations and in having 25% fewer items. She then conducted an experiment with male and female high school students from a blue-collar neighborhood in which she manipulated the sex of a competitor. Cohen reasoned rather ingeniously that for those students high in fear of success, if the Oedipal conflict were the underlying cause, then competition with the same-sex other would, because of the similarity to the same-sex retaliatory parent, raise more anxiety about retaliation and success. This would lead to a greater degree of sabotage than would competition with an opposite-sex opponent. Accordingly, Cohen staged a preliminary 10-person competition on a memory test (tachistoscopically flashed objects). After the preliminary contest, each subject was separately taken aside and told that he or she had done very well, and was now in a final 2-person competition to win the contest and 10 dollars. The sex of the opponent was randomly assigned so that there were both same-sex and opposite-sex pairs. The decrement in performance from the preliminary memory score to the score in the final competition was the dependent measure of self-sabotage.

Indeed, success fearing subjects' sabotage showed a greater decrement in performance in the same-sex than in the opposite-sex competition and in general more sabotage than those low in fear of success, who presumably have resolved their Oedipal difficulties. The experiment is open to an alternative interpretation: only the degree of competitiveness was really manipulated by the same-sex versus opposite-sex competition, in that more similar people are presumably better matched in ability and therefore the competition between them is greater than when they are dissimilar. Cohen's experiment is nevertheless a noteworthy attempt to establish *a priori* the influence of so intangible a variable as the Oedipus complex.

Whatever the potential criticisms of these studies, it would be imprudent to let them detract from the enormous contribution they made in demonstrating that empirical research was possible and fruitful with a notion (fear of success) that while observable, had not been made amenable to scientific investigation. Despite their intended differences, the Pappo and Cohen scales correlate very highly with each other (.88) and are reliable (.90 to .92) and essentially interchangeable as research instruments.

Building on this earlier work, three social psychologists, Canavan-Gumpert, Garner, and Gumpert, and many of their students continued to develop both the research and the underlying ideas. Their continuation of the research bears the earmarks of social psychology, in that the work is an analysis of fear of success from a person–situation interaction model in a Lewinian tradition. In the subsequent research program they enlarged the concept of fear of success to include three achievement related motives: the motive to succeed, the unconscious motive to avoid success, and the motive to avoid failure. Further, they enlarged the situational perspective of the success fearer to include failure. With this broadened perspective and a classic conflict model (avoid failure, consciously approach success/unconsciously avoid success), they were able to delineate motivational tendencies and behavioral predictions for success fearers as a function of where they stood subjectively with respect to failure or success. A classic approach–avoid conflict is at the heart of the success fearer's dilemma, with the modification that the success-avoidant motive is unconscious and only inferable from the avoidant behavior of the success fearer in that region. Thus, the success fearer who is unambivalent about failure moves away from failure but vacillates toward and away from success in much the same way that a laboratory rat, who is hungry, moves toward and away from an electrified grid which holds cheese:

Failure (−) -- (+/−) Success

Near failure, the success fearer, though anxious, experiences the motive to avoid the humiliation of failure and thus moves effectively out of the failure zone. Safe from failure, but not close to success, the success fearer (like many other people) entertains a strong desire to succeed, anticipates that success will be gratifying, and usually performs at the same level as nonsuccess fearers. As in the approach–avoid conflict, the pull of the success motive recedes, and the repellent quality of the avoidance motive takes precedence as the success becomes imminent. Thus as the success draws near, the success fearer, now under the influence of the unconscious motive to avoid success, usually experiences anxiety, impaired concentration and immobilization, and frequently sabotages the success.

The success fearer's conflict differs from the totally typical approach–avoid conflict only in that the avoidance motive or the reason for it is not conscious. Thus the success fearer, for the purpose of intrapsychic defense, must rationalize the sabotage or success avoidance. Typical rationalizations include seeing the self-sabotage as externally inflicted or citing another motive, as did a researcher who had spent countless years solving a problem and when he had, claimed he was too bored to bother publishing the findings. Thus he protected himself from the rewards of his success.

Examples of typical success fearers follow. One student, evaluated as doing poorly in a Ph.D. program, got the top grade on the qualifying exams, and then proceeded to lose all the copies of her dissertation to a thief who simply snatched the elegant briefcase in which they were residing from an unlocked car. The student was shocked that anyone could have been so cruel as to steal all the copies of her dissertation. She simply did not see that she had virtually invited the theft of the briefcase, which from the thief's point of view happened to be stuffed with paper. A dieter successfully lost all the pounds between herself and her ideal-size jeans; when she could just close the zipper, she was inexplicably seized by an uncontrollable desire to raid the local bakery. Kaplan (1979) describes as having fear of romantic success individuals whose sexual adjustment before marriage is excellent but who respond to the success of the marriage with a disorder she calls failure of sexual desire. Interestingly, she regards impotence, frigidity, and premature ejaculation as much easier problems for the sex therapist to help solve, but she sees failure of sexual desire as a deep-seated problem.

There are innumerable stories, beyond coincidence when taken as a group, of debilitating accidents which prevent artists, performers, and athletes from engaging in that crucial contest or performance. It is not that clinicians do not believe in bad luck, but the critical question "Why now?" frequently leads to the suspicion of fear of success over bad luck. Thus, in everyday life it is important to look at the timing of changed motives and plans, psychosomatic illnesses, unanticipated pregnancies, and accidents as convenient, if not invited, fates.

In addition to the three achievement-related motives, success fearers, as previously indicated, are characterized by the following five traits: low self-esteem, unstable self-esteem, a preoccupation with evaluation, a preoccupation with competition, and a tendency to repudiate their competency. These characteristics of success fearers are conceptualized as a defensive strata which serve to express indirectly the success fearer's unconscious ambivalence about being independent and willfully responsible for succeeding. These characteristics enable success fearers unconsciously to manipulate themselves into situations, for example, procrastination, which permit them to strive for success with minimal perceived personal responsibility; that is, they see their behavior as responsive to an external threat rather than internal initiative. These characteristics provided the underlying rationale for the items on the questionnaires that first Pappo and later Cohen designed to measure fear of success.

A success in this conceptualization can be any goal an individual sets out to accomplish. Though the goals success fearers sabotage are usually conventional, such as scholastic, work, and romantic goals, they can also include athletic, artistic, appearance, and hedonistic or acquisitive goals. Success fearers thus can be found on baseball fields, in the stock market, in politics, and at diet and fitness workshops, as well as in poetry contests, in Gamblers' Anonymous meetings, and in love. They simply must have chosen a goal that they want and have worked to achieve, and then they have sabotaged that goal unintentionally as it drew near. People who allow themselves to succeed and then become depressed or otherwise deprive themselves of the rewards of the success are also considered success fearers, though this manifestation has been given less attention.

Earlier research had already established that success fearers sabotaged their performances in anticipation of winning a competition and in the face of imminent task success and that under ordinary performance conditions they did not differ from nonsuccess fearers. In a first group of studies, Canavan-Gumpert *et al.*, (1978a) set out to establish the antecedents of fear of success and that success fearers were also failure avoiders.

THE ANTECEDENTS OF FEAR OF SUCCESS

In order to investigate the antecedents of fear of success, it was necessary first to construct a scale to measure fear of success in children and also to do a validation experiment that demonstrated that fairly young children fear success and, like their adult counterparts, sabotage an imminent success. The Children's Fear of Success Scale was constructed essentially by simplifying and making age appropriate many of the statements on the Pappo and Cohen scales. Then, with age-appropriate materials, Pappo's original experiment was replicated with third through fifth graders in a suburban elementary school. It was impractical due to potential limitations in reading ability to go to a younger age than 8. The study of both boys and girls replicated the results of the Pappo experiment; children high in the Children's Fear of Success Scale showed performance decrements when served with success feedback, and the two groups did not differ in response to average feedback. Many of the teachers at the school confided interest in the work, noting that they had believed that some students feared success but that they were afraid to label it that; instead, they had been calling the reversals of improving students fear of failure, a misnomer they confessed to be relieved to be rid of.

In order to investigate the antecedents of fear of success directly, it was decided to observe children high and low in fear of success in interaction with one of their parents in an achievement-related context. The design of the study involved inviting, by random selection, an equal number of fathers and mothers of boys and girls who were both high and low in the fear of success. In the procedure of the observational study, the parent was asked simply to note whether his or her child's performance in the situation was typical. Under the pretext of studying how children do different kinds of tasks, the child was presented with a series of Scrabble letters in the form of a large word like "chrysanthemum" and asked to construct as many smaller words from the letters as was possible in a timed period. It was clearly stated that only the words produced by the child himself or herself would count. There were three trials of two words each. The first trial was followed by average feedback, the second by success feedback. The study was conducted in the library of a heterogenous urban elementary school. Two trained observers, blind to the fear of success category of the child, coded the parent–child interaction.

While the study showed no effects due to either the sex of the child or the sex of the parent, there was an overall performance difference. The success-fearing boys and girls who were accompanied by the same-sex parent performed at a lower level on the word construction task than did the success-fearing children accompanied by the opposite-sex parent. They also performed at a lower level than any of the nonsuccess fearing children. This result obviously gives some support to Cohen's notions about the importance of the Oedipus complex in the origins of fear of success.

Perhaps somewhat more astonishing, at least under public observation, were the parent behaviors. The parents of success-fearing children were more likely to be active and intrusive in their interactions with their child. They were more likely to criticize their child, give hints and instructions, and make comments about the child to the experimenter, although they were *not* more likely to give praise or encouragement. In addition, it was only the parents of success-fearing children who gave the child words, moved the child's Scrabble letters, and in several instances actually pushed the child aside and started making the words themselves. By contrast, the parents of nonsuccess fearing children sat quietly and calmly observed.

These intrusive behaviors on the part of success fearers' parents of both sexes, while more congruent with the notions of conflict about independence and security than they are with the Oedipal notions, tell us something specific about how independence is preempted, criticized, and indeed, prevented. The parents' intrusive behavior can be seen as both competitive with the children and as indicating that the parents are somewhat psychologically unseparated from their children, insofar as they seem to regard their children's performances as extensions of their own performances and to feel personally apprehensive about the quality of the child's performance. While one might deem it normal for a parent to feel personally evaluated as a function of the child's performance, it is important to remember in this study that it was explicitly stated that only the child's own words counted toward the score and that the parents of nonsuccess fearing children were content not to interfere. The correlation between these children's fear of success scores and the fear of success scores of the accompanying parent was .40, a positive and moderate correlation (Gumpert, Canavan-Gumpert, & Garner, 1978).

In another study of family interaction, the same correlation, .41, was found between the fear of success scores of both parents. Apparently success fearers tend to marry success fearers, to a moderate degree. In addition, the parents of success fearers were more likely to agree to a postexperimental question stating that all in all they had mixed feelings about their desire for their children to be successful (Canavan-Gumpert *et al.*, 1978a; Gumpert, Canavan-Gumpert, & Garner, 1978).

FEAR OF SUCCESS AND FEAR OF FAILURE

The question was frequently raised whether fear of success was not simply fear of failure, that is, that success fearers near success simply feared that they would fail to succeed, got anxious, and thus performed poorly. This question is, on the face of it, more compelling if we consider (1) the high correlation between fear of success and measures of text anxiety, which are frequently seen as measures of fear of failure; and (2) the fact that most of the success fearers fall into the fear of failure quadrant on the Atkinson measures which assess need for achievement versus fear of failure (Boardman, Gumpert, & Canavan-Gumpert, 1982). Since this model of fear of success describes success fearers as both fearing success and sabotaging when success is near *and* as fearing failure but improving to avoid failure when failure is near, an experiment manipulating both success and failure was conducted (Canavan-Gumpert *et al.*, 1978a) to demonstrate that success fearers have both motives and that the motives are different, since success fearers are predicted to sabotage success but to improve after failure.

The task was presented as a test of whether undergraduates, raised in a television generation, were still able to communicate the music and meaning of poetry in reading aloud. The participants, who were either high or low on the Cohen measure of fear of success, stood before a one-way mirror and recited from memory and then read a stanza of a Dylan Thomas poem. The experimenter then delivered randomly assigned false feedback from the bogus judges from the English department who presumably stood behind the one-way mirror. In order for the judges to be certain of their evaluation, the participants were asked to read another stanza. Finally, for an ostensibly different purpose, the subjects were then asked to complete another task—four cards on the Witkin Embedded Figure Test. The dependent measures in the experiment were the pretest to posttest differences in the number of stutters, stammers, and slurs in the poetry reading and the number of correctly memorized words, as well as the performance on the Embedded Figure Test.

As predicted, the success fearers showed a performance decrement after success and a performance increment after failure, while the reverse was true for the individuals who were not success fearers. In addition, the success fearers who had received success feedback and sabotaged their success performed better on the Embedded Figure Test, presumably a reinstigation of their desire to do well after the sabotage. Thus we see that while the success fearers are anxious in the face of evaluation, the anxiety or energy is put to very different use depending on whether success or failure is the perceived threat.

Success Fearers in Everyday Life

A series of field studies (Garner, Gumpert, Canavan-Gumpert, & Headen, 1978) provide further corroboration for the duality of fear of success and fear of failure in success fearers. In an introductory psychology course taught by programmed instruction, where students could take the tests on their own schedule and in which a special test had to be taken at the end in order to get an A, success-fearing as compared to non-success-fearing students procrastinated, put off the tests until the end, and were less likely to take the special test required to get an A. The transcripts of success-fearing students as compared to non-success-fearing students showed much greater performance vacillation or "spotty records": more categories of grades, withdrawals, and the like, were required to describe their transcripts, and this vacillation was reflected in their having a lower grade point average. In response to questionnaire items success fearers reported greater indecisiveness and conflict: they found it more difficult to choose a major and were more dissatisfied with the major they did choose, and they were more likely to change majors, and even to take leaves of absence from school.

In another survey success fearers reported experiencing a series of conflicts to a greater degree than the nonsuccess fearers. A factor analysis reduced the 33 conflicts to 5 factors, presented in the order in which success fearers experienced them:

1. *Conflict over competence and adequacy* (Wanting to be decisive and assertive but fearing that I am not)
2. *Conflict over intrinsic versus extrinsic orientation* (Living up to my own ideas of myself versus doing what important others expect of me)
3. *Conflicts over adult pursuits and values* (Being more achievement oriented versus being more relaxed and unconcerned about middle-class values)
4. *Conflicts over achievement versus interpersonal issues* (Wanting to combine marriage, family, and career, but fearing it is too much to handle)
5. *Conflicts between achievement and rejection* (Getting ahead in life but fearing that will alienate other people)

In a study of male and female law students (Curtis, Zanna, & Campbell, 1975), those high on Pappo's measure of fear of success reported wanting to volunteer answers in class but not doing so, being less satisfied with law and more satisfied with previous experience, lower law board scores, and lower ratings of their ability at logical abstract thought. However, these students neither reported nor expected lower grades, nor were they less likely to report their high grades to classmates.

Taken as a whole these data clearly present the success fearers as procrastinating, indecisive, conflicted in their motives, and vacillating in their behavior toward and then away from success. As we shall see, in those circumstances where success avoidance can only be accomplished by failure, such as drinking alcohol for an alcoholic or resuming compulsive eating and thus gaining weight, the vacillation swings between failure and success without the ability to accept either.

THERAPEUTIC SITUATIONS: SETUPS OF DEFEAT FOR SUCCESS FEARERS

Though somewhat oversimplified, the guidelines in therapeutic and change programs are the following: anticipate success, reward success, ignore failure, and present successful models for identification. While these rules assist normal people in change efforts, they are not likely to be effective with success fearers who sabotage success, flee successfully from failure, feel anxious about imagining success, and feel inferior to rather than identified with people doing better than themselves. Two field studies (Garner *et al.*, 1978) illustrate these points. The first was conducted with female clients at a diet workshop. As compared with participants low in fear of success, those high in fear of success missed more meetings, experienced anxiety at imagining themselves attaining their goal of slimness, and felt more anxiety at hearing of others' progress as well as concommitant anxiety and dissatisfaction with their own progress. The success-fearing dieters came to the workshop less overweight and at an average younger age than the non-success-fearing dieters. Thus, the typical reward strategies had the reverse effect for the success fearers. That the success fearers came younger and lighter, that is, sooner, is a positive sign, but one which is best understood as a consequence of their particular sensitivity to failure.

A more acute picture of vacillating between success and failure was found in a group of men in a detoxification center. On the average their fear of success scores, as was also true of the dieters, were much higher than comparable groups of men and women who were neither alcoholic nor in a diet workshop. In response to an open-ended question inquiring when they were likely to drink, all the men reported depressing events like loss of a job, interpersonal rejection, and frustration. Only the success-fearing alcoholics, however, reported drinking to celebrate promotions, successes, and positive family events. Certainly for an alcoholic to toast to success with alcohol is sabotage. Finally, success-fearing alcoholics reported more detoxifications. Every detoxification after the first is simultaneous evidence of sabotage of an earlier success of achieving sobriety as well as moving away from the failure of drunkenness. A related group that has received much attention, adult children of alcoholics, were found in a college sample to have higher fear of success than their counterparts from nonalcoholic homes. This was particularly true if the alcoholic parent and the student were the same sex (Canavan-Gumpert, 1985).

Lall (1981) conducted a laboratory experiment to confirm the finding in the field studies that the affirmation of one's ability to succeed leads to sabotage of the success for the success fearer but to success enhancement for the nonsuccess fearer; and that paradoxically, derogation of one's ability to succeed leads to an ability to maintain the success for the success fearer but to a loss of confidence and performance deterioration in the nonsuccess fearer.

Based on the idea that the rewarding of success leads to sabotage by success fearers, while the disavowal of success leads to an ability to maintain the success, an experiment was systematically conducted in which individuals high and low in the fear of success were all given success feedback on a reading task. The experimental manipulations of self-affirmation, self-derogation, and a control period on a distraction task were utilized in order to show that success fearers can sustain success better in the face of self-derogation and that self-affirmation, rather than building confidence, leads to an increased tendency to sabotage.

The results of the experiment clearly revealed that the success-fearing subjects who read self-affirming statements aloud from a preestablished group of statements were more likely to sabotage their success than the control group. Also, the success-fearing subjects who, despite the success, read self-derogating statements from a preestablished set, in fact, sustained their success and improved in a second performance. The prepared statements were used to equalize the manipulations for all subjects. As had been anticipated, when asked to produce their own statements, success fearers produced more self-derogating and fewer self-affirming statements than did subjects low in fear of success, whose production pattern was reversed.

In addition to reconfirming the well-established finding that success fearers sabotage their success, this experiment shows that the sabotaging tendencies are enhanced by self-affirming responses and paradoxically reduced by self-derogation. It is common experience to those who know success fearers well that they frequently fear or postulate the proximity of failures the observer cannot corroborate. This study gives a first clue that success fearers lead a fairly complex intrapersonal emotional life, trying to scare themselves, as it were, with a serviceable motive—fear of failure—into backing into success. Their tendency to procrastinate has the same effect. It moves them away from a success region into a failure region, from which they can then succeed or at least avert a failure by calling on their motive to avoid failure. Buried in this convoluted pattern is the success fearers' very strong motive to succeed coupled with their inability to be directly responsible for their success. Thus, it is the buried desire to succeed which sensitizes success fearers to "select" certain situations (threat of failure, deadlines) that lead to the internal psychological reactions (fear of failure, self-derogation) which then allow and motivate them to actually succeed.

It would not be surprising to find that success fearers who succeed have taken longer to get to their goals, have incurred more pain along the way, and have achieved a lesser level of success than might be expected of their non-success-fearing counterparts. The following descriptions of two successful success fearers illustrate this point. One professor, outstanding as a graduate student, got his Ph.D. 2 years late because he lost a trunk full of handwritten notes made from texts in a foreign country. Upon completion of the Ph.D., he took a post in a conservative department at a first-rate university but was not tenured because he blatantly espoused liberal political opinions and wore only purple clothes. Several years later he almost missed a final tenure chance at a lesser university when he refused to reduce a huge manuscript to a conventional-sized book, guaranteed to secure him tenure, because he was afraid of losing a prizewinning book in the process. In another instance an aspiring applicant, interviewing at a top medical school, felt that since her integrity was on the line, she had to express her opinions on the evils of modern medicine. She became a physician after graduating from a lesser medical school and only after taking several leaves of absence for a curious back ailment.

The whole pattern of research so far compels us to ask under what conditions can success fearers succeed without sabotaging?

WHEN SUCCESS FEARERS CAN AND CANNOT SUCCEED WITHOUT SABOTAGING SUCCESS

Canavan-Gumpert *et al.* (1978a) attempted to provide the conditions under which success fearers could succeed without sabotaging. Their experiment was based on the reasoning that if success feedback were not explicitly delivered while success fearers gradually improved in their task scores, then perhaps they could tolerate the continued improvement—a sort of success. Subjects high and low in fear of success completed four trials at a task, after each of which they received successively increasing bogus task scores in percentile form. Actual performance for both groups gradually improved until the fourth bogus score, reported in the 92nd percentile, at which time the success fearers sabotaged their performance; the nonsuccess fearers did not. This result indicated that the success fearers' fear of success and of potential competition was sufficient for them to project those consequences, even in this fairly neutral situation.

This finding led to the postulation that an active manipulation would be necessary to counteract their fear. Since competition and evaluation figure so prominently in the dynamics of the success fearer, a cooperative structure was selected where each member's success contributed to the success of the others and could not plausibly be used as grounds for anticipatory retaliation or rejection from the other members.

Accordingly, a laboratory experiment was conducted (Canavan-Gumpett, Garner, & Gumpert, 1978b) in which college students high or low in fear of success performed a task as a member of either a cooperative or a competitive group. In the competitive group each person's performance contributed to a team score which was compared to the team scores of other teams. After the first round each subject, unknown to the others, was given feedback that he or she had the highest score in the group. In the posttest performance which followed, the success fearers who were in the competitive group, as anticipated, sabotaged their success, while the nonsuccess fearers improved. In the cooperative condition, the success fearers were in fact able to maintain their pretest performance without sabotage, although they didn't improve. There were no significant differences in the mean performances between subjects high and low in fear of success in a third performance, in which subjects in the cooperative condition represented their team in a competition against other team representatives to determine the best team; subjects in the competitive condition represented themselves to determine the best player. An analysis of responses on the postexperimental questionnaire indicated that while the manipulation of cooperation and competition showed the appropriately reliable differences between conditions, these differences were much stronger for nonsuccess fearers. Nonsuccess fearers more readily perceived the cooperative condition as much more cooperative than did the success fearers, who seemed to have a difficult time perceiving a situation as cooperative. Another postexperimental questionnaire item posed an additional intriguing issue. Success fearers were asked whether while in the final competition they thought of the other team members or of their own performance. They indicated that they concentrated on their own performance, suggesting that perhaps rather than working for the team to deflect success anxiety from themselves, they used the protection of the cooperative team as an opportunity to reveal, at least to themselves, their motive to excel.

The difficulty of producing a strong cooperative manipulation for the success fearers in a laboratory led to the study of success fearers in already existing cooperative groups. The first choice, the Boston Symphony, declined on the grounds that they did not fear success. Some of the Boston College athletic teams, however, were in fact enthusiastic about being studied. Accordingly, responses to the fear of success scale and performance scores were obtained from members of the lacrosse, baseball, and basketball teams. In addition, based on a hunch, the coaches were asked to name the two best clutch players on each team. It was anticipated that the more cooperative the teams, the better the success fearer's performances would be. Further, the success fearers were expected to be overrepresented among the clutch players (a good guess on theoretical grounds; a statistical long shot with an $n = 6$).

The prediction about the clutch players was based on the notion that, like procrastination, the clutch is a situation in which fear of success is pitted against fear of failure. In a cooperative situation, fear of success is neutralized by the cooperative structure, but the fear of failure should be as active, if not more so, as in any other situation. In addition, the success fearer's motive to do well is unencumbered by the fear of success. Thus, all the performance vectors point to good performance in this situation. On two of the three teams the success fearers' performances were in fact *significantly better* than those of the nonsuccess fearers. On the third team, basketball, where some intragroup competition is fairly likely, the success fearers in fact did not perform worse than the nonsuccess fearers on points earned, but they did not perform better. The success-fearing basketball players did, however, show a higher performance on assists, passing the ball to another player who got the points.

All six of the clutch players were high in fear of success. It is worth noting here that the average fear of success score of the college athletes did not differ from the average score of male students in the same school who were not athletes. Perhaps success fearers are not afraid to compete or try out for a success in which they join, rather than get separated from, people, as is common in most successes, including graduation or getting released from prison or a psychiatric hospital.

Though one is admonished not to look a gift horse in the mouth, these results, given the track record for success fearers, seemed too good to be true. None of the previous studies nor any of the theory gave any reason to believe that success fearers might be any more able than nonsuccess fearers. Why then at their best should they do better than nonsuccess fearers? Within the context of the theory, one possible reason is that their extreme antipathy for failure leads them to better performance when faced with failure, while the performance of nonsuccess fearers tends to deteriorate in the face of failure. For the nonsuccess fearer, success breeds success and failure breeds failure, and this does not differ much as a function of whether the context is cooperative or competitive. For the success fearer, success breeds sabotage and failure breeds success in the competitive context, but in the cooperative context, both success and failure lead to success. There is yet another possibility, which is that for the success fearer, more motives than achievement are invested in the achievement endeavors.

Schmid (1987) began his experiment by asking the question "What is the active ingredient in cooperation that enables the success fearers to do so well?" Two distinguishable though closely associated possibilities occurred. The first was that since each member's success contributes to the group's success in cooperation, the group members would have no reason to react negatively with rejection or retaliation to the success of a member. Thus fear of success is not activated. The more cooperative a group, the more this would be so. The second possibility is the assumption, frequently true, that in a cooperative group the members like each other, and presumably in a competitive group the members dislike and/or envy one another in proportion to the degree of success of the offending party.

With these ideas in mind, Schmid completed a dissertation in which he independently manipulated cooperative versus competitive group structure and information that group members did or did not particularly like each other, as well as success and average performance feedback on a word construction task. The subjects were male and female high school students who were either high or low in the fear of success. What he found overall was that the success fearers performed better as a main effect of both the liking variable and the cooperation variable but that the liking variable was stronger. The cooperation plus liking variable was strongest, but of interest here is that the competition plus liking condition was about as strong as the cooperation plus not-liking condition. The best performance of the nonsuccess fearers, on the other hand, was accounted for almost entirely by the success versus average feedback variable, whereas success feedback led to better performances on the part of the nonsuccess fearers.

This last study, oddly, takes us back to the first conflict between Pappo and Cohen of whether the success fearer's conflict originates in the pre-Oedipal separation–individuation conflict, in which the child requires the empathic, supportive, positive regard of the mother or mothering one as a precondition for independence and mastery, or whether, as Cohen contended with Freud, the conflict is Oedipal in nature. The two explanations are of course straw men for the fruitful generation of hypotheses, but the effectiveness of the liking manipulation even in the competitive group structure is too compelling not to remind us of the pre-Oedipal separation–individuation conflict, if for no other reason than that in cooperation the success fearer is not alone.

Still another experiment (Bordini, Gumpert, & Canavan-Gumpert, 1982) demonstrates that the operation of the liking variable is indeed complex. Male and female groups of same-sex composition were joined on the pretext of performing an impression formation task. After each of the four members took 5 minutes to tell the others something about himself or herself, each of the group members rated each of the others on characteristics such as intelligence, attractiveness, and sense of humor, as well as associating each member with a model of automobile. The impressions were collected and bogus feedback was privately delivered to each member, randomly putting him or her into either a competitive social acceptance or competitive social rejection condition. In the acceptance condition the subject was told that he or she was rated as most popular by all the other group members due to the overall high characteristic ratings. The subject in the rejection condition was told that he or she had received the lowest ratings in the group and that the other members had expressed some reservations about him or her.

After the feedback the subjects were asked to complete a posttest performance measure (Wesman Personnel Classification Test; Wesman, 1947), which was presented as a follow-up to the pretest measure they had completed along with the Cohen Fear of Success Scale 2 weeks earlier. The results showed that the success-fearing subjects who had just received the group popularity feedback showed a decrement from their pretest performance on the academic task, while the success-fearing subjects who had just received rejecting feedback, in fact, showed task improvement. The reverse was true for the nonsuccess fearers; their performance improved after competitive acceptance and worsened after rejection.

Taken in the context of the other research, this study can, with some guardedness, be interpreted as an extension of Cohen's study to demonstrate that competitive success, paradoxically, even in popularity, raises the success-avoidant anxiety of success fearers so that they sabotage even a different performance, in this case one in the academic realm. Similarly, the positive anxiety released in conjunction with a social failure, the group rejection, led to an unusually effective performance in another sphere, the academic. This experiment admittedly raises more questions than it answers, but it is nevertheless intriguing in that it suggests that success fearer's usual responses of sabotage of success and improvement after failure can be transferred from one domain to another, in this case from the social to the academic. The experiment also suggests that for success fearers, being liked or being popular is similar to other successes, and not acceptable under competitive conditions. It is hard to ignore the similarity of this dilemma to the Oedipal dilemma, in the sense of the same-sex competition about being preferred, with the subsequent fear of retaliation. Certainly some of this element must exist for the children of alcoholics, whose fear of success is very high, if the same-sex parent is alcoholic.

Schmid's study demonstrated that either cooperation or liking provides the conditions under which success fearers can succeed without sabotage. Taken together with the findings that being competitively accepted leads to sabotage and that in the clutch the success fearers think of their own performance rather than the group's, Schmid's study leads to another speculation: success fearers are looking for the right degree of liking, which like a good enough mother is not an affiliative end in itself but rather a precondition for the development of independence strivings. It seems plausible to posit that success fearers enter the achievement arena with an insecurity or esteem deficit which makes it necessary to get something in the situation as a precondition to being motivated to show their best performance. Either cooperation or liking provides that security for them. The nonsuccess fearers, on the other hand, bring that sense of security and of being liked with them, as evidenced by their being unaffected by the cooperation or the liking variable, but instead being motivated to perform better by the success manipulation.

The next important question is whether the cooperation–liking variable is an end in itself, that is, do success fearers do well in order to be liked? Or is it a protective step along the way to further achievement of independence? That is, as suggested above, does being liked provide a kind of protection against retaliation and rejection which in turn provides the space for the emergence of independent, perhaps even competitive, achievement motivation?

This section on the neurotic fear of success closes with two bits of data pertinent to these questions, which are compelling issues for future research. The first pertains to the study of the effects of manipulated cooperation and competition on the performance of success fearers (Canavan-Gumpert *et al.*, 1978b). In the last round, in which the subjects either represented their team or themselves in the final competition, while there were no significant differences in the mean performances, there was an interesting and significant performance difference, similar to the clutch player finding. The performance task was scored in terms of the number of errors subjects made. When the performance data were analyzed by the number of subjects in each condition who turned in perfect, errorless performances, a clear difference emerged. Of the 44 subjects in the experiment, 6 turned in perfect performances. Of those 6 subjects, 5 were success fearers in cooperative groups, and the remaining 1 was not a success fearer.

Second, on the Mehrabian scales measuring fear of rejection and need for affiliation (Mehrabian, 1970), the correlation between fear of success and fear of rejection was $r = .62$. Surprisingly, there was no correlation between fear of success and need for affiliation. Success fearers do not particularly crave affiliation but are quite afraid of rejection, and while representing a cooperative group in a final competition, they think about their own performance rather than that of the other group members. In addition, success fearers turn in excellent performances in this situation or in the cooperative and liking conditions of Schmid's experiment. Putting these findings together, it seems very likely that in liking or in cooperation, success fearers find protection and permission to develop further independence rather than an affiliative goal just for its own sake. Obviously these propositions require more specific formulation and testing.

FEAR OF SUCCESS IN SOCIAL PSYCHOLOGY

Despite an epic history in the annals of social psychology, the notion of fear of success, first introduced by Horner (1968), has only recently begun to be established as a systematic body of research, primarily in the work of Zuckerman and his colleagues (Zuckerman & Allison, 1976; Zuckerman *et al.*, 1980; Zuckerman & Wheeler, 1975). Like the proverbial caveat of killing two birds with one stone, the notion that women, but not men, fear success seemed to explain why the theory of achievement motivation had not been able to predict the behavior of women while simultaneously illuminating the uncomfortable observation that women did not achieve as highly as men.

Unfortunately, the idea almost fell under the weight of so great a promise, perhaps because of its inherent constraining requirements. Horner's ideas began as a set of testable hypotheses requiring a good deal of systematic thinking and research: the development of a reliable and valid instrument to measure fear of success, the theoretical relation of fear of success to the need for success, the fear of failure in the theory of achievement motivation, and then, an empirical study relating the three motives in men and women to predicted achievement-related behaviors. What appeared instead was (1) an intuitively appealing projective measure based on one stimulus cue ("After first-term finals Anne (John) finds herself (himself) at the top of her (his) medical school class"), to which 65% of the women and only 9% of the men told stories that revealed fear of success according to a present–absent scoring criterion, and (2) one study showing that women high in fear of success on this measure performed worse in a mixed-sex group testing situation (competitive) than they did in a testing situation in which they worked alone (noncompetitive), while the reverse was true for women low in fear of success. These preliminary findings were transformed in the heat of excitement about their plausibility into the solid empirical truths that women, but not men, feared success and that the success-fearing women withdrew from success in competitive situations. Thus was launched an ill-prepared inquiry into fear of success and achievement behavior. The virtual shower of research during the next years bogged down in controversy and confusion over whether women did in fact fear success more than men and also over whether fear of success systematically affected achievement-related behavior. Despite a revised measure to improve reliability (Horner *et al.*, 1973), little confirmation or advance beyond the 1968 research was attained. Among a number of reviews of this work, those of Tresemer (1974, 1976, 1977) and Zuckerman and Wheeler (1975) were particularly patient, painstaking, and, in fact, pained.

In brief summary, on the basis of the review of scores of studies, Tresemer and Zuckerman and Wheeler concluded that the Horner measure of fear of success (1) is not reliable, (2) frequently shows high scores for men as well as women, (3) is better understood as a measure of sex-role stereotypes than fear of success, (4) has not been related to a theory of achievement motivation in a clear fashion, and (5) has poor predictive validity. Finally, a careful scrutiny of the experiment reveals that it is seriously flawed. Zuckerman and Wheeler go so far as to say that the data can as easily be interpreted in the opposite direction: women high in fear of success do better in competitive situations.

Despite these devastating criticisms, Zuckerman and Allison (1976) remained respectful of the promise and intuitive appeal of Horner's original intent and set themselves the task of designing another measure of fear of success, one that was objective and suitable for both men and women. The Fear of Success Scale (FOSS) presents 27 items in a 7-point agree–disagree format. The statements were generated to describe the benefits of success, the costs of success, and the preferability of alternatives to success. FOSS shows adequate internal reliability (.71); in a series of studies it shows a correlation with the Horner measure from slightly positive to none, and a correlation with the Mehrabian (1968) measure of resultant achievement motivation from slightly negative to none. Finally, some studies show women scoring higher than men, and others reveal no differences between the sexes on FOSS.

Two experimental studies predicted and found differential behavior for both sexes as a function of their being high or low in fear of success. Zuckerman and Allison (1976) found that by varying low and high motivational conditions for the performance of anagrams, the high fear of success subjects performed worse. This result withstood a covariance analysis by the Mehrabian (1968) resultant achievement motivation score, thus eliminating low achievement motivation as an alternative interpretation. In addition, the high fear of success subjects felt it was less important to do well on the task, and they made more internal attributions for failure and external attributions for success than did low fear of success subjects, who tended to attribute success internally and failure externally. It should be noted, however, that the subjects high in fear of success actually varied little in their attributions. Regardless of success or failure, their attributions were at the neutral or very slightly internal point.

A second experiment (Zuckerman *et al.*, 1980) reasoned that, for individuals low in fear of success who presumably desire to maximize success and minimize failure, successful task outcomes lead to an enhancement of perceived personal competence, with a concommitant increase in task-related intrinsic motivation as well as desire to extend one's realm of control over the task. Failing outcomes reduce perceived competence and lead to task withdrawal, a reduction of intrinsic motivation, and relinquishment of control over the task. Since success fearers attribute success externally, it was anticipated that success would not increase their sense of competence and thus would not lead to an increase in intrinsic motivation or to an increase in desire to control the task.

Accordingly, Zuckerman *et al.* (1980) varied success/failure and choice/no choice (of the particular tasks) and then measured the amount of free time invested in the tasks, the amount of choice subjects desired on the anticipated next set of tasks, and the internal or external attribution of success and failure. As anticipated, both the male and female subjects low in fear of success, compared to the subjects high in fear of success, evidenced more intrinsic motivation, made more internal attributions under success, and more external attributions under failure. Subjects low in fear of success chose to maintain the degree of choice that had led to their success and to change the degree of choice that had led to failure; subjects high in fear of success did not show this pattern. Finally, under failure, subjects high and low in fear of success did not differ on any of the dependent measures. Success fearers consistently rated their performances lower than did nonsuccess fearers, though in fact there turned out to be no reliable differences.

In summary, Zuckerman and his colleagues have a reliable measure of fear of success which is not predictably correlated with either Horner's measure or with the Mehrabian measure of achievement motivation and which does not show reliable sex differences (the range of correlations was mentioned earlier). It does reliably predict different behavior for individuals low in fear of success as compared to those high in fear of success. Overall, these behavioral differences are that subjects low in fear of success perform better, perceive they perform better, make internal attributions about their performances under success and external attributions under failure, and in general behave in a fashion that maximizes their self-perceptions and their investments in behaviors which lead to and ensure success and its gratifying rewards, while those who fear success do not.

The experimental results are reported in this odd fashion in order to highlight a consistent peculiarity in most of the experimental data: the subjects high in fear of success do not differ on the dependent variables as a result of either the independent or intervening variables. Manipulation of success and failure, high or low motivational instructions, and choice or no choice did not differentially affect success fearer's performances. Taken as a whole the data show the nonsuccess fearers to be responsive to the independent variables in a way which is self- and success-enhancing. The success fearers are not responsive, which, in not taking advantage of opportunity, is self-defeating. It is almost as though the success fearers do not perceive that they have control over their outcomes and have made a commensurately lesser investment in the importance of and effort required to achieve success. Yet in a certain sense, the external control issue aside, perhaps this pattern of unresponsiveness to success is what was measured by FOSS: success has a lot of costs, fewer benefits, and other things are more important.

In any event, the work of Zuckerman and his colleagues has lifted the measurement of fear of success out of the entanglement of infinite arguments about projective tests into an arena where further research on the convergent and divergent relationships of FOSS to other individual differences variables (the need to affiliate and external locus of control come to mind) and further experimental research will result in a clearer, more developed conceptual framework. The production of a reliable measure, now independent of the old history and able to predict a variety of achievement-related behaviors, constitutes a solid, interesting, and promising beginning.

RELATIONSHIPS AMONG FEAR OF SUCCESS AND FEAR OF FAILURE MEASURES

Two studies (Gelbort & Winer, 1985; Griffore, 1977) of the relationship among measures of fear of success [Horner (FOS), Zuckerman (FOSS), and Pappo (NFOS)] and a presumed measure of fear of failure [the Alpert–Haber (1960) Debilitating Anxiety Scale (DAS)] in a multitrait–multimethod matrix show variable correlations among the measures of fear of success: Horner and Zuckerman (−.26, n.s.), Pappo and Horner (both n.s.), Zuckerman and Pappo (n.s., +.29). Correlations between the DAS and measures of fear of success were fairly stable, however: Zuckerman and DAS (+.23, +.43), Pappo and DAS (+.59, +.54), and Horner and DAS (n.s., +.18). One study (Gelbort & Winer, 1985) included the Birney *et al.* Hostile Press measure of fear of failure (Birney, Burdick, & Teevan,

1969), which was not related to the Pappo measure but showed a positive relation to the Horner measure (+.41), a negative relationship to the Zuckerman measure (−.26), and no relationship to the DAS, the other measure of fear of failure. The authors of both studies concluded that there was poor convergent validity among the measures of fear of success; thus, the measures of fear of success were probably measuring different rather than similar underlying constructs. In addition, they concluded that there was poor convergent validity among the measures of fear of failure, indicating that they, too, were tapping different underlying constructs. Finally, these authors warned that the consistent and somewhat high correlations of fear of success and fear of failure (most notably NFOS and DAS) and FOSS and DAS led to the inadvisability of assuming that fear of success is distinguishable from fear of failure.

A third study (Sadd, Lenauer, Shaver, & Dunivant, 1978) of the relationships among objective measures of fear of success found similarly high correlations between measures of fear of success and measures of test anxiety. (The measures used were Cohen, Pappo, and Zuckerman and Allison's measures of fear of success and three measures of test anxiety, including the Alpert-Haber (1960) facilitating and debilitating anxiety scales and the Sarason (1972) test anxiety scale.) In order to identify and thus disentangle underlying dimensions that the fear of success and the test anxiety scales might have in common, they completed a first-order factor analysis, which produced factors describing each of the measures, and then a second-order factor analysis which, using all the items on all the measures, produced essentially five new scales or factors:

Factor 1. Concern about negative consequences of success (reflects concern about jealousy, criticism, exploitation, and burdensome responsibility following success). First-order factors from the Zuckerman and Allison scale and from both the Pappo and the Cohen scales loaded highly on this factor.

Factor 2. Self-depreciation and insecurity (reflects failure to live up to one's own standards, self-consciousness, unassertiveness, and behavioral manifestations of insecurity). This factor is composed solely of factors from the Pappo and Cohen measures.

Factor 3. Test anxiety (reflects anxiety in specific testing situations). All of the first-order factors from all of the test anxiety scales and none of the components from any of the other scales load on this factor.

Factor 4. Attitudes toward success in medical school (is not pertinent to this discussion). None of the pertinent scales loaded on this factor.

Factor 5. Extrinsic motivation to excel (concerned with the extreme importance of success, status, and power). First-order factors from the Zuckerman and Allison scale and from the Pappo scale loaded on this factor.

In the final phase of this fine study, the authors related subjects' scores on each of the newly derived factors to their responses to a questionnaire asking them to indicate whether they suffered certain psychological and psychosomatic symptoms. Eighteen symptoms, including disturbance in sleep and eating habits, feelings of anxiety, loneliness, guilt, worthlessness, inability to concentrate, and inability to go on, were among those listed. Subjects who were high on Factor 2 (insecurity) indicated the greatest number of symptoms (14) dominated by feelings of worthlessness; subjects high on Factor 3 (test anxiety) indicated the second greatest number (10); high scores on Factor 1 (negative consequences of success) and Factor 5 (extrinsic motivation to excel) were related to few symptoms (3 and 2, respectively). The study taken as a whole shows that the deep conflict and anxiety of the neurotic success fearers is not shared by individuals who score as success fearers on the Zuckerman scale. It also shows that the individuals who have a great deal of anxiety and insecurity also have situational anxiety measured by test anxiety. However, as the orthogonality of the factors suggests, the underlying dimensions—deep insecurity and test anxiety—are different, though highly correlated.

One might draw the conclusion from these data that the test anxiety scales measure anxiety, not fear of failure, and that the Cohen and Pappo scales measure a deeper, more intense, and extensive amount of anxiety, insecurity, and conflict, but not specifically fear of success. It is important to note that these findings are consistent with the fact that the items on both the Pappo and Cohen scales were generated to tap low and unstable self-esteem, preoccupation with evaluation and competition, and repudiation of competency. These characteristics are conceived of as a defensive strata to protect the success fearer from the anxiety of being responsible for succeeding.

The relatively low, though frequently significant, correlations between the Zuckerman and Allison measures of fear of success and the measures of test anxiety, as well as the absence of first-order factors from the Zuckerman and Allison scale on Factor 2 (insecurity and self-depreciation), suggest that much anxiety has been resolved or avoided by these individuals by their depreciation of success. Yet as indicated in Factor 1 (negative consequences of success), the Zuckerman and Allison scale measures an avoidance motive toward success. High scores on Factor 2 describe individuals with feelings of worthlessness, guilt, loneliness, and indecisiveness, which suggest deep conflict less easily resolved. Thus, the neurotic fear of success scales which load on this factor describe individuals caught in conflict and vacillation who must enter the achievement arena to gain any sense of self-esteem, yet, because of their unconscious conflicts, sabotage their successes when they are imminent and thus perpetuate the conflict. It is perhaps more appropriate to say that the individuals who score high on the Zuckerman and Allison measure are success avoiders, while the individuals who score high on the Pappo and Cohen measures are, because of their insecurity and conflict, both success seekers and success fearers, as well as failure avoiders.

One final point. The findings in the Sadd *et al.* (1978) study suggests that the neurotic fear of success may be synonymous with general neuroticism. In order to investigate this possibility, Gumpert, Garner, Canavan-Gumpert, and Schmid (1978) conducted a study in which a group of male and female college students completed both the Cohen Fear of Success Scale and the entire Minnesota Multiphasic Personality Inventory (MMPI; Dahlstrom, Welsh, & Dahlstrom, 1972). Success fearers showed higher scores on Scale 2 (Depression), Scale 6 (Paranoia), Scale 7 (Psychasthenia), Scale 8 (Schizophrenia), and Scale 10 (Social Introversion). A composite profile constructed from the scores on the clinical scales of the success fearers in the top quartile of fear of success yields a classic 7-8/8-7, with Depression (Scale 2) third highest. The profile types (Graham, 1977) which best discriminate between high and low scores on fear of success are: type 7-8 (chronic feelings of inadequacy, inferiority, and insecurity); type 8-9 (individuals with high pressure and need to achieve but who, because of low self-esteem, limit their involvement in competitive achievement situations resulting in mediocre accomplishments); and type 2-7 (individuals who have a strong need for achievement and recognition of their accomplishments and who feel guilty when they fall short of their high goal aspirations). Thus, the success fearers are neurotic in specific rather than general ways. Their problems revolve around feelings of low and unstable self-esteem, a strong need to achieve, and unstable and conflicted motivation to achieve. Clearly these findings are consistent with the work on the neurotic fear of success.

With few exceptions (Birney *et al.*, 1969), the term *fear of failure* has been a misnomer or, as in the case of the work of Atkinson and his colleagues (1966), a contrived category. The most widely used measures, the Mandler–Sarason Test Anxiety Scale (Sarason, 1972) and the Alpert–Haber Debilitating Anxiety Scale (Alpert & Haber, 1960), are really, as their titles tell us, measures of anxiety and evaluation apprehension. It is thus not so surprising, after all, if these measures and their underlying constructs correlate positively with measures of neurotic fear of success, which are, in the main, measures of insecurity and conflict.

Unfortunately, it was not until recently that the notion that people would really fear success was an everyday thought. If we see anxiety and anxiety about evaluation (success or failure) as the core construct of all this controversy, then it seems less problematic. Unwittingly, scales are frequently identified formally and informally by the stimuli (success, failure) or behavior (self-sabotage, achievement behavior) they address. Once these semantic problems are laid bare, the correlation between (misnamed) measures of fear of success and (misnamed) measures of fear of failure is illuminating or even obvious. Surely, as in the work presented on the neurotic fear of success, one who might more appropriately be called high in evaluation apprehension might be shown to fear both failure and success but under different stimulus conditions and with different responses. The scales are most likely identifying the same people—anxious people. It is the task of the researcher to state an underlying theory about these people which postulates and provides a test of the conditions under which their anxiety will manifest itself as a fear of success or a fear of failure. It is probably time that we loosened, as another author put it (Hyland, Curtis, & Mason, 1985), the "bedeviling" grip that the theory of achievement motivation has had on this area of research.

With respect to the relationship among fear of failure and fear of success and a need for success, this is particularly important for two reasons. First, high need achievement versus high fear of failure is a contrivance arrived at by the particular crossing of scores on the Thematic Apperception Test (TAT) measure of Need Achievement and a test anxiety scale. Neither individual difference category exists in people in relatively pure form; otherwise, there would be one presumably unidimensional measure. Second, the TAT measure of achievement motivation requires the production of competitive imagery to obtain high scores. Although competitive orientation *and* low performance anxiety or their opposites are highly useful constructed categories in predicting risk and competitiveness, they may not be the best way to divide up a group to identify people who have particular fears of failure or of success.

One could argue that work on achievement behavior has been too long in the hold of the theory of achievement motivation (Atkinson & Feather, 1966; Atkinson & Raynor, 1974; Feather, 1982). Thus the validity of and room for other work to develop has been constrained by the requirement that it fit in or defend itself, too soon, against the Atkinson work. By requiring that the motive to succeed include a desire to compete and by excluding anxiety, a "pure" motive, the need to achieve, is constructed. By ruling out people who do not want to compete and by including anxiety, another pure motive, fear of failure, is constructed. This contrived state of affairs, together with the lack of recognition that a test anxiety scale may measure evaluation apprehension that is as pertinent to success as it is to failure, has led to a picture where we assume, because it can be constructed to be so, that people are composed of unidimensional motivational systems—either they fear failure or they want to succeed. Rather, in a full set of people, at least 75% of them can be better described as having some degree of conflict among three motives (fear of failure, need to succeed, fear of succeeding). This conflict may be resolved ahead of time fairly consciously and lead to a stable part of the personality (Zuckerman's FOSS). For others, the conflict may be unconscious and not resolved. Instead it will be played out differently, depending on the situational factors which energize or neutralize it (Canavan-Gumpert *et al.*, 1978a). That a measure cannot predict fear of success and fear of failure puts research requirements on how people can be, rather than asking how it is that they are. Why can't people fear success and fear failure, without researchers insisting that the two fears are the same thing? Certainly in the domain of affiliation people are allowed to fear isolation and commitment. They may be the same people but they are not the same fears.

Finally, much of the conflict experienced by people over competitive achievement may be illuminated by bringing the affiliation motive back into perspective, both as a motivator of people's behavior and as constituting a desirable goal which may be in conflict with competitive success. Some people, in moderating or recoiling from a competitive success, may be successfully achieving a two-pronged goal of doing reasonably well while also getting on well with other people. The truth of the matter is that in certain competitions for promotions and romantic partners, unlike Sunday afternoon tennis games, the person who loses is distressed and unhappy, and if the winner is sensitive he or she recognizes that distress as a cost of his or her own success. In line with this reasoning, Gilligan's work (1982) on feminine psychology suggests that women take special account of the feelings of others in their thinking and behavior.

While for some the (neurotic) fear of success involves self-sabotage and is self-defeating, for others (the social psychological concept) it may represent a careful attempt to weave one's way successfully enough in the interpersonal world, to do well, and yet not unduly hurt or offend others. In 1870 John Greenleaf Whittier had a young girl express these gentle sentiments:

"I am sorry that I spelt the word:
I hate to go above you,
Because," —her brown eyes lower fell,—
"Because, you see, I love you!"

He lives to learn, in life's hard school,
How few who pass above him.
Lament their triumph and his loss,
Like her, —because they love him.
(J.G. Whittier, "In School Days")

STATE OF THE THEORY AND IMPLICATIONS FOR FUTURE RESEARCH

Building on the early work of Pappo and Cohen, Canavan-Gumpert *et al.* (1978a) and the students and colleagues working with them have, during the 1970s and 1980s, produced a dozen experiments and field studies on the neurotic fear of success. These studies clearly support the underlying theory and demonstrate that children and adults of both sexes who are identified as success fearers sabotage an imminent success and improve in their performances when threatened with failure. In innumerable applied settings, schools, and athletic teams, and in various therapeutic and self-help oriented situations, they show procrastination, indecision, and vacillating behavior. Cooperation and supportive group acceptance seem to relieve their anxiety and insecurity and permit them to perform astonishingly well. Important questions for future research must investigate the question of whether and how success fearers can acquire an independent sense of security and identity or whether certain supportive social relationships are a prerequisite for them to be able to use their abilities productively. These questions parallel the most pressing questions that psychoanalysts and clinical psychologists are attempting to solve in the theories of self-psychology. Kohut (1971, 1984), Masterson (1985), and Miller (1981) are optimistic that a relationship with a "good enough psychotherapist" can result in a psychologically separate and secure self.

The social-psychological notion of feminine fear of success seems to have fallen by the wayside, although some clinicians, notably Krueger (1984), have applied notions related to the neurotic fear of success specifically to women in an enlightening fashion. The reformulation of fear of success by Zuckerman and Allison is a solid beginning point from which to develop theory and research about individuals who avoid rather than fear high levels of success in favor of maintaining internal balance and good social relationships. Future research in this area might fruitfully include a study of the affiliation needs of these individuals as well as address the question of the costs of foreclosing on success, not only in terms of accomplishments, but as Zuckerman *et al.* (1980) have demonstrated, in intrinsic motivation, self evaluation, and feelings of personal efficacy.

Finally, research on both neurotic fear of success and fear of failure has made it clear that grave problems in both theory and measurement exist in the general area of achievement motivation. Scales purported to measure the neurotic fear of success and fear of failure have been shown actually to measure different types of underlying insecurity and anxiety. The misnaming of these scales has caused untold confusion. The unraveling of this confusion has reaffirmed that it is prudent to name a personality measure accurately. In this connection, the section on neurotic fear of success might better be called insecurity and ambivalence about achievement. This confusion in the name of measures of neurotic fear of success and fear of failure has also pointed to the importance of emphasizing the underlying theory in predicting how individuals who score high on a particular measure will behave.

It is perhaps time to reflect on whether the entrepreneurial spirit, which formed the foundation for the conceptualization of achievement motivation and fear of failure in the fifties, has not given way to a new set of issues in the eighties. These issues might be described as the problems involved in acquiring a stable and positive sense of self and how that task contributes to and is affected by people's relationships with achievement and with other people (Canavan, 1986).

REFERENCES

Alpert, R., & Haber, R. N. (1960). Anxiety in academic achievement situations. *Journal of Abnormal and Social Psychology, 61*, 207–215.

Atkinson, J. W. (1957). Motivational determinants of risk-taking behavior. *Psychological Review, 64*, 359–372.

Atkinson, J. W., & Feather, N. T. (Eds.). (1966). *A theory of achievement motivation*. New York: Wiley.

Atkinson, J. W., & Raynor, J. O. (Eds.). (1974). *Motivation and achievement*. Washington, DC: Winston.

Birney, R. C., Burdick, H., & Teevan, R. C. (1969). *Fear of failure*. New York: Van Nostrand-Reinhold.

Boardman, S., Gumpert, P., & Canavan-Gumpert, D. (1982, August). *Fear of success, fear of failure, and need achievement*. Paper presented at the 90th Annual Convention of the American Psychological Association, Washington, DC.

Bordini, E., Gumpert, P., & Canavan-Gumpert, D. (1982, August). *Social acceptance, social rejection, and self-sabotage in success-fearers*. Paper presented at the 90th Annual Convention of the American Psychological Association, Washington, DC.

Canavan, D. (1986, August). *Psychological separateness in male and female college students*. Paper presented at the Twelfth International Conference on Improving University Teaching, Heidelberg, Germany.

Canavan-Gumpert, D. (1985, July). *A preliminary profile of the students who are adult children of alcoholics*. Paper presented at the Eleventh International Conference on Improving University Teaching, Utrecht, The Netherlands.

Canavan-Gumpert, D., Garner, K., & Gumpert, P. (1978a). *The success-fearing personality: Theory and research*. Lexington, MA: Lexington Books.

Canavan-Gumpert, D., Garner, K., & Gumpert, P. (1978b, August). *When success-fearers*

succeed: The effects of cooperation and competition. Paper presented at the 86th Annual Convention of the American Psychological Association, Toronto, Canada.
Cohen, N. W. (1974). *Explorations in the fear of success*. Unpublished doctoral dissertation, Columbia University, New York.
Curtis, R., Zanna, M. P., & Campbell, W. W. (1975). Sex, fear of success, and the perceptions and performance of law school students. *American Educational Research Journal, 11*, 187–197.
Dahlstrom, W. G., Welsh, G., & Dahlstrom, L. E. (1972). *An MMPI handbook* (Vol. 1, Clinical interpretation). Minneapolis: University of Minnesota Press.
Feather, N. T. (Ed.). (1982). *Expectations and actions*. Hillsdale, NJ: Erlbaum.
Freud, S. (1959). Some character-types met with in psychoanalytic work. In E. Jones (Ed.), *Sigmund Freud: Collected papers*, (Vol. IV, pp. 318–344). New York: Basic Books. (Original work published 1915)
Garner, K., Gumpert, P., Canavan-Gumpert, D., & Headen, S. (1978, August). *Field studies of conflict and self-sabotage in success-fearers*. Paper presented at the 86th Annual Convention of the American Psychological Association, Toronto, Canada.
Gelbort, K. R., & Winer, J. L. (1985). Fear of success and fear of failure: A multitrait–multimethod validation study. *Journal of Personality and Social Psychology, 48*, 1009–1014.
Gilligan, C. (1982). *In a different voice*. Cambridge, MA: Harvard University Press.
Graham, J. D. (1977). *The MMPI: A practical guide*. New York: Oxford University Press.
Griffore, R. J. (1977). Validation of three measures on fear of success. *Journal of Personality Assessment, 41*, 417–421.
Gumpert, P., Canavan-Gumpert, D., & Garner, K. (1978, August). *Fear of success and family dynamics*. Paper presented at the 86th Annual Convention of the American Psychological Association, Toronto, Canada.
Gumpert, P., Garner, K., Canavan-Gumpert, D., & Schmid, C. E. (1978, August). *MMPI profiles of success-fearers*. Paper presented at the 86th Annual Convention of the American Psychological Association, Toronto, Canada.
Horner, M. S. (1968). *Sex differences in achievement motivation and performance in competitive and non-competitive situations*. Unpublished doctoral dissertation, University of Michigan, Ann Arbor. An abridged portion, "The measurement and behavioral implications of fear of success in women," can be found in J. W. Atkinson and J. O. Raynor (Eds.), (1974). *Motivation and achievement*. Washington, DC: Winston and Sons.
Horner, M. S., Tresemer, D. W., Berens, A. E., & Watson, R. I., Jr. (1973). *Scoring manual for an empirically derived scoring system for motive to avoid success*. Unpublished manuscript, Harvard University, Cambridge.
Horney, K. (1937). *The neurotic personality of our time*. New York: Norton.
Hyland, M., Curtis, C., & Mason, D. (1985). Fear of success: Motive and cognition. *Journal of Personality and Social Psychology, 49*(6), 1669–1677.
Kaplan, H. S. (1979). *Disorders of sexual desire*. New York: Simon & Schuster.
Kohut, H. (1971). *The analysis of the self. A systematic approach to the psychoanalytic treatment of narcissistic personality disorders*. New York: International Universities Press.
Kohut, H. (1984). *How does analysis cure?* Chicago: University of Chicago Press.
Krueger, D. W. (1984). *Success and the fear of success in women*. New York: Free Press.
Lall, M. (1981). *The effects of self-affirmation and self-derogation on the performance of success-fearers*. Unpublished doctoral dissertation, Boston College, Chestnut Hill.
Mahler, M., Pine, F., & Bergman, A. (1975). *The psychological birth of the human infant: Symbiosis and individuation*. New York: Basic Books.
Masterson, J. F. (1985). *The real self*. New York: Brunner/Mazel.

McClelland, D. C., Atkinson, J. W., Clark, R. A., & Lowell, E. L. (1976). *The achievement motive*. New York: Irvington. (Original work published 1953)

Mehrabian, A. (1968). Male and female scales of the tendency to achieve. *Educational and Psychological Measurement, 21,* 493–502.

Mehrabian, A. (1970). The development and validation of measures of affiliative tendency and sensitivity to rejection. *Educational and Psychological Measurement, 30,* 417–428.

Menninger, K. A. (1938). *Man against himself*. New York: Harcourt Brace.

Miller, A. (1981). *Prisoners of childhood. The drama of the gifted child and the search for the true self*. New York: Basic Books.

Pappo, M. (1972). *Fear of success: A theoretical analysis and the construction and validation of a measuring instrument*. Unpublished doctoral dissertation, Columbia University, New York.

Sadd, S., Lenauer, M., Shaver, P., & Dunivant, N. (1978). Objective measurement of fear of success and fear of failure: A factor analytic approach. *Journal of Consulting and Clinical Psychology, 46,* 405–416.

Sarason, I. G. (1972). Experimental approaches to test anxiety: Attention and the uses of information. In C. D. Spielberger (Ed.), *Anxiety: Current trends in theory and research* (Vol. II, pp. 383–403). New York: Academic Press.

Schmid, C. E. (1987). *The effects of performance feedback, social acceptance and cooperative–competitive group situations on the performance of success-fearing persons*. Unpublished doctoral dissertation, Boston College, Chestnut Hill.

Sullivan, H. S. (1953). *The interpersonal theory of psychiatry*. New York: Norton.

Tresemer, D. (1974, March) Fear of success: Popular but unproven. *Psychology Today, 7*(10), 82–85.

Tresemer, D. (1976). The cumulative record of research on "Fear of Success." *Sex Roles, 2*(3), 217–236.

Tresemer, D. (1977). *Fear of success*. New York: Plenum.

Wesman, A. G. (1947). *Wesman Personnel Classification Test*. San Antonio, Texas: Psychological Corporation.

Winnicott, D. W. (1965). *The maturational processes and the facilitating environment. Studies in the theory of emotional development*. New York: International Universities Press.

Zuckerman, M., & Allison, S. N. (1976). An objective measure of fear of success: Construction and validation. *Journal of Personality Assessment, 40,* 422–430.

Zuckerman, M., Larrance, D. T., Porac, J. F. A., & Blanck, P. D. (1980). Effects of fear of success on intrinsic motivation, causal attribution, and choice behavior. *Journal of Personality and Social Psychology, 39,* 503–513.

Zuckerman, M., & Wheeler, L. (1975). To dispel fantasies about the fantasy-based measure of fear of success. *Psychological Bulletin, 82,* 932–946.

CHAPTER 8

CHOOSING TO SUFFER OR TO . . . ?

EMPIRICAL STUDIES AND CLINICAL THEORIES OF MASOCHISM

REBECCA CURTIS

Whether 'tis nobler in the mind to suffer
The slings and arrows of outrageous fortune
Or to take arms against a sea of troubles
And by opposing end them.
For who would bear the whips and scorns of time,
The oppressor's wrong, the proud man's contumely,
the pangs of disprized love, the law's delay,
The insolence of office, and the spurns
That patient merit of the unworthy takes,
When he himself might his quietus make
With a bare bodkin? Who would fardels bear,
To grunt and sweat under a weary life
But that the dread of something after death,
The undiscover'd country, from whose bourn
No traveller returns—puzzles the will,
And makes us rather bear those ills we have
Than fly to others that we know not of?
Thus conscience does make cowards of us all.
Shakespeare's *Hamlet*, act III, scene 1

She had consented to go away, to leave her home. Was that wise? She tried to weigh each side of the question. . . . Down far in the avenue she could hear a street organ playing. She knew the air. Strange that it should come that very night

REBECCA CURTIS • Department of Psychology, Adelphi University, Garden City, New York 11530.

to remind her of the promise to her mother, her promise to keep the home together as long as she could.... She stood up in a sudden impulse of terror. Escape! She must escape! Frank would save her. He would give her life, perhaps love, too. But she wanted to live. Why should she be unhappy? She had a right to happiness.... She felt her cheek pale and cold and, out of a maze of distress, she prayed to God to direct her to show her what was her duty. The boat blew a long mournful whistle into the mist. If she went, to-morrow she should be on the sea with Frank, steaming towards Buenos Ayres. Their passage had been booked. Could she still draw back after all he had done for her? Her distress awoke a nausea in her body and she kept moving her lips in silent fervent prayer. A bell clanged upon her heart. She felt him seize her hand:

All the seas of the world tumbled about her heart. He was drawing her into them: he would drown her. She gripped with both hands at the iron railing.

—Come!

No! No! No! It was impossible. Her hands clutched the iron in frenzy. Amid the seas she sent a cry of anguish!

—Eveline! Evvy!

He reached beyond the barrier and called to her to follow. He was shouted at to go on but still he called to her. She set her white face to him, passive, like a helpless animal. Her eyes gave him no sign of love or farewell or recognition.

Joyce's "Eveline" (1914/1969)

That people seek pleasure and avoid pain is an idea accepted by most psychologists, researchers, and clinicians, as well as any naive person on the street. Why people and animals would then apparently "choose" to suffer in various situations has been an enigma which has fascinated psychologists, philosophers, theologians, and poets. To be hurt or to hurt another is the choice in the minds of Shakespeare's Hamlet and Joyce's Eveline. It is also the choice facing the Bible's Abraham, Melville's Ahab, and Dostoevsky's "Man From Underground," among many others. What experiences lead to such a limited perception of life's alternatives? The situations leading to the first of these alternatives—the "choice" to suffer—is the focus of this chapter.

The puzzle of "masochistic" behavior can be explained in such a way that it becomes uninteresting by simply attributing it to a destructive instinct or to reinforcement history, or it can be examined much more thoroughly in an attempt to understand the precise conditions under which it occurs in laboratory settings, the family environment, and the other life experiences of many. Recent laboratory and clinical observations have converged upon some common conditions and themes which are articulated later in this chapter.

Although the focus in the current volume is upon research with humans, the empirical research with people on the "choice to suffer" is sparse when the "self-handicapping" paradigm (discussed by Berglas in Chapter 11, this volume) is excluded. Because there is a much larger body of work on self-punitive behavior in animals, and because these experiments provide considerable information regarding the conditions under which masochistic-like behavior occurs, the research with animals is reviewed as well. Although it may not be difficult to understand why the empirical and clinical observations have rarely been considered simultaneously, it is more surprising that the research by social psychologists and psychologists interested in learning and conditioning has not been examined conjointly. The current review attempts to integrate the findings of both of these bodies of empirical research with the major hypotheses of clinicians. Neither sexual masochism, psychotic masochism, nor "self-injurious behavior" which involves physical self-mutilation or harm (and appears frequently to result from neurological damage) is discussed in this chapter. The chapter focuses instead upon the more general kinds of masochistic behavior in social situations.

SUFFERING "THE SLINGS AND ARROWS OF OUTRAGEOUS FORTUNE": EXPERIMENTAL STUDIES OF MASOCHISM AND "CHOOSING" TO SUFFER

The present review considers three different areas of experimental research regarding masochism—research from the perspective of learning theorists, research from the perspective of developmental theory, and research from the perspective of social psychology. Although the present review attempts to consider all of the studies of masochism conducted with human participants, only the major findings of the research on masochism in animals is presented. More exhaustive surveys of the literature on masochistic-like behavior in animals can be found in Sandler (1968), Brown (1969), Melvin (1971), and Renner and Tinsley (1976).

Research from the Learning and Behavioral Perspective

The earliest studies of masochistic-like behavior are those of Masserman (1946). Masserman reports Erofeyeva's (cited in Masserman) observations that a dog fed only after a mild shock to its leg would soon learn to withstand the pain calmly and eventually give "indications of welcoming the 'unpleasant' experience preliminary to the feeding" (p. 110). If the current was made so strong as to cause tissue destruction, however, the dog's reactions immediately reversed and the dog would not tolerate even weak electrical stimuli. The dogs avoided painful stimuli that resulted in tissue injury which exceeded the gain from the satisfaction of hunger. Masserman also reports Slutskaya's (cited in Masserman) demonstration "that human infants could be made to show pleasurable anticipation of a previously resented needle-prick if it were repeatedly followed by feeding, provided only that the stimulus was not made excessively painful" (p. 110).

In Masserman's own studies cats first learned to depress a switch for food, then to depress the switch to administer shock to themselves before feeding. When barriers were put in the way of their feeding, some animals continued to depress the switch, receiving only the shock.

Masserman (1946) postulated that painful experiences came to represent part of the "sign-gestalt" for the satisfaction of biological needs and eventually were sought for their own sake. He asserted that the repeated seeking of painful experiences may not indicate an actual "'joy in pain'—a semantic and dynamically meaningless paradox—but rather (a) a compulsive urge to reexplore danger in order to dispel anxiety, or (b) (a compulsive urge to) attain symbolic goals" (p. 56). Work similar to that of Masserman (1946) was later conducted by Keller and Schoenfeld (1950) and by Green (1972). In the Keller and Schoenfeld study, shock became a secondary reinforcer after accompanying the presentation of food and, in the study by Green, after accompanying reinforcing electrical stimulation of the brain. Mowrer (1950) used Horney's (1939) term *vicious circle* to describe the behavior of rats taught to press a bar to turn off shock but later shocked for pressing the bar. The rats would then continue to press the bar to turn off the shock, regardless of its effect, thus perpetuating the "vicious-circle." Mowrer described this behavior as self-defeating, "yet self-perpetuating instead of self-eliminating" (p. 351).

Several experiments confirmed the observation that aversive stimulation would make behaviors more resistant to extinction (Gwinn, 1949; Solomon, Kamin, & Wynne, 1953; Whiteis, 1956) or increase responding when paired with reinforcement (Holz & Azrin, 1961). Nevertheless, some investigators (Imada, 1959; Moyer, 1955; Seward & Raskin, 1960) did not replicate this finding in similar situations. Therefore, Brown (1965, 1969; Brown, Anderson, & Weiss, 1965; Brown, Martin, & Morrow, 1964) began a program of research designed to clarify the variables affecting self-punitive responses. The basic paradigm of these studies as described by Brown (1965) first involves the training of animals to escape or avoid electric shock in a starting box and straight alleyway by running into a safe goal box. After this behavior has been firmly established, the subjects are given up to approximately 60 extinction trials on which no further shocks are received. For experimental subjects, however, shocks are introduced in the alley or goal box, though not in the starting box. Thus the rats may remain in the starting box without receiving any more shocks. The shocked animals persist in running through the electrified alley section significantly longer than the control rats never administered shock in the alley. It is this behavior which is self-punitive and "masochistic like" (Brown, 1965, p. 65). Brown cites Mowrer's (1950) views regarding why the rats should engage in this type of "vicious circle" behavior. Mowrer argued that the running persists even when it results in shock because fear has been conditioned in the starting box and fear reduction reinforces running. The fear aroused in the starting box is more noxious than the electric shock experienced in the alleyway. Brown suggests that an interpretation such as this can be applied to other instances of self-punitive behavior. He suggests that the religious fanatic, for example, may be a person who finds feelings of guilt and shame more painful than flagellation itself.

Since these early experiments, many researchers have investigated the percentage of punished extinction trials, the percentage of shocked acquisition trials, the intensity of the punishment, the strength of the response, and the length of the punishment zone (Sandler, 1968). The best explanation for the behavior still appears to be that the rats run from areas high in aversiveness to areas lower in aversiveness (Matthews & Babb, 1985). From the rats' avoidance of it initially, it appears that the shock is aversive and not pleasurable.

Dreyer and Renner (1971) subsequently criticized these studies on self-punitive behavior in rats because the methodology employed did not allow an adequate demonstration of preference for the behavior resulting in shocks. Dreyer and Renner and Renner and Tinsley (1976) reported conducting several experiments with both animals and humans using a paradigm in which the subjects were made aware that their own responses were turning on the shock—the human subjects informed by verbal instructions and the animal subjects made aware by blocking the response leading to punishment and forcing the response leading to nonpunishment. Renner and Tinsley (1976) concluded that the rats in the previous research were simply lacking important information about contingencies: "They were caught in a vicious circle of confusion, not in a vicious circle of fear" (p. 194). They conclude that "the key to breaking the circle was *knowledge*" (p. 194). Renner and Tinsley suggest that self-punitive behavior should not be labeled as masochistic unless the behavior is evoked in situations which meet the following conditions:

> (a) there are alternative behaviors available; (b) the individual is aware of these alternatives and their outcomes; and (c) our social normative values tell us the behavior is bizarre. (p. 196)

As the review of clinical theories of masochism indicates, it is unlikely that people would engage in self-punitive behavior if they knew of alternative behaviors which would achieve their desired outcomes and knew how to perform them. The way, however, to attain objectives as vague as the "sense of individuality" desired by Dostoevsky's (1864/1960) antihero from *Notes from the Underground* (quoted in the introduction to this volume) is not easily communicated by verbal instructions or a few trials of response blocking. Before we examine the clinicians' impressions of masochism, however, it is important to look at Harlow's comparative–developmental research and the research of experimental social psychologists.

Research from the Comparative–Developmental Perspective

Harlow and his associates (Harlow, 1962; Harlow & Harlow, 1971; Rosenblum & Harlow, 1963) also conducted studies in which masochistic behavior was observed. In the well-known studies of infant–mother attachment, air blasts had been found to be extremely aversive to infant monkeys. In a study by Rosenblum and Harlow (1963) of six monkeys deprived of their real mothers since birth, two were given surrogate wire and terrycloth mothers which periodically blasted compressed air out of many holes pierced in their frames, and four were given surrogate wire and terrycloth mothers without the aversive aspect. The two monkeys blasted with air by the surrogate mothers spent significantly more time on the surrogate mothers than the four control monkeys. Harlow and Harlow (1971) commented:

> Whenever the mother vented from her body streams of compressed air at high pressure, the babies were distraught. Their hair was blown flat to their cranium and away from their body; they closed their eyes and they screamed. Nevertheless, they never left the mother's body but instead clung to the mother with frenzied zeal while the ordeal was in progress. (p. 205)

RESEARCH FROM THE SOCIAL-PSYCHOLOGICAL PERSPECTIVE

The social-psychological research on masochism comes primarily from work on expectancy confirmation, although a study by Stone and Hokanson (1969) was designed to apply some of Skinner's (1953) ideas concerning masochism to the problem of coping with another's aggression. In addition, several studies from research on the resolution of conflict provide experimental evidence regarding the effects of masochistic strategies upon the partner's behavior.

Carlsmith and Aronson (1963) had postulated that the confirmation of expectancies was more pleasant than their disconfirmation. In a test of their hypothesis, experimental participants tasted a random sequence of bitter and sweet solutions. They found that when participants developed expectancies regarding whether the next trials' solution would be bitter or sweet, they judged the solutions to taste more unpleasant when their expectancies were disconfirmed. Thus, bitter solutions were rated more bitter, sweeter solutions less sweet.

Aronson and Carlsmith (1962) then questioned whether or not people would make their performance match their expectations, even if it meant lowering their performance by changing right answers to wrong answers. Their data confirmed this prediction. There was some difficulty replicating this finding if the initial answers of participants were made salient or recalled (Brock, Edelman, Edwards, & Schuck, 1965, Experiments 3, 7; Lowin & Epstein, 1965; Waterman & Ford, 1965) or if an audience was present (Ward & Sandvold, 1963). Brock *et al.* (1965, Experiment 1 & 2), however, replicated Aronson and Carlsmith's findings, and Cottrell (1965) replicated their findings both with and without an audience. Maracek and Mettee (1972) found that this type of sabotage was more likely to occur if participants who performed very well after developing a low expectation for their performance expected to be tested again in front of an audience than if they did not expect to be tested again. They interpreted this finding as indicating that people were unlikely to raise their self-evaluations if they were possibly going to need to lower them again in the future. Baumeister, Cooper, and Skib (1979) found that participants were likely to sabotage their performance when a good performance was correlated with a personality quality which was undesirable.

Aronson, Carlsmith, and Darley (1963) went on to investigate whether people would choose an unpleasant task over a neutral one if the unpleasant task was the one they were expecting. Their results showed that people who were expecting to taste bitter drinking solutions were more likely to choose to do so than were people who had not been given the unpleasant expectation. The other participants were more likely to choose a neutral task of comparing the weights of various objects. Foxman and Radtke (1970) replicated this finding. Walster, Aronson, and Brown (1966) subsequently found that experimental participants who were expecting an unpleasant event (tasting grasshoppers) shocked themselves more during a waiting period than participants who were expecting a pleasant event (tasting ice cream). Walster *et al.*, included another condition in which the tasting assignment was going to be determined later by a coin toss, thus creating a 50% probability of assignment to the unpleasant condition. Those participants behaved similarly to the participants with the pleasant expectation. Curtis, Rietdorf, and Ronell (1980), however, found that men who were waiting for an unpleasant event which was probably going to occur took more shock during the waiting period than men who were waiting for an unpleasant event which was certainly going to occur. Both groups also took more shock than men waiting for a pleasant event. Curtis, Mariano, and Gersh (1979) had previously found that a 90% probability of shock produced greater physiological arousal than a 99%, 50% or 10% probability of shock.

The experiments by Walster *et al.* (1966) and by Curtis *et al.* (1980) are important in that they demonstrate more than a simple expectancy confirmation or "self-fulfilling prophecy." These experiments show that people who hold expectations that one type of unpleasant event is going to occur will hurt themselves in other ways during the anticipation period. Further research (Curtis, Smith, & Moore, 1984) revealed that participants given the opportunity to shock themselves expected better outcomes in two different future situations than participants who were not in a condition in which they were asked to shock themselves. The participants acted in a way consistent with Reik's (1941) idea that masochists feel they are entitled to their pleasures as long as they suffer for them. People apparently believe that if they suffer they will be rewarded, as Lerner's (1980) "just world" theory postulates. Zuckerman (1975) had previously found that students who believed in a just world were more likely than those who did not to volunteer to help right before their exams, but not earlier in the semester to help both psychology experimenters and blind students. He interpreted these results as indicating that when rewards are desired, people who believe in a just world try to be deserving in order to get these rewards, even though the "deserving" behavior (helping others in this case) is not related in any obvious way to the satisfaction of their needs or wishes.

Curtis, Nyberg, and Smith (1982) and Ferrari and Curtis (1987) also found that people would punish themselves for past failures. In the Curtis *et al.* experiment, participants who had already tasted unpleasant foods self-administered more shock than participants who were still expecting to taste the unpleasant foods. In the Ferrari and Curtis experiment, participants were led either to be successful on two tasks or to fail at two or five tasks. Participants who had failed at five tasks subsequently self-administered significantly more shock than participants who had failed at two tasks or had been successful. The amount of shock taken was not related to either their belief in a just world or depression. Cohen and Tennen (1985) found, however, that male students who were either depressed or noncontingently reinforced (helpless) engaged in more self-punitive behavior (blasting themselves with noise) than anxious, contingently reinforced, or nondepressed–nonanxious participants. Levey (1983) had also found that depressed students were more likely to self-handicap by choosing to play a piece of music which had supposedly been found to interfere with task performance as opposed to a piece of music which would probably facilitate their performance.

Comer and Laird (1975) found differences between the attributions of people who chose to engage in an unpleasant activity after having anticipated doing so and people who chose the more pleasant alternative. Those participants who chose to engage in the unpleasant activity (tasting a worm) made changes in their attributions about *themselves* during the waiting period, either deciding that they were brave or that they deserved to suffer, whereas participants who chose not to engage in the unpleasant activity made changes in their attributions about the *situation*, deciding that tasting the worm wouldn't be so bad after all.

Questionnaire studies on masochism have been conducted by Leary (1957) and Shore, Clifton, Zelin, and Myerson (1971). Leary's analysis of interpersonal and intrapsychic processes found that patients weighted heavily on the masochism dimension had few psychosomatic disorders except for neurodermatological ones. The masochistic patients stayed in therapy longer than hysterical, narcissistic, psychosomatic, or managerial patients and were motivated for therapy, but not for change. Shore *et al.* conducted a factor analysis of items in a masochism questionnaire and identified three different types of masochists: (1) "victims," who were in an intense relationship with someone who mistreated them emotionally or physically; (2) "doers," who were engaged in altruistic self-sacrifice and self-effacement; and (3) "somatizers," who presented medically unsubstantiated physical complaints.

Questionnaires have also been developed which measure people's general tendencies toward chronic self-destructiveness (Kelley *et al.*, 1985) and self-handicapping (Rhodewalt, Saltzman, & Wittmer, 1984). The scale developed by Kelley *et al.* taps four characteristics: carelessness, poor health maintenance, evidence of transgressions, and lack of planfulness. Those who scored high in chronic self-destructiveness were found to be more frequently in treatment for drug or alcohol abuse, to report having cheated in courses, to have delayed in getting a medical test for cancer, and to have received more fines for driving violations. Rhodewalt *et al.* (1984) found that athletes who scored high on a self-handicapping scale did not practice as much before important meets as athletes with lower scores on this scale, although there were no differences in the amount of practice before unimportant meets. They interpreted these results as indicating that those who scored high on the self-handicapping scale wished to protect their self-esteem. (For more research regarding self-handicapping, see Chapter 11 by Berglas in the current volume.) The correlations among these four questionnaires are not known.

Stone and Hokanson's (1969) research was designed from a different perspective—that of Skinner's operant-conditioning approach. It was designed in an attempt to test Skinner's (1953) idea that aversive stimuli become positively reinforcing, in the sense of actually reducing physiological arousal, if they have been presented simultaneously with another positive reinforcer. Stone and Hokanson arranged a two-person "game" situation in which the experimental participant was administered mild shock by the confederate. The subject was given the choice of retaliating or administering a mild shock to himself. Retaliation resulted in a shock from the confederate on the next trial, whereas self-administered shock resulted in points instead of shock on the next trial. Results showed that the participants not only learned to shock themselves, thus avoiding future retaliation, but that the self-shock reduced the participants' arousal as measured by peripheral vasodilation.

Several studies from research on the resolution of conflict provide information on people's reactions to masochistic strategies of interaction. Solomon (1960) studied the effects of three strategies of interaction in a two-person prisoner's dilemma game: an unconditionally benevolent strategy, a conditionally benevolent strategy, and an unconditionally benevolent strategy. Solomon found that his unconditionally benevolent accomplices were exploited by the experimental participants. Deutsch, Epstein, Canavan, and Gumpert (1967) found exploitation of participants who used what they called a "turn the other cheek" strategy. This strategy consisted of choosing a peg in a game which gave a point to the partner, but not one to the participant himself or herself. Research has generally shown that victims are derogated (Simmons & Lerner, 1968; Lerner, 1980), so that masochistic behavior would appear to be successful only to the extent that a person finds derogation reinforcing in the sense revealed by Stone and Hokanson (1969). Knight and Weiss (1980), however, found that victims are seen as more honest and independent.

The experimental literature regarding "choosing to suffer" in humans and masochism in animals demonstrates the effects of exposure to aversive stimuli or, in the case of humans, to verbal statements that aversive stimuli will be experienced in the future. In these research studies, stimuli such as shock, air blasts, or unpleasant-tasting foods are used. Although people who have experienced sexual and physical abuse certainly develop what has been labeled masochistic behavior (Montgomery, 1985; Symonds, 1979), many people who have not experienced physically aversive stimuli have been observed by clinicians to develop what they have called self-defeating or masochistic behavior. Reports and inferences regarding the experiences in relationships which have led to such behaviors are reviewed next.

In summary, the experimental research on masochism demonstrates six principles regarding the conditions under which masochistic behavior occurs:

1. Masochistic behavior occurs after exposure to aversive stimuli or, in the case of humans, verbal statements that aversive stimuli will be experienced in the future. The research indicates two different ways in which self-punitive responses can be learned and maintained:
   (a) when very desired positive reinforcers have been paired with aversive stimuli so that the organism learns that aversive stimuli accompany positive ones;
   (b) when the organism has learned a behavior that is fear reducing and continues to engage in that behavior in response to fear even when that behavior no longer provides relief from aversive stimulation and may even be aversive itself.
2. In the latter situations described above it is not appropriate to say that the organism is seeking pleasure and avoiding pain but rather that it is going, subjectively, from an area of high aversiveness to an area of lower aversiveness.
3. New responses, not resulting in as much punishment as the old ones, will not be attempted as long as the organism cannot discriminate a new situation as a different one in which different contingencies may be oper-

ating. The arousal produced by the aversive situation makes well-learned (self-punitive) responses the dominant ones. Unless the arousal in the initial aversive situation is reduced by the presentation of positive stimuli or, in the case of humans, verbal statements making the situation less aversive, new ways of coping will not be attempted.

4. Because the experience of aversive stimulation after an anticipation period appears to be more aversive than the experience of the same aversive stimulation without the waiting period, animals and humans learn to engage in self-punitive responses to avoid waiting for the aversive stimulation. If organisms frequently experience reinforcement after suffering, but rarely experience reinforcement without suffering, they may self-punish in situations of pleasure when no suffering would occur without their own intervention, having learned that such behavior reduces the length of the aversive anticipation period.
5. Having learned that reinforcement follows suffering, humans may also engage in self-punitive behaviors in an attempt to gain desired rewards in situations in which there is no relationship between suffering and reward.
6. The experience of suffering and/or the expectation of suffering may lead to changes in the self-statements made by people, and these self-statements may provide guidance regarding their style of relating to others.

These negative self-statements, such as "I am a victim" or "I have to suffer more than most people," may be less aversively arousing than confusion regarding the person's role and relationships with others. Thus, these self-statements may be fear reducing, and eliminating them may be fear arousing. They may also have positively reinforcing qualities derived from inappropriate implications of religious ideas regarding suffering and rewards. As the clinical literature demonstrates, new self-statements, and a new sense of identity in relationship to others, must be learned along with behaviors resulting in less suffering in order to prevent a person from being aversively aroused by a feeling of inconsistency, fraud or phoniness, or a confused sense of identity when trying out the new behaviors.

"THE UNDISCOVER'D COUNTRY": CLINICAL AND PHILOSOPHICAL IDEAS REGARDING MASOCHISM

Having reviewed the research literature regarding the choice to suffer, let us turn to the clinical theories of masochism. Although the major theories on this subject are considered, an exhaustive examination of this literature is not attempted. Reviews can also be found in Panken (1973) and Menaker (1979a). Many articles published in the past decade in psychoanalytically oriented journals cannot be discussed in the current chapter due to lack of space. (Some psychoanalytic ideas regarding masochism are also discussed briefly in the chapters in this volume by Berglas, Canavan, Strauman, and Widiger and Frances.)

The purpose of this review, as stated previously, is to integrate the findings regarding the situations affecting the choice to suffer in experimental research with the situations elucidated by clinical theory leading to similar behaviors. it should be pointed out that the review here is one informed by recent developments in psychoanalytic theory of the object relations and self-psychology groups. Experimental and clinical psychologists with little interest in psychoanalytic theory should recognize that this theory has been a major intellectual force in our century. The thinking has been refined so as to discard the less tenable aspects, including those largely derived from particular behaviors of Freud's time, and to supplement the deficiencies, especially those related to mother–child interactions and the parents' behaviors generally. Within psychoanalytic theory, the use of a "drive" construct is slowly withering away, just as it did in learning theory two decades ago, not because of a lack in belief in motivation, but because of the lack of theoretical precision. Analytic theory has come to focus more upon the reciprocal interactions of people (frequently referred to as "objects" in the philosophical tradition of the subject–object distinction) and thus more upon "situational" as opposed to "dispositional" variables. Thus psychoanalytic theory has become more "social," in recent years along with the socialization of the rest of clinical psychology. In the present review it is argued that all of the observations since Freud share the idea that the individual must give up a part of the self, that is, that the individual must refrain from engaging in various assertive, achievement, or self-efficacious behaviors in order to obtain the love of the parent or to help the parent take care of him or her.

Krafft-Ebing (1896/1978), the first modern writer to deal with this subject, wrote only about sexual masochism (a disorder named after Leopold Sacher-Masoch, the author of a novel entitled *Venus in Furs*). Krafft-Ebing considered masochism to be a form of "perversion" in which the sexual instinct was "directed to ideas of subjugation and abuse by the opposite sex" (p. 87). He considered deep-rooted masochism beginning at an early age to be congenital in origin (pp. 87, 137), but a mild degree of masochism or sadism to be acquired through associations (pp. 137, 142). Of note in light of the ideas presented in the current review, however, is his discussion of Rousseau's masochism. Although he believed Rousseau's desire for subjugation to and humiliation by a woman to be the basis of Rousseau's masochism, he comments: "Flagellation only awakened ideas of a masochistic nature. In these ideas lies the psychological nucleus of his interesting study of *self*" (p. 11, italics added).

Freud's theory of masochism changed over time from a theory focused upon inner instinct and the fear of being beaten to that of a basic destructive instinct (the "death" instinct). In "A Child is Being Beaten" (1919/1981), Freud's theory of masochism focuses upon children's fantasies of being beaten, presumably due to their repressed sense of guilt for their aggressive feelings toward their fathers. In Freud's revised (1924/1981) theory of masochism, as described in "The Economic Problem in Masochism," "moral masochism," based upon an unconscious sense of guilt, is differentiated from "sexual" and "feminine" masochism, the latter being related to the repression of aggressiveness and a natural state for females, resulting from their constitution but also, admittedly, from their role in society (p. 163).

Freud's idea regarding the origin of the child's aggressive fantasies is that these fantasies stem, of course, from the child's innate sexual desires for the parent of the opposite gender, as opposed to frustrations resulting from actual beatings or psychological castration of power or creative energy. Freud notes, however, that in seeking relief from the feelings of guilt aroused by these fantasies, people may develop a general behavioral style in which they elicit punishment "from the great parental authority of Fate": The masochist then "must do something inexpedient, act against his own best interests, ruin the prospects which the real world offers him, and possibly destroy his own existence in the world of reality" (1930/1981, pp. 126–127).

Freud's (1920/1981) ideas regarding the repetition compulsion are also relevant to masochism, although he does not explicitly connect the two theories. He states that the repetition compulsion takes precedence over the pleasure principle and leads people to repeat the original trauma to the extent that they engage in self-injurious life behavior. Whatever was repressed (or its opposite) is repeated without the person's knowing it (1914/1981, p. 150; 1939/1981, p. 76). In the case of masochism the aggressive fantasies and sense of guilt are repressed if people are unable to discharge the aggression outwardly (1933/1981, pp. 109–110). Freud, believing that he had failed to isolate the genesis of masochism, eventually proposed (1930/1981) that forces toward both creation and self-destruction were basic biological processes inherent in all forms of life.

Many of Freud's followers unfortunately relied upon the notion of instinct, eliminating in their minds the need to describe the subtle, complex interactions between parents and children which lead to the development and maintenance of masochistic behaviors. Their observations, however, offer additional insight regarding the beliefs, behaviors, and self-statements of masochists and provide support for the idea that individuals learn to refrain from self-efficacious behaviors in order to satisfy other, initially more important, needs.

Alexander's (1935) theory suggested that people believe they may satisfy otherwise forbidden impulses if they pay the penalty of suffering. In this regard his theory is somewhat similar to recent ideas about belief in a just world (Lerner, 1980). Later ideas about the self are foreshadowed by Wittels' (1937) idea that "the masochist wishes to prove the futility of one part of his person in order to live the more secure in the important other part" (p. 143).

Horney (1939) regards masochism as a way to "get rid of the self with all of its conflicts" and to achieve oblivion. She asks, "Could one . . . define masochism as essentially a striving toward the relinquishment of self?" (p. 248), and she concludes that one can in some cases, but not in others. She notes that the masochist "feels he is incapable of living without the presence, benevolence, love, friendship of another person as he is incapable of living without oxygen" (p. 251). The masochist may "exclude from awareness the fact that the partner is not and never will be the appropriate person to fulfill his expectations" (p. 251). Similar ideas are explained more fully by Menaker (1979a) and Panken (1973). Also of interest, Horney points out that the masochist blames his or her lack of achievement on other people or circumstances, including illness, and is afraid to stick his or her neck out, thus never actually achieving anything involving any risk of failure.

Reich (1933) maintained that Freud made a mistake in changing his theories of neurosis and masochism from ones of conflict between instinct and the outer world to ones of conflict between instinct and a *need* for punishment. He was critical of Freud's new theory which he saw as eclipsing the primary source of suffering—the frustrating and punishing outer world. He foreshadows other theorists in suggesting that the pleasure in masochistic suffering comes from the relief that a greater punishment is not forthcoming.

Reich (1933) describes a process by which the masochist provokes others by complaining to the point of causing them to act in a way which provides a rational foundation to the reproach—"See how badly you are treating me" (p. 243). The masochist then feels "I am right in hating you." Reich points out that a deep disappointment in love lies behind the provocation (p. 243). The masochist becomes inordinately afraid of the loss of love and attention, which Reich attributes to the experience of being left alone and deserted in early childhood. Frequently, the masochist thinks, "If I am not loved, then I am not worthy of being loved and have, therefore, to be really stupid and ugly" (p.254). Whether or not one accepts Reich's ideas of desertion or lack of love, it seems reasonable that a child who failed to have his or her needs met on repeated occasions in a significant relationship would generalize this expectation to other relationships. Although Reich depicts with clarity some of the phenomena associated with masochistic characters, his theory does not elaborate upon the ways in which specific behaviors are reinforced. Presumably, the rageful crying of the baby and the later complaining are eventually or intermittently reinforced by the parent.

Reik (1941) does not accept the unconscious need for punishment as the masochist's primary motive, but he instead focuses upon the masochist's desire for compensation by future glory in the appreciative judgments of posterity. He believes that masochists expect to attain their gratification even if they are "punished, abused, and beaten" (p. 163). Masochists believe they are failing because their efforts to succeed were not appreciated. There is a part of themselves that feels they are incapable of succeeding in the present. When they try their hardest, they unconsciously find the worst conditions possible. They seem "to follow the line of the greatest resistance...instead of the line of greatest advantage" (p. 256). "Any approach to success, any beckoning chance, is avoided because then the forbidden aggressive and imperious tendencies could break through and the inevitable punishment threatens" (p. 334). Reik states that "the suffering then becomes the sign and expression of one's own value" (p. 258). According to Reik's theory, the early "ill treatments and humiliations by a person who has become the object of love are replaced by blows of fate, various suffering and privations, voluntary and involuntary renunciations, awkward and self-damaging behavior" (p. 304). The masochist's expectation of imminent calamity is similar to that of the obsessional neurotic. The difference is that the neurotic renounces satisfaction because of his anxiety, whereas the masochist pays for his satisfaction by suffering in advance (p. 425). Reik's suggestion for therapy is to help the person master the overwhelming anxiety and help the person to feel better able to "fear frustrations and external failures" (p. 380).

For Bieber (1966) sadism and masochism are defensive adaptations to threat. In sadism "the victim is a personified representative of a variety of irrationally perceived threats; he must then be dominated, injured, neutralized, or destroyed" (p. 263). For the sadist, there is "a sense of triumph in subjugating an irrationally perceived enemy or in extinguishing a threat" (p. 263). Bieber agrees with Reich that masochistic acts are defenses against even greater injury by another. The expectation of injury is almost always irrational, although masochistic behavior may be a maladaptive way of coping with a realistic threat. He notes that "for the masochistic pattern to become established, it must have had adaptive value at some time, even though it is essentially maladaptive" (p. 267).

Bieber (1966) describes two types of parent psychopathology which foster masochism: hostility and ambivalence toward a child and the acting out of masochism through a child. In the latter situation the parent may identify with the child and "hope to fulfill his own frustrated ambitions through the success of his offspring, only to become as anxious about the child's achievement as he was of his own" (p. 267).

Bieber's (1966) review is insightful in its recognition of sadistic and masochistic behaviors as responses to threat, but he fails to elaborate upon the interactions with parents which lead to masochistic behaviors to the extent that Menaker (1979a) and Panken (1967, 1973) do later. Although Bieber recognizes the role of masochistic behaviors in severe work inhibitions and the fear of success, he relates these problems to the fear of competition with rivals which seems to be rooted in Freud's ideas regarding the Oedipal conflict. He thus misses the focus which Menaker and Panken place upon the child's fear of the psychological consequences for the mother (or caretaker) of the child's assertion of his or her own individual aspirations. Bieber's (1966) view of the underlying psychopathology is surprisingly purely a cognitive one. He describes the pathology as consisting "of irrationally held beliefs and belief systems associated with erroneous expectations of injury" (p. 269). The therapy involves pointing out the patient's false premises, their origins, and their current meanings. He notes, however, the difficulty in altering the person's belief that he or she will not be injured.

Menaker's (1942, 1953) ideas, and those of Panken (1973), focus upon the child's protection of the mother's need to dominate by sacrificing his or her own autonomy. In order to do this the child must dampen the creative assertion of his or her own personality (cf. Rank, 1968). For Menaker (1953), if the mother's love is insufficient, the masochistic reaction on the part of the child is to sacrifice "its own worth" to sustain the illusion of mother love, "without which life itself is impossible" (p. 219). Panken provides an excellent clinical example of a patient's noneffective behavior which appears to be a provocation to induce the other person to prove his or her superiority (p. 60). She argues that the woman learned this behavior to protect herself from her mother.

Sack and Miller (1975) conclude from their review of clinical theories and empirical research regarding masochism that behavior in which people do not act in their own best interests may be described as masochistic, but it may not involve the seeking of suffering in a motivational sense in which suffering has acquired an incentive value of its own. They believe the use of the term in such a broad sense has resulted in conceptual vagueness. They also conclude that the mechanisms regarding masochistic behavior are many and varied, with no singular dynamic feature. Their suggestions for therapy include pointing out and challenging the patient's masochistic behavior and supporting the masochism when it is "utilized as an adaptive measure of defense" (p. 256). It is difficult to understand why they would make the latter suggestion unless they are referring to short-term therapy.

Sack and Miller's (1975) failure to find a singular mechanism underlying masochistic behavior is not shared by Warren (1985). Warren's review is philosophical in nature and does not attempt to include empirical research. Her point of view is that masochists derive a sense of identity and self-worth from pain. Because giving up pain and inner conflict means giving up a part of their identity, masochists have a great deal of difficulty changing. Warren distinguishes between masochists who are aware of their contribution to their own pain and those who are not, citing Kierkegaard's (1849/1955) contrast between defiant and passive despair. She notes that writers on masochism either reduce it to ordinary behavior, which seems not odd enough to be interesting, or leave it too odd to be comprehensible.

Maintaining a cohesive self-representation is also considered by Stolorow (1975) to be one of the functions of masochistic activity. In developing masochistic behavior, Saretsky (1976) has described the role of parents who give love only if the child sacrifices his or her own individuality. Becker (1973, 1975) described how the perpetuation of values is the way many people attempt to gain a sense of immortality. Thus, parents may require children to forgo developing an independent set of their own values in order to obtain a sense of immortality, or to deny death.

The clinical theories of masochism lead us to the conclusion that children are punished for engaging in assertive, efficacious (Bandura's 1977 term) behaviors which lead to fear or anxiety on the part of their caretakers. Among the behaviors which elicit negative reactions on the part of the caretakers are those particular behaviors which may be necessary not only for achievement but also for a basic sense of self-worth.

Rather than accept the severe disappointment and frustration as a consequence of the limitations of the caretaker, the child learns behaviors which reduce the caretaker's anxiety and thus the caretaker's ineffective nurturance and even punitive behaviors. Masochistic personalities develop considerable control over other people, but as a consequence apparently believe that when their own needs are not met, it is because their own behavior is at fault. When their needs are met, they believe that pain must precede or follow the satisfaction.

The psychoanalytic theories and the ideas of Becker (1973, 1975) suggest that many children sense that behaving in a manner inconsistent with their parents' values will "kill" their parents, or result in their parents' loss of a perception of meaning to their lives, that is, their psychological death. For such parents, their values apparently provide a sense of guidance regarding their roles and obligation in life dearer to them than life itself, which by definition implies creative growth and change. An attempt at psychological infanticide by the parents leads to a vicious cycle of anxiety regarding a perceived choice between either hurting another or oneself—between either psychological patricide (or matricide) or psychological suicide on the part of the child. Fulfilling one's own needs without interfering with the parents' fulfilling theirs is not easily accomplished in such a situation. From the complementary perspective of the parent, the difficulty of fulfilling one's own needs and fulfilling those of a child will also be recognized by those readers who have spent a considerable amount of time as the sole caretaker of an infant.

STATE OF THE THEORY ON CHOOSING TO SUFFER AND IMPLICATIONS FOR FUTURE RESEARCH

The research regarding masochism in animals demonstrates that self-punitive behaviors can be learned by the pairing of positive or fear-reducing stimuli with aversive ones and indicates how such behavior can develop without the secondary reinforcement value of providing a sense of individuality, or a sense of identity, which is being argued occurs in at least some human self-punitive behavior. Different factors may, of course, lead to similar behaviors among humans and animals for different reasons. Furthermore, the animal and human laboratory studies with shock, noise, and air blasts as aversive stimuli do not identify for us the nature of the aversive stimuli occurring naturalistically in human relationships which produce masochistic behavior.

Theory regarding the choice to suffer must be expanded in three areas: (1) the extent to which the choice to suffer is self-protective or involves self-statements related to the person's sense of identity; (2) the conditions under which self-punitive responses are learned in humans—specifically, the situations with caretakers and significant others which are anxiety arousing, the nature of the threatening stimuli, the nature of the original reinforcers, and the nature of the fear-reducing responses; and (3) the most effective ways to eliminate the maladaptive beliefs, behaviors, and anxiety and to substitute more self-enhancing ways of being in both threatening and nonthreatening situations.

SELF-PROCESSES

The only experimental studies indicating directly that self-statements or self-protective strategies are involved in the choice to suffer are those of Baumeister *et al.* (1979), Comer and Laird (1975), and Maracek and Mettee (1972). The questionnaire studies of Kelley *et al.* (1985) and of Rhodewalt *et al.* (1984) also indicate that people who make statements consistent with the idea of being a victim sabotage their health and performance. The self-statements of people who choose to suffer should be examined in light of recent social-psychological theory regarding the self, such as self-discrepancy theory (Higgins, Strauman, & Klein, 1986), and recent research regarding changes in self-statements over time (Goldfried & Robins, 1983). The research and theory presented in this chapter suggest that people who choose to suffer may have discrepancies between what Higgins *et al.* (1986) have called the "ought-self" and the "actual self," at least before they engage in self-punitive behavior.

The factor analyses conducted by Shore *et al.* (1971) suggest that the self-statements of people who choose to suffer may be composed of three different types. The group of people Shore *et al.* called "doers" should have positive self-statements as well as statements of self-reproach. Victims should have fewer positive self-statements, report feeling more helpless, and have more negative self-statements. Curtis *et al.* (1984) have suggested that people who choose to suffer may expect a lower overall level of good outcomes in life than people who do not choose to suffer and are symptom-free. The literature reviewed in the present chapter suggests that such people have experienced more unpleasant situations than people without any psychopathological symptoms.

Situations Leading to Self-Punitive Responses

Most people who choose to suffer are likely unaware of the precise nature of the fear-arousing situations in which their self-punitive responses are learned. If they are aware of the situations in which the responses are learned, they are likely unaware that the anxious expectations they are bringing into new situations are leading to responses which others would consider inappropriate and which, in turn, may be creating self-fulfilling prophecies (see Chapter 3 on expectancy confirmation in this volume). Because the fear-arousing situations are likely to be subtle anxiety reactions on the part of the parents, which may differ only slightly, if at all, from cultural norms, the fear-arousing stimuli may be difficult to discern and verbally express. Instead of being afraid of physical abuse or religious threats, a child may be made anxious when the parents are concerned with a loss of a sense of meaning in life resulting from a child's psychological separation, or a child may be made anxious when the parents are concerned about a subtle loss of social or economic status desired for themselves or the child. Awareness of a person's current interactional pattern can be increased in a therapy setting, and exploration can then take place regarding the nature of the fear aroused before the maladaptive behavior ensues. Other ways of coping can be modeled by the therapist or learned from other members in a group therapy setting. Research tools, such as Benjamin's (1984) Structural Analysis of Social Behavior (SASB) inventory, may also be of use in identifying a person's maladaptive interactional patterns.

It is assumed that the most effective and efficient way to learn how to balance fulfillment of one's own needs and those of other people in the larger social unit is to experience such a relationship with a "good enough" (Winnicott, 1965) parent or caretaker. Although laboratory studies such as those of Beebe

(1986) and Stern (1985) are very valuable, the question always remains as to how representative these interactions are of the more important and difficult interactions in daily life. For example, a parent may do an admirable job of balancing these needs when unimportant issues are at stake but be less available or more impinging when more important, anxiety-provoking issues arise. Ideally, longitudinal studies of caretaker–infant or caretaker–child interactions in the home should be examined in relation to reports or observations of self-punitive behaviors and other coping strategies in adulthood. Self-punitive behavior may not become noticeable until the young adult attempts to marry someone of whom the parents disapprove or develops political or religious beliefs antithetical to those of the parents.

The Differences Between Choosing To Suffer (Masochism), Self-Handicapping, and Self-Defeating Behavior

The term *self-defeating behavior* encompasses a large variety of behaviors, including choosing to suffer, self-handicapping, and other behaviors. As was stated in the introductory chapter of this volume, self-defeating behaviors are defined as behaviors leading to a lower reward–cost ratio than is available to the person through alternative behaviors. The person may be unaware that an alternative strategy exists, or aware that an alternative behavior is available for achieving the desired outcome, but unable to execute the behavior. A further differentiation can be made between people who are aware that they are choosing to suffer in some way and people who are not aware of making such a choice. In addition, distinctions can be made between people who are aware of the positive outcomes they are obtaining by making a sacrifice and those who are not aware of any such rewards and between people who are aware of how they are harming themselves and people who are not aware. Four groups result from this differentiation: (1) people who are aware of something they are getting and something they are paying, such as Dostoevsky's (1864/1960) self-conscious narrator in *Notes from the Underground*; (2) people who are aware of something they are getting but not what they are sacrificing, such as people who take irrational risks regarding their health, employment, or relationships; (3) people who are aware of something they are sacrificing but not what they are gaining from the sacrifice, including a wide variety of self-defeating behaviors such as eating disorders and sabotaged opportunities for success; and (4) people who are not aware of what they are getting or what they are sacrificing, representing a group of people who have not achieved the outcomes they are capable of obtaining but who do not reflect accurately upon their capabilities and the possibilities available to them. Many self-handicapping strategies fall into this category. Masochists are people who choose to suffer, who choose to get what they want by paying more than other observers believe is necessary. Thus, a greater degree of awareness is present in masochistic behavior than in self-handicapping or other self-defeating behaviors.

INCREASING THE LIKELIHOOD OF CHOOSING NOT TO SUFFER MASOCHISTICALLY

CHANGING THE AFFECT

Changing self-punitive behavior by encouraging inhibition of the self-minimizing, self-destructive behaviors and supporting more positive behaviors and self-descriptions can not take place without confronting the anxiety which occurs when the masochist does not engage in self-defeating behavior. Because any relationship, but particularly a close one, is anxiety producing and a stimulus for relief-producing, self-effacing behaviors, masochists are anxious that a much more threatening situation is going to occur if submission and humiliation are not experienced.

If a therapist attempts to change the behaviors and self-statements of the masochist, the masochist will sabotage the most effective of these attempts. As the anxiety increases from the expectation that a more threatening situation will occur, the probability increases that a self-destructive response will occur to reduce the anxiety. Thus, for example, a masochistic person who has been supported effectively to apply for a new job may have an automobile accident en route to the interview. In relationships in which masochists are not being ill-treated, they will (1) develop a variety of fears and engage in self-destructive behaviors which they will see as caused by the relationship, and (2) hurt themselves by ending the relationship if they are unsuccessful at expectancy-confirming behaviors, which may have been effective in obtaining pain from other people in the past. Thus, Menaker (1979b) has pointed out that masochists frequently undermine effective therapeutic treatment. She argues that traditional psychoanalysis will be unsuccessful with them (1) because it ignores the role of corrective experiences, such as awareness of affects which were previously inaccessible and which do not occur as the result of interpretation; (2) because rapid social changes affecting identification processes affect the character of psychic structure and must affect the nature of the treatment; and (3) because knowledge regarding the deficiencies in the normal process of separation and individuation has legitimized technical procedures other than the use of interpretation. These procedures include the mirroring types of interventions Kohut (1971, 1977; Kohut & Wolf, 1978) has advocated in his theory of self-psychology (Menaker, 1981). Menaker therefore suggests that the psychoanalytically oriented therapist step out of the traditional analytic stance which results in a perception of the therapist as omnipotent. If the masochist views the therapist as more powerful in the situation, self-destructive responses occur, and the masochist views the therapeutic relationship as responsible. Thus, Menaker recommends that therapists be unafraid to show their own personalities in order to actively support the person's realistic perceptions rather than encourage the transference of previously learned paranoid perceptions and thus the inevitable masochistic reactions.

It has been argued here and demonstrated experimentally that self-destructive behaviors occur when they are less aversive than remaining in another more aversive situation. Thus, if masochists are neither treated poorly nor treat themselves poorly, they become anxious that a much more threatening situation is going to occur. As they learn to reward themselves more, they may need to be allowed to gradually diminish the ways in which they hurt themselves, so that they do not become unbearably anxious. Warren (1985) has theorized that if masochists do not have their identity as victims, they lose their sense of identity entirely. To not know who one is, where one belongs, or how one should act is terrifying.

In Joyce's story, Eveline becomes panicked that if she does not remain at home unhappily forever, an even worse fortune awaits her—that of drowning. In therapy masochists report fears of being drowned, of being swallowed up, of being lost in the world, or of becoming oblivious to life if they contemplate giving up their masochistic relationships. These are symbolic representations of their fear of losing their identity. This anxiety must be reduced if the masochist is to be freed from repeating the dominant, self-destructive response. Masochists must allow themselves to experience this anxiety if they are to gain a new, positive identity. This is the experience of losing the self to gain it discussed by Kierkegaard (1849/1955) and Christians (Matthew 16:25; Mark 8:35; Luke 9:24) and of "not being" in existential and Eastern philosophy. If the therapist is available to experience this "drowning" with the client, the client is more easily desensitized to this threat. Verbal labeling of the fear of losing a sense of identity will also be therapeutic.

Changing the Beliefs

A change to self-efficacious behaviors requires an integration of approaches aimed at changing affects and beliefs as well as behaviors. In order for the reformed masochist to develop a new, positive sense of identity, the masochist must engage in behaviors which will make positive self-statements veridical.

After the loss of identity as a victim has been grieved and the possibility of behaving in new ways occurs to masochists, they may still, however, remain inhibited from engaging in new self-enhancing behaviors by beliefs communicated to them during their socialization regarding the moral obligations of all people to others. Although Bieber (1966) has argued that the belief system of the masochist must be changed, he was referring to the masochist's beliefs that pain must accompany pleasure and that submission and self-minimization are necessary in order to be loved. These expectations of the masochist must clearly be altered. If the analytic theories about the origins of masochistic behavior in the interactions with the caretakers are correct, however, it is not simply the masochists' beliefs about what to expect in relationships that must change but also the masochists' moral beliefs about the circumstances in which it is acceptable to hurt another person. The parents or caretakers who have required their children to sacrifice their own aspirations or capabilities in order for the parents to achieve theirs *will* feel hurt by their children's new self-efficacious behaviors. Thus came Hamlet's pangs of conscience and Eveline's prayer for moral direction. Therefore, three types of beliefs held by masochists must be changed: (1) self-beliefs, which have already been discussed; (2) expectations regarding pleasure and pain in relationships with others, discussed in this chapter and by Bieber; and (3) moral beliefs about duties to significant others who psychologically or physically hurt other people.

To change the third type of belief, the therapist must actively convey a sense of morality that does not negate the importance of obligations to others but emphasizes the adaptive value of a morality which does not require anyone to sacrifice his or her potential for growth and change. How to balance the needs of self and others, the needs for what Spence (1985) called autonomy and belonging, or what Bakan (1966) called agency and communion, is a difficult moral dilemma facing masochists—Eveline, Hamlet, and all of us, of course. Family therapists have long been aware of the sacrifice by the identified patient for continuous functioning of the others in the family. By labeling it and, in many cases, presenting it to the family with its positive connotations, they have enabled the family to change the self-defeating ritual (Selvini-Palazzoli, Cecchin, Prata, & Boscolo, 1978, p. 42). How to establish and maintain interactions which reduce the extent of the suffering experienced and the suffering caused is an immense task facing all social groups for which the insights of research findings and clinical observations will continue to be very valuable.

SUMMARY

This chapter has reviewed the major findings of empirical research by learning theorists and social psychologists and the observations and theories of psychoanalysts regarding choosing to suffer. The research with animals indicates that animals learn self-punitive responses when they provide relief from more highly aversive situations. Animals, however, do not engage in these responses to the extent of actually harming themselves physically. The research by social psychologists indicates that people choose to suffer if they have been led to expect to suffer and that people believe their suffering will improve future outcomes. People are more likely to choose to suffer if their self-evaluations are at stake. Psychoanalytic theories of masochism focus upon the feelings of aggression toward the parents and the fear of psychological annihilation.

People may learn self-punitive behaviors to escape a variety of threatening situations. Together, the empirical findings and clinical theories suggest that people sometimes learn self-punitive responses which allay their parents' and their own anxiety while simultaneously preserving their own sense of self. Part of their identity, however, is that of the victim. In order to refrain from self-minimizing behaviors and beliefs, a person who has learned to choose to suffer must experience the anxiety of the threatening situation which is usually avoided. It is argued that this anxiety is sometimes related to the loss of a self-defeating identity and to the decision to act in opposition to strongly socialized beliefs about obligations to others.

ACKNOWLEDGMENTS

The author wishes to thank Esther Menaker and George Stricker for their helpful comments on an earlier draft of this chapter.

REFERENCES

Alexander, F. (1935). *The psychoanalysis of the total personality*. (B. Glueck, Trans.). New York: Nervous and Mental Disease Publishing Co. (Coolidge Foundation)

Aronson, E., & Carlsmith, J. M. (1962). Performance expectancy as a determinant of actual performance. *Journal of Abnormal and Social Psychology, 65*, 178–182.

Aronson, E., Carlsmith, J. M., & Darley, J. M. (1963). The effects of expectancy on volunteering for an unpleasant experience. *Journal of Abnormal and Social Psychology, 66*, 220–224.

Bakan, D. (1966). *The duality of human existence*. Chicago: Rand McNally.

Bandura, A. (1977). Self-efficacy: Toward a unifying theory of behavioral change. *Psychological Review, 84*, 191–215.

Baumeister, R. F., Cooper, J., & Skib, B. A. (1979). Inferior performance as a selective response to expectancy: Taking a dive to make a point. *Journal of Personality and Social Psychology, 37*, 424–432.

Becker, E. (1973). *The denial of death*. New York: Free Press.

Becker, E. (1975). *Escape from evil*. New York: Free Press.

Beebe, B. (1986). Mother–infant mutual influence and precursors of self and object representation. In J. Masling (Ed.), *Empirical studies of psychoanalytic theories, 2* (pp. 27–48). Hillsdale, NJ: The Analytic Press.

Benjamin, L. S. (1984). Principles of prediction using Structural Analysis of Social Behavior (SASB). In R. A. Zucker, J. Aronoff, & A. J. Rabin (Eds.), *Personality and the Prediction of Behavior* (pp. 121–174). New York: Academic Press.

Bieber, I. (1966). Sadism and masochism. In S. Arieti (Ed.), *American Handbook of Psychiatry* (Vol. 3, pp. 259–270).

Brock, T. C., Edelman, S. K., Edwards, D. C., & Schuck, J. R. (1965). Seven studies of performance expectancy as a determinant of actual performance. *Journal of Experimental Social Psychology, 1*, 295–310.

Brown, J. S. (1965). A behavioral analysis of masochism. *Journal of Experimental Research in Personality, 1*, 65–70.

Brown, J. (1969). Factors affecting self-punitive locomotor behavior. In B. Campbell & R. M. Church (Eds.), *Punishment and aversive behavior* (pp. 467–514). New York: Appleton-Century-Crofts.

Brown, J. S., Anderson, D. C., & Weiss, C. G. (1965). Self-punitive behavior under conditions of massed practice. *Journal of Comparative and Physiological Psychology, 60*, 451–453.

Brown, J. S., Martin, R. C., & Morrow, M. W. (1964). Self-punitive behavior in the rat: Facilitative effects of punishment on resistance to extinction. *Journal of Comparative and Physiological Psychology, 57*, 127–133.

Carlsmith, J. M., & Aronson, E. (1963). Some hedonic consequences of the confirmation and disconfirmation of expectancies. *Journal of Abnormal and Social Psychology, 66*, 151–156.

Cohen, R. E., & Tennen, H. (1985). Self-punishment in learned helplessness and depression. *Journal of Social and Clinical Psychology, 3*, 82–96.

Comer, R., & Laird, J. D. (1975). Choosing to suffer as a consequence of expecting to suffer: Why do people do it? *Journal of Personality and Social Psychology, 32*, 92–101.

Cottrell, N. (1965). Performance expectancy as a determinant of actual performance: *Journal of Personality and Social Psychology, 2*, 685–691.

Curtis, R. C., Mariano, A., & Gersh, W. D. (1979). Probabilities of an aversive event and physiological correlates of stress. *Psychological Reports, 44*, 247–256.

Curtis, R., Nyberg, S., & Smith, P. (1982, April). *Choosing to suffer: Punishment for the past or hope for the future.* Paper presented at the annual meeting of the Eastern Psychological Association, Baltimore, MD.

Curtis, R. C., Rietdorf, P., & Ronell, D. (1980). "Appeasing the gods"? Suffering to reduce probable future suffering. *Personality and Social Psychology Bulletin, 6*, 234–241.

Curtis, R. C., Smith, P., & Moore, R. (1984). Suffering to improve outcomes determined by both chance and skill. *Journal of Social and Clinical Psychology, 2*, 165–173.

Deutsch, M., Epstein, Y., Canavan, D., & Gumpert, P. (1967). Strategies of inducing cooperation: an experimental study. *Journal of Conflict Resolution, 11*, 345–60.

Dostoevsky, F. (1960). *Notes from the Underground* (R. E. Matlaw, Trans.). New York: E. P. Dutton. (Original work published 1864)

Dreyer, P., & Renner, K. E. (1971). Self-punitive behavior, masochism or confusion? *Psychological Review, 78*, 333–337.

Ferrari, J. R., & Curtis, R. C. (1987, April). *Choosing to suffer after failure: Self-administered shock and number of failures experienced.* Paper presented at the annual meeting of the Eastern Psychological Association, New York.

Foxman, J., & Radtke, R. (1970). Negative expectancy and the choice of an aversive task. *Journal of Personality and Social Psychology, 15*, 253–257.

Freud, S. (1981). Remembering, repeating and working-through (Further recommendations on the technique of psychoanalysis II). In J. Strachey (Ed.), *The standard edition of the complete psychological works of Sigmund Freud* (Vol. 12, pp. 145–156). (Original work published 1914)

Freud, S. (1981). A child is being beaten. In J. Strachey (Ed.), *The standard edition of the complete psychological works of Sigmund Freud* (Vol. 17, pp. 177–204). (Original work published 1919)

Freud, S. (1981). Beyond the pleasure principle. In J. Strachey (Ed.), *The standard edition of the complete psychological works of Sigmund Freud* (Vol. 18, pp. 7–64). (Original work published 1920)

Freud, S. (1981). The economic problem in masochism. In J. Strachey (Ed.), *The standard edition of the complete psychological works of Sigmund Freud* (Vol. 19, pp. 159–170). London: Hogarth Press. (Original work published 1924)

Freud, S. (1981). Civilization and its discontents. In J. Strachey (Ed.), *The standard edition of the complete psychological works of Sigmund Freud* (Vol. 21, pp. 64–145). (Original work published 1930)

Freud, S. (1981). Anxiety and instinctual life. In J. Strachey (Ed.), *The standard edition of the complete psychological works of Sigmund Freud* (Vol. 22, pp. 81–111). (Original work published 1933)

Freud, S. (1981). Moses and monotheism: Three essays. In J. Strachey (Ed.), *The standard edition of the complete psychological works of Sigmund Freud* (Vol. 23, pp. 3–107). (Original work published 1939)

Goldfried, M. R., & Robins, C. (1983). Self-schemas, cognitive bias, and the processing of therapeutic experiences. In P. C. Kendall (Ed.), *Advances in cognitive-behavioral research and therapy* (Vol. 2, pp. 33–80). New York: Academic Press.

Green, P. (1972). Masochism in the laboratory rat: An experimental demonstration. *Psychonomic Science, 27*, 41–44.

Gwinn, G. T. (1949). The effects of punishment on acts motivated by fear. *Journal of Experimental Psychology, 39*, 260–269.

Harlow, H. H. (1962). The heterosexual affectional system in monkeys. *American Psychologist, 17*, 1–9.

Harlow, H. H., & Harlow, M. K. (1971). Psychopathology in monkeys. In H. D. Kimmel (Ed.), *Experimental psychopathology: Recent research and theory* (pp. 203–229). New York: Academic Press.

Higgins, E. T., Strauman, T., & Klein, R. (1986). Standards in the process of self-evaluation: Multiple affects from multiple stages. In R. M. Sorrentino & E. T. Higgins (Eds.), *Handbook of motivation and cognition: Foundations of social behavior* (pp. 23–63). New York: Guilford Press.

Holz, W. C., & Azrin, N. H. (1961). Discriminative properties of punishment. *Journal of the Experimental Analysis of Behavior, 4*, 225–232.

Horney, K. (1939). *New ways in psychoanalysis*. New York: Norton.

Imada, H. (1959). The effects of punishment on avoidance behavior. *Japanese Psychological Research, 52*, 27–38.

Joyce, J. (1969). *Dubliners*. New York: The Modern Library. (Original work published in 1914)

Keller, F. S., & Schoenfeld, W. N. (1950). *Principles of psychology: A systematic text in the science of behavior*. New York: Appleton-Century-Crofts.

Kelley, K., Byrne, D., Przybyla, D. P. J., Eberly, C., Eberly, B., Greendlinger, V., Won, C. K., & Gorsky, J. (1985). Chronic self-destructiveness. Conceptualization, measurement, and initial validation of the construct. *Motivation and Emotion, 9*, 135–151.

Kierkegaard, S. (1955). *Fear and trembling and the sickness unto death* (W. Lowrie, Trans.). Garden City: Doubleday. (Original work published 1849)

Knight, P. A., & Weiss, H. M. (1980, September). *Benefits of suffering: Communicator credibility, benefiting, and influence*. Paper presented at the annual meeting of the American Psychological Association, Montreal, Canada.

Kohut, H. (1971). *The analysis of the self*. New York: International Universities Press.

Kohut, H. (1977). *The restoration of the self*. New York: International Universities Press.

Kohut, H., & Wolf, E. (1978). The disorders of the self and their treatment: An outline. *International Journal of Psycho-Analysis, 59*, 413–426.

Krafft-Ebing, R. (1978). *Psychopathia sexualis* (F. S. Kalf, Trans.). New York: Stein & Day. (Original work published 1896)

Leary, T. (1957). *Interpersonal diagnosis of personality*. New York: Ronald Press.

Lerner, M. J. (1980). *The belief in a just world: A fundamental delusion*. New York: Plenum.

Levey, C. A. (1983). *Self-handicapping behavior: When and why do people engage in it?* Unpublished doctoral dissertation, Adelphi University. (University Microfilms, 8319708-1983)

Lowin, A., & Epstein, G. F. (1965). Does expectancy determine performance? *Journal of Experimental Social Psychology, 1*, 244–255.

Maracek, J., & Mettee, D. R. (1972). Avoidance of continued success as a function of self-esteem level, of esteem certainty, and responsibility for success. *Journal of Personality and Social Psychology, 22*, 98–107.

Masserman, J. H. (1946). *Principles of dynamic psychiatry*. Philadelphia: Saunders.

Matthews, M. D., & Babb, H. (1985). Self-punitive behavior: Effects of percentage of shocked acquisition trials and percentage of goal-shocked extinction trials. *The Psychological Record, 35*, 535–547.

Melvin, K. B. (1971). Vicious circle behavior. In H. D. Kimmel (Ed.), *Experimental psychopathology: Recent research and theory* (pp. 95–115). New York: Academic Press.

Menaker, E. (1942). The masochistic factor in the psychoanalytic situation. *Psychoanalytic Quarterly, 11*, 171–186.
Menaker, E. (1953). Masochism: a defense reaction of the ego. *Psychoanalytic Quarterly, 22*, 205–220.
Menaker, E. (1979a). *Masochism and the emergent ego: Selected papers of Esther Menaker*. New York: Human Sciences Press.
Menaker, E. (1979b). The issues of symbiosis and ego-autonomy in the treatment of masochism. In G. D. Goldman, D. S. Millman, & K. Hunt (Eds.), *Parameters in psychoanalytic psychotherapy* (pp. 127–139). Dubuque, IA: Kendall Hunt Publishing.
Menaker, E. (1981). Self-psychology illustrated on the issue of moral masochism: Clinical implications. *American Journal of Psychoanalysis, 41*, 297–305.
Montgomery, J. D. (1985). The return of the masochistic behavior in the absence of the therapist. *Psychoanalytic Review, 72*, 503–511.
Mowrer, O. H. (1950). *Learning theory and personality dynamics*. New York: Ronald Press.
Moyer, K. E. (1955). A study of some of the variables of which fixation is a function. *Journal of Genetic Psychology, 86*, 3–31.
Panken, S. (1967). On masochism: A re-evaluation. *Psychoanalytic Review, 54*, 135–147.
Panken, S. (1973). *The joy of suffering*. New York: Jason Aronson.
Rank, O. (1968). *Will therapy and truth and reality* (J. Taft, Trans.). New York: Alfred Knopf. (Original works published 1929, 1936)
Reich, W. (1933). *Character analysis*. New York: Orgone Institute Press.
Reik, T. (1941). *Masochism in modern man*. New York: Farrar and Straus.
Renner, K. E., & Tinsley, J. B. (1976). Self-punitive behavior. In G. H. Bower (Ed.), *The Psychology of Leaning and Motivation* (Vol. 10, pp. 156–198). New York: Academic Press.
Rhodewalt, F., Saltzman, A. T., & Wittmer, J. (1984). Self-handicapping among competitive athletes. The role of practice in self-esteem protection. *Basic and Applied Social Psychology, 5*, 197–210.
Rosenblum, A., & Harlow, H. H. (1963). Approach–avoidance conflict in the mother-surrogate situation. *Psychological Reports, 12*, 83–85.
Sack, R. L., & Miller, W. (1975). Masochism: A clinical theoretical overview. *Psychiatry, 38*, 245–257.
Sandler, J. (1968). Masochism: An empirical analysis. In D. S. Hommes (Ed.), *Reviews of research in behavior pathology* (pp. 76–86). New York: Wiley.
Saretsky, T. (1976). Masochism and ego identity in borderline states: *Contemporary Psychoanalysis, 12*, 433–445.
Selvini-Palazzoli, M. S., Cecchin, G., Prata, G., & Boscolo, L. (1978). *Paradox and counterparadox* (E. V. Burt, Trans.). New York: Jason Aronson. (Original work published 1975)
Seward, J. P., & Raskin, D. C. (1960). The role of fear in aversive behavior. *Journal of Comparative and Physiological Psychology, 53*, 328–335.
Shakespeare, W. (1934). *Hamlet*. Cambridge, England: The University Press.
Shore, M. F., Clifton, A., Zelin, M., & Meyerson, P. G. (1971). Patterns of masochism: An empirical study. *British Journal of Medical Psychology, 44*, 59–66.
Simmons, C. H., & Lerner, M. (1968). Altruism as a search for justice. *Journal of Personality and Social Psychology, 9*, 216–225.
Skinner, B. F. (1953). *Science and human behavior*. New York: MacMillan.
Solomon, L. (1960). The influence of some types of power relationships and game strategies upon the development of interpersonal trust. *Journal of Abnormal and Social Psychology, 61*, 223–230.
Solomon, R. L., Kamin, L. J., & Wynne, L. C. (1953). Traumatic avoidance learning: The outcomes of several extinction procedures with dogs. *Journal of Abnormal and Social Psychology, 48*, 291–302.

Spence, J. T. (1985). Achievement American style: The rewards and costs of individualism. *American Psychologist, 40,* 1285–1295.
Stern, D. N. (1985). *The interpersonal world of the infant: A view from psychoanalysis and developmental psychology.* New York: Basic Books.
Stolorow, R. D. (1975). The narcissistic function of masochism (and sadism). *International Journal of Psychoanalysis, 56,* 441–448.
Stone, L. J., & Hokanson, J. E. (1969). Arousal reduction via self-punitive behavior. *Journal of Personality and Social Psychology, 12,* 72–79.
Symonds, A. (1979). Violence against women: The myth of masochism. *American Journal of Psychotherapy, 33,* 161–173.
Walster, E., Aronson, E., & Brown, Z. (1966). Choosing to suffer as a consequence of expecting to suffer: An unexpected finding. *Journal of Experimental Social Psychology, 2,* 400–406.
Ward, W. D., & Sandvold, K. D. (1963). Performance expectancy as a determinant of actual performance: A partial replication. *Journal of Abnormal and Social Psychology, 67,* 293–295.
Warren, V. (1985). Explaining masochism. *Journal for the Theory of Social Behavior, 15,* 103–129.
Waterman, A. S., & Ford, L. H. (1965). Performance expectancy as a determinant of actual performance: Dissonance reduction or differential recall? *Journal of Personality and Social Psychology, 2,* 464–467.
Whiteis, U. E. (1956). Punishment's influence on fear and avoidance. *Harvard Educational Review, 26,* 360–373.
Winnicott, D. W. (1965). *The maturational processes and the facilitating environment.* New York: International Universities Press.
Wittels, F. (1937). The mystery of masochism. *Psychoanalytic Review, 24,* 139–149.
Zuckerman, M. (1975). Belief in a just world and altruistic behavior. *Journal of Personality and Social Psychology, 31,* 972–976.

CHAPTER 9

TOWARD AN UNDERSTANDING OF SELF-DEFEATING RESPONSES FOLLOWING VICTIMIZATION

RONNIE JANOFF-BULMAN AND CAROL E. THOMAS

Victims—of crime, violence, abuse, disease, serious accidents, natural disasters—generally experience considerable psychological distress. It is not difficult to comprehend common victim reactions such as disbelief, confusion, fear, anxiety, and hypervigilance. Typically, we recognize that bad things happen, but we never truly believe they will happen to us; when misfortune strikes, we are shocked, confused, and anxious. In addition to these "comprehensible" reactions, victims also often manifest responses, generally patterns of thought, that appear far more incomprehensible to others. The victim appears to be adding insult to injury, to be choosing to suffer even more than appears warranted by the actual victimization.

Following victimization, there are two very common responses that appear to fall into this category of what might be deemed "self-defeating behaviors." First, victims experience intrusive, recurrent thoughts about the negative event. Rather than look forward and attempt to cope with the exigencies of daily existence, victims frequently find themselves looking back and continually reexperiencing the event, reliving the unpleasantness and suffering as a result. The second seemingly self-defeating response of victims is self-blame, a very common reaction of individuals who have experienced violence, crime, disease, or serious accidents. Even in cases that outsiders would clearly agree were not the fault of the victim, one nevertheless sees a great deal of self-blame by the victim.

RONNIE JANOFF-BULMAN AND CAROL E. THOMAS • Department of Psychology, University of Massachusetts-Amherst, Amherst, Massachusetts 01003.

In this chapter we maintain that these two relatively common responses—intrusive, recurrent thoughts and self-blame—play an important, productive role in the coping efforts of victims. These responses may appear self-defeating but are rather highly appropriate, deriving from adaptive impulses within the victim. Unfortunately, in some instances, repetitive thoughts and self-blame may, in the end, become maladaptive and self-defeating, in spite of the positive motivations underlying their initiation. Thus, the intrusive, repetitive thoughts of victims may take on a life of their own, causing considerable stress and anxiety and interfering with victims' attempts to adapt to their posttrauma existence. Similarly, self-blame may become a generalized response involving considerable self-esteem deficits, and low self-esteem following victimization may lead to such clearly maladaptive behaviors as substance abuse and suicide. Nevertheless, to more fully understand the self-defeating forms of recurrent thoughts and self-blame, it is important to examine the ways in which they may begin as adaptive responses to victimization. With this in mind, we first present a general framework within which to fit these victim reactions.

BACKGROUND MODEL OF REACTIONS TO VICTIMIZATION

We maintain that the psychological distress experienced by victims is largely attributable to the challenging and potential breakdown of their very basic assumptions about the world (Janoff-Bulman, 1985; Janoff-Bulman & Frieze, 1983). Each of us maintains a coherent set of assumptions about ourselves and the world that perseveres, generally unchallenged by everyday experience. These assumptions are organized into an internally consistent conceptual system that affords us psychological equilibrium in a complex and constantly changing world; they provide us with a means of structuring and understanding our environment and allow us to perceive the world as orderly and predictable.

THE ROLE OF A COHERENT CONCEPTUAL SYSTEM

Several psychologists have addressed the existence and importance of people's conceptual systems. Parkes (1971, 1975), for example, used the phrase "assumptive world," which he defined as a "strongly held set of assumptions about the world and the self which is confidently maintained and used as a means of recognizing, planning, and acting.... Assumptions such as these are learned and confirmed by the experience of many years" (1975, p. 132). Bowlby (1969) referred to "world models" as working models of the self and the environment that enable an individual to plan, set goals, and function effectively. In his discussion of "structures of meaning," Marris (1975) described the significance of basic principles that are abstract enough for us to apply to any event we encounter; these basic principles or structures "make life continuously intelligible" (p. 20).

Epstein's (1973, 1980, 1984, 1985) cognitive-experiential self-theory is particularly instructive with regard to the internal structure of the conceptual system.

He maintains that an individual's theory of reality is subdivided into a self-theory and a world theory. Each of these subtheories consists of a hierarchical arrangement of higher- and lower-order postulates, wherein "higher order postulates are broad generalizations that are highly abstract" and "lower order postulates are narrow beliefs that are directly tied to experience" (1985, p. 292). "Central" postulates are higher-order postulates derived early in life from emotionally significant experiences. Considerably resistant to change, they are essentially our most basic assumptions and, as such, reflect highly abstract, generalized theories about the nature of the world and ourselves. Invalidation of these postulates has serious consequences for the integrity of the whole conceptual system. However, because they are not readily subjected to the direct test of experience, central postulates are very difficult to invalidate. Furthermore, the conceptual system guides our perceptions and directs our actions at a preconscious level, where it is relatively inaccessible to introspection.

The basic assumptions that comprise our conceptual system generally serve us well and ordinarily are not scrutinized and challenged. Rather, paralleling social-psychological findings related to schemas (Fiske & Taylor, 1984), these basic assumptions are quite resistant to major changes; they provide the lenses through which we view our world, and they can selectively focus or alter perceptions so that they may be readily assimilated into our conceptual system (for further discussion of this parallel with schemas, see Janoff-Bulman, in press-a, and Janoff-Bulman & Timko, 1987). Sometimes, however, people are confronted with information—usually the result of intensely emotional experiences—that cannot be readily assimilated into our most basic assumptions about ourselves or our world. In fact, the emotional intensity of the experience may be due to the violation of one or more basic assumptions that is posed by the experience (Epstein, 1984). Victimization frequently represents just such an experience. The "data" representing the victimization often cannot be readily assimilated, and victims' basic assumptions about themselves and their world may be seriously challenged, threatening a state of cognitive disintegration. Traumatic events may force us to recognize, objectify, and examine our most basic assumptions about ourselves and the world. The very assumptions that previously afforded psychological stability are seriously questioned, and victims' perceptions are marked by threat, danger, insecurity, and self-questioning. The victim's task following victimization involves rebuilding a core of basic assumptions that can account for the traumatic event and reestablish order within the conceptual system.

In the philosophy of science, Kuhn's (1962) conception of "paradigm shift" may be used to illustrate the process of upheaval and restructuring of the assumptive world. A *paradigm* is a framework within which to conduct science, in the same sense that our conceptual system or "assumptive world" is a framework within which to conduct everyday living. In their pursuit of knowledge, scientists are often unaware of the paradigm they are using, even though these basic theories provide the framework for all of their scientific work. During the period Kuhn refers to as "normal science," the prevailing paradigm is generally accepted until particularly pressing anomalies challenge its fundamental aspects. When it cannot account for this new scientific data, the inadequacies of the paradigm are revealed, and a crisis within the scientific community ensues. Historically, the response to this crisis has been a scientific revolution, culminating in a paradigm shift; the old paradigm is discarded and a new one embraced. However, not all anomalies result in the complete abandonment of the established paradigm; as many are eventually assimilated through an additive adjustment rather than an entire shift. In either case, "the anomalous has become the expected" (Kuhn, 1962, p. 53) insofar as it has now been assimilated and explained by the paradigm in use.

Three Core Assumptions Challenged by Victimization

In a parallel manner, the experience of victimization often generates data that cannot be accounted for by the conceptual system maintained by the victim. Three core assumptions of this system that are particularly threatened by traumatic experiences concern the benevolence of the world, the meaningfulness of the world, and the worthiness of the self (Janoff-Bulman, in press-b; cf. Janoff-Bulman, 1985; Janoff-Bulman & Frieze, 1983). Deriving first from early object relations (see Janoff-Bulman, in press-b, for a discussion of this issue) and generally receiving support throughout one's childhood, these postulates occupy a central position in one's conceptual system, representing the metaphysical hard core surrounded by a protective belt of less-central postulates (see Lakatos, 1974). More specifically, this core includes the assumption that the world—both the impersonal world and people—is benevolent; that is, we believe that outcomes are generally positive and that people are basically good. A second basic postulate is the assumption that the world is a meaningful place (Janoff-Bulman & Frieze, 1983; Janoff-Bulman, 1985; Silver & Wortman, 1980). According to the latter assumption, events in the world make sense, in that they can be explained in accordance with accepted "social laws" (Janoff-Bulman & Frieze, 1983; Janoff-Bulman, 1985). In our society, such social laws include principles of justice and control. Justice is invoked when there is a belief that people get what they deserve and deserve what they get (see Lerner, 1980, for his discussion of the just-world theory); that is, we can make sense of events by believing particular outcomes were deserved. We may also understand events by examining people's direct behavioral control over outcomes. In other words, we may make sense of an outcome through an understanding of people's actions or omissions immediately prior to the event. These cultural orientations minimize the likelihood that the world will be perceived as a place where randomness prevails; a random world is a meaningless one. A third basic assumption is self-evaluative; we believe that we are worthy, decent people (Janoff-Bulman & Frieze, 1983; Janoff-Bulman, 1985; also see Taylor & Brown, 1988).

These three basic assumptions are among the most basic in our conceptual system, and together they provide an individual with a sense of relative invulnerability (Janoff-Bulman, in press-b). The likelihood of bad outcomes is apt to be underestimated, and those negative outcomes that are acknowledged as likely are nevertheless perceived as likely to happen only to others, and not to oneself. After all, given one's positive sense of self, the negative outcomes would not be deserved (i.e., the self is perceived as decent and worthy), and, in addition, they would be avoided through proper behaviors and precautionary actions. We thus walk around with an illusion of invulnerability and unrealistic optimism (Janoff-Bulman & Lang-Gunn, 1988; Perloff, 1983; Taylor & Brown, 1988; Weinstein, 1980; Weinstein & Lachendro, 1982). When an individual is victimized, a common immediate response is, "I never thought it could happen to me" (Bard & Sangrey, 1979). Victims are forced to confront their own vulnerability, and simultaneously they are forced to confront many of their formerly unchallenged, unexamined core assumptions, including the benevolence and meaningfulness of the world, as well as their self-worth.

Victimization calls into question some of the most central postulates of people's assumptive worlds. Victims experience a "loss of equilibrium. The world is suddenly out of whack. Things no longer work the way they used to" (Bard & Sangrey, 1979, p. 14). The psychological stability afforded by an intact conceptual system is threatened, and normal functioning is seriously compromised. The major coping task of victims is to reestablish or rebuild a core of basic assumptions that is able to assimilate the data of their traumatic experience (Janoff-Bulman, 1985; Janoff-Bulman & Frieze, 1983). The adaptive value of repetitive thoughts and self-blame lie in their contribution to this process of arriving at a viable postvictimization conceptual system, for they play a facilitative role in the cognitive integration of old assumptions and new information.

INTRUSIVE, RECURRENT THOUGHTS

> I have trouble keeping the whole thing from coming into my mind. There are just so many thoughts running through. Once at work the thought came into my mind and hit me and I lost my breath, the feeling was so intense. (rape victim; Burgess & Holmstrom, 1974, p. 40)

There is little question that recurrent thoughts—in the form of intrusive ideas and images, ruminations and preoccupations, and nightmares—are commonly reported following victimization. These recurrent thoughts and images continue long after the termination of the actual victimizing event, and reexperiencing the event in this way is emotionally painful for victims. On the basis of his research with a wide variety of victims of traumatic events, Horowitz (1982) maintains that such intrusive symptoms are virtually universal among those who have expected serious, negative life events. These recurrent thoughts and images occur regardless of the type of traumatic event and regardless of dispositional factors such as personality (Horowitz, 1976, 1982; Horowitz, Wilner, Kaltreider, & Alvarez, 1980), and they are now recognized as a primary diagnostic criterion of posttraumatic stress disorder (American Psychiatric Association, 1980). Why do individuals continue to reexperience their traumatic victimizations? What impulse in the human organism could account for the more or less universal nature of these painful events? Do they reflect some basic masochism, in that they consistently induce unwanted suffering, or do they reflect a more adaptive impulse?

Freud (1920/1959) himself attempted to tackle these questions, for he found himself puzzled by the repetitive dreams reported by soldiers who were suffering from traumatic neuroses during World War I. The soldiers' traumatic events were reexperienced in these dreams, and Freud recognized that these unbidden images clearly were not instances of wish fulfillment, which operates on the basis of the pleasure principle. Rather, the dreams were so frightening to the soldiers that they often did not want to go to sleep. Up to this point, Freud has assumed all dreams could be accounted for by wish fulfillment; now he was confronting evidence seemingly to the contrary. In response, Freud posited a fundamental motivation that he named the "repetition compulsion." Although he noted that such dreams represent an attempt at mastery by producing the "anxiety whose omission was the cause of the traumatic neurosis" (Freud, 1920/1959, p. 60), in the end he nevertheless revised his theory of personality in accordance with a more maladaptive view of the repetitive symptoms. He posited that there are life and death instincts that are primary human motives. Freud (1920/1959) attributed the repetition compulsion, evidenced by the frightening dreams of the traumatic neurosis, to the death instinct (for more complete discussions, see Epstein, 1981, 1983, and Horowitz, 1976).

The Adaptive Value of Recurrent Thoughts

The frightening dreams of Freud's soldiers and the recurrent, intrusive thoughts of a wide variety of trauma victims do not coincide with a view of human behavior that is ruled by the pleasure principle. These symptoms are unpleasant and result in suffering by victims. Nevertheless, recurrent thoughts derive from an adaptive impulse, in response to the human organism's need for a stable, integrated conceptual system (Epstein, 1980, 1981, 1984; Janoff-Bulman, 1985; Janoff-Bulman & Frieze, 1983). Following victimization, assumptions about the benevolence and meaningfulness of the world are seriously questioned, as are positive self-evaluations. The assumptive worlds that had served victims so well in the past, that had been built up over many years of experience, are now unable to account for the data of the victimizing experience. The event cannot be readily assimilated. To simply give up one's core assumptions is to risk complete cognitive disintegration (Epstein, 1979); yet, the data derived from the victimization are too intense to ignore. Somehow, the new, emotionally powerful information must be slowly assimilated; both the old assumptions and the new information must be worked on, massaged, and gradually merged.

It is in the service of this ultimate assimilation of the new data and accommodation of the core assumptions that the recurrent thoughts, ruminations, and unbidden images of trauma victims must be understood. That they are repeatedly, even compulsively, brought into consciousness is evidence that the traumatic event has not been assimilated; yet, this process of repeatedly thinking about the event also contributes to the gradual assimilation of the new data. It is as if the mind is working on the new information, trying to get it to fit one's assumptive world. This view is consistent with the work of Horowitz (1976, 1980, 1982), who maintains that *"active memory storage has an intrinsic tendency towards repeti-*

tion of representation of contents until the contents held in active memory are actively terminated" (Horowitz, 1976, p. 93). He goes on to write that *"this tendency to repetition of representation is part of a general tendency toward completion of cognitive processing, and hence that completion of cognitive processing is what actively terminates a given content in active memory storage"* (Horowitz, 1976, p. 93). Completion of cognitive processing occurs when there is an integration of new information and old inner models (see Horowitz, 1976, 1980, 1982). When there is a good enough fit, recurrent, intrusive thoughts cease and, according to Horowitz, the new information moves from active memory to inactive memory.

Repetitive, intrusive thoughts provide for gradual, progressive modifications of new and old information. The material is continually recycled, with the possibility of continual reexamination and reinterpretation. Eventually, in the optimal case, the victimization data and old assumptions merge to create a new, viable conceptual system. This assimilation process is not necessarily an easy one. Given that intrusive thoughts are themselves quite stressful and anxiety provoking (Horowitz, 1982; Silver, Boon, & Stones, 1983), it is somewhat remarkable that repeatedly reliving the event can actually prove successful in terms of cognitive integration and the reduction of stress. Past research has demonstrated that a stimulus such as a loud tone will result in habituation if it is not too intense, but it will result in sensitization if it is intense (Sokolov, 1963). Similarly, in the case of traumatic victimization, the intensity of the recurrent thoughts must be modulated so as to effect integration of the new information with one's core assumptions. It is not surprising, then, that among trauma victims, recurrent, intrusive thoughts alternate with periods of denial and numbness (Horowitz, 1976, 1980, 1982), which provide a means of tempering the emotional intensity experienced. Denial plays an extremely important role in the coping process of victims, for it enables them to deal with the event in manageable doses (Epstein, 1983; Horowitz, 1976; Janoff-Bulman & Timko, 1987). As Janoff-Bulman and Timko (1987) maintain

> A dramatic unmodulated attack on the primary postulates of one's assumptive world is controlled by the process of denial, which allows the individual to face slowly and gradually the realities of the external world and incorporate them into his or her internal world. (p. 145)

It is unlikely that denial would be regarded as a self-defeating response following victimization. In general, it does not lead to greater suffering by victims but rather reduces their stress and discomfort; denial appears to operate in accordance with the pleasure principle. This is not the case with recurrent, intrusive thoughts. They are painful and appear to increase, not decrease, suffering. They seem so self-defeating; why not simply forget the event and go on with one's life? For good or ill, it is the intrusive thoughts themselves that often enable the person to get past the event and go on with his or her life, for it is these repetitive thoughts that, in the end, aid the process of cognitive integration. Recurrent thoughts and ruminations replay the victimization so that it can eventually be assimilated, and the victim's assumptive world can once again be a stable, viable conceptual system.

In the case of successful adjustment, the intrusive, repetitive thoughts should become increasingly less stressful and anxiety provoking, as well as increasingly less frequent. They should essentially cease once the victimizing event is integrated into one's assumptive world. This does not mean the victim will not think about the event; rather, the autonomous repetition of the event will markedly decrease, and recollections will occur primarily when the victim is in situations that serve as associational triggers of the event (Horowitz, 1976). A successful resolution of the integration process would incorporate the new data, but it would not completely overwhelm the prior positive perceptions of the world and the self. Thus, an adaptive resolution would involve maintaining generally positive views but recognizing that bad things can and do happen; that although the world is generally benign and most people are caring and good, there are instances of malevolence and people who are bad; that although most events are comprehensible in terms of justice and/or control, and are therefore meaningful and predictable, it is simply impossible to make sense of some events; that although the self is worthy and decent, imperfections are inevitable. The individual thereby retains the ability to enjoy life, while also accepting its limitations (Epstein, in press). In essence, the victim may be a bit sadder, but far wiser.

When Recurrent Thoughts are Self-Defeating

The success of integrating the new information and one's prior assumptions rests largely with the possibility of finding a fit between the two. There may be instances when this is a particularly difficult task, and in such cases the intrusive, repetitive thoughts remain extremely stressful and, in fact, interfere with successful coping. These are the instances in which the stimulus (i.e., the repetitive thoughts) are too intense, resulting in sensitization rather than habituation (Epstein, 1983; Sokolov, 1963). In these instances, the tremendous, unabating anxiety associated with the intrusive, recurrent thoughts derives not solely from the fear, and even terror, associated with the actual victimization but from the implicit recognition of how widely discrepant the information is from one's prior core assumptions. In other words, there is fear associated with confronting the very real possibility of serious physical injury or mortality; in addition, there is anxiety associated with a view of the world that is not only new but very threatening—so threatening, in fact, that massaging it to fit one's prior assumptions seems largely beyond the realm of possibilities.

Factors that maximize the discrepancy between old assumptions and new information are likely to minimize the adaptive value of intrusive, repetitive thoughts. Recurrent thoughts will not abate and will result in increasingly greater stress and anxiety for the victim. The degree of discrepancy between the old and new will depend on the nature of the prior assumptive world, the nature of the data from the victimization, and on new, incoming information that may provide additional material relevant to one's basic conceptual system. Regarding the nature of one's prior assumptions, it appears that the more exaggerated one's positive views are prior to the victimization, the more difficult it will be to assimilate the traumatic experience. As Perloff (1983) has argued, victims who feel most invulnerable to negative outcomes prior to their experience have the most difficulty coping after victimization (also see Wortman, 1976, regarding the danger of high expectations of control in the face of uncontrollable outcomes). If the world is assumed to be unquestionably benign and meaningful, and one's self is assumed to be completely worthv, then the personal experience of victimization will represent a particularly powerful blow to one's conceptual system. To the extent that one's assumptions have been challenged, even minimally, in the past, one's conceptual system will reflect a more realistic, perhaps less Pollyannish view of the world and self. The assumptive world would still be overwhelmingly positive in outlook but would retain greater flexibility, perhaps by providing the individual with the ability to make more distinctions through more complex assumptions about the world and self. This type of conceptual system could most readily accommodate to new information. An assumptive world characterized by extremely positive basic assumptions that have never been challenged, and are therefore apt to be most simplistic, will present the greatest difficulties for victims confronting the task of cognitive integration. In such cases, intrusive, recurrent thoughts of the victimization may become self-defeating, remaining extremely frequent and stressful and interfering with one's day-to-day functioning.

The nature of the data to be assimilated is also important when considering those instances in which repetitive thoughts are apt to be self-defeating. Some types of data are no doubt more difficult to assimilate than others. The extent to which a threat is posed by the victimization experience depends not only on the number and importance of the basic assumptions that are challenged but also on the ability of the victim to interpret the new information in less threatening ways. For example, there is considerable evidence that victims are often able to reevaluate their experience in a positive light. This type of interpretation generally involves finding some meaning in the traumatic event (Bulman & Wortman, 1977; Silver & Wortman, 1980; Taylor, 1983), such as learning some important lesson—about oneself, about others, or about what's really important in life. Some people are able to construe their victimization positively, thereby minimizing the threat to one's prior assumptive world. It is not that these victims would have chosen to be victimized but, rather, once victimized, they are able to interpret their experience as having been worthwhile in some way. They may feel they have discovered some great personal strength, or realized how much their loved ones care for them, or recognized how important their family and friends are. The world is not totally malevolent or meaningless if the victimization can be reevaluated as positive to some extent. When victimizations cannot be reinterpreted positively in any way, the data from the experience will certainly provide a greater threat to one's prior conceptual system.

Other interpretations of the victimization may also have an impact on ease of assimilation (see the discussion of self-blame that follows); overall, to the extent that the event can be interpreted in ways consistent with one's already existing basic assumptions, repetitive thoughts will cease and the event will be assimilated. Not only may people differ in the ease with which they are able to reevaluate events, but certain events may simply be more difficult to interpret in a way that minimizes the cognitive threat that is posed. The concentration camp experience, for example, was an extreme victimization that was particularly difficult to reinterpret in any positive way (e.g., Benner, Roskies, & Lazarus, 1980).

In addition to the nature of one's core assumptions and the nature of data from the victimization, there are ongoing experiences in victims' lives that coincide with the process of cognitively coping with the victimization. In other words, while the victim is trying to assimilate the victimization experience, other events in the victim's life may affect the process. It seems very likely that victims who receive a great deal of social support from others in their lives will have an easier time assimilating their experience. Victims who do not receive social support are more likely to manifest the self-defeating form of intrusive, repetitive thoughts, the type that does not decrease in frequency or intensity and reflects an inability to complete the task of cognitive integration. A common response of nonvictims is to blame victims for their fate (Lerner, 1980; Ryan, 1971), ignore them (Reiff, 1979), and see them as losers (Bard & Sangrey, 1979). In spite of any teachings of our Judeo-Christian heritage, victims are often not regarded with any compassion. However, there is a great deal of evidence that support from family, friends, the helping professions, and the community-at-large has a strong positive impact on the process of recovery of victims (e.g., Bard & Sangrey, 1979; Burgess & Holmstrom, 1976; Cobb, 1976; Silver & Wortman, 1980; Symonds, 1980).

One means by which this impact may be felt is in terms of the process of cognitive integration from victimization. If victims are given a great deal of support by others during the readjustment period, they are essentially being given information that contradicts their traumatic experience; that is, they are being provided with evidence that the world can be benevolent, that there are people that are good, that justice and deservingness can operate in one's life, that they themselves are worthy of care and concern. By combining their information with their former assumptions and the data from their victimization, victims are likely to be able to assimilate the victimization in an adaptive way. Described in greater detail above, this involves viewing the world and oneself positively, while simultaneously recognizing limitations and imperfections. Assuming that one's core assumptions were positive, and that the social support provides a positive view of oneself and the world, the victim's assumptive world would be positive, but the data from the victimization would be integrated in terms of particular types of experiences or particular types of people, rather than general assumptions reflecting negative views of the world and oneself. If victims are blamed and ignored by others, they would be receiving information consistent with their traumatic experience—that the world is bad and meaningless, and that they are unworthy. In light of people's cognitive tendencies to maintain existing assumptions (see work on schemas, Fiske & Taylor, 1984), assimilating their victimization experience would continue to be difficult. Intrusive, repetitive thoughts would be more likely to continue as extremely stressful, frequently occurring experiences, and a coherent conceptual system would be lacking.

In spite of the tendency to persevere in maintaining some parts of one's old assumptions, it is nevertheless the case that some victims do, in fact, reestablish an assumptive world that bears little or no resemblance to their prior conceptual system. These victims essentially replace their prior assumptions with new basic postulates derived from their traumatic experience. This new set of assumptions is extremely threatening and, as such, is not easily embraced. Nevertheless, having some coherent system—no matter how negative—may be better than having none. The individual may thus have a stable, integrated system, but one that has core assumptions involving the malevolence of the world and people, the meaningless and randomness of the world, and the unworthiness of the self. There is clearly a cost involved in resolving the cognitive coping task in this way. The victim is likely to be very anxious, even paranoid, and his or her behavior will reflect a state of extreme hypervigilance. The rape victim who does not leave her home, and the disease victim who becomes a hypochondriac, certain that every minor symptom spells disaster, have probably established an assumptive world based primarily upon the data from their victimization. Intrusive, repetitive thoughts generally will not be a problem for these victims, for they are no longer struggling with the process of assimilation. Nevertheless, chronic anxiety will permeate their lives, for their world views are dominated by perceptions of danger and vulnerability.

SELF-BLAME

Recurrent thoughts represent cognitive responses that generally do not seem to be under volitional control. Although they may appear self-defeating, one can nevertheless argue that the trauma victim is not actually choosing to suffer, even if he or she does in fact suffer as a result. The decision rests instead with the nature of the human organism and its information-processing functions. Such is not the case when considering self-blame, for this attribution appears to be under far greater volitional control. If self-blame causes greater suffering, it would appear that the victim has chosen to suffer and is engaging in an incomprehensible self-defeating behavior. Is self-blame self-defeating, or is there evidence that it is, in fact, an adaptive response to victimization?

THE ADAPTIVE VALUE OF SELF-BLAME

Self-blame is a common response to a wide variety of victimizations; the tendency to accept blame is common among victims of rape (Burgess & Holmstrom, 1974; Medea & Thompson, 1974; Weis & Weis, 1975), battering (Frieze, 1979; Hilberman & Munson, 1978; Walker, 1979), other crimes (Bard & Sangrey, 1979; Frieze, Hymer & Greenberg, 1984; Geis, 1981), disease (Abrams & Finesinger, 1953; Bard & Dyk, 1956; Davis, 1963; Friedman, Chodoff, Mason, & Hamburg, 1977; Timko & Janoff-Bulman, 1985), natural disasters (Wolfenstein, 1957), and serious accidents (Bulman & Wortman, 1977). Victims often seem unnecessarily willing to blame themselves, at least in part, for their victimization; perhaps the pervasiveness of this response reflects a positive attempt to cope following the traumatic event.

As in the case of intrusive, repetitive thoughts, the adaptive value of self-blame derives from the attribution's role in facilitating the process of cognitive integration. In the case of recurrent thoughts, the data from the victimizing event is considered and reconsidered until, ultimately, it can fit what already comprises one's assumptive world. This process involves not only massage of the new information but change and accommodation of the old assumptions as well. In the case of self-blame, however, far less accommodation of prior assumptions is necessitated. Self-blame involves perceiving the traumatic incident in such a way that the new information is made minimally threatening to one's conceptual system. In other words, the prior assumptions can remain more or less intact, and the new data can be readily assimilated into one's old, stable system. In order to understand how self-blame might operate in this fashion, it is important to focus first on the nature of self-blame and, more specifically, the type of self-blame that is apt to be adaptive.

Janoff-Bulman (1979) posited that there are (at least) two distinct types of self-blame—one that focuses on behavior, labeled "behavioral self-blame," the other that focuses on character or personality, labeled "characterological self-blame." The former involves blaming a modifiable factor, whereas the latter involves blaming more stable, enduring qualities of a person. This distinction is reflected in the differences between the following two statements by rape victims: "I should not have gone back to his apartment" versus "I am a very bad judge of character." Note that the differences between these statements in terms of behavior and character are apparent in the past versus present tense of the verb used in each case; behavioral self-blame is generally related in the past tense, reflecting the implicit modifiability of the behavior, and characterological self-blame is generally related in the present tense, reflecting the continuing definition of one's self in terms of the selected character trait. One's behaviors are perceived as more controllable and changeable than one's character traits; behavioral self-blame is control oriented and does not involve esteem deficits. Characterological self-blame, on the other hand, is a more generalized blame response and involves lowered self-esteem. The difference in perceived controllability of the factor blamed (i.e., behavior versus character) led Janoff-Bulman (1979; also see Wortman, 1976) to propose that behavioral self-blame may be an adaptive response to victimization, for it would enable victims to minimize their sense of vulnerability following the traumatic incident. They would be able to maintain that by altering their behaviors in the future, they would be capable of avoiding a recurrence of the event. Further, a general belief in controllability over negative outcomes would be maintained. Given that discomfort over vulnerability and fear of repetition of the trauma are extremely common reactions following victimization (Horowitz, 1982), behavioral self-blame would be an adaptive, stress-reducing response to the event. It is important to recognize that it is not behavioral self-blame that is adaptive, but behavioral self-blame in the absence of characterological self-blame that is adaptive. People can believe they have done stupid things without believing they are stupid people; however, the opposite is unlikely, for people who believe they are stupid are likely to believe they have done stupid things. People who engage in characterological self-blame almost necessarily also engage in behavioral self-blame, but these are not the individuals whose responses are adaptive. Behavioral self-blamers who do not also engage in characterological self-blame are regarded as engaging in the most adaptive attributional strategy (Janoff-Bulman, 1979; Janoff-Bulman & Lang-Gunn, 1988). Empirical research has generally found that behavioral self-blame is, in fact, an adaptive response to victimization, in that it is associated with positive coping outcomes (e.g., Affleck, Allen, Tennen, McGrade, & Ratzan, 1985; Affleck, McGrade, Allen, & McQueeney, 1985; Baum, Flemming, & Singer, 1983; Bulman & Wortman, 1977; Fischer, 1984; Peterson, Schwartz, & Seligman, 1981; Tennen, Affleck, & Gershman, 1986; Tennen, Affleck, Allen, McGrade, & Ratzan, 1984; Timko & Janoff-Bulman, 1985; cf. Kiecolt-Glaser & Williams, 1987; Meyer & Taylor, 1986).

Although the adaptive value of behavioral self-blame was originally posited in terms of its implications for control and perceived vulnerability (Janoff-Bulman, 1979), this probably represents an incomplete analysis of the adaptive nature of the attribution. Rather, a more thorough understanding involves the implications of behavioral self-blame for the victim's conceptual system. By engaging in behavioral self-blame, victims essentially eliminate the need to alter their basic assumptions about the world in order to assimilate the data from their victimization. By focusing on oneself as the cause of the victimization, yet not generalizing the self-blame beyond specific behavioral acts or omissions, the victim is able to maintain a view of the world as meaningful and benign and a view of the self as positive and worthy. The world can continue to be perceived as meaningful, for the social law of controllability is upheld; when the victim asks "Why me?" (Janoff-Bulman & Lang-Gunn, 1988) he or she can make sense of the event by pointing to particular behaviors that contributed to the negative outcome. The victim's view of the impersonal world and other people can remain essentially unaffected; in spite of a possible new realization that bad things can happen, the victim is likely to continue to view the world as benign, for such negative outcomes will be perceived as avoidable. Further, the victim's self-esteem should remain unscathed, for behavioral self-blame is not a generalized attribution to the core of the self; one's positive sense of self is thereby left intact.

By engaging in behavioral self-blame, victims can minimize the cognitive work involved in establishing a stable, coherent conceptual system. The data from the traumatic event can be readily assimilated, for it does not pose a serious threat or challenge to the victim's existing assumptive world; change and accommodation of basic assumptions are not unnecessary. From this perspective, it is unlikely that those who engage in behavioral self-blame will experience intrusive, repetitive thoughts to any considerable extent, for the task of conceptual integration should be resolved with a minimum of cognitive effort. For individuals who do experience frequent intrusive, recurrent thoughts and images, it is possible that one way in which the task of integration is ultimately resolved is by arriving at an interpretation of the traumatic event that involves some behavioral self-blame. The data from the victimizing incident would then be more easily assimilated, and intrusive, repetitive thoughts should cease.

When Self-Blame is Self-Defeating

Unfortunately, self-blame following victimization does not always focus on behaviors. Rather, victims may instead engage in characterological self-blame and may thereby suffer from markedly decreased self-esteem following the traumatic incident. Low self-esteem can result in a number of clearly self-destructive behaviors, including suicide and substance abuse. Characterological self-blame seems very self-defeating, particularly when considered in light of the adaptive value of behavioral self-blame. Why don't victims simply choose to attribute the victimization to their behavioral acts or omissions? What factors lead victims to generalize to their more basic, core beliefs about the self?

Victimizations that occur again and again are likely to change specific behavioral self-blame attributions to more global characterological attributions. In cases such as battering or incest, the female victim may initially engage in behavioral self-blame; she may select as a cause of the incident a behavior that immediately preceded the abuse (see Miller & Porter, 1983). By changing her behavior, the victim believes she can avoid a recurrence of the event. When the battering or incest recurs, the victim may again go through the same cognitive strategy. In the end, however, behaviors are apt to cease to be the focus of one's self-blame; no behavior change seems the "right one" to eliminate the abuse. After a number of instances, the victim may generalize from her discrete behaviors to her character and thereby begin to question her own self-worth. In reaction to repeated victimizations, the victim of battering or incest is likely to move from a more situational response to a dispositional one, experiencing a marked decrease in self-esteem as she does so. Low self-esteem is commonly found among victims of battering (e.g., Hilberman & Munson, 1978; Walker, 1979) and incest (e.g., Gold, 1986; Herman, 1981; Shapiro, 1987); this low esteem is no doubt attributable in part to maladaptive strategies of self-blame (i.e., characterological self-blame) by victims.

It is certainly the case that many victimizations do not represent "chronic" states such as battering and incest; rather, many are discrete, single events. In these instances, one would expect victims to engage in behavioral rather than characterological self-blame, given the adaptive value of the former attribution. Nevertheless, certain factors may work against behavioral self-blame and may increase the likelihood of a more self-defeating response—characterological self-blame. First, some victims may not regard behaviors (or behavioral omissions) as "big" enough causes of such serious negative events. It appears that people use a resemblance criterion for cause and effect (Nisbett & Ross, 1980), and this criterion includes resemblance in terms of size or magnitude (Janoff-Bulman, in press-b). Just as "great events ought to have great causes" (Nisbett & Ross, 1980, p. 116), victimizations, which seem extremely large given their huge impact, ought to have "large" causes. Perhaps behaviors are simply not big enough or major enough to warrant serious consideration as causes of such overwhelming outcomes. However, one's character, or generalized sense of self, may be a cause of appropriate magnitude.

Second, it is certainly the case that it is easier to invoke behaviors as the cause of some victimizations as compared to others. Whereas the woman who is raped while hitchhiking may find it relatively easy to focus on her behavior, the woman who is raped while sleeping in her bed in her locked home will have a far more difficult time doing so. Likewise, whereas the disease victim who has never attended to his or her health may focus on past behaviors (e.g., smoking, lack of exercise, poor diet), this would be more difficult for the disease victim who has always taken excellent care of himself or herself. The paralyzed accident victim who has decided to drive while drunk will have an easier time engaging in behavioral self-blame than the paralyzed accident victim who was driving safely and carefully and was hit by another car. Victims who have engaged in the safest, most cautious behaviors are often the ones who have the most difficulty coping; thus, in a study of rape victims, Scheppele and Bart (1983) found that the women who had the most difficult time psychologically were those who had been following their personal rules for avoiding rape and were therefore in a "safe" situation at the time of the attack. Clearly, situations differ in terms of how compelling a victim's behaviors are as a cause of the victimizing event. There are outcomes which simply do not lend themselves to behavioral explanations. In such cases, victims may nevertheless look to themselves to explain their misfortune; that is, they may regard themselves as deserving the outcome because of the kind of people they are (i.e., characterological self-blame). If behavioral self-blame seems unwarranted, why engage in this maladaptive form of self-blame? Why not explain the victimization without self-blame?

In part, the propensity to blame oneself may be a reflection of societal views about victims. Given the tendency of people in our society to blame victims (Lerner, 1980; Ryan, 1971; Symonds, 1980), individuals may internalize this blame when they become victims. More central to an understanding of the pervasiveness of self-blame is the victim's search for meaning following the traumatic event (Bulman & Wortman, 1977; Silver *et al.*, 1983; Silver & Wortman, 1980). In their attempts to make sense of their experience, victims struggle with the question of why the negative outcome happened to them in particular (Janoff-Bulman & Lang-Gunn, 1988). They do not seek an answer to "Why?" but rather to "Why me?" It is the selective incidence of the event that they feel compelled to explain. The rape victim does not want to know why rape occurs but why it occurred to her; the accident victim does not want to know why serious automobile accidents happen but why it happened to him. By invoking "social laws" such as justice or controllability, the "Why me?" question is answered; it was because of something the victim did or failed to do (controllability) or it was because he or she deserved it (justice). To explain the selective incidence of traumatic events, victims naturally turn to themselves—it happened to them, so there must be something about them that accounts for the outcome. If behavior is not invoked as an explanation, for reasons discussed previously, one's more general sense of self is apt to be blamed. In turn, the victim is likely to experience the marked decrease in self-esteem that would naturally follow a belief that one deserved the victimization.

By engaging in characterological self-blame, victims perceive themselves more negatively. However, they are able to maintain their basic assumptions about the meaningfulness and, to some extent, the benevolence of the world. If an outcome is regarded as deserved, the world can still make sense, and events can seem orderly and predictable. For many, the need to see the world as meaningful may be even more basic than the need to evaluate oneself positively (Wortman, 1976). Thus, although characterological self-blame is self-defeating, in that it results in decreased self-esteem, it must nevertheless be understood in the context of one's set of core assumptions.

NEGATIVE PRIOR ASSUMPTIONS

Throughout this chapter we have discussed responses to victimization when the prior conceptual system of the victim reflected a positive world view, that is, when the victim's prior conceptual system is comprised of assumptions about the benevolence of the world and people, the meaningfulness of the world, and the worthiness of the self. Given that most people operate on the basis of an illusion of invulnerability and unrealistic optimism (Janoff-Bulman & Lang-Gunn, 1988; Perloff, 1983; Taylor & Brown, in press; Weinstein, 1980; Weinstein & Lachendro, 1982), it seems reasonable to conclude that most people also hold positive basic assumptions about the world and the self. Nevertheless, unquestionably there are people whose conceptual systems reflect considerable pessimism, people who, at the time of victimization, already have negative views of themselves and the world. These are individuals who are likely to have lived in an environment that has not been benign—one in which other people have not been caring and responsive and negative events have seemed a part of one's daily existence. Experiences of childhood abuse and neglect, for example, may lead children to hold basic assumptions reflecting negative views of themselves and the world, assumptions that will form the core of their conceptual system in adulthood. Individuals with negative core assumptions are likely to be as committed to maintaining their assumptive world as are individuals with more positive views; that is, threats to these individuals' basic postulates would not come from victimization experiences but rather from very positive outcomes.

Further, just as individuals with positive, benign assumptions implicitly validate their basic assumptions by finding supportive data in their lives (e.g., evidence of their self-worth, evidence of the goodness of people), individuals with negative assumptions no doubt try to validate their assumptions as well. This can be very problematic, for such people may place themselves in situations that virtually guarantee negative outcomes and self-devaluation. Generally they are not aware of their reasons for doing so, but their self-defeating behaviors enable them to maintain a stable, coherent albeit negative conceptual system. Freud recognized that people tend to repeat their past mistakes in life (Epstein, 1981). And, as "the Greeks noted a long time ago, people appear to be controlled by a daemonic fate that forces them to behave consistently in self-destructive ways" (Epstein, 1981, p. 35). Thus, children who are victims of violence frequently find themselves in violent families as adults as well (e.g., Hilberman, 1980).

People try to retain their basic postulates about the world and themselves, for to do otherwise would be to threaten the breakdown of one's basic conceptual system, a certain path to intense psychological disequilibrium. Such a state of psychological distress would follow, whether the prior assumptions reflected a positive, optimistic view of the world or a negative, pessimistic view of the world. After victimization, a major coping task of the victim is to reestablish a viable, coherent set of basic assumptions. For most people, the experience must be integrated into a conceptual system that has been based upon positive beliefs about the world and the self. Behaviors that appear self-defeating following victimization, including intrusive, repetitive thoughts and self-blame, actually derive from adaptive impulses. They help maintain the integrity of the victim's conceptual system by allowing the successful integration of old assumptions and new information. Generally, this is no easy task, given the victim's positive prior assumptions and the intensely negative experience of victimization.

REFERENCES

Abrams, R. D., & Finesinger, J. E. (1953). Guilt reactions in patients with cancer. *Cancer, 6*, 474–482.

Affleck, G., Allen, D. A., Tennen, H., McGrade, B. J., & Ratzan, S. (1985). Causal and control cognitions in parent coping with a chronically ill child. *Journal of Social and Clinical Psychology, 3*, 369–379.

Affleck, G., McGrade, B. J., Allen, D. A., & McQueeney, M. (1985). Mothers' beliefs about behavioral causes for their developmentally disabled infant's condition: What do they signify? *Journal of Pediatric Psychology, 10*, 193–303.

American Psychiatric Association. (1980). Diagnostic and statistical manual of mental disorders (DSM III) (3rd ed.). Washington, DC: Author.

Bard, M., & Dyk, R. B. (1956). The psychodynamic significance of beliefs regarding the cause of serious illness. *Psychoanalytic Review, 43*, 146–162.

Bard, M., & Sangrey, D. (1979). *The crime victim's book.* New York: Basic Books.

Baum, A., Flemming, R., & Singer, J. E. (1983). Coping with victimization by technological disaster. *Journal of Social Issues, 39*, 119–140.

Benner, P., Roskies, E., & Lazarus, R. S. (1980). Stress and coping under extreme conditions. In J. E. Dimsdale (Ed.), *Survivors, victims, and perpetrators: Essays on the Nazi holocaust* (pp. 215–258). Washington, DC: Hemisphere.

Bowlby, J. (1969). *Attachment and loss: Vol. 1. Attachment.* London: Hogarth.

Bulman, R. J., & Wortman, C. B. (1977). Attributions of blame and coping in the "real world": Severe accident victims react to their lot. *Journal of Personality and Social Psychology, 35*, 351–363.

Burgess, A., & Holmstrom, L. (1974). *Rape: Victims of crisis.* Bowie, MD: Brady.

Burgess, A., & Holmstrom, L. (1976). Coping behavior of the rape victim. *American Journal of Psychiatry, 13*, 413–417.

Cobb, S. (1976). Social support as a moderator of life stress. *Psychosomatic Medicine, 38*, 300–314.

Davis, F. (1963). *Passage through crisis: Polio victims and their families.* Indianapolis, IN: Bobbs-Merrill.

Epstein, S. (1973). The self-concept revisited, or a theory of a theory. *American Psychologist, 28*, 404–416.

Epstein, S. (1979). The ecological study of emotions in humans. In P. Pliner, K. R. Blanstein, & I. M. Spigel (Eds.), *Advances in the study of communication and affect: Vol. 5. Perception of emotions in self and others* (pp. 47–83). New York: Plenum.

Epstein, S. (1980). The self-concept: A review and the proposal of an integrated theory of personality. In E. Staub (Ed.), *Personality: Basic issues and current research* (pp. 82–132). Englewood Cliffs, NJ: Prentice-Hall.

Epstein, S. (1981). The unity principle versus the reality and pleasure principles, or the tale of the scorpion and the log. In M. D. Lynch, A. A. Norem-Hebeisen, & K. Gergen (Eds.), *Self-concept: Advances in theory and research* (pp. 27–37). Cambridge, MA: Ballinger.

Epstein, S. (1983). Natural healing processes of the mind: Graded stress inoculation as an inherent coping mechanism. In D. Meichenbaum & M. E. Jaremko (Eds.), *Stress reduction and prevention* (pp. 39–66). New York: Plenum.

Epstein, S. (1984). Controversial issues in emotion theory. In P. Shaver (Ed.), *Review of personality and social psychology: Emotions, relationships, and health* (pp. 64–88). Beverly Hills, CA: Sage.

Epstein, S. (1985). The Implications of cognitive-experiential self-theory for research in social psychology and personality. *Journal for the Theory of Social Behavior, 15*(3), 283–310.

Epstein, S. (in press). The self-concept, the traumatic neurosis, and the structure of personality. In D. J. Ozer, J. M. Healy, & A. J. Stewart (Eds.), *Perspectives on personality: Self and emotion*. Greenwich, CT: JAI Press.

Fischer, C. T. (1984). A phenomenological study of being criminally victimized: Contributions and constraints of qualitative research. *Journal of Social Issues, 40*, 161–178.

Fiske, S. T., & Taylor, S. E. (1984). *Social cognition*. Reading, MA: Addison-Wesley.

Freud, S. (1959). *Beyond the pleasure principle*. New York: Bantam Books. (First German edition, 1920)

Friedman, S. B., Chodoff, P., Mason, J. E., & Hamburg, D. A. (1977). Behavioral observations on parents anticipating the death of a child. In A. Monat & R. Lazarus (Eds.), *Stress and coping* (pp. 349–374). New York: Columbia University Press.

Frieze, I. H. (1979). Perceptions of battered wives. In I. H. Frieze, D. Bar-Tal, & J. S. Carroll (Eds.), *New approaches to social problems: Applications of attribution theory* (pp. 79–108). San Francisco; Jossey-Bass.

Frieze, I. H., Hymer, S., & Greenberg, M. S. (1984). Describing the victims of crime and violence. In S. S. Kahn (Ed.), *Victims of crime and violence* (pp. 19–78). Final report of the APA task force on the victims of crime and violence. Washington, DC: American Psychological Association.

Geis, G. (1981). Victims of crimes of violence and the criminal justice system. In B. Galaway & J. Hudson (Eds.), *Perspectives on crime victims* (pp. 62–72). St. Louis: Mosby.

Gold, E. R. (1986). Long-term effects of sexual victimization in childhood: An attributional approach. *Journal of Consulting and Clinical Psychology, 54*, 471–475.

Herman, J. L. (1981). Father–daughter incest. Cambridge, MA: Harvard University Press.

Hilberman, E. (1980). Overview: The "wife-beater's wife" reconsidered. *American Journal of Psychiatry, 137*, 1336–1347.

Hilberman, E., & Munson, K. (1978). Sixty battered women. *Victimology, 2*, 460–471.

Horowitz, M. J. (1976). *Stress response syndromes*. New York: Aronson.

Horowitz, M. J. (1980). Psychological response to serious life events. In V. Hamilton & D. Warburton (Eds.), *Human stress and cognition* (pp. 235–266). New York: Wiley.

Horowitz, M. J. (1982). Stress response syndromes and their treatment. In L. Goldberger & S. Breznitz (Eds.), *Handbook of stress* (pp. 711–732). New York: Free Press.

Horowitz, M. J., Wilner, N., Kaltreider, K., & Alvarez, W. (1980). Signs and symptoms of post-traumatic stress disorder. *Archives of General Psychiatry, 37*, 85–92.

Janoff-Bulman, R. (1979). Characterological versus behavioral self-blame: Inquiries into depression and rape. *Journal of Personality and Social Psychology, 37*(10), 1798–1809.

Janoff-Bulman, R. (1985). The aftermath of victimization: Rebuilding shattered assumptions. In C. R. Figley (Ed.), *Trauma and its wake* (pp. 15–35). New York: Brunner/Mazel.

Janoff-Bulman, R. (in press-a). Assumptive worlds and the stress of traumatic events: Applications of the schema concept. *Social Cognition*.

Janoff-Bulman, R. (in press-b). Understanding people in terms of their assumptive worlds. In D. J. Ozer, J. M. Healy, and A. J. Stewart (Eds.), *Perspectives on personality: Self and emotion*. Greenwich, CT: JAI Press.

Janoff-Bulman, R., & Frieze, I. H. (1983). A theoretical perspective for understanding reactions to victimization. *Journal of Social Issues, 39*, 1–17.

Janoff-Bulman, R., & Lang-Gunn, L. (1988). Coping with disease and accidents: The role of self-blame attributions. In L. Y. Abramson (Ed.), *Social cognition and clinical psychology* (pp. 116–147). New York: Guilford Press.

Janoff-Bulman, R., & Timko, C. (1987). Coping with traumatic life events: The role of denial in light of people's assumptive worlds. In C. R. Snyder & C. Ford (Eds.), *Coping with negative life events: Clinical and social psychological perspectives* (pp. 135–159). New York: Plenum.

Kiecolt-Glaser, J. K., & Williams, D. (1987). Self-blame, compliance, and distress among burn patients. *Journal of Personality and Social Psychology, 53*, 187–193.

Kuhn, T. S. (1962). *The structure of scientific revolutions*. Chicago: University of Chicago Press.

Lakatos, I. (1974). Falsification and the methodology of scientific research programs. In I. Lakatos & A. Musgrave (Eds.), *Criticism and the growth of knowledge* (pp. 91–196). London: Cambridge University Press.

Lerner, M. J. (1980). *The belief in a just world*. New York: Plenum.

Marris, P. (1975). *Loss and change*. Garden City, NY: Anchor/Doubleday.

Medea, A., & Thompson, K. (1974). *Against rape*. New York: Farrar, Straus & Giroux.

Meyer, C. B., & Taylor, S. E. (1986). Adjustment to rape. *Journal of Personality and Social Psychology, 50*, 1226–1234.

Miller, D. T., & Porter, C. A. (1983). Self-blame in victims of violence. *Journal of Social Issues, 39*, 141–154.

Nisbett, R. E., & Ross, L. (1980). *Human inference: Strategies and shortcomings of social judgment*. Englewood Cliffs, NJ: Prentice-Hall.

Parkes, C. M. (1971). Psycho-social transitions: A field of study. *Social Science and Medicine, 5*, 101–115.

Parkes, C. M. (1975). What becomes of redundant world models? A contribution to the study of adaptation to change. *British Journal of Medical Psychology, 48*, 131–137.

Perloff, L. S. (1983). Perceptions of vulnerability to victimization. *Journal of Social Issues, 39*(2), 41–62.

Peterson, C., Schwartz, S. M., & Seligman, M. E. P. (1981). Self-blame and depressive symptoms. *Journal of Personality and Social Psychology, 41*, 253–259.

Reiff, R. (1979). *The invisible victim: The criminal justice system's forgotten responsibility*. New York: Basic Books.

Ryan, W. (1971). *Blaming the victim*. New York: Vintage Books.

Scheppele, K. L., & Bart, P. B. (1983). Through women's eyes: Defining danger in the wake of sexual assault. *Journal of Social Issues, 39*, 63–81.

Shapiro, S. (1987). Self-mutilation and self-blame in incest victims. *American Journal of Psychotherapy, 41*, 46–54.

Silver, R. L., Boon, C., & Stones, M. H. (1983). Searching for meaning in misfortune: Making sense of incest. *Journal of Social Issues, 39*, 81–101.

Silver, R. L., & Wortman, C. B. (1980). Coping with undesirable life events. In J. Garber & M. E. P. Seligman (Eds.), *Human helplessness: Theory and application* (pp. 279–340). New York: Academic Press.

Sokolov, Y. N. (1963). *Perception and the conditioned reflex*. New York: MacMillan.

Symonds, M. (1980). The "second" injury to victims. *Evaluation and Change*, 36–38.

Taylor, S. E. (1983). Adjustment to threatening events: A theory of cognitive adaptation. *American Psychologist, 38*, 1161–1173.

Taylor, S. E., & Brown, J. D. (1988). Illusion and well-being: A social psychological perspective on mental health. *Psychological Bulletin, 103*, 193–210.

Tennen, H., Affleck, G., Allen, D. A., McGrade, B. J., & Ratzan, S. (1984). Causal attributions and coping with insulin-dependent diabetes. *Basic and Applied Social Psychology, 5*, 131–142.

Tennen, H., Affleck, G., & Gerschman, K. (1986). Self-blame among parents of infants with perinatal complications: The role of self-protective motives. *Journal of Personality and Social Psychology, 50*, 690–696.

Timko, C., & Janoff-Bulman, R. (1985), Attributions, vulnerability, and psychological adjustment: The case of breast cancer. *Health Psychology, 4*, 521–544.

Walker, L. E. (1979). *The battered woman*. New York: Harper & Row.

Weinstein, N. D. (1980). Unrealistic optimism about future life events. *Journal of Personality and Social Psychology, 39*, 806–820.

Weinstein, N. D., & Lachendro, E. (1982). Egocentrism as a source of unrealistic optimism. *Personality and Social Psychology Bulletin, 8*, 195–200.

Weis, K., & Weis, S. (1975). Victimology and the justification of rape. In I. Drapkin & E. Viano (Eds.), *Victimology: A new focus* (Vol. 3, pp. 3–27). Lexington, MA: Lexington Books.

Wolfenstein, M. (1957). *Disaster: A psychological essay*. Glencoe, IL: The Free Press.

Wortman, C. B. (1976). Causal attributions and personal control. In J. H. Harvey, W. J. Ickes & R. F. Kidd (Eds.), *New Directions in Attributions Research* (Vol. 1, pp. 23–52). Hillsdale, NJ: Erlbaum.

CHAPTER 10

LEARNED HELPLESSNESS

CHRISTOPHER PETERSON AND LISA M. BOSSIO

Learned helplessness in people entails two stories: an account of the controversial attempts in the experimental laboratory to produce a phenomenon akin to that observed in dogs following uncontrollable shocks and an account of the enthusiastic extrapolations of the helplessness phenomenon to explain our failures to adapt. We find this pattern striking, since one might expect greater acceptance of "basic" science and greater skepticism concerning "applied" science. Because we see the opposite pattern, we must conclude that scientists and citizens alike feel a strong need to explain why people engage in puzzling acts of self-injury. The learned helplessness phenomenon provides us with one possible answer.

We have several purposes here. First, we explain what is meant by learned helplessness. Second, we discuss how we might evaluate the way in which the learned helplessness model is applied to particular instances of maladaptive behavior. Third, we survey six popular areas of application and evaluate them using the criteria we propose.

TWO DECADES OF LEARNED HELPLESSNESS

It's been but 20 years since graduate students studying animal learning at the University of Pennsylvania discovered and explained the helplessness phenomenon among dogs (Overmier & Seligman, 1967; Seligman & Maier, 1967). But in these 20 years, learned helplessness has become a fixture within psychology.

Interestingly enough, learned helplessness was a serendipitous discovery (Seligman, 1975). The psychologists who first stumbled across the phenomenon

CHRISTOPHER PETERSON • Department of Psychology, University of Michigan, Ann Arbor, Michigan 48109. LISA M. BOSSIO • 4707 Fairway Drive, Rohnert Park, California 94928.

were interested in Pavlovian-operant transfer, which means they juxtaposed methods respectively used to investigate these types of learning. Dogs were immobilized in a hammock and given a series of random shocks that they could neither avoid nor escape. Twenty-four hours later, the dogs were placed in a shuttlebox, where the simple response of crossing a barrier in the middle would terminate the shock.

The dogs did not learn this simple escape response. Indeed, they rarely initiated any escape attempts at all. When they did occasionally move to the other side of the box, they did not follow with a shuttle on the next trial, suggesting that the dogs did not attend to the course of events. Further, the dogs showed few signs of overt emotionality. Instead, they sat and passively endured the shock. Dogs that were not exposed to uncontrollable shocks the day before encountered no difficulty in learning how to escape shock in the shuttlebox.

These first studies with dogs were published in 1967, which the reader may recognize as the same year that Ulric Neisser's *Cognitive Psychology* appeared, helping to stimulate psychology's cognitive revolution. The reader may not know, however, that Neisser worked on this book while on leave at the University of Pennsylvania. As students there, Maier, Overmier, and Seligman could not help but be influenced by the cognitive ideas that filled the air. Learned helplessness has become popular in no small way because these original researchers proposed a cognitive interpretation of the phenomenon. It was the right thing to say at the right time.

According to their account, helplessness in animals results from their learning during exposure to uncontrollable shocks that responses and outcomes are independent. Regardless of what their response is, shocks come and go on a random schedule. This learning is represented as an expectation that future responses and outcomes will be independent of each other as well. When generalized to new situations, like the shuttlebox, this expectation of helplessness produces the observed deficits in motivation, learning, and emotion that comprise the helplessness phenomenon.

Learned helplessness in animals continues to be a thriving area of research, and some of the most intriguing work here looks at the impact of uncontrollable events on physiology. So, helpless rats are analgesic—they do not feel pain as readily or as deeply as nonhelpless rats, presumably because of their increased endorphin levels (Maier & Jackson, 1979). And helpless rats show immunosuppression—they don't fight off disease as successfully as nonhelpless rats (Laudenslager, Ryan, Drugan, Hyson, & Maier, 1983; Sklar & Anisman, 1979; Visintainer, Volpicelli, & Seligman, 1982).

The fact that physiology is implicated in helplessness does not argue against a cognitive (or psychological) interpretation, since the phenomenon is not produced by the physical trauma of bad events. Animal studies typically use a yoking procedure to create two groups of animals exposed to physically identical shocks, with the critical difference being that the first group has control over their onset or offset while the second group does not (Maier & Seligman, 1976). Relative to animals exposed to no shock whatsoever (controllable or uncontrollable), only animals in the second group display helplessness deficits, and only animals in the second group show physiological effects of the shocks. Whether or not shocks are controllable is not a property of the shocks *per se* but of the relationship between the animal and the shock. Uncontrollability is therefore not something that can be reduced below a psychological level. Helplessness must have a cognitive representation.

Unlike the animal studies, human applications have not always been as attentive to showing that cognition matters above and beyond trauma. The yoking procedure that is standard in animal studies is difficult if not impossible to implement in field studies with human subjects, and researchers are often guilty of not even attempting a reasonable facsimile. Why? Perhaps because it is so "obvious" that people's expectations can produce difficulties for them. However, human passivity can certainly be produced by trauma.

Even though there were difficulties to be expected in researching the phenomenon using people, researchers soon made the attempt. Their studies closely followed the animal procedures, exposing people to events that could or could not be controlled (like bursts of noise delivered through headphones) and seeing the effect on their performance of tasks that indeed could be mastered (like unscrambling anagrams). Many human studies showed that uncontrollable events did indeed disrupt subsequent performance (e.g., Hiroto & Seligman, 1975), but the consensus in the literature was that human helplessness was more complicated than the original hypothesis implied (see reviews by Miller & Norman, 1979; Roth; 1980; and Wortman & Brehm, 1975).

Among those laboratory subjects who encountered uncontrollable events, a variety of reactions occurred. Some subjects showed full-blown helplessness (i.e., difficulty in solving problems, lack of motivation, and bad mood), but more common was a circumscribed reaction under the sway of factors which had no conceptual status in helplessness theory. For instance, studies found that helpless behavior only occurred when the test task was administered in the same room where uncontrollable events were encountered, when the same experimenter conducted both phases of the experiment, and so on.

Data like these inspired Abramson, Seligman, and Teasdale (1978) to revise helplessness theory (as applied to people) to take into account human cognitive capacities. Although a person's expectation remained critical in producing helplessness, Abramson *et al.* addressed the determinants of this expectation. Where the original helplessness theory assumed that the route from uncontrollable events to an expectation of helplessness was simple and automatic, the reformulated theory proposed that other factors intervened. To give a full account of learned helplessness, one must incorporate these other factors, particularly the individual's causal interpretation of the original uncontrollable events.

The new theory suggests that when people encounter bad events that elude their control, they ask themselves "Why?" The answer affects their subsequent reaction, not only whether helplessness ensues, but also the nature of any helplessness that is produced. There are three dimensions of a person's causal explanations which are deemed important. Each dimension is assigned a particular role in influencing one's subsequent reactions.

First, if the person points to an *internal* cause of the bad events ("I made a mistake"), his or her self-esteem falls. This is not the case if an *external* cause is implicated. Second, if the person explains bad events with a *stable* cause ("it runs in my family"), then deficits are long lasting. This does not happen if the event is attributed to an *unstable* cause. Third, if the person offers an explanation in terms of *global* factors ("it's the human condition"), then helplessness is pervasive. An explanation in terms of a more specific cause leads to accordingly circumscribed deficits.

People most at risk for helplessness following uncontrollable events are those who explain them using internal, stable, and global causes. The actual characteristics of the events obviously influence the sort of explanations offered, but so too does a person's habitual tendency to explain events in one way or another. Peterson and Seligman (1984) call this individual difference *explanatory style*, and with all other things being equal, people explain bad events in a characteristic way.

Explanatory style is typically measured with a self-report questionnaire designed for this purpose: the Attributional Style Questionnaire (ASQ; Peterson *et al.*, 1982). The ASQ presents subjects with hypothetical events to be explained—for instance, "you have been looking for a job unsuccessfully for some time." Subjects imagine the event actually happening to them and write down what they think would be the one major cause of this event if it happened. Then they use 7-point scales to rate the cause they have provided according to its internality (versus externality), stability (versus instability), and globality (versus specificity). Ratings are averaged across the different ASQ events to provide an overall estimate of an individual's explanatory style.

By reformulating helplessness theory along attributional lines, Abramson *et al.* (1978) not only increased its fit to the laboratory data but also extended its scope by introducing personality factors. In its original version, helplessness theory spoke only to the "main effects" of bad events. When explanatory style was added, helplessness theory allowed psychologists to predict who was at particular risk following uncontrollability (i.e., those who offered internal, stable, and global explanations). It also helped them to explain why these people were disrupted (i.e., because their causal explanations determined their expectations of helplessness) and to intervene in a helpful way with people exhibiting helplessness (i.e., by changing their causal explanations with cognitive therapy techniques; see Seligman, 1981).

In short, the attributional reformulation made helplessness the province not only of the experimental psychologist but of the clinician as well. And so helplessness theory became popular as an explanation for failures of adaptation that involved passivity. The availability of the ASQ further bolstered the popularity of the theory, since it is an instrument that is easy to administer and possesses good validity (Tennen & Herzberger, 1986).

The story of helplessness is hardly this simple, though, because not all psychologists interested in the phenomenon left the experimental laboratory. Those who stayed have raised some hard questions about what goes on when people experience uncontrollable events. Some psychologists who apply helplessness notions outside the laboratory seem unaware that considerable controversy exists on the inside. Here are some of the issues that have been raised.

First, subjects in a laboratory experiment may show little recognition that outcomes are uncontrollable (e.g., Peterson, 1978). In other words, the psychological event that sets the learned helplessness process into operation (the recognition of noncontingency) appears much more unusual than helplessness theory implies.

Second, along similar lines, other evidence suggests that most people possess benign illusions of control, tendencies to see events as due to their actions when in actuality they are not. Individuals who are depressed do not have this illusion; they see the response–outcome relationships accurately (Alloy & Abramson, 1979). Note that these data completely reverse the predictions of helplessness theory, which holds that "normal" people should judge contingencies correctly, while people with problems like depression should entertain mistaken beliefs.

Third, Frankel and Snyder (1978) argue that uncontrollable events produce helplessness not because the person believes in his or her own ineffectiveness in dealing with them but because he or she gives up in order to save face. From the outside, this process is much the same as learned helplessness, but from within, the process looks quite different. Helplessness theory does not view passivity as motivated or instrumental, yet Frankel and Snyder's egotism hypothesis opts for this view (see also Miller, 1985).

Fourth, another alternative explanation of helplessness observed in the laboratory has been proposed by Kuhl (1981). He suggests that people become debilitated by uncontrollable events because they ruminate about them. The ruminations interfere with their subsequent task performance because the individuals are distracted. Again, this looks much the same as learned helplessness from the outside, but the inner process differs.

Fifth, Tennen (1982) concludes that the cognitive factors hypothesized by helplessness theory to mediate the phenomenon (i.e., contingency judgments, expectations, and causal explanations) have yet to be satisfactorily demonstrated in the laboratory. In many studies which explicitly set out to assess these constructs, helplessness deficits follow uncontrollable events in apparent independence of them.

What is the implication of these questions as far as applications of helplessness ideas are concerned? Not that helplessness fails to exist—uncontrollable events can reliably produce deficits. Not that cognitions are unimportant—remember, "uncontrollability" must have a cognitive representation. Rather, we have yet to grasp exactly what the helpless person is thinking. All the criticisms and questions concerning the laboratory phenomenon have to do with the nature of the cognitions that link uncontrollable events with the observed deficits. The attributional reformulation takes one step toward a more complex view of the helpless person's cognitions, but we expect the need for still further steps. Applications of helplessness ideas should thus be regarded more tentatively than they usually are, since our understanding of the basic helplessness phenomenon is still evolving.

CRITERIA FOR LEARNED HELPLESSNESS

As the term *learned helplessness* has come to be understood, we use three criteria to recognize the phenomenon. First, learned helplessness is present when a person or animal displays *inappropriate passivity*: failing through lack of mental or behavioral action to meet the demands of a situation where effective coping is possible. Second, learned helplessness follows in the wake of *uncontrollable events*. As we emphasized earlier, bad events *per se* do not cause learned helplessness. Trauma may produce unfortunate reactions, including passivity, but trauma-induced helplessness is not of the "learned" variety. Third, learned helplessness is mediated by particular *cognitions* which are acquired during a person's exposure to uncontrollable events and then inappropriately generalized to new situations. As we noted above, the exact nature of these cognitions is unclear.

EVALUATING APPLICATIONS OF LEARNED HELPLESSNESS

These criteria can be used to judge the degree to which a particular behavior represents learned helplessness. What would the ideal instance of self-defeating behavior (as learned helplessness) look like? First, the person would act in an inappropriately passive way, and this qualification is critical. Someone may be passive in all sorts of situations for all sorts of reasons, but "learned helplessness" is reserved for passivity in situations where activity indeed brings forth the desired results. We imagine that a great deal of passivity in this world is instrumental: someone is rewarded for passivity and/or punished for activity. What results is a motionless individual whose inactivity is appropriate granted the prevailing contingencies.

Maier's (1970) animal experiment is instructive in this regard. He used the standard learned helplessness procedure with dogs: pretreatment followed by a test task. The pretreatment employed three groups (controllable shock, uncontrollable shock, or no shock) with an interesting wrinkle. In order for the dogs in the controllable group to escape the shock, they had to respond by doing nothing. If the animals moved, they were shocked. If they held still, the shock was terminated. Here is the logic of this design. *If* learned helplessness is a matter of reinforcement for holding still, then animals in the controllable condition (where reinforcement follows when they do nothing) should be as debilitated on the test task as those in the uncontrollable condition.

But this is not what happened. The dogs with control over the shocks readily learned the test task, showing that learned helplessness is not the same as reinforcement for holding still. This is important because it shows that the phenomenon among animals is not motivated by instrumental considerations. We know of no comparable study with people, which is unfortunate, because it leaves unanswered the question of whether human helplessness, as demonstrated in or out of the laboratory, is strictly analogous to animal helplessness.

What results is an occasional misinterpretation of human helplessness, one encountered even in published articles. Some writers assume that people "learn" helplessness because they are reinforced for dependency, inactivity, and so on. This is not what learned helplessness means. It is not that the person learns a particular behavior but rather an expectation; the person learns that responses and outcomes will be independent in the future. It is the expectation that produces helplessness.

Perhaps it is so "obvious" that human helplessness is cognitive that no one has undertaken Maier's (1970) study with human subjects, but this is not the only question thereby left unexamined. To argue that human helplessness is present, we must demonstrate passivity in an environment that truly is responsive. This demonstration is not only theoretically important but also practically so. Of course, interventions will differ if the problem of passivity stems from an inappropriately generalized expectation versus an environment that punishes activity.

Let's consider an argument common in the literature that describes applications of learned helplessness. Passivity in situation A is labeled learned helplessness because the desired outcomes have eluded one's control in the past. But as long as our attention remains on situation A, where outcomes are still noncontingent, we cannot be sure that learned helplessness is present. Only when passivity is generalized to a second situation B (a responsive one) can we say with certainty that learned helplessness is at work.

Second, the person whose behavior is to be described as learned helplessness would have experienced a history of uncontrollable events. As we have noted, the learned helplessness model accords importance to the uncontrollability of events, not to their other traumatizing properties. In the experimental laboratory, uncontrollability and controllability can be teased apart from the physical properties of shock with a yoking procedure. In the real world, it is not so simple. Nevertheless, it is important that the researcher attempt to show that uncontrollability matters.

The attributional reformulation makes this task easier by emphasizing that objective uncontrollability is not debilitating in the absence of perceived uncontrollability. Only when the person believes that the events are uncontrollable does helplessness follow. So, researchers should ascertain whether "helpless" individuals perceive their life events as uncontrollable. The more they perceive them to be beyond their control, the more helplessly they should behave.

If all subjects experience the same general event, individual differences in beliefs should predict a variation in their subsequent impairment. This is the strategy followed in a study of people's depressive reactions following the breakup of a romance (Peterson, Rosenbaum, & Conn, 1985). All subjects experience the same event (breakup), but they differed in terms of the control they perceived. These perceptions predicted the degree to which they were upset: the less control, the greater the depressive symptoms.

Third, if someone's self-defeating actions are to be well described as learned helplessness, then their passivity would be mediated by their beliefs about helplessness. Learned helplessness is a cognitive phenomenon, although the exact representation of these cognitions is unclear. And sometimes merely asking the person about his or her beliefs isn't sufficient (cf. Nisbett & Wilson, 1977).

Indeed, one reason that the attributional reformulation has caught on is that people can tell researchers readily about their causal beliefs. We recognize that causal attributions are not as close to actual helplessness deficits as are expectations. But we have found that explanatory style is a construct quite easy to operationalize and hence more useful to study. Perhaps expectations are overly influenced by the disorder they are being used to predict (cf. Dohrenwend, Dohrenwend, Dodson, & Shrout, 1984). Explanatory style, in contrast, appears stable—over months and even years (Peterson & Seligman, 1987). Manipulations of mood do not affect explanatory style (Mukherji, Abramson, & Martin, 1982).

Several researchers caution us about accepting a subject's statements about expectations at face value. Rothbaum, Weisz, and Snyder (1982), for instance, introduce a notion they call *secondary control*, which they contrast with primary control, the sort of control with which helplessness theory concerns itself. Primary control refers to one's ability to make events literally happen or not happen. In contrast, secondary control is a means of blunting the effects of bad events by how we think about them. It can be described as a form of cognitive control. Rothbaum *et al.* (1982) enumerate several strategies of secondary control, one of which involves expecting the worse course of events. In other words, low expectations may have benefits.

Norem and Cantor (1986) provide a similar idea in *defensive pessimism*. This is the tendency of some people to entertain low expectations, not because these are realistic estimates, or even sincere ones, but as a way of harnessing anxiety. In their research, defensive pessimists are those individuals with a past history of success in a particular domain (like academic performance) coupled with extremely low expectations about their future success. These people are prone to rumination, and their strategy of expecting the worse puts an end to the rumination, allowing them—interestingly—to perform well.

At any rate, the expectations of the defensive pessimist and of the person attempting secondary control play a different role than the expectations of other individuals. The former are motivated. A researcher may court confusion by treating all reported expectations as functionally the same.

Explanatory style, to date, appears less tricky, apparently not disrupted by self-presentation. For instance, Seligman (1986) gave research subjects a detailed description of the sort of outcomes that can be predicted from explanatory style. He then administered the ASQ to them under the instructions to produce answers like those of people with these good outcomes. In other words, subjects were asked to fake "good" answers. Did their knowledge of the potential purpose of the test results influence the answers? Not at all, in contrast to more transparent personality measures that are not able to survive a challenge like the one posed in this research.

In sum, we now have a good notion of what constitutes learned helplessness. People whose self-defeating actions can be described in these terms are inappropriately passive. They do not initiate effective coping in situations where it would clearly win them relief. They have a history of uncontrollable bad events. And they have abstracted from this past experience a belief that the future will be the same. These beliefs produce their passivity.

The best way to demonstrate the applicability of learned helplessness is longitudinally, since helplessness theory—in both its original and reformulated versions—is a theory of process. The theory demands that we look at how events unfold over time if we want to be the most confident that learned helplessness is present. Unfortunately, longitudinal demonstrations are rare. Cross-sectional studies are much more common. Contemporaneous correlations (such as between causal explanations and passivity) are consistent with helplessness predictions, but they are obviously weak support, since other possibilities exist (cf. Peterson & Seligman, 1984).

Many applications of learned helplessness are middling ones, neither good nor bad, demonstrating some of the criteria for learned helplessness but not all. So, these applications should not be fully accepted, just as they should not be fully dismissed. The ubiquitous recommendation that "more research is needed" of course follows, but at least the explicit criteria for recognizing learned helplessness provide a direction for this future research to take.

In the next section, we survey half a dozen applications of learned helplessness to instances of self-defeating behaviors, evaluating them against the three criteria. But first, let us illustrate the extremes of such applications. Depression is an excellent example of learned helplessness. By far the most research in the helplessness tradition has tested Seligman's (1974, 1975) hypothesis that learned helplessness models reactive depression, allowing us to evaluate depression in terms of the three criteria.

Does depression satisfy all three criteria? We believe that it does. Depression involves maladaptive passivity; this is part of its very definition (American Psychiatric Association, 1980). Depression also follows bad events, particularly those that people judge to be uncontrollable (e.g., Thoits, 1983). And depression is mediated by cognitions of helplessness, hopelessness, and pessimism (e.g., Beck, 1967). Explanatory style is a consistent covariate of depressive symptoms (e.g., Sweeney, Anderson, & Bailey, 1986) and a demonstrable risk factor (e.g., Peterson & Seligman, 1984).

There has been criticism of the use of learned helplessness to explain depression (see representative objections by Coyne & Gotlib, 1983). We believe that this criticism is often misdirected, reflecting a misunderstanding of what it means to claim that learned helplessness helps to explain depression (or any failure of adaptation, for that matter). To propose that helplessness is a model of depression is not to suggest that it *is* depression. Models and the phenomena they explain exist at different levels of abstraction, and so equivalence can never occur and hence should not be expected.

In judging the goodness of a model (vis-à-vis some phenomenon), one must ascertain whether the essential features of the model capture something about the phenomenon. The learned helplessness model has three essential features, and all are clearly present in the case of depression. Insofar as these features tell us something about the symptoms, etiology, and therapy for depression (see Peterson & Seligman, 1985), we believe they speak meaningfully to the disorder.

Someone wishing to criticize learned helplessness as a model of depression must argue that one or more of the criteria for learned helplessness are not present and/or not relevant in depression. Arieti and Bemporad (1978) take this route by proposing that the ostensible passivity of depressives is instrumental; that is, depressed people act in a helpless way in order to manipulate others. We know of no research that in any way bears out this argument (see Coates & Wortman, 1980, for a review of the reactions that depressives elicit from others), but at least this criticism grapples with the adequacy of the model.

Other criticisms are simply irrelevant. To dismiss learned helplessness as inapplicable to depression because research in support of it uses college students, for instance, is no kind of argument at all. The point is not whether helpless college students resemble depressives in all ways but whether they share essential features. At any rate, these ideas help with the task at hand: evaluating applications of learned helplessness. The rules for evaluation must be made clear, or else endless arguments will ensue. We think this lesson can be learned well from the controversy surrounding learned helplessness and depression (see Peterson, 1985).

The very worst examples of learned helplessness rarely make it into the psychological literature. However, we refer the reader to two humorous articles in *The Worm Runner's Digest*, one applying learned helplessness to dead pigeons (Gamzu, 1974) and the other applying it to rocks (Brewster & Wilson, 1976). These end up being instructive, because they illustrate the folly of assuming that any instance of inactivity necessarily implicates learned helplessness (see also Maier, 1974).

Here is a serious, bad example from a book we once read (the reference escapes us). The authors attributed the woes of the Philippines to the frequent monsoons that buffet the islands. According to this argument, the monsoons induced learned helplessness in the residents. We are hardly expert on the Philippines, but we know enough to say that this is a weak argument, since none of the criteria for learned helplessness are documented.

Although we know that the Philippines over the years have suffered a fair share of turmoil, is passivity the best way to describe these problems? (The success of the Aquino revolution, with its grass-roots support, hardly strikes us as evidence of passivity.) And even if passivity is a good description, is it inappropriate passivity? Did the Philippine citizens act passively even though they lived in a responsive world, or was their passivity instrumental, a means of avoiding trouble in a dangerous political climate?

Similarly, is it the uncontrollability of the monsoons or the physical damage they do that creates passivity (if passivity indeed exists)? Although it is impossible to perform an experiment in which controllable and uncontrollable monsoons are yoked, it is possible to study different parts of the islands where monsoons are equally uncontrollable but not equally destructive. If learned helplessness is operative, then passivity should occur regardless of damage. Or people could be interviewed concerning their perceptions of the uncontrollability of the monsoons. Those who perceive less control should act more passively. In either case, the authors did not provide pertinent information.

A SURVEY OF APPLICATIONS

In the remainder of the chapter, we survey a range of behaviors that on the surface look self-defeating and that theorists have hypothesized to be examples of learned helplessness. We evaluate each application in terms of the three learned helplessness criteria. A summary table is included in which we note our judgment of each application with respect to each criterion (see Table 1).

ACADEMIC ACHIEVEMENT

Next to depression, the best-known application of learned helplessness is to school achievement. We can think of at least two reasons for this popularity. First, more so than in many domains of life, school represents a situation where there are right and wrong answers and where one's efforts indeed matter. So, school is a particularly close approximation to the laboratory setting where learned helplessness was first described. It should allow a straight-forward generalization of helplessness ideas.

Second, with the attributional reformulation, helplessness research converges with Weiner's (1974, 1978, 1979, 1985) impressive investigations of the attributional determinants of performance. Weiner began his work in the achievement motivation tradition, to which he gave a cognitive twist, just as Maier and Seligman began in the animal learning tradition, giving it the same twist. It is interesting how both lines of work agree on the importance of attributions.

Dweck (1975; Dweck & Reppucci, 1973) was the first to apply helplessness ideas to academic achievement. In her research, she started with children designated as "helpless" versus "mastery-oriented" by virtue of their responses to a questionnaire asking about the reasons for academic success and failure. Helpless children are those who attribute failure to their lack of ability. When working at problems, they employ ineffective strategies, report negative feelings, expect to do poorly, and ruminate about irrelevant matters (e.g., Diener & Dweck, 1978).

TABLE 1. Applications of Learned Helplessness

	Criteria of learned helplessness		
Phenomenon	Inappropriate passivity	History of uncontrollability	Mediating cognitions
Academic achievement	shown	shown	shown
Aging	not shown	shown	shown
Battered women	not shown	not shown	shown
Child abuse	not present	shown	not shown
Institutionalization	not shown	not shown	shown
Mental retardation	shown	shown	not shown

When these children encounter failure, they fall apart, and any prior successes by them have little effect (Dweck & Reppucci, 1973).

Dweck (1975) found that attribution retraining—where students who attribute failure to a lack of ability are taught to attribute it instead to a lack of effort—indeed improves reactions to failure. Since this is a cognitive intervention, its success further strengthens the argument that school failures exemplify learned helplessness. Other cognitive interventions effective against school failure have been discussed by Wilson and Linville (1982, 1985), Sowa and Burks (1983), and Brustein (1978), among others.

Furthermore, there are studies which show a link between helplessness constructs and academic outcomes for college students. At the beginning of a school year, Kamen and Seligman (1986) administered the ASQ to two groups of students at the University of Pennsylvania: freshman and upperclassmen. They also obtained their SAT scores as an estimate of their ability. Does explanatory style predict grades at the end of the year, even when ability is held constant? Results for the upperclassmen were straightforward and suggest that learned helplessness is involved in school failure. Habitual explanations of bad events in terms of internal, stable, and global causes predicted poor academic performance, even when SAT scores were held constant.

But among freshmen, explanatory style predicted grades only among the less able of the sample. One interpretation of this latter finding is that freshmen students at the university simply did not encounter enough bad events for explanatory style to make any difference. Introductory courses tend to have larger enrollments than upper-level courses and tend as a result to use multiple-choice examinations to assign grades. The high-SAT freshmen studied by Kamen and Seligman (1986) may well have breezed through these objective examinations. Since failure was never encountered, the manner in which it was explained was irrelevant. In contrast, the low-SAT freshmen no doubt stubbed their toes during their first year at college. Those who made upbeat explanations for the bad events they encountered kept trying to excel, while those who made pessimistic explanations gave up.

A similar study among freshmen students at Virginia Tech obtained clearer results (Peterson & Barrett, 1987). As judged by their SAT scores, these students were much more average than the Ivy League freshmen studied by Kamen and Seligman (1986). We found that explanatory style for bad events indeed predicted poor grades for these freshmen during their first year at college, above and beyond the effect of SAT scores. We also determined the number of times each of the students in our sample sought out academic advising during the year. As to be expected if they were helpless, students who explained bad events with internal, stable, and global causes tended not to go to an advisor. In turn, not going to an advisor was associated with poor grades.

So, research into academic achievement seems to satisfy pretty well two criteria of learned helplessness: passivity and cognition. What about the third criterion? A study by Kennelly and Mount (1985) provides us with some pertinent evidence. These researchers studied 86 students in the sixth grade. They devised and administered a measure called the Teacher Contingency Scale, which asked students for their perceptions of the degree to which their teachers delivered rewards and punishments in a contingent versus noncontingent fashion. They also measured the student's beliefs about the causes of success and failure, their actual academic performance (grades), and whether or not they were seen by their teachers as helpless.

Perceptions of the noncontingency of punishment did not relate to the other variables, but perceptions of the noncontingency of reward were strongly correlated with helplessness on the part of the students ($r = .48$). Further, children who thought that academic outcomes were beyond their control were rated by their teachers as helpless. All these variables in turn predicted their actual academic performance.

From a learned helplessness perspective, the piece that doesn't fit is the fact that only the perceived noncontingency of rewards related to the other variables. Other studies find the opposite pattern: perceived noncontingency of punishments (but not rewards) predicts poor academic performance (e.g., Kennelly & Kinley, 1975; Yates, Kennelly, & Cox, 1975). Perhaps matters differ from classroom to classroom. Regardless, these studies considered together suggest a good fit between learned helplessness and passivity as evidenced in the classroom.

Johnson's (1981) study further implicates the criteria of learned helplessness in school failure. She compared three groups of male students, all between 9 and 12 years of age. One group consisted of average students, the second group was composed of chronically failing students, and the third group was students who had been chronic failures but were presently enrolled in remedial classes. All subjects completed an attribution questionnaire, a self-concept measure, and an experimental task that indexed their persistence.

In this study, all three criteria of learned helplessness were assessed—history of bad events, cognition, and passivity. Consistent with the argument that chronic failure in school involves learned helplessness, all these variables covaried—and with low self-esteem as well. On all measures, the chronic failures scored lowest. Finally, remedial instruction showed some signs of alleviating helplessness.

AGING

Recent work in gerontology increasingly reminds us that aging is as much psychological as it is physical. Several theorists have proposed that some of the disabilities and deficiencies associated with old age reflect learned helplessness (cf. Rodin, 1986; Schulz, 1980). By now we know what to look for in evaluating this claim: maladaptive passivity, a history of uncontrollable events, and cognitions about helplessness.

Do older people experience lack of control? In an obvious sense, yes. As one ages, one almost inevitably experiences an increasing number of uncontrollable events: loss of friends and family members to death, loss of one's job, loss of income, and so on. But in a less obvious sense, yes as well. Consider the widespread stereotypes that society holds regarding the elderly (Solomon, 1982, p. 283):

> the need for more bedside nursing, memory loss, physical problems... limited interests... poor physical condition... not important to their families... negative personality traits... mental and physical deterioration... conservative, insecure, lonely, meddlesome, and pessimistic.

Even professionals may entertain these beliefs, which means they respond not to the needs of an older person (i.e., contingently on the person's behavior) but instead to the stereotype. This is the appropriate antecedent for learned helplessness.

On the other hand, arguing against this possibility is the suggestion that health care professionals do not treat the elderly in a noncontingent fashion but rather in a systematic way that reinforces their passivity (Solomon, 1982). As we have seen, this is not what learned helplessness means.

Thomae (1981) described a study of 174 men and women whose average age was 75. They completed a measure of the degree to which they saw the events in their life as beyond their control. Their responses to this measure predicted their life satisfaction as well as how forthrightly these people responded to stressful events. These results were mostly independent of objective measures of resources available to the subject (like income), which argues for the importance of cognitions in producing deficits in old age.

In studies with similar procedures, Langer and Rodin (1976) and Schulz (1976) found that an intervention that enhanced the sense of control among the institutionalized elderly led to improved physical and psychological health. Other studies similarly show that control-enhancing interventions can improve task performance among the elderly (e.g., Kennelly, Hayslip, & Richardson, 1985).

How does aging fare as an example of learned helplessness? We think it qualifies as a middling example. Passivity may be present, but it may be instrumental. Cognitions of helplessness are present among those who show the greatest debilitation. A history of uncontrollable events may precede helplessness by the elderly, but this is not clearly shown.

Battered Women

Not all couples marry and live happily ever after. Physical violence occurs in 15% or more of all marriages (e.g., Kalmuss & Struss, 1982). The question of course arises as to why women remain with husbands who beat them (Gelles, 1976). Contrary to what one might expect, the frequency or severity of beating is not strongly related to whether a wife leaves an abusing husband (Pageglow, 1981). Theorists have thus searched for other reasons. Two unsurprising factors have been implicated: psychological commitment to the marriage and economic dependence (e.g., Strube & Barbour, 1983). But some theorists have further suggested that learned helplessness may be involved (e.g., Peterson & Seligman, 1983).

How good is such an application? On the face of it, the decision to stay in an abusive relationship looks like maladaptive passivity. Battered women reportedly feel unable to control the beatings they receive and further believe that societal agents like police and social service agencies are unhelpful (e.g., Gayford, 1975; Martin, 1976). However, we must remember that the decision to stay may reflect instrumental considerations. If a woman cannot afford to leave a marriage, then she stays—not because she is helpless, but because it is her only alternative.

Follingstad (1980) reported a case study of a battered woman that ostensibly conforms to the helplessness model. She describes a woman who is weak and ineffectual. However, Follingstad betrays some confusion about learned helplessness by arguing that "battered women. . . find a passive style a sensible one and frequently their only perceived alternative" (p. 295). In other words, she attributes passivity to a mechanism other than learned helplessness. Further, "the consequence for ineffectual change attempts by battered women is typically increased abuse" (p. 295). Follingstad (1980) concludes that the passivity observed in battered women is a result of the abuse rather than an antecedent. This is no doubt a reasonable conclusion, but her case study poorly exemplifies learned helplessness.

Walker (1977-1978, 1979, 1983) makes more extensive use of the model to explain the passivity of battered women. She argues that traditional socialization imparts to women a belief in their own helplessness. Further, she finds that a large proportion of abused wives were abused as children, which satisfies—among these subjects at least—the requirement that uncontrollable events precede helpless behavior.

But we think matters are again misunderstood. Walker (1977-1978) says "the message they received was that in order to be successful and popular with boys, it was necessary to give their power away" (p. 529). Such socialization produces helplessness, to be sure, but this is not learned helplessness as we conceive it. And Walker (1983) continues to write about something different than helplessness when she concludes that "the battered woman's terror was appropriate and her fears that separation would make the violence worse were accurate" (p. 47).

In sum, we think the passivity observed among battered women is a middling example of learned helplessness. Passivity is present, but it may well be instrumental. Cognitions of helplessness are present, as is a history of uncontrollability. But there may also be a history of explicit reinforcement for passivity. Taken together, these results do not constitute the best possible support for concluding that battered women show learned helplessness.

Child Abuse

Several theories have argued that one of the factors involved in why parents abuse their child is learned helplessness (on the part of the parents), engendered by their inability to control the child's crying. Just on the face of it, this seems implausible. Although uncontrollable crying is an antecedent of abuse (Parkin, 1975), abuse itself is hardly maladaptive passivity. Maladaptive—yes, passivity—no. Indeed, in a narrow sense, child abuse is instrumental, since a child sufficiently brutalized will stop crying. Helpless animals are less likely to make aggressive responses, just as they are less likely to make any responses

(Seligman, 1975). But (in the case of humans) if uncontrollable crying by babies produces helplessness in their parents (e.g., Donovan, 1981; Donovan & Leavitt, 1985; Kevill & Kirkland, 1979), then this should be expressed in neglect of the child, not in active abuse.

Learned helplessness applications have been popular in a number of areas because they are optimistic. To say that someone has learned to be helpless is to avoid blaming the person for the misfortune he or she experiences. It is also to provide a ready target for intervention. When we argue against interpreting some phenomenon as learned helplessness, as in the present case of child abuse, we hope it is clear that we are not suggesting that one instead invoke masochism or similar psychoanalytic convolutions as an explanation. We're merely saying that learned helplessness doesn't work too well. Indeed, we suspect that the most plausible alternative in cases where learned helplessness fares poorly as an explanation of self-defeating actions is even more mundane: locally prevailing rewards and punishments. These also provide a ready target for intervention.

Institutionalization

Learned helplessness research originated in animal learning, but it finds an interesting parallel in the sociological literature. Similarities between helplessness (at an individual level) and alienation (at an institutional level) certainly exist. In both cases, events are seen as independent of the person's actions; estrangement is represented in cognitive terms; and passivity ensues. Not surprisingly, then, researchers have used the learned helplessness phenomenon to explain why some institutions produce listlessness, apathy, and poor morale more than others.

So, Thoreson and Eagleston (1983) argue that our typical educational systems lead to unnecessary stress among children and adolescents by giving them tasks that they lack the resources to meet. They use the example of athletics. Schools emphasize not aerobic exercises that can benefit all students (like jogging, swimming, or bicycling) but competitive sports that can be mastered only by the physically elite (like football, basketball, and baseball). What results from this emphasis is helplessness, a lack of activity on the part of the typical student, which recurs later in life as a failure to master other demands, such as the need for exercise to maintain health and combat stress.

Along these lines, Winefield and Fay (1982) reported an interesting study of students in traditional high schools versus those from a school with an "open" format. (Note: Rosen, 1977, shows that open-format schools enhance a student's sense of control over academic outcomes). In a standard learned helplessness experiment, students from these schools were exposed to solvable or unsolvable problems and then tested on a second (controllable) task. Following solvable problems, students from neither school had difficulty. But students from the traditional school were impaired following unsolvable problems, whereas students from the open school were not.

Similarly, DeVellis (1977) argued that the passivity, submissiveness, and learning difficulty often seen among the institutionalized retarded are produced not by retardation but by the institution itself (see also Floor & Rosen, 1975). He points to three sources of noncontingency: (1) the behavior of the staff, which attends not to the needs of individuals but to matters of convenience (as by always placing a nonambulatory person near the bathroom); (2) the behavior of the individual's peers, which may be unresponsive to what he or she does; and (3) seizures and other physical conditions that are imposed on the person.

Martinko and Gardner (1982) argue that learned helplessness can explain maladaptivity in work organizations, such as low productivity, low quality, absenteeism, turnover, passivity, withdrawal, and dissatisfaction. A person is likely to perceive uncontrollability when organizations are centralized bureaucracies with formal rules (e.g., Aiken & Hage, 1966; Blauner, 1964). And workers often regard salaries and benefits as unrelated to performance (e.g., Kerr, 1975; Lawler, 1966).

Yet another example of how learned helplessness may operate within an institution is presented by Malcomson (1980), who argues that hospitals may produce apathy and listlessness among nurses by ignoring their attempts to make policy recommendations. Although formal data are not presented, she recounts personal experiences of uncontrollable events, passivity, and helpless cognitions. However, Malcomsen (1980) shows that by now familiar misunderstanding of learned helplessness when she states that the helplessness *per se* is reinforced. She quotes a head nurse's recommendation: "You will learn that nothing you do or say makes any difference here *or you will be one of the ones who will only last six months*" (p. 252; emphasis added).

Still on the subject of hospitals, Taylor (1979) proposes that they produce helplessness in patients by conceiving of them not as active agents but as broken machines. Patients do not have their actions responded to in a contingent fashion. Raps, Peterson, Jonas, and Seligman (1982) supported this argument by showing that patients in a general medical hospital became more depressed and exhibited greater problem-solving deficits as their length of hospitalization increased, even as their health improved.

The problem with most of these analyses is twofold. First, they do not explicitly look at whether outcomes are viewed as uncontrollable. The case can be made, perhaps more persuasively, that institutions contingently punish active responding (Goffman, 1961). Certainly, this produces helplessness, but not of the learned variety. Second, in few cases does a researcher show that the putative helplessness generalizes from one situation to another, which is the real test of a helplessness explanation (cf. Peterson, Zaccaro, & Daly, 1986). In sum, we think the case of institutionalization as learned helplessness has not been well made.

Mental Retardation

Our final instance of a phenomenon approached from the perspective of learned helplessness is the passivity observed among mentally retarded and learning-disabled individuals (e.g., Canino, 1981; DeVellis & McCauley, 1979; Lowenthal, 1986; Stamatelos & Mott, 1983). Research by Weisz (1979; Raber & Weisz, 1981) in particular implicates helplessness among the retarded. He starts with the observation that retarded individuals accumulate failures as they age (cf. Cromwell, 1963; Zigler & Balla, 1976), more so than nonretarded individuals. This hypothesis was confirmed by observing feedback that teachers gave to retarded individuals. Compared to the nonretarded, retarded students are given more negative feedback, relatively and absolutely. Further, the negative feedback is more apt to be intellectually relevant.

This type of experience, as it accumulates, implies that the retarded will be susceptible to helplessness, a finding confirmed by Weisz, who found that retarded students are disrupted by failure particularly as they get older. This interaction is important, since it shows that as experience with uncontrollability (in everyday life) accumulates, so too does one's propensity to act helpless in the face of failure.

One problem here is the failure of Raber and Weisz (1981) to find that retarded children are prone to make attributions in terms of ability. Indeed, relative to the nonretarded, they are more likely to attribute failure to lack of effort as opposed to lack of ability. Perhaps effort is differently construed here, but on the face of it, this fails to support the argument that learned helplessness is involved in mental retardation. In sum, we see again a middling example of learned helplessness in this phenomenon. Two of the criteria are present (passivity and uncontrollability), but the third (cognition) has not been convincingly demonstrated.

CONCLUSIONS

We have reviewed six phenomena that theorists propose as examples of learned helplessness. By our analysis, which involved checking each against a prototypic case of learned helplessness (i.e., maladaptive passivity, history of uncontrollable events, and cognition of helplessness), only one fares well: academic achievement. Several others prove to be decent but not outstanding examples: aging, battered women, institutions, and mental retardation. Child abuse, however, is a poor example of learned helplessness.

Here then are our conclusions: First, learned helplessness plays a role in various self-defeating behaviors. Second, its role is probably not as ubiquitous as some have believed. Third, learned helplessness can prove useful, even in those cases where it is not an outstanding example, if it directs our attention away from inner "pathology" and onto more mundane constructs like situational contingencies and cognitions. These provide a readier target for intervention. Fourth, we must nevertheless keep in mind that examples can show a range of fit. If we treat all examples as equally compelling, we risk the credibility of the learned helplessness model.

REFERENCES

Abramson, L. Y., Seligman, M. E. P., & Teasdale, J. D. (1978). Learned helplessness in humans: Critique and reformulation. *Journal of Abnormal Psychology, 87*, 49–74.

Aiken, M., & Hage, J. (1966). Organizational alienation: A comparative analysis. *American Sociological Review, 31*, 497–507.

Alloy, L. B., & Abramson, L. Y. (1979). Judgment of contingency in depressed and non-depressed college students: Sadder but wiser? *Journal of Experimental Psychology, 108*, 441–487.

American Psychiatric Association. (1980). *Diagnostic and statistical manual of mental disorders* (3rd ed.). Washington, DC: Author.

Arieti, S., & Bemporad, J. (1978). *Severe and mild depression*. New York: Basic Books.

Beck, A. T. (1967). *Depression: Clinical, experimental, and theoretical aspects*. New York: Hoeber.

Blauner, R. (1964). *Alienation and freedom: The factory worker and his industry*. Chicago: University of Chicago Press.

Brewster, R. G., & Wilson, M. E. (1976, December). Learned helplessness in pet rocks (*Roccus pettus*). *The Worm Runner's Digest*, pp. 111–113.

Brustein, S. C. (1978). Learned helplessness. *Journal of Instructional Psychology, 5*, 6–10.

Canino, F. J. (1981). Learned helplessness theory: Implications for research in learning disabilities. *Journal of Special Education, 15*, 471–484.

Coates, D., & Wortman, C. B. (1980). Depression maintenance and interpersonal control. In A. Baum & J. E. Singer (Eds.), *Advances in environmental psychology* (Vol. 2, pp. 149–187). Hillsdale, NJ: Erlbaum.

Coyne, J. C., & Gotlib, I. H. (1983). The role of cognition in depression: A critical appraisal. *Psychological Bulletin, 94*, 472–505.

Cromwell, R. L. (1963). A social-learning theory approach to mental retardation. In N. R. Ellis (Ed.), *Handbook of mental deficiency* (pp. 41–91). New York: McGraw-Hill.

DeVellis, R. F. (1977). Learned helplessness in institutions. *Mental Retardation, 15*, 10–13.

DeVellis, R. F., & McCauley, C. (1979). Perception of contingency and mental retardation. *Journal of Autism and Developmental Disorders, 9*, 261–270.

Diener, C. I., & Dweck, C. S. (1978). An analysis of learned helplessness: Continuous changes in performance strategy and achievement cognitions following failure. *Journal of Personality and Social Psychology, 36*, 451–462.

Dohrenwend, B. S., Dohrenwend, B. P., Dodson, M., & Shrout, P. E. (1984). Symptoms, hassles, social supports, and life events: The problem of confounded measures. *Journal of Abnormal Psychology, 93*, 222–230.

Donovan, W. L. (1981). Maternal learned helplessness and physiologic response to infant crying. *Journal of Personality and Social Psychology, 40*, 919–926.

Donovan, W. L., & Leavitt, L. A. (1985). Simulating conditions of learned helplessness: The effects of interventions and attributions. *Child Development, 56*, 594–603.

Dweck, C. S. (1975). The role of expectations and attributions in the alleviation of learned helplessness. *Journal of Personality and Social Psychology, 31*, 674–685.

Dweck, C. S., & Reppucci, N. D. (1973). Learned helplessness and reinforcement responsibility in children. *Journal of Personality and Social Psychology, 25*, 109–116.

Floor, L., & Rosen, M. (1975). Investigating the phenomenon of helplessness in mentally retarded adults. *American Journal of Mental Deficiency, 79*, 565–572.

Follingstad, D. R. (1980). A reconceptualization of issues in the treatment of abused women: A case study. *Psychotherapy: Theory, Research, and Practice, 17*, 294–303.

Frankel, A., & Snyder, M. L. (1978). Poor performance following unsolvable problems: Learned helplessness or egotism? *Journal of Personality and Social Psychology, 365*, 1415–1423.

Gamzu, E. R. (1974, December). Learned laziness in dead pigeons. *The Worm Runner's Digest*, pp. 86–87.

Gayford, J. J. (1975). Wife battering: A preliminary survey of 100 cases. *British Medical Journal, 1,* 194–197.

Gelles, R. J. (1976). Abused wives: Why do they stay. *Journal of Marriage and the Family, 38,* 659–668.

Goffman, E. (1961). *Asylums*. Garden City: NY: Anchor.

Hiroto, D. S., & Seligman, M. E. P. (1975). Generality of learned helplessness in man. *Journal of Personality and Social Psychology, 31,* 311–327.

Johnson, D. S. (1981). Naturally acquired learned helplessness: The relationship of school failure to achievement behavior, attributions, and self-concept. *Journal of Educational Psychology, 73,* 174–180.

Kalmuss, D. S., & Straus, M. A. (1982). Wife's marital dependency and wife abuse. *Journal of Marriage and the Family, 44,* 277–286.

Kamen, L. P., & Seligman, M. E. P. (1986). [Attributional style and academic performance.] Unpublished data, University of Pennsylvania.

Kennelly, K. J., Hayslip, B., & Richardson, S. K. (1985). Depression and helplessness-induced cognitive deficits in the aged. *Experimental Aging Research, 11,* 169–173.

Kennelly, K. J., & Kinley, S. (1975). Perceived contingency of teacher-administered reinforcements and academic performance of boys. *Psychology in the Schools, 12,* 449–453.

Kennelly, K. J., & Mount, S. A. (1985). Perceived contingency of reinforcements, helplessness, locus of control, and academic performance. *Psychology in the Schools, 22,* 465–469.

Kerr, S. (1975). On the folly of rewarding A, while hoping for B. *Academy of Management Journal, 18,* 769–783.

Kevill, F., & Kirkland, J. (1979). Infant crying and learned helplessness. *Journal of Biological Psychology, 21,* 3–7.

Kuhl, J. (1981). Motivational and functional helplessness: The moderating effect of state versus action orientation. *Journal of Personality and Social Psychology, 40,* 155–170.

Langer, E. J., & Rodin, J. (1976). The effects of choice and enhanced personal responsibility for the aged: A field experiment in an institutional setting. *Journal of Personality and Social Psychology, 34,* 191–198.

Laudenslager, M. L., Ryan, S. M., Drugan, R. C., Hyson, R. L., & Maier, S. F. (1983). Coping and immunosuppression: Inescapable but not escapable shock suppresses lymphocyte proliferation. *Science, 221,* 568–570.

Lawler, E. E. (1966). The mythology of management compensation. *California Management Review, 9,* 11–22.

Lowenthal, B. (1986). The power of suggestion. *Academic Therapy, 21,* 537–541.

Maier, S. F. (1970). Failure to escape traumatic shock: Incompatible skeletal motor responses or learned helplessness? *Learning and Motivation, 1,* 157–170.

Maier, S. F. (1974, December). Reply to "Learned laziness in dead pigeons" by Gamzu. *The Worm Runner's Digest*, 88.

Maier, S. F., & Jackson, R. L. (1979). Learned helplessness: All of us were right (and wrong): Inescapable shock has multiple effects. In G. H. Bower (Ed.), *The psychology of learning and motivation* (Vol. 13, pp. 155–218). New York: Academic Press.

Maier, S. F., & Seligman, M. E. P. (1976). Learned helplessness: Theory and evidence. *Journal of Experimental Psychology, 105,* 3–46.

Malcomson, K. (1980). Learned helplessness: A phenomenon observed among the nursing staff of "City Hospital." *Perspectives in Psychiatric Care, 18,* 252–255.

Martin, D. (1976). *Battered wives*. San Francisco: Glide Publications.

Martinko, M. J., & Gardner, W. L. (1982). Learned helplessness: An alternative explanation for performance deficits? *Academy of Management Review, 7,* 195–204.

Miller, A. (1985). A developmental study of the cognitive basis of performance impairment after failure. *Journal of Personality and Social Psychology, 49*, 529–538.

Miller, I. W., & Norman, W. H. (1979). Learned helplessness in humans: A review and attribution theory model. *Psychological Bulletin, 86*, 93–119.

Mukherji, B. R., Abramson, L. Y., & Martin, D. J. (1982). Induced depressive mood and attributional patterns. *Cognitive Therapy and Research, 6*, 15–21.

Neisser, U. (1967). *Cognitive psychology*. Englewood Cliffs, NJ: Prentice-Hall.

Nisbett, R., & Wilson, T. D. (1977). Telling more than we can know: Verbal reports on mental processes. *Psychological Review, 84*, 231–259.

Norem, J. K., & Cantor, N. (1986). Defensive pessimism: Harnessing anxiety as motivation. *Journal of Personality and Social Psychology, 51*, 1208–1217.

Overmier, J. B., & Seligman, M. E. P. (1967). Effects of inescapable shock upon subsequent escape and avoidance learning. *Journal of Comparative and Physiological Psychology, 63*, 23–33.

Pageglow, M. D. (1981). Factors affecting women's decisions to leave violent relationships. *Journal of Family Issues, 2*, 391–414.

Parkin, J. M. (1975). The incidence and nature of child abuse. *Developmental Medicine and Child Neurology, 17*, 641–646.

Peterson, C. (1978). Learning impairment following insoluble problems: Learned helplessness or altered hypothesis pool? *Journal of Experimental Social Psychology, 14*, 53–68.

Peterson, C. (1985). Learned helplessness: Fundamental issues in theory and research. *Journal of Social and Clinical Psychology, 3*, 248–254.

Peterson, C., & Barrett, L. C. (1987). Explanatory style and academic performance among university freshmen. *Journal of Personality and Social Psychology, 53*, 603–607.

Peterson, C., Rosenbaum, A. C., & Conn, M. K. (1985). Depressive mood reactions to breaking up: Testing the learned helplessness model of depression. *Journal of Social and Clinical Psychology, 3*, 161–169.

Peterson, C., & Seligman, M. E. P. (1983). Learned helplessness and victimization. *Journal of Social Issues, 39*, 103–116.

Peterson, C., & Seligman, M. E. P. (1984). Causal explanations as a risk factor for depression: Theory and evidence. *Psychological Review, 91*, 347–374.

Peterson, C., & Seligman, M. E. P. (1985). The learned helplessness model of depression: Current status of theory and research. In E. E. Beckham & W. R. Leber (Eds.), *Handbook of depression: Treatment, assessment, and research* (pp. 914–939). Homewood, IL: Dorsey.

Peterson, C., & Seligman, M. E. P. (1987). Explanatory style and illness. *Journal of Personality, 55*, 237–265.

Peterson, C., Semmel, A., von Baeyer, C., Abramson, L. Y., Metalsky, G. I., & Seligman, M. E. P. (1982). The Attributional Style Questionnaire. *Cognitive Therapy and Research, 6*, 287–299.

Peterson, C., Zaccaro, S. J., & Daly, D. C. (1986). Learned helplessness and the generality of social loafing. *Cognitive Therapy and Research, 10*, 563–569.

Raber, S. M., & Weisz, J. R. (1981). Teacher feedback to mentally retarded and nonretarded children. *American Journal of Mental Deficiency, 86*, 148–156.

Raps, C. S., Peterson, C., Jonas, M., & Seligman, M. E. P. (1982). Patient behavior in hospitals: Helplessness, reactance, or both? *Journal of Personality and Social Psychology, 42*, 1036–1041.

Rodin, J. (1986). Aging and health: Effects of the sense of control. *Science, 233*, 1271–1276.

Rosen, C. E. (1977). The impact of an open campus program upon high school students' sense of control over their environment. *Psychology in the Schools, 14*, 216–219.

Roth, S. (1980). A revised model of learned helplessness in humans. *Journal of Personality, 48*, 103–133.

Rothbaum, F., Weisz, J. R., & Snyder, S. S. (1982). Changing the world and changing the self: A two-process model of perceived control. *Journal of Personality and Social Psychology, 42*, 5–37.

Schulz, R. (1976). Effects of control and predictability on the physical and psychological well-being of the institutionalized aged. *Journal of Personality and Social Psychology, 33*, 563–573.

Schulz, R. (1980). Aging and control. In J. Garber & M. E. P. Seligman (Eds.), *Human helplessness: Theory and applications* (pp. 261–277). New York: Academic Press.

Seligman, M. E. P. (1974). Depression and learned helplessness. In R. J. Friedman & M. M. Katz (Eds.), *The psychology of depression: Contemporary theory and research* (pp. 83–113). Washington, DC: Winston.

Seligman, M. E. P. (1975). *Helplessness: On depression, development, and death*. San Francisco: Freeman.

Seligman, M. E. P. (1981). A learned helplessness point of view. In L. P. Rehm (Ed.), *Behavior therapy for depression: Present status and future directions* (pp. 123–141). New York: Academic Press.

Seligman, M. E. P. (1986). [The ASQ is not transparent.] Unpublished data, University of Pennsylvania.

Seligman, M. E. P., & Maier, S. F. (1967). Failure to escape traumatic shock. *Journal of Experimental Psychology, 74*, 1–9.

Sklar, L. S., & Anisman, H. (1979). Stress and coping factors influence tumor growth. *Science, 205*, 513–515.

Solomon, K. (1982). Social antecedents of learned helplessness in the health care setting. *Gerontologist, 22*, 282–287.

Sowa, C. W., & Burks, H. M. (1983). Comparison of cognitive restructuring and contingency-based instructional models for alleviation of learned helplessness. *Journal of Instructional Psychology, 10*, 186–191.

Stamatelos, T., & Mott, D. W. (1983). Learned helplessness in persons with mental retardation: Art as a client-centered treatment modality. *Arts in Psychotherapy, 10*, 241–249.

Strube, M. J., & Barbour, L. S. (1983). The decision to leave an abusive relationship: Economic dependence and psychological commitment. *Journal of Marriage and the Family, 45*, 785–793.

Sweeney, P. D., Anderson, K., & Bailey, S. (1986). Attributional style in depression: A meta-analytic review. *Journal of Personality and Social Psychology, 50*, 974–991.

Taylor, S. E. (1979). Hospital patient behavior: Reactance, helplessness, or control? *Journal of Social Issues, 35*(1), 156–184.

Tennen, H. (1982). A re-view of cognitive mediators in learned helplessness. *Journal of Personality, 50*, 526–541.

Tennen, H., & Herzberger, S. (1986). Attributional Style Questionnaire. In D. J. Keyser & R. C. Sweetland (Eds.), *Test critiques* (Vol. 4, pp. 20–32). Kansas City, KS: Test Corporation of America.

Thoits, P. A. (1983). Dimensions of life events that influence psychological distress: An evaluation and synthesis of the literature. In H. Kaplan (Ed.), *Psychosocial stress: Trends in theory and research* (pp. 33–103). New York: Academic Press.

Thomae, H. (1981). Expected unchangeability of life stress in old age: A contribution to a cognitive theory of aging. *Human Development, 24*, 229–239.

Thoreson, C. E., & Eagleston, J. R. (1983). Chronic stress in children and adolescents. *Theory into Practice, 22*, 48–56.

Visintainer, M. A., Volpicelli, J. R., & Seligman, M. E. P. (1982). Tumor rejection in rats after inescapable versus escapable shock. *Science, 216*, 437–439.

Walker, L. E. (1977–1978). Battered women and learned helplessness. *Victimology, 2*, 525–534.

Walker, L. E. (1979). *The battered woman*. New York: Harper & Row.

Walker, L. E. (1983). The battered woman syndrome study. In D. Finkelhor, R. J. Gelles, G. T. Hotaling, & M. A. Straus (Eds.), *The dark side of families* (pp. 31–48). Beverly Hills, CA: Sage.

Weiner, B. (Ed.). (1974). *Achievement motivation and attribution theory*. Morristown, NJ: General Learning Press.

Weiner, B. (1978). Achievement strivings. In H. London & J. E. Exner (Eds.), *Dimensions of personality* (pp. 1–36). New York: Wiley.

Weiner, B. (1979). A theory of motivation for some classroom experiences. *Journal of Educational Psychology, 71*, 3–25.

Weiner, B. (1985). An attributional theory of achievement motivation and emotion. *Psychological Review, 92*, 548–573.

Weisz, J. R. (1979). Perceived control and learned helplessness among retarded and nonretarded children: A developmental analysis. *Developmental Psychology, 15*, 311–319.

Wilson, T. D., & Linville, P. W. (1982). Improving the academic performance of college freshmen: Attribution therapy revisited. *Journal of Personality and Social Psychology, 42*, 367–376.

Wilson, T. D., & Linville, P. W. (1985). Improving the performance of college freshmen with attributional techniques. *Journal of Personality and Social Psychology, 49*, 367–376.

Winefield, A. H., & Fay, P. M. (1982). Effects of an institutional environment on responses to uncontrollable outcomes. *Motivation and Emotion, 6*, 103–112.

Wortman, C. B., & Brehm, J. (1975). Responses to uncontrollable outcomes: An integration of reactance theory and the learned helplessness model. In L. Berkowitz (Ed.), *Advances in experimental social psychology* (Vol. 8, pp. 278–336). New York: Academic Press.

Yates, R., Kennelly, K., & Cox, S. H. (1975). Perceived contingency of parental reinforcements, parent–child relations, and locus of control. *Psychological Reports, 36*, 139–146.

Zigler, E., & Balla, D. (1976). Motivational factors in the performance of the retarded. In R. Koch & J. C. Dobson (Eds.), *The mentally retarded child and his family: A multidisciplinary handbook* (2nd ed., pp. 369–385). New York: Bruner/Mazel.

Part III

WHEN SITUATIONAL RESPONSES BECOME PERSONALITY DISPOSITIONS

CHAPTER 11

SELF-HANDICAPPING BEHAVIOR AND THE SELF-DEFEATING PERSONALITY DISORDER

TOWARD A REFINED CLINICAL PERSPECTIVE

STEVEN BERGLAS

I'm a proud man and I'm proud of what I've accomplished. . . . I'm not a beaten man; I'm an angry and defiant man. I've said that I bend but I don't break. And believe me, I'm not broken.

Now clearly under present circumstances [where the press is making me the issue], this campaign cannot go on. I refuse to submit my family and my friends. . . and myself to further rumors and gossip. It's simply an intolerable situation.

I believe I would have been a successful candidate. And I know I could have been a very good President, particularly for these times. But apparently now we'll never know.

Gary Hart (May 8, 1987)

With these words, Gary Hart, the undisputed front-runner for the 1988 Democratic presidential nomination, withdrew from the race 25 days after announcing his candidacy and less than a week after polls showed him with 65% of the vote

STEVEN BERGLAS • McLean Hospital/Harvard Medical School, Belmont, Massachusetts 02178.

in strategically crucial Iowa.* The public, particularly the press, had no trouble "diagnosing" what had happened. The May 18, 1987, cover of *Newsweek* trumpeted, "Gary Hart Self-Destructs." That same week, Michael Kramer wrote a cover story for *U.S. News & World Report* that claimed, "Hart's tendency toward self-destruction has been on display for years" (Kramer, 1987).

Given the alleged events that led to his withdrawal from the presidential race—for example, his putative weekend tryst in a Washington, D.C. townhouse with Donna Rice and the publicity it received—who could blame the press for its conclusion? According to a number of published reports, Hart did defy a *New York Times* reporter who asked about his alleged womanizing to "put a tail on me." More damaging still may have been his posing for photographs—wearing a now famous "monkey business crew" shirt with drink in hand and Ms. Rice on lap—that found their way to the cover of the June 2, 1987, *Enquirer*. And although evidence pointing to an illicit sexual encounter still remains largely circumstantial, is there any doubt that Hart was *politically* self-defeating if not self-*destructive*?†

Oddly enough, there are doubts aplenty regarding the meaning and diagnosis of Gary Hart's behavior when mental health professionals voice their opinions. The press may call Hart's behavior "masochistic," but clinicians won't. The Work Group to Revise DSM-III (1985) initially intended to use *masochistic* as the name for a personality disorder that encompassed chronic or repetitious behavior patterns comparable to Hart's public involvement with Ms. Rice and its sequela, but they opted against it. Because of the historic association of the term with psychoanalytic views of female sexuality and the implication that a person with the disorder derives unconscious pleasure from suffering, the diagnosis was renamed *self-defeating personality disorder* (SDPD; American Psychiatric Association, 1987).

Alas, what's in a name? That which we call self-defeat by any other name would be an expression of the same drive or serve the same function. Or would

*The discussion of Gary Hart's behavior during the campaign for the 1988 Democratic presidential nomination is not intended as a psychological diagnosis. I have never met nor spoken with Mr. Hart, and I firmly believe that it is impossible to diagnose a psychological disorder on the basis of secondhand information or from quotes obtained from media sources. It is, however, often the case that individuals who exhibit behaviors comparable to Mr. Hart's involvement with Ms. Rice are suffering from a psychological disorder, most probably a self-defeating personality disorder. Any and all references to behaviors comparable to Mr. Hart's are made solely to illustrate a behavioral style that may reflect a personality disorder, not to evaluate him or his mental status.

†On December 15, 1987, more than 2 months after this chapter was completed and revised, Gary Hart reentered the race for the 1988 Democratic presidential nomination. After initially regaining his front-runner status, his fortunes dimmed considerably as the February 8 Iowa caucuses neared. Mr. Hart's ability to reenter the 1988 Democratic primaries with an initially warm reception in no way mitigates the arguments made in this chapter about individuals who engage in self-handicapping behaviors and may, in fact, lend support to the contention that self-handicapping strategies function to preserve preexisting favorable competency images.

it? While few mental health professionals, apart from the most die-hard psychoanalytic conservatives, hold to the notion that a death instinct or drive to engage in self-destructiveness is part of our biological endowment, there is little, if any, agreement regarding the purpose served by engaging in any of the myriad behaviors classified as masochistic, self-destructive, or self-defeating.

By omitting any reference to what psychoanalysts refer to as "primary" or "erotogenic" masochism—the capacity for sexual pleasure in pain (Maleson, 1984)—the provisional SDPD diagnosis would appear to have carved for itself a unique niche in the psychiatric nomenclature. Yet careful examination of the diagnostic criteria for SDPD reveals that the behaviors in question are virtually identical to descriptions of individuals once identified as suffering from "moral masochism" (e.g., Freud, 1924; Maleson, 1984) or self-debasing masochistic behaviors designed to achieve "victory through defeat" (Reik, 1941; Stolorow, 1975).

The SDPD diagnosis also overlaps quite extensively with a concept that I advanced several years ago called a "self-handicapping disorder" (Berglas, 1985). This didactic formulation was put forth to describe and establish verifiable criteria for one frequently observed form of self-defeating behavior that affords strategic benefits to those who suffer from it. One unique aspect of self-handicapping behavior (Berglas, 1985; Berglas & Jones, 1978; Jones & Berglas, 1978) is that it *appears* to be self-destructive—for example, getting drunk prior to an important job interview—but instead protects a highly favorable but fragile competence image from negative feedback.

The purpose of the discussion that follows is to examine the ways in which the SDPD diagnosis is linked to psychoanalytic formulations of masochism as well as cognitive/social psychological models of strategic self-protective behavior. A more important issue to consider is whether or not this provisional diagnosis has overstepped its bounds or intended function by amalgamating a number of distinct disorders within one conceptual framework. It may be that self-defeating behaviors are better understood as falling along a continuum from neurotic disorders to enduring patterns of maladaptive behavior, and, if so, the provisional SDPD diagnosis might cloud this point. To address these issues, the specific diagnostic criteria proposed for the SDPD is examined to determine where and how this concept converges with what is known about self-protective strategies such as self-handicapping behavior (Berglas, 1985) and psychodynamic formulations of masochistic behavior.

PERSPECTIVES ON MASOCHISM

For better or worse, the SDPD is rooted in psychodynamic formulations of masochism. Originally conceived as a sexual perversion in which suffering is associated with sexual gratification (Krafft-Ebing, 1901/1950), the concept is currently applied to elements of psychological processes ranging from the neurotic to the pathological. The one point of consensus among mental health professionals is that the individual who behaves masochistically seems to contradict the basic psychological truth that the fundamental driving force in human behavior is the attainment of pleasure, self-preservation, or the pursuit of self-interests (see also Chapter 8 by Curtis and Chapter 12 by Widiger and Frances in this volume).

According to Sack and Miller (1975), masochism's blurred conceptual boundaries may be rooted in Krafft-Ebing's (1901/1950) original formulation. They note that while Krafft-Ebing maintained that physical punishment was common in masochistic perversion, it was less important than the relationship that existed between the tormenter and the tormented. Thus, from its conception, the "forebear" of the SDPD—the concept of sexual masochism—was not restricted to cases in which physical pain was necessary for sexual arousal or fulfillment. Instead, as originally conceived, masochism focused on complex experiences of enslavement, passivity, or general suffering as an integral part of its clinical picture.

The Freudian Perspective

Freud (1919) introduced the drive concept of masochism to explain the sexual phenomena he observed in children, yet he allowed for multiple uses of the term in other aspects of his writings. At times, Freud (1924) appeared to view masochism as an aspect of personality functioning or character trait that reflected the existence of a punishing superego. Elsewhere he argued that masochistic behavior was a function of an individual's biological endowment as well as being an expression of feminine qualities.

Freud's most useful contribution to an understanding of the SDPD can be found in his discussions of psychoanalytic technique—specifically, the transference neurosis. In these writings Freud (1920) identified the "repetition compulsion" that appeared to him to be one form of masochistic process. Simply stated, Freud noticed that the normal lives of neurotics revealed a tendency to pursue fates—owing to "a demonic trait in their destiny"—that would always end in some form of psychological suffering.

On occasion, Freud maintained that the repetition compulsion served an adaptive function by preparing the person to better tolerate the reliving of formerly devastating events (Freud, 1920, 1924). He claimed that the recapitulation of traumatic events in an attempt to master them can occur covertly through dreams or obsessive ideation or by acting them out in life or psychotherapy. Since it is assumed that childhood traumas are best mastered in the context of a therapeutic relationship (the transference neurosis), repetition compulsions can, if not treated, persist as lifelong patterns of behavior.

Yet in other portions of his writings Freud claimed that the propensity to repeatedly create situations or establish relationships that would result in self-inflicted pain was biologically determined and a direct manifestation of Thanatos—the death instinct. Even in discussions of "moral masochism" (Freud, 1924)—self-inflicted humiliations and interpersonal abuse—he failed to dissociate this process from drives identical to those that prompted masochistic sexual perversions (see Maleson, 1984). Moreover, Freud (1924) claimed that the hypermoralistic and self-punitive posture assumed by moral masochists was the expression of an unconscious wish to be beaten by the father—a relationship deemed virtually identical to having a passive (feminine) sexual relationship with him.

This assertion that masochistic behaviors are essentially feminine acts was Freud's most unfortunate contribution to the confusion surrounding the concept. Although he intended to differentiate three distinct expressions of a so-called masochistic disorder—(1) primary, or erotogenic, (2) feminine, and (3) moral (cf. Caplan, 1984; Maleson, 1984)—Freud's (1924) belief in a feminine nature underlying all masochism overshadowed the balance of his theory (see also Curtis, Chapter 12, this volume).

Caplan's (1984) insightful analysis of this issue notes that Freud equated "feminine" and "masochistic" when he claimed that sexual masochists' fantasies place them in a "characteristically female situation"—being castrated, copulated with, or giving birth to a baby. The inflammatory implications of this assertion, compounded by the fact that Freud's disciples (most notably, Helene Deutsch, 1944) once perpetuated it, still, to this day, impedes attempts to understand the complexity of masochistic processes.

The Interpersonal Perspective

Most psychodynamic and psychoanalytic theories of masochism no longer support Freud's controversial positions on the feminine attitude or his metaphysical discourse on the death instinct. There is, however, support for the contention that masochistic behaviors are expressed in relationships, mirroring Freud's (1920, 1924) insights regarding the repetition compulsion. More specifically, a prevailing perspective on masochistic behavior contends that it can function as a mechanism for strengthening and structuring interpersonal relationships (see Sack & Miller, 1975).

It is widely recognized that displays of suffering—through failures, physical illness, or various pains—frequently elicit responses of sympathy or pity. This process, known as *secondary gain* (e.g., Fenichel, 1945), goes beyond Freud's assumption of "demonic traits" in explaining the widespread occurrence of behaviors that appear governed by repetition compulsions. When a masochist's ostensibly painful symptoms secure desirable interpersonal rewards, they are likely to be repeated. Moreover, if these same behaviors induce others to feel strong or superior, they are likely to elicit nurturance or support (see Leary, 1957). Masochists reinforced for their suffering are likely to exaggerate or dramatize their pain so that their needs for rescue seem even more compelling.

The contention that masochism is a mechanism for structuring or securing relationships derives further support from clinical observations of individuals with masochistic interpersonal styles pairing off with narcissistic, exploitative, and punitive partners [see Perry & Flannery's (1982) discussion of sadomasochistic relationships]. The consensus among the theories that have examined this unique symbiosis points to the masochist's dependency and need for an involvement with another individual in a manner that permits him or her to be in a subordinate or inferior position.

Presumed Etiology

Attempts to explain the pursuit of sadomasochistic relationships typically focus on the patterns of childrearing that masochists experienced. One popular perspective holds that masochists are the products of abusive mothers (Berliner, 1947; Menaker, 1953). Basically, because the masochist grows up without ever being exposed to appropriate caregivers, he or she develops a "peculiar blind spot for judging others' abuses...and misidentifies cruelty for love" (Sack & Miller, 1975, p. 247). Given this history, the masochistic individual gravitates toward a punishing relationship because it is familiar and the only kind of intimacy he or she finds comforting.

A similar perspective contends that masochistic interpersonal transactions attempt to create (or preserve in fantasy) the relationship that dependent children strive to maintain with idealized parents (Stolorow, 1975). This view also assumes that the person who behaves in a masochistic fashion experienced abusive parenting but adds the assumption that the abuse generated extreme anger. For this individual, masochistic behaviors are assumed to have a dual function. By stunting personal development, sacrificing competence, and deprecating his or her self-worth to theirs, the individual can deny his or her hostility toward those who might punish him or her, and simultaneously elevate them to roles where they are expected to provide nurturance and protection. Thus, the masochist attempts to secure a symbiotic relationship with a powerful individual by self-debasement that insures the desired status/power differential.

The Grandiose Masochist as an Aggressor

An intriguing aspect of the dyadic relationships achieved by those who exhibit masochistic behaviors is that their victim status often results in their gaining ultimate "victory" or control over their partner. Sack and Miller (1975) have noted that "masochistic behavior can be used as a weapon" (p. 247), and they find that some clinicians view the aggressive component of this process in a strong enough light to justify calling the dynamic "sadomasochism" (see also Perry & Flannery, 1982). Regardless of which aspect of the process is prepotent, it is clear that the goal of many masochist transactions is to *hurt* significant others.

Mild forms of this dynamic have been noted by Berne (1964) and Brody (1964). According to Berne, many dyadic relationships—games, as he views them—are structured to permit players to claim "existential advantages" from being in a position where they surrender to the demands of others. In one of his classic games, "If It Weren't For You," people voluntarily endure abusive relationships for a number of reasons, including the benefits derived from blaming their shortcomings, failures, and dissatisfaction on their dominating partners.

Brody (1964) has observed a similar dynamic in patients characterized as "help-rejecting complainers." These individuals, many of whom enter treatment as victims of abuse, greet problem-focused interventions (such as advice, assistance, or support) with hostility and rebuke that can afford them enormous power in certain contexts. Not only does the masochistically inclined individual accuse and hurt others by devaluing their best efforts, he or she also protects himself or herself against retaliation by self-righteously proclaiming the superiority of his or her suffering. As Haley (1969) noted, "You cannot defeat a helpless opponent; if you strike him and your blows are unreturned, you can only suffer feelings of guilt...as well as doubt about who is the victor" (p. 39). Moreover, when self-effacing or help-rejecting behaviors do elicit malevolence from another, the suffering individual can "win" by virtue of "moral superiority."

In line with this perspective, Stolorow (1975) contends that masochists often derive feelings of omnipotence as a direct consequence of being the victim of an abuser's punishing behavior. For example, he cites several theorists who found, in their masochistic patients, "variations of a fantasy...that in their perverse activities the sadistic partner would be weakened by his exertions and the masochist, the 'victim,' would emerge unscathed, thus proudly demonstrating his superior strength and affirming his omnipotence" (p 445). Lowenstein (1957) also commented that behaving in a masochistic fashion, specifically passive–aggressive sulking ("the weapon of the weak"), can be an enormously powerful mechanism for controlling interpersonal relationships. As Reik (1941) noted, behind the suffering of many masochistic interactions lurks fantasies of victory through defeat.

The Narcissistic Function of Masochism

One of the more interesting theories advanced to account for the paradox of masochistic behavior is Stolorow's (1975) "narcissistic" formulation. Borrowing heavily from the work of Kohut (1971, 1972), he argues that

> masochistic activities may, in certain instances, represent abortive...efforts to restore and maintain the structural cohesiveness, temporal stability and positive affective colouring of a precarious or crumbling self-representation...such efforts in the service of maintaining the self-representation would constitute the "narcissistic function" of masochistic manifestations. (pp. 441–442)

A number of psychodynamically oriented theorists support Stolorow's contention. The close association between masochistic phenomena and narcissistic pathology is strongly suggested by developmental studies that trace the origins of masochistic tendencies to disruptions in the earliest mother–child interactions (e.g., Berliner, 1947; Menaker, 1953), when insufficient development of, or damage to, the self-representation is likely to occur. What these studies and other theories (e.g., M'Uzan, 1973) imply is that many individuals who engage in masochistic behaviors fear that their defective self-representation—the unconscious, preconscious, and conscious representations of the bodily and mental self (Hartmann, 1950/1964)—will be unable to function in the face of stressful circumstances. According to Stolorow, the narcissistic function of masochism relieves this anxiety and stabilizes and restores the favorable aspects of the individual's self-representation.

When Stolorow discusses the interpersonal aspects of masochistic behavior, he argues that it supports Kohut's (1971) contention that individuals with defective self-representations attempt to solidify a sense of self-identity and self-esteem by forming intimate, interdependent relationships ("merging") with aggrandized people ("idealized parent imago"). As noted above, two types of masochistic behaviors are ideally suited to this end. On one hand, debasing oneself in relationship to another can serve to establish a dominant–submissive symbiosis in which the dependent (masochistic) partner is nurtured, protected, and, presumably, provided with a structure with which to bolster his or her fragile self-esteem. On the other hand, when masochistic behaviors achieve victory through defeat, Stolorow argues that the victim bolsters a defective sense of self-esteem when fantasized victories over an idealized aggressor are attributed to the self as though they were actual triumphs.

SELF-ESTEEM PROTECTION: THE SELF-HANDICAPPING FORMULATION

Stolorow's (1975) view of masochistic behavior as actions directed at restoring or maintaining a positive sense of self-esteem helps to explain the paradox of acting in ways that appear to contradict self-interests. It appears as though the individual who behaves masochistically is attempting to attain gratification and fulfillment, but these goals are not revealed in overt behaviors. The true function of ostensibly self-defeating behaviors, according to this perspective, can only be understood with reference to how suffering can help an individual deal with threats to his or her self-esteem.

Self-handicapping behaviors (Berglas, 1985; Jones & Berglas, 1978) function in an identical manner. They are, first and foremost, one of several modes of impression management available to those intent on sustaining a positive self-image (see Schlenker, 1980). Self-handicapping behaviors are unique among self-presentational tactics in their capacity to structure the context within which evaluations take place so as to obscure the diagnosticity of evaluative feedback or preempt its utility altogether. Instead of manipulating self-disclosures, the self-handicapper controls impressions by getting into situations or circumstances that may look painful or problematic but, paradoxically, sustain a lofty image of competence.

Self-handicapping is accomplished in one of two ways: (1) by finding or creating impediments that make successful performances less likely, or (2) by withdrawing effort in order to invite probable failure (Berglas, 1985). After the enactment of either tactic, the validity of subsequent evaluations is obscured. The self-handicapper's true abilities cannot be assessed because extraneous factors (impediments, lack of effort) have prevented their manifestation. If and when this state of judgmental ambiguity is created, the self-handicapper has achieved his or her tactical goal: the preservation of the favorable competence image attained prior to the evaluative interaction.

In response to the fear of damaging an inflated self-conception, the self-handicapper reaches out for impediments or exposes himself or herself to incapacitating circumstances that inhibit his or her capacity to succeed again. When this occurs, according to Kelley's (1971) *discounting* principle, the self-handicapper is not blamed for failure owing to the presence of multiple plausible causal agents capable of accounting for the unwanted failure. Should a self-handicapper succeed despite his or her self-imposed burdens, Kelley's (1971) *augmentation* principle predicts that his or her competency image would be enhanced. When an individual triumphs despite the presence of multiple plausible inhibitory causes, the role of ability (a facilitative cause) is judged greater. By self-handicapping, the person intent upon preserving an image of being successful creates a truly no-lose situation (Berglas, 1985).

Self-handicapping behaviors can be further differentiated from other self-protective strategies by their timing: they occur following a success and in anticipation of threats to the esteem gains derived from success feedback. It is important to recognize that the self-handicapper's ostensibly self-defeating behavior is a proactive coping strategy initiated in anticipation of losing his or her favorable but fragile competence image. Seen in terms of a cost–benefit analysis, the cost of a self-imposed hardship or burden is well worth the benefits derived from maintaining a lofty sense of self-esteem.

Self-handicapping behaviors occur only in response to successes deemed noncontingent (Berglas, 1985, 1986a; Berglas & Jones, 1978). Noncontingent successes are so named because they are not justified by, or contingent upon, a person's instrumental behaviors (see Abramson, Seligman, & Teasdale, 1978). When success is contingent upon instrumental behaviors, an individual develops an experiential base of knowledge regarding how previous rewards have been earned and what behaviors are required to replicate reward-winning performances in the future (Berglas, 1986a). This type of feedback enhances self-esteem because it increases knowledge about one's abilities and the range of challenges that are acceptable and nonthreatening (Bandura, 1977; Erikson, 1963). Noncontingent success provides none of this information and, in fact, generates feelings of anxiety or distress.

Noncontingent success is aversive for a number of reasons (for a complete discussion of this issue, see Berglas, 1986a). The most disruptive form of noncontingent success is externally based (Berglas, 1986a, 1987). Externally based noncontingent success is attributable to factors that have nothing to do with a person's internal dispositions or abilities such as intelligence, tenacity, or interpersonal skills. Extraneous factors such as beauty, irrelevant past successes, or the ascribed status of being born into the right family can secure rewards purportedly reserved for those who *achieve* significant goals (Berglas, 1985, 1986a).

When someone receives externally based noncontingent success, he or she is left wondering, "Was I successful for what I did or for who I am?" Succeeding in this manner leaves "victims" with no clear understanding of how success came about and, most important, what can be done to sustain success over time. If, for example, a person is successful because of political connections, control over rewards is lodged in those who afford the person his or her in-crowd status. Should political winds shift, through no personal fault, the recipient of the externally based form of noncontingent success will end up an embarrassed loser. "Successful" is a dispositional attribution (Jones & Davis, 1965; Kelley, 1967), and people so labeled are expected to sustain that image over time regardless of when, why, or how they are evaluated (Berglas, 1986a).

Support for the self-handicapping formulation comes from both laboratory and clinical reports. In the first empirical investigation of this phenomenon, Berglas and Jones (1978) employed a test–retest paradigm to create an analog of self-handicapping, with alcohol as a means of protecting a favorable but fragile competence image. Male subjects who received noncontingent success on a test of intelligence elected to receive a performance-inhibiting, versus performance-enhancing, drug prior to a promised retesting of their intellectual abilities (this effect did not apply to females). Subsequent investigations have replicated this effect in investigations involving placebo self-handicapping "drugs" (e.g., Gibbons & Gaeddert, 1984; Kolditz & Arkin, 1982) as well as alcoholic beverages (Tucker, Vuchinich, & Sobell, 1981).

Although there have been no formal studies of the incidence and prevalence of self-handicapping behavior within DSM-III diagnostic groupings, there exists strong anecdotal evidence that a number of symptom presentations may be best diagnosed as reflective of a self-handicapping disorder (see Berglas, 1985, 1986b). Berglas (1986a) describes the case of a professional hockey player who began a career of self-handicapping alcohol abuse following receipt of a contract that made him the highest paid athlete on earth. According to this individual (as well as reports from collateral informants), his motivation to "hit the bottle" began when he feared that he could not perform in accordance with the expectations derived from this excessive contract. The athlete went on to note that alcohol relieved his performance anxiety and allowed him to believe that he would "never fall from the [exalted] level I was at" (p. 202).

Since identifying self-handicapping behaviors as a distinct class of strategic self-protective behaviors, clinicians have described, or referred to me, a number of individuals that were thought to be self-handicapping alcohol abusers, as well as patients who exploited chronic procrastination, panic attacks, asthma, insomnia, and even eating disorders such as anorexia nervosa or morbid obesity, to protect previously held lofty competence images from potential disconfirmation in social or vocational evaluations. Although it is clear that psychiatric symptoms are frequently multiply determined, it is often easy to determine that disorders develop, or are manifest, at times that leave little doubt as to their self-protective intent (see Berglas, 1985, for a complete discussion of this issue).

GARY HART: FORMER FRONT-RUNNER...AND SELF-HANDICAPPER?

The term *political*—of, pertaining to, or concerned with the science, organization, or activities of government—is closely related to the concept *politic*, which connotes "shrewd," "crafty," "sly," and "cunning." The political arena is, unquestionably, a field in which advancement is often a function of externally based noncontingent success, and those "politic" enough to "earn" that success will advance.*

There are no quantifiable determinants for political success, nor are there techniques that a person can learn to train for a political career. "Proving grounds" for our most powerful politicians range from spacecraft and the ministry to Hollywood movie lots. Winning a political race is not comparable to winning a footrace. Only athletic runners who start with equal opportunities to win experience contingent success. Political victories have a great deal in common with noncontingent success experiences in the sense that they are rarely, if ever, attributable to the internal dispositions of the politician. In politics there is one inescapable truth: Getting to the top is more a function of *who* someone is, than *what* he has done.

Prior to his May 8 withdrawal from the Democratic presidential race, Gary Hart had a long history of battling against the political reality of winning or losing because of who you are—the so-called character issue. In a *New York Times Magazine* story published less than one week before his withdrawal, Hart is quoted as telling reporters, "Please keep your mind open to the possibility that I'm not weird" (Dionne, 1987, p. 28). Yet the press insisted that he was. Reports kept surfacing about his extramarital affairs as well as chronic falsehoods regarding his age, resume, and circumstances of his name change. When, in his withdrawal speech, Hart commented, "I was going to be the issue," he was basically correct, but he obscured one significant point. In his withdrawal speech he was apparently actively exploiting the controversy over whether or not the press was justified in prying into his involvement with Donna Rice as a smokescreen to cloud scrutiny of the Hart-the-man issue.

By pointing a finger of blame at the harassment reporters subjected him to—claiming he was withdrawing from the race because he could no longer permit the fourth estate to disrupt the equanimity of his personal life—Hart found his handicap. He wasn't "a beaten man," he claimed, he was withdrawing in response to "an intolerable situation" created by journalists who are "hunters [of] Presidential candidates." As front-runner for the Democratic nomination and a victim of the journalistic aggression, Hart could use a self-handicapping strategy to make his most important claim: "I know I could have been a very good President." His audience was left to complete the sentence with, "had it not been for this intolerable situation you found yourself in." (Dionne, 1987)

Concluding that Hart's withdrawal from the race for the 1988 Democratic presidential nomination was a self-handicapping strategy is made easier by summarizing the defining features, or diagnostic criteria, of this self-protective tactic: 1) a history of noncontingent success, (2) an impending evaluation that threatens to negate previously acquired self-esteem gains, and (3) access to a performance impediment or incapacitating circumstances that prevent an indi-

*I thank Paul Chodoff, M.D., for pointing out that successful politicians often possess internal strengths such as perseverance, industriousness, toughness, and, in certain cases, altruism, and that their success are often attributed to these factors. His insight has led me to temper my opinion about the nature of political success, but not abandon it. A political success is more often than not noncontingent, despite noteworthy exceptions.

vidual from behaving in a manner that reflects his or her true competencies (see Berglas, 1985).

Even Hart's most avid apologist would be hard pressed to deny that his political career, particularly the events that followed his ascendancy to the role of Democratic front-runner, was peppered with events that met these criteria. The circumstance that prevented him from manifesting his presumed ability (to be president) occurred *following* receipt of success feedback (the poll showing his control of 65% of the vote in Iowa). Yet, as noted above, most political successes have a noncontingent flavor to them, and in Hart's case—with his public battles against the "character" issue—it is safe to assume that all gains were probably experienced as somewhat ill-gotten.

Hart was successful in the polls prior to his reported association with Donna Rice, but the primary elections scheduled prior to November, 1988, were guaranteed to threaten his front-runner status. One could argue that by blaming a hostile press for his withdrawal, Hart succeeded in quitting while ahead (see Berglas, 1985). Far from self-destructing, Hart left himself in a position where, at a minimum, he can write a book (for a high six-figure advance), function as a speaker (for Croesian fees), and never again face the Hart-the-man controversy unless he chooses to once again run for political office. More important, the particular self-defeating behaviors he engaged in permitted him to retain the attributions of competence garnered prior to his withdrawal, because it appeared as though he was the victim of an external handicap (journalistic harassment).

THE SELF-DEFEATING PERSONALITY DISORDER

WHAT ARE PERSONALITY DISORDERS?

It is one thing to conclude that Gary Hart, or anyone else, engaged in a self-handicapping strategy. It is a different matter entirely to assert that self-handicapping or any single instance of self-protective or self-defeating behavior is reflective of a personality disorder. In order to infer the presence of a personality disorder—as opposed to a personality trait or enduring characteristic—certain core characteristics must be manifest. The revision of the third edition of the American Psychiatric Association's *Diagnostic and Statistical Manual of Mental Disorders* (DSM-III-R, 1987) distinguishes personality traits and disorders as follows:*

> Personality *traits* are enduring patterns of perceiving, relating to, and thinking about the environment and oneself, and are exhibited in a wide range of important social and personal contexts. It is only when *personality traits* are inflexible and maladaptive and cause either significant functional impairment or subjective distress that they constitute *Personality Disorders*. The manifestations of Personality Disorders are often recognizable by adolescence or earlier and continue through most of adult life, though they often become less obvious in middle or old age. (APA, 1987, p. 335 [emphasis mine]).

*The following excerpts are reprinted by permission from the *Diagnostic and Statistical Manual of Mental Disorders, Third Edition, Revised*. Copyright 1987 American Psychiatric Association.

Vaillant and Perry (1985), in their overview of these phenomena, add to this definition by providing a clinical picture of patients with personality disorders. One of their findings with particular relevance to the present discussion is that all personality disorders occur in an interpersonal context and are elicited by interpersonal conflicts. If neurotic symptoms are the modes by which an individual copes with unbearable desires or fears, Vaillant and Perry see personality disorders as the modes by which one copes with unbearable interpersonal relationships or demands. Thus, consistent with Freud's (1920, 1924) assertions concerning repetition compulsions, the current perspective on personality disorders maintains that they are characterized by vicious cycles of interpersonal discord that reflect entrenched, maladaptive styles of dealing with social stressors and those who create them.

Returning to the question of Gary Hart's purported self-defeating propensity, it is clear that in at least one crucial way he appears to be manifesting a personality disorder. Hart's presumably "diagnostic" behaviors were all public displays of political naïveté judged self-defeating because he had been a politician for so long. From provoking a *New York Times* reporter to tail him, to battling with the fourth estate about his character and qualifications to run for office, it is clear that Hart acted in a disordered manner with significant members of the public. Both he and his confidants maintain that the private person was much different—presumably, more agreeable—which lends further support to the contention that his "Rice-related" behaviors may have reflected a personality disorder.

Self-Defeating Personality Disorders

According to DSM-III-R, a self-defeating personality disorder (SDPD) is:

> . . . a pervasive pattern of self-defeating behavior, beginning by early adulthood and present in a variety of contexts. The person may often avoid or undermine pleasurable experiences, be drawn to situations or relationships in which he or she will suffer, and prevent others from helping him or her, as indicated by at least five of the [criteria presented]. (APA, 1987, p. 373)

For the purposes of the discussion that follows, I have grouped and reordered the SDPD diagnostic criteria (see Table 1) according to a conceptual system that provides a functional analysis of the behavioral patterns manifest by the individual thought to suffer this disorder. This, of course, in no way contradicts the DSM-III-R (APA, 1987) committee members who conceived the SDPD and its diagnostic criteria. Rather, the purpose of this proposed trifurcation is to analyze this disorder in a manner that may help to inform therapeutic strategies and, in the case of individuals who do not meet five of the proposed eight criteria, suggest the neurotic conflicts that brought them to the attention of clinicians.

A secondary concern of this conceptualization is to simplify comparisons between the SDPD and what has been written about masochistic behaviors and other ostensibly self-defeating behavioral styles, such as self-handicapping (Berglas, 1985). It is clear that self-handicapping and masochistic behaviors are

TABLE 1. A Proposed Trifurcation of the Self-Deating Personality Disorder[a]

I. Self-protective
- 1.(1) Chooses people and situations that lead to disappointment, failure, or mistreatment even when better options are clearly available
- 2.(3) Following positive personal events (e.g., new achievement), responds with depression, guilt, or a behavior that produces pain (e.g., an accident)
- 3.(6) Fails to accomplish tasks crucial to his or her personal objectives despite demonstrated ability to do so (e.g., helps fellow students write papers, but is unable to write his own)

II. Self-aggrandizing (narcissistic)
- 4.(2) Rejects or renders ineffective the attempts of others to help him or her
- 5.(4) Incites angry or rejecting responses from others then feels hurt, defeated, or humiliated (e.g., makes fun of spouse in public, provoking an angry retort, then feels devastated)
- 6.(8) Engages in excessive self-sacrifice that is unsolicited by the intended recipients of the sacrifice

III. Secondary gain
- 7.(5) Rejects opportunities for pleasure or is reluctant to acknowledge enjoying himself or herself (e.g., despite having adequate social skills and the capacities for pleasure)
- 8.(7) Is uninterested in or rejects people who consistently treat him or her well (e.g., is unattracted to caring sexual partners)

[a]The original numbering used in DSM III-R appears in parentheses.

conceptually related to the proposed SDPD; dividing this disorder into its component features should reveal the extent of this relatedness.

Self-Protective Component of the SDPD

Criteria 1, 3, and 6, proposed for the SDPD in DSM-III-R and regrouped under the heading "Self-Protective" in Table 1, read as follows:

> [1.] [the person] chooses people and situations that lead to disappointment, failure, or mistreatment even when better options are clearly available
> [2.] following positive personal events (e.g., new achievement), [the person] responds with depression, guilt, or a behavior that produces pain (e.g., an accident)
> [3.] [the person] fails to accomplish tasks crucial to his or her personal objectives despite demonstrated ability to do so

The pattern of behavior represented by each of these criteria most closely resembles self-handicapping behavior and the purely didactic self-handicapping disorder proposed elsewhere (Berglas, 1985; see the Appendix at the end of this chapter, for the diagnostic criteria established for this disorder), provided they are timed appropriately. Appropriately, in this context, means a time that will enable an individual to preserve the attributions drawn from prior successes without the need to replicate past successes.

For example, the individual who "chooses people and situations that lead to disappointment [or] failure," is self-handicapping if the choice occurs following success and prior to an evaluative interaction. Moreover, this is exactly the function of the second self-protective SDPD criterion component ("following positive personal events the person responds with a behavior that produces pain") and can be the goal of criterion 3 as well. The sequelae of these self-defeating acts can be exploited to create the impression that their impact is blocking an individual from sustaining a successful career or relationship. These behaviors are thought to be self-*protective* because the individuals who exhibit them following success typically have a number of reasons to assume that subsequent evaluations will result in failure and loss of esteem, without the effects of self-imposed impediments to success (Berglas, 1985; Berglas & Jones, 1978).

Returning once again to Mr. Hart, it is apparent that his "Rice-related" behaviors conform to the style reflected by the self-protective component of the SDPD: (1) the alleged affair—the most flagrant of his purported years of womanizing—occurred within a week of his learning that national polls documented his front-runner status in Iowa (criterion 2), (2) he cancelled a weekend campaign appearance to meet Rice in Washington after provocatively challenging a reporter to put a tail on him (criteria 1), and (3) he withdrew from a political race that, prior to the "Monkey Business" fiasco, he clearly seemed capable of winning (criteria 3).

Behaviors subsumed by the self-protective component of the SDPD can also function in a distinct, ostensibly more "masochistic," manner when they are timed to occur in *anticipation* of success. In contrast to those occasions when these behaviors follow success—the hallmark of self-handicapping strategies—behaving in a self-defeating fashion prior to reaching a goal (criterion 3) can function in the service of reducing anxieties identified by Freud (1923) and others (e.g., Tresemer, 1977) as stemming from a fear of success. This neurotic disorder has unfortunately been branded "feminine," partially as a consequence of research that focused on the achievement-related concerns of women (e.g., Horner, 1972). Yet fearing the consequences of success is neither necessarily female nor masochistic. Succeeding can expose an individual to a range of adverse consequences (Berglas, 1986a).

For example, jealousy and envy are two of the interpersonal consequences that successful people suffer after achieving significant goals. In addition, every success raises expectations for increasingly proficient performances over time, thereby heightening the likelihood of failure and the experience of distress (see Marecek & Mettee, 1972). It is also widely recognized that experiencing success can evoke intense intrapsychic conflicts for individuals who have failed to resolve Oedipal fixations (Cavenar & Werman, 1981). Given the potential for incurring these adversities as a result of achieving success, avoiding this ambivalent outcome by defeating oneself *a priori* can be a very adaptive maneuver (see Berglas, 1986a, for a complete discussion of this issue).

Thus, it appears as though certain behavior patterns subsumed by the SDPD have either of two self-protective functions depending upon when they emerge. While some theorists (e.g., Adler, 1930) claim that all symptoms have a self-protective function and others, most notably Horney (1937), have asserted that all masochists accuse others for their suffering while excusing themselves from blame, the present formulation is far more restrictive. By establishing when an individual exhibits certain self-defeating behaviors, it is possible to differentiate his or her conflicts, fears, or character pathology from a number of similar yet distinct disorders.

The Self-Aggrandizing (Narcissistic) Component of the SDPD

Criteria 2, 4, and 8, proposed for the SDPD in DSM-III-R, regrouped under the heading "Self-Aggrandizing (Narcissistic)" in Table 1, read as follows:

> [4.] [the person] rejects or renders ineffective the attempts of others to help him or her
> [5.] [the person] incites angry or rejecting responses from others and then feels hurt, defeated, or humiliated
> [6.] [the person] engages in excessive self-sacrifice that is unsolicited by the intended recipients of the sacrifice

Designating these SDPD criteria the "self-aggrandizing" component creates an apparent contradiction. Behaviorally, they place the "victim" in anything but a self-aggrandized posture. Actually, their function appears to be to heighten the power, status, or significance of another individual vis-à-vis the victim. Yet virtually all psychodynamic formulations of masochistic behavior maintain that this self-debasement is in exchange for various psychological rewards (see Sack & Miller, 1975). Most often, the individual who behaves like a help-rejecting complainer (criterion 4; Brody, 1964), martyr (criterion 5), or passive–aggressive provocateur (criterion 6) sets the stage for feelings of moral superiority and victory through defeat (Reik, 1941).

This primary focus on status relationships stands in marked contrast to the behaviors subsumed by the "self-protective" component, which seem focused on personal achievement concerns. Whereas the tendency to engage in self-protective self-defeating behavior appears motivated by a concern with *preserving* self-esteem gains, individuals whose behaviors conform to the self-aggrandizing component of the SDPD appear motivated by concerns over a *negative* or severely damaged self-esteem in need of rebuilding or repair (see Stolorow, 1975).

As noted above, Stolorow's (1975) formulation of the narcissistic function of masochism contends, in line with Kohut (1972), that an unstable or defective self-representation can be restored or solidified by merging with aggrandized people (idealized parent imago) and that engaging in masochistic behaviors is one means of achieving that end. According to Stolorow, emerging unscathed from an involvement with an idealized sadistic, abusive, or dominating partner strengthens the self-representation of those victims because they are able to attribute these victories to their own capacity to triumph over others.

The additional benefit derived by achieving a passive triumph over idealized power figures is that the self-defeating individual need not confront the aggressive component of his or her self-representation. Controlling a relationship, and ultimately dominating another person with passive self-sacrifice (criterion 6), permits fantasies of moral superiority (over an abuser) to emerge. Not only does the self-defeating individual "win" (narcissistic repair), he or she is a better person for not acting upon his or her aggressive urges (self-aggrandizement).

Similarly, the self-defeating tendency to "incite angry or rejecting responses from others" and "reject or render ineffective the attempts of others to help" (criteria 5 and 6) bears a strong similarity to the devaluing behavior characteristic of individuals suffering severe narcissistic disturbances or, in the extreme, borderline personality disorders (Kernberg, 1975). By creating a rift with a significant other, the devaluing individual defends against wishes for nurturance and support that are extremely terrifying and inconsistent with an idealized sense of self (Adler, 1970). Thus, rather than feeling helpless and abandoned, individuals who engage in self-aggrandizing self-defeating behaviors deny dependency and, by acting in a manner that should provoke abandonment, gain control over a morbid fear.

The Secondary Gain Component of the SDPD

Criteria 5 and 7, proposed for the SDPD in DSM-III-R, regrouped under the heading "Secondary Gain" in Table 1, read as follows:

> [7.] [the person] rejects opportunities for pleasure or is reluctant to acknowledge enjoying himself or herself
> [8.] [the person] is uninterested in or rejects people who consistently treat him or her well

When a behavior pattern is designated a "personality disorder," it is assumed that it occurs within an interpersonal context and involves a routinized—typically aversive—pattern of interacting with another individual (Vaillant & Perry, 1985). In the case of the behaviors subsumed by the secondary gain component of the SDPD, it is assumed that they are central to a pattern of ongoing social interaction with an individual(s) who will respond to the victim's rejection of him or her, or pleasurable outcomes, in a predictable manner. If one criteria of the proposed SDPD diagnosis is to reject people who *consistently* treat him or her well, it is clear that the victim has succeeded in forming stable relationships with others who reinforce his or her rejection with nurturance. When rewards or benefits are secured as a result of manifesting a *failed* interpersonal status in a relationship that is sustained beyond the point at which symptoms first emerge, these favorable outcomes are called secondary gain (Fenichel, 1945; White & Gilliland, 1975).

The secondary gain component of the SDPD is most easily differentiated from ostensibly self-defeating behaviors designed to protect a favorable competence image. Although both tactics secure rewarding outcomes, it appears as though the motivation to secure secondary gain stems from a sense of incompetence that must be hidden, as opposed to the favorable but fragile self-conception that motivates self-handicapping or comparable behaviors (Berglas, 1985).

Behaviors reflective of the secondary gain component may be symptomatic of a reaction formation born of intense Oedipal hostility or feared Oedipal victory. The behavior pattern characterized by the secondary gain component is totally devoid of the abusive elements that characterize the other proposed dimensions. All of the self-imposed pain that characterizes this dimension of the SDPD results from passive self-denial, reflecting a sense or need for powerlessness or incompetence that may be attributable to unresolved fears of how acting in a competent manner vis-à-vis one's same-sex parent might be received.

According to Fenichel (1945), much of the behavior designed to secure secondary gain "brings all the advantages of passive receptive behavior. 'Now I am not the one who has to act; they have to do it for me.' " (p. 461). This passive, helpless, and anhedonic posture is ideal for the individual who fears retaliation for expressions of power, but it stands in marked contrast to the self-handicapper who by *actively* assuming behavioral impediments thwarts the diagnosticity of future evaluations that may strip him or her of esteem gains (self-protective component) or to the self-defeating individual who eschews controlling impressions or his or her capacity to succeed in favor of grandiose fantasies derived from merging with idealized others (self-aggrandizing component).

Another distinguishing feature of self-defeating individuals characterized by the secondary gain component of the SDPD is their apparent tolerance of dependency needs. Remaining in a relationship where others are perennially attempting to nurture them or introduce opportunities for pleasure suggests a passive resignation to the need for receiving care or the belief that the only way in which to secure rewarding relationships is to assume a subordinate role. This tolerance is remarkably dissimilar to the active denial of feelings of dependency that characterize self-defeating types who devalue, or provoke hostilities from, significant others (self-aggrandizing component).

IMPLICATIONS OF THE PROPOSED TRIFURCATION

A REVISED NOMENCLATURE?

The preceding trifurcation of the SDPD is only one among many potential ways in which the diagnostic criteria of this disorder can be divided into component features. For example, one potentially useful component of the SDPD omitted from the preceding trifurcation is a "depressive" feature. Beck's (1967) early work on depression hypothesized a strong correlation between masochism—which he defined as self-imposed suffering (p. 170) or self-defeating patterns (p. 178)—and this disorder. More recent statements of his cognitive triad of depression (e.g., Beck, 1976) suggest that both a depressed person and one suffering a SDPD would *express* comparably negative views about the self, the external world, and anticipated events. Unfortunately, even if both individuals were to manifest virtually identical self-report behavior, it would be impossible to determine if a given depressed person and one suffering a SDPD *felt* the same degree of self-doubt or self-contempt. Should an individual's SDPD be dominated by self-protective concerns, he or she might express depressive self-statements in a strategic attempt to avoid future evaluative interactions following a significant achievement.

Yet keeping in mind the ways in which a given SDPD may be dominated by self-protective, self-aggrandizing (narcissistic), secondary gain (dependent), or even depressive features suggests that consideration be given to identifying component features of this and other personality disorders as part of the standard DSM-III-R nosology. More specifically, it might be useful to qualify the SDPD in a manner comparable to that used to identify subtypes of adjustment disorders (APA, 1987). For this diagnostic grouping, DSM-III-R allows for a number of adjustment disorders reflecting the dominant aspects of a patient's symptom picture. Among other features, types of adjustment disorders include anxious mood, physical complaints, and work (or academic) inhibition (APA, 1987, p. 331).

DMS-III-R employs a subtyping analysis of adjustment disorders because symptoms of the disorder are varied, and each specific type of adjustment disorder "presents a predominant clinical picture; many of the types are partial syndromes of specific disorders" (APA, 1987, p. 329). The preceding trifurcation of the SDPD, particularly the component representing a "purely" self-protective feature related to self-handicapping behaviors, suggests that personality disorders may also be profitably understood as having subtypes or as encompassing partial syndromes of specific disorders.

Therapeutic Concerns

Regardless of whether or not the DMS-III nomenclature ever reflects a subtyping of personality disorders, it is still useful to consider how this type of analysis can inform therapeutic decision making. Presently, DSM-III makes no claim that its Axis II categorizations (the personality disorders classification) have etiological or treatment implications. Hypothesis about "dynamics" were intentionally excluded from the development of DSM-III—a purely descriptive taxonomy—because they are considered unscientific, unobservable inferences (Benjamin, 1987). Yet a growing number of researcher/clinicians are voicing concern over the fact that Axis II of DSM-III could be refined to enhance both clinical significance as well as interobserver reliability (Frances & Cooper, 1981; Widiger & Frances, 1985).

The preceding trifurcation of the SDPD is consistent with the growing interest in classifying personality disorders into distinct subtypes (Board of Mental Health, 1985) with an eye toward heightening their clinical utility.* This didactic

*Anyone concerned with personality disorders should examine ongoing research projects designed to develop more specific behavioral criteria for DSM-III personality disorders (most notably Widiger & Frances, 1985, as well as the seminal research of Benjamin, 1974, 1987) that code clinical observations for use in assigning patients to subgroup-specific treatment protocols.

formulation, like others developed for alcohol abuse disorders (Berglas, 1986b) and self-protective disorders resulting from the adverse effects of success (see, Berglas, 1986a), can, as heuristics, heighten a clinician's capacity to predict patients' typical patters of interpersonal functioning and response to various psychotherapeutic interventions (cf. Frances & Cooper, 1981). Specifically, if it can be determined that an individual presenting for treatment with SDPD features or the qualifications for an SDPD diagnosis has a clinical picture dominated by one of the three SDPD component styles, a therapist's capacity to anticipate resistances and the patient's ability to work in psychotherapy should be heightened significantly (see also, the discussion of "prototypic acts" by Widiger & Frances, 1985).

For example, in their survey of treatments appropriate for patients with passive–aggressive symptoms, Perry & Flannery (1982) note the benefits and limitations of assertiveness training. Their work has direct relevance to the SDPD in general and the discussion of the present trifurcation in particular. Their discussion of patients caught in sadomasochistic relationships suggests that these individuals will utilize assertiveness training in many areas of functioning, but this particular intervention is insufficient to alter their primary sadomasochistic involvement. Knowing this, clinicians referred SDPD patients whose presenting complaints were dominated by secondary gain concerns would be wise to initiate couples therapy for the patient and his or her partner and/or adopt a psychodynamically oriented approach to the patient's involvement with his or her partner during "individual" psychotherapy sessions.

Psychodynamic treatments are the choice in those instances where an SDPD is dominated by unconscious fantasies such as those articulated in Stolorow's (1975) formulation. In these cases—self-aggrandizing (narcissistic) types—the patient's ties to idealized sadistic objects coupled with intolerance of nurturance must be explored. Establishing that a patient's clinical picture is dominated by the self-aggrandizing (narcissistic) component of the SDPD should inform therapists of developments likely to occur in the transference, particularly if and when reassurance and support is offered. In contrast to patients dominated by secondary gain concerns, likely to engage in passive–aggressive resistance (Perry & Flannery, 1982), self-aggrandizing (narcissistic) patients can be expected to cover their ambivalence toward idealized objects with devaluation (Adler, 1970) or other comparably active defenses.

Cognitive behavior therapy techniques (e.g., Beck, 1976) coupled with insight-oriented therapy are most appropriate for patients characterized by self-protective concerns. Those self-protective SDPD patients who meet the criteria for a self-handicapping disorder (Berglas, 1985; see also the Appendix, at the end of this chapter) are recognized as initiating self-defeating strategies in response to irrational interpretations of the expectations born of success. Techniques that attack these irrational beliefs can reduce their anxieties and help remove the need to engage in self-defeating tactics designed to protect their favorable but fragile self-conception (Berglas, 1985, 1986a; Berglas & Jones, 1978). However, behavioral strategies that emphasize any form of skills training (e.g., Kelly, 1955) should be actively avoided with these patients owing to the manner in which enhancing behavioral competency compounds the threats that fuel their self-protective concerns (Berglas, 1985, 1986b).

When it can be established that a patient's self-defeating behavior is more proactive than reactive to success [Table 1, 3.(6)], psychodynamically oriented interventions assume a greater importance owing to the presumed existence of excessive guilt over Oedipal conflicts or victories (Freud, 1923; Fenichel, 1945). Yet these patients also benefit from cognitive behavior therapy since they must learn to discriminate "illicit" achievement strivings from legitimate real-world competencies while being kept from therapeutic interventions that threaten to overwhelm their tolerance of success (Berglas, 1985; 1986a).

A Word about Defense Mechanisms

According to Vaillant and Perry (1985), "defenses are unconscious mental processes that the ego uses to resolve conflicts among the four lodestars of the inner life—instinct (wish or need), reality, important people, and conscience (p. 964). The DSM-III-R definition is far less elegant: "[Defense mechanisms are] patterns of feelings, thoughts, or behaviors that are relatively involuntary and arise in response to perceptions of psychic danger. They are designed to hide or to alleviate the conflicts or stressors that give rise to anxiety" (APA, 1987, p. 393). Both definitions suggest that defense mechanisms will figure prominently in the expression of personality disorders for two reasons: (1) they are an individual's "automatic" response to conflict and (2) they are deemed mechanisms in the sense that they function without conscious effort and are typically immutable despite situational variation (Perry & Cooper, in press). Thus, the clinician confronted with the task of helping a person suffering a SDPD could benefit by anticipating the defense mechanism(s) that individual is likely to employ.

Although it is generally agreed that there is no one-to-one relationship between defenses and diagnosis, research has shown that there are some significant associations with important clinical implications (e.g., Vaillant, 1977). According to most accepted taxonomies of defense mechanisms, the defenses that appear to characterize most individuals suffering a SDPD are rated as either "immature" or "image distorting," both representative of significant degrees of psychosocial impairment (Perry & Cooper, 1987). The reason why these defenses suggest a poor prognosis is that they are "action" defenses that evoke negative responses from others and perpetuate a sense of depression and futility in the user. The one exception to this rule appears to be those individuals whose SDPD is characterized by self-protective concerns.

Meissner (1980) describes a mature,neurotic defense, he calls "controlling"—"excessive attempts to manage or regulate events or objects in the environment in the interest of minimizing anxiety and solving internal conflicts" (p. 691)—that captures the essential features of both self-handicapping disorders (Berglas, 1985) and SDPDs characterized by self-protective concerns. Although this may, at first glance, be confused with "action" or "acting out" defenses since it involves actively structuring the environment, it can be easily differentiated from the more primitive action defenses by the fact that the intended targets of controlling defenses are inanimate. Thus, the self-handicapper who gets into an accident need not harm another for his or her behavior to have its intended effect upon an audience. When controlling defenses are contrasted with a devaluing defense mechanism that involves directing hostility toward significant others, the higher level of functioning implied by controlling becomes obvious.

Since controlling defenses appear to be reflective of an individual's learning to cope with stress by manipulating aspects of the environment (Berglas, 1985), behavioral interventions would appear to be the therapeutic strategy of choice. However, as noted earlier, individuals suffering an SDPD with self-protective concerns will react poorly to behavioral therapies that involve skills training likely to increase already intimidating performance expectancies. However cognitive-behavior therapies (e.g., Beck, 1976) that can train an individual to substitute rational, adaptive interpretations for irrational reactions to stress-provoking demands may prove an effective means of enabling individuals characterized by controlling defenses to move "upward" to more mature defense reactions.

If we recall Stolorow's (1975) views regarding the narcissistic function of masochism, namely, restoring an unstable or defective self-representation through self-defeating behaviors that permit an individual to merge with an idealized parent imago, it appears likely that individuals suffering an SDPD with self-aggrandizing (narcissistic) concerns will most likely present for treatment with defenses including omnipotence, projective identification, devaluation, idealization and, possibly, splitting. These so-called narcissistic or image-distorting defenses are typically either defenses against hostility, rage, retaliation, and so forth or reparative efforts to regulate self-esteem or a weak sense of identity (Perry & Cooper, 1987).

Since with patients suffering an SDPD characterized by self-aggrandizing (narcissistic) concerns it may be impossible to determine which, if either, function is more prominent, it appears prudent to assume that both aspects of their image-distorting defenses will emerge in treatment. As a general rule of thumb one can assume that patients defending against hostility and rage would respond well to interventions aimed at clarifying and interpreting their reactions, while when patients are in the process of attempting to shore up a defective self-representation, an empathic and mirroring approach would be advised.

Finally, it is likely that patients suffering an SDPD characterized by the secondary gain component will manifest a hypochondriacal defensive style (see Vaillant & Perry, 1985). It is important to note that as a defense mechanism, hypochondriasis is often an attempt to deal with wishes for dependency and functions to unite an individual with a caring other in a sadomasochistic relationship. Since the individual who incessantly voices complaints that cannot be relieved may in fact be attempting to punish his or her partner with his or her pain and discomfort, the clinician encountering this defense should immediately target the reinforcing aspects of the patient's primary relationships—not the patient in isolation—for treatment (see Perry & Flannery, 1982).

While the proposed trifurcation of the SDPD can enhance the likelihood of a successful treatment outcome by informing the assignment of patients to various treatments, this work is obviously just a beginning. The SDPD as presently constructed intentionally omits references to a variety of behavior patterns comparable to the psychoanalytic concept of erotogenic masochism (Maleson, 1984), which is often part of the clinical picture presented by self-defeating types. Moreover, it is has been shown that self-defeating behaviors figure prominently in the initiation and maintenance of substance abuse disorders (e.g., Berglas, 1986b) as well as other personality disorders (Benjamin, 1987), reflecting the need to employ multiaxial formulations of personality disorders (Millon, 1981) or taxonomies with subtypes more refined than the one suggested here. As therapeutic techniques grow more sophisticated and specialized, we need nosological systems capable of matching treatment strategies to a patient's idiosyncratic needs.

SUMMARY

The concept of self-defeating behaviors and the diagnostic criteria for DSM-III-R's (APA, 1987) provisional self-defeating personality disorder may be more valuable to mental health professionals if seen as representing a number of self-defeating types as opposed to one unidimensional disorder. It was argued that there are at least three components to the SDPD, as currently construed by the American Psychiatric Association, each dominated by a distinct function. The self-protective component, closely related to the author's research on self-handicapping behavior (e.g., Berglas, 1985, 1986b), is displayed most frequently by individuals who have achieved a favorable but fragile competence image and then initiate self-defeating behaviors. Another component of the SDPD, that of self-aggrandizing (narcissistic), is displayed most frequently by individuals thought to be concerned with restoring or maintaining the structural cohesiveness of a precarious self-representation (Stolorow, 1975). The third component of the SDPD, secondary gain, is manifested by individuals who participate in sadomasochistic relationships for extended periods of time.

Attention was also given to the defense mechanisms thought to characterize each of the three components of SDPD, and suggestions were made for treatment planning based upon a trifurcated diagnosis of self-defeating personality disorders.

ACKNOWLEDGMENTS

The presentation of the ideas developed in this chapter was substantially improved as a function of suggestions made by Rebecca Curtis, Ph.D. The author also thanks Gerald Adler, M.D., for an important contribution to this project.

APPENDIX: DIAGNOSTIC CRITERIA FOR SELF-HANDICAPPING DISORDER*

1. An original or recurrent disorder wherein the functioning of the person in areas of *performance requirements* (e.g., job, school, parenting) breaks down to the point of complete restriction or incapacitation as a result of some behavior or set of behaviors (e.g., drinking, refusing to sleep, overt self-sabotage) initiated prior to some known anticipated performance requirement. This behavior may continue through the performance requirement in question, but in order to qualify as self-handicapping, may not be chronic. The significant psychological distress caused to the person experiencing this disorder is characterized by the following *affective* symptoms:

   > ...recurrent debilitating apprehensiveness, marked anticipatory anxiety, and a sense of impending doom, all related to performance expectations.

   The affective component of this disorder occurs in the absence of medical illness or physical deterioration capable of accounting for this experienced distress, and most importantly, *does not* meet the criteria for diagnosis of anxiety neurosis.

   The ego defensive structure of self-handicapping is most closely identified with the mechanism of *controlling*. Excessive attempts to manage or regulate events or objects in the environment in the interest of minimizing anxiety and solving conflicts. Functionally, self-handicapping behavior "removes" an individual from situations which are evaluative and/or involve performance expectations when these expectations, or the person's investment in maintaining highly favorable evaluations, become extreme. The symptoms of self-handicapping render an individual incapable of performing "as expected," and in doing so allay his anxiety until the next expected performance.

2. A. The duration of behavioral symptoms which incapacitate the self-handicapper (e.g., alcohol and drug abuse) must clearly be time-limited with no appearance of chronicity. In those cases where substance abuse is the dominant symptom, physical dependence must be clearly ruled out as the primary diagnosis.

   B. Symptoms commonly presented by individuals suffering self-handicapping disorders include: Alcohol abuse, anxiolytic abuse, psychogenic pain, accident proneness, headaches, and asthma. Procrastination attributable to one of the preceding symptoms or external constraints is a common associated feature of self-handicapping disorders.

3. The time of initial onset of the disorder must be contemporaneous with one event from the following list:

*From Berglas (1985).

A. Indication through some formal notification that one's competence will be examined, assessed, or the like. Examples:
   1. Structured competition
   2. School examination
   3. Job interview
   4. Periodic job review
   5. Heightened vocational responsibility

B. Change of status to a position of greater responsibility, greater power, or both, which may impose tests to one's competency image. Examples:
   1. Age-related *rite de passage*
   2. Recovery from a Debilitating illness
   3. Graduation
   4. Job promotion or transfer
   5. Marriage
   6. Parenthood or increased parenting requirements
   7. Major financial gain
   8. Increased social responsibility

4. To qualify as a self-handicapping disorder, there must be one of the following manifestations of POSITIVE self-esteem present in the premorbid personality for at least 6 months prior to the onset of symptoms:
   A. The successful negotiation of any of the status advances or examinations listed above in 3A or 3B,
   B. Acknowledged potential for success (e.g., aware of IQ or past achievement),
   C. Major investment in future planning (material or interpersonal)

5. Exclusionary criteria ruling out the diagnosis of self-handicapping involves the experience of any two events from the lists appearing above in 3A or 3B WITHOUT the occurrence of some manifestation of impaired functioning and severe dysphoria.

   A diagnosis of self-handicapping is also ruled out when it is apparent that "secondary gains" is motivating the presentation of symptoms. It is assumed that self-handicapping behaviors are NOT designed to evoke pity, attention, sympathy, etc., as we assume disordered behaviors aimed at obtaining secondary gain are.

   Self-handicapping behaviors (symptoms) render an individual unable to perform "up to potential." This incapacitation, which precludes an accurate assessment of underlying abilities and preserves a belief in underlying strengths, is the aim of self-handicapping. Individuals with self-handicapping disorders protect their self-esteem by not engaging in performances which threaten to expose them to failure or loss of esteem; they do not self-handicap for supplementary gains.

REFERENCES

Abramson, L. Y., Seligman, M. E. P., & Teasdale, J. D., (1978). Learned helplessness in humans: Critique and reformulation. *Journal of Abnormal Psychology, 87*, 49–74.

Adler, A. (1930). *Problems of neurosis*. New York: Cosmopolitan Book Corporation.

Adler, G. (1970). Valuing and devaluing in the psychotherapeutic process. *Archives of General Psychiatry, 22*, 455–461.

American Psychiatric Association. (1987). *Diagnostic and statistical manual of mental disorders* (3rd ed., rev.). Washington, DC: Author.

Bandura, A. (1977). Self-efficacy: Toward a unifying theory of behavior change. *Psychological Review, 84*, 191–215.

Beck, A. T. (1967). *Depression: Clinical, experimental, and theoretical aspects*. New York: Harper & Row.

Beck, A. T. (1976). *Cognitive therapy and emotional disorders*. New York: International Universities Press.

Benjamin, L. S. (1974). Structural analysis of social behavior. *Psychological Review, 81*, 392–425.

Benjamin, L. S. (1987). Use of the SASB dimensional model to develop treatment plans for personality disorders. I: Narcissism. *Journal of Personality Disorders, 1*(1), 43–70.

Berglas, S. (1985). Self-handicapping and self-handicappers: A cognitive/attributional model of interpersonal self-protective behavior. In R. Hogan & W. H. Jones (Eds.), *Perspectives in personality* (Vol. 1, 235–270.) Greenwich, CT: JAI Press.

Berglas, S. (1986a). *The success syndrome: Hitting bottom when you reach the top*. New York: Plenum.

Berglas, S. (1986b). A typology of self-handicapping alcohol abusers. In M. J. Saks and L. Saxe (Eds.), *Advances in applied social psychology* (Vol. 3, pp. 29–56). Hillsdale, NJ: Erlbaum.

Berglas, S. (1987). Self-handicapping and psychopathology: An integration of social and clinical perspectives. In J. E. Maddux, C. D. Stoltenberg, & R. Rosenwein (Eds.), *Social processes in clinical and counseling psychology* (pp. 113–125). New York: Springer-Verlag.

Berglas, S., & Jones, E. E. (1978). Drug choice as a self-handicapping strategy in response to noncontingent success. *Journal of Personality and Social Psychology, 36*, 405–417.

Berliner, B. (1947). On some psychodynamics of masochism. *Psychoanalytic Quarterly, 16*, 459–471.

Berne, E. (1964). *Games people play: The psychology of human relationships*. New York: Castle Books.

Board of Mental Health, National Institute of Medicine (1985). Research on mental illness and addictive disorders. *American Journal of Psychiatry 142* (suppl.)

Brody, S. (1964). Syndrome of the treatment-rejecting patient. *Psychoanalytic Review, 51*, 75–84.

Caplan, P. J. (1984). The myth of women's masochism. *American Psychologist, 39*(2), 130–139.

Cavenar, J. O., & Werman, D. S. (1981). Origins of the fear of success. *American Journal of Psychiatry, 138*(1), 95–98.

Dionne, E. J., Jr. (1987, May 3). Gary Hart: The elusive front-runner. *The New York Times Magazine*, pp. 28–36, 40, 70).

Deutsch, H. (1944). *The psychology of women* (Vol. 1). New York: Grune & Stratton.

Erikson, E. H. (1963). *Childhood and society* (2nd ed.). New York: Norton.

Fenichel, O. (1945). *The psychoanalytic theory of neurosis*. New York: Norton.

Frances, A. & Cooper, A. M. (1981). Descriptive and dynamic psychiatry: A perspective on DSM-III. *American Journal of Psychiatry, 138*(9), 1198–1202.

Freud, S. (1919). A child is being beaten. A contribution to the study of the origin of sexual perversions. In *Collected Papers* (Vol. II, pp. 172–201). New York: Basic Books.

Freud, S. (1920). Beyond the pleasure principle. In J. Strachey (Ed.), *The standard edition of the complete psychological works of Sigmund Freud* (Vol. 18, pp. 7–64). London: Hogarth Press.

Freud, S. (1924). The economic problem of masochism. In J. Strachey (Ed.), *The standard edition of the complete psychological works of Sigmund Freud* (Vol. 19, pp. 159–170). London: Hogarth Press.

Freud, S. (1949). Some character-types met with in psychoanalytic work. In *Collected Papers* (Vol. IV, pp. 318–344). London: Hogarth.

Gibbons, F. X., & Gaeddert, W. P. (1984). Focus of attention and placebo utility. *Journal of Experimental Social Psychology, 20,* 159–176.

Haley, J. (1969). *The power tactics of Jesus Christ.* New York: Avon Books.

Hartmann, H. (1964). Comments of the psychoanalytic theory of the ego. In *Essays on Ego Psychology* (pp. 113–141). New York: International Universities Press. (Original work published 1950)

Horner, M. S. (1972). Toward an understanding of achievement-related concerns in women. *Journal of Social Issues, 28,* 157–176.

Horney, K. (1937). *The neurotic personality of our time.* New York: Norton.

Jones, E. E., & Berglas, S. (1978). Control of attributions about the self through self-handicapping strategies: The appeal of alcohol and the role of underachievement. *Personality and Social Psychology Bulletin, 4,* 200–206.

Jones, E. E., & Davis, K. E. (1965). From acts to dispositions: The attribution process in person perception. In L. Berkowitz (Ed.), *Advances in experimental social psychology* (Vol. 2, pp. 219–266). New York: Academic Press.

Kelley, H. H. (1967). Attribution theory in social psychology. In D. Levine (Ed.), *Nebraska Symposium on Motivation* (pp. 192–238). Lincoln: University of Nebraska Press.

Kelley, H. H. (1971). *Attribution in social interaction.* Morristown, NJ: General Learning Press.

Kelly, G. A. (1955). *The psychology of personal constructs* (Vol. 2). New York: Norton.

Kernberg, O. (1975). *Borderline conditions and pathological narcissism.* New York: Jason Aronson.

Kohut, H. (1971). *The analysis of the self.* New York: International Universities Press.

Kohut, H. (1972). Thoughts on narcissism and narcissistic rage. In *The search for the self.* New York: International Universities Press.

Kolditz, T. A., & Arkin, R. M. (1982). An impression management interpretation of the self-handicapping strategy. *Journal of Personality and Social Psychology, 43,* 492–502.

Krafft-Ebing, R. V. (1950). *Psychopathia sexualis: A medico-forensic study.* New York: Pioneer Publications. (Original work published 1901)

Kramer, M. (1987, May 18). The self-destruction of Gary Hart. *U.S. News & World Report,* p. 25.

Leary, T. (1957). *Interpersonal diagnosis of personality.* New York: Ronald Press.

Lowenstein, R. (1957). A contribution to the psychoanalytic theory of masochism. *Journal of the American Psychoanalytic Association, 5,* 197–234.

Maleson, F. G. (1984). The multiple meanings of masochism in psychoanalytic discourse. *Journal of the American Psychoanalytic Association, 32,* 325–356.

Marecek, J. & Mettee, D. R. (1972). Avoidance of continued success as a function of self-esteem, level of esteem certainty, and responsibility for success. *Journal of Personality and Social Psychology, 22,* 98–107.

Meissner, W. W. (1980). Theories of personality and psychopathology: Classical psychoanalysis. In H. I. Kaplan, A. M. Freedman, & B. J. Sadock (Eds.), *Comprehensive textbook of psychiatry/III* (3rd ed., pp. 631–728). Baltimore, MD: Williams & Wilkins.

Menaker, E. (1953). Masochism—a defense reaction of the ego. *Psychoanalytic Quarterly, 22,* 205–220.

Millon, T. (1981). *Disorders of personality. DSM-III: Axis II*. New York: Wiley-Interscience.

M'Uzan, M. de (1973). A case of masochistic perversion and an outline of a theory. *International Journal of Psycho-Analysis, 54*, 445–467.

Perry, J. C., & Cooper, S. H. (1987). Empirical studies of psychological defense mechanisms. In R. Michels & J. O. Cavenar (Eds.), *Psychiatry*, Chapter 30 (pp. 1–19). Philadelphia: Lippincott.

Perry, J. C. & Flannery, R. B. (1982). Passive–aggressive personality disorder: Treatment implications of a clinical typology. *Journal of Nervous and Mental Disease, 170*(3), 164–173.

Reik, T. (1941). *Masochism in modern man*. New York: Farrar & Strauss.

Sack, R. L., & Miller, W. (1975). Masochism: A clinical and theoretical overview. *Psychiatry, 38*, 244–257.

Schlenker, B. R. (1980). *Impression management*. Monterey, CA: Brooks/Cole.

Stolorow, R. D. (1975). The narcissistic function of masochism (and sadism). *International Journal of Psychoanalysis, 56*, 441–448.

Tresemer, D. W. (1977). *Fear of success*. New York: Plenum.

Tucker, J. A., Vuchinich, R. E., & Sobell, M. B. (1981). Alcohol consumption as a self-handicapping strategy. *Journal of Abnormal Psychology, 90*, 220–230.

Vaillant, G. E. (1977). *Adaption to life*. Boston: Little, Brown.

Vaillant, G. E., & Perry, J. C. (1985). Personality disorders. In H. I. Kaplan & B. J. Sadock (Eds.), *Comprehensive textbook of psychiatry* (4th ed., pp. 958–986). Baltimore, MD: Williams & Wilkins.

Widiger, T. A., & Frances, A. (1985). The DSM-III personality disorders: Perspectives from psychology. *Archives of General Psychiatry, 42*, 615–623.

White, R. B., & Gilliland, R. M. (1975). *Elements of psychopathology: The mechanism of defense*. New York: Grune & Stratton.

CHAPTER 12

CONTROVERSIES CONCERNING THE SELF-DEFEATING PERSONALITY DISORDER

THOMAS A. WIDIGER AND ALLEN J. FRANCES

INTRODUCTION

The revision of the third edition of the American Psychiatric Association's (APA) Diagnostic and Statistical Manual of Mental Disorders (DSM-III-R; APA, 1987) contains a new diagnosis, the self-defeating personality disorder (SDPD). SDPD, however, was not included within the text along with the other personality disorders. It was placed in an appendix with other "proposed diagnostic categories needing further study" (APA, 1987, p. 367). This placement was in response to the controversy generated by the proposal to include a masochistic personality diagnosis. In this chapter, we provide an overview of the controversy. We begin with a description of the historical precedents for the diagnosis and the development of the DSM-III-R SDPD criteria set. We then present the major arguments against its inclusion, followed by a discussion of the relevant empirical literature. We conclude with a brief overview that highlights fundamental empirical issues.

THOMAS A. WIDIGER • Department of Psychology, University of Kentucky, Lexington, Kentucky 40506-0044. ALLEN J. FRANCES • Department of Psychiatry, New York Hospital, Cornell Medical Center, Payne Whitney Clinic, New York, New York, 10021.

HISTORICAL PRECEDENTS

Precedents for the concept of a self-defeating personality disorder are present in the psychoanalytic, psychological, and psychiatric literature.

PSYCHOANALYSIS

The term *masochism* was originally coined by Krafft-Ebing (1901/1950) in reference to a psychosexual disorder. Freud (1924/1961) extended the concept to include erotogenic masochism, feminine masochism, and moral masochism. The latter most clearly related to personality functioning, describing a readiness to incur failures or accidents and to lash oneself with self-reproaches as the result of a harsh conscience. W. Reich (1933/1976) described a masochistic character as displaying chronic subjective feelings of suffering, with annoying complaints and demands, self-debasement, provocation, self-inflicted pain, awkward and ataxic social behavior, and an intense passion for tormenting others. He rejected Freud's biological model of etiology, and suggested instead that masochism can "be explained on the basis of the fantasized or actual nonfulfillment of a quantitatively inordinate demand for love" (p. 271). The masochist was intensely anxious and fearful of being left alone due to an early and severe disappointment in a parental figure. Suffering acted as a continual demand for proof of love.

Horney (1939) suggested that a masochistic character entailed two main trends. The first was a tendency toward self-minimization, the result of which was to feel unattractive, helpless, insignificant, inefficient, stupid, and worthless. The second was a clinging dependency, with a feeling that one was incapable of living without the presence and benevolence of another person. Hostility was expressed indirectly, by "representing himself as victimized and harmed, by spitefully letting himself go to pieces…, killing himself on the offender's doorstep" (p. 262). Horney (1935/1967) suggested that sociocultural factors (e.g., a false assumption that women were inferior and their economic dependence on men), as well as physiological factors (e.g., greater physical strength in men and the act of being penetrated in intercourse), predisposed women to masochism relative to men.

Contemporary psychoanalytic theory views masochism as a multidetermined disorder serving a variety of defensive functions, including guilt and narcissism (Kass, MacKinnon, & Spitzer, 1986; Shainess, 1979). The broader formulation of a "depressive character" (Bemporad, 1985; Chodoff, 1972) includes many of the masochistic traits but places more emphasis on pessimism and self-blame and less on self-inflicted pain and self-punishment. Some masochists may have accepted and introjected overly punishing, abusive, or restrictive treatment during childhood as a justifiable reflection of their own self. The parental figure is subsequently experienced as an internal part or aspect of oneself and/or is abstracted as a severe, harsh, or cruel fate, destiny, or God (Asch, 1986). Masochists may suffer from continued guilt and low self-esteem because they have accepted the denigrating, demeaning, and malicious way they were treated as reflecting their worth and value as a person, and it may only be by suffering and pain that they believe they will deserve love or approval.

Psychology

There are a number of precedents for an SDPD within psychology. One of Murray's (1938) 20 basic human needs was "abasement," characterized by a desire to submit passively to external force, to accept injury, blame, criticism, and punishment, to become resigned to fate, to blame, belittle, or mutilate oneself, and to seek and enjoy pain, punishment, illness, and misfortune. High scorers on the Abasement scale of the popular Personality Research Form (which measures Murray's need system) are described as humble, self-effacing, accepting of undeserved blame and criticism, and tending to expose themselves to situations in which they are in an inferior position (Jackson, 1974).

Millon (1983) described a "negativistic" personality syndrome, characterized by irritability, behavioral contrariness, and discontented self-image (pessimism, disgruntlement, and disillusionment and feeling misunderstood, unappreciated, and demeaned by others). He found that 24% of patients in a national sample of various clinical settings were assessed as possessing this negativistic personality style.

A self-defeating personality style is also found in the interpersonal circumplex, originally formulated by Freedman, Leary, Ossorio, and Coffey (1951). The self-effacing style is characterized by a modest, unpretentious reserve when it is at a normal level of intensity. "In its maladaptive extremes it becomes a masochistic self-abasement" (Leary, 1957, p. 282). The masochistic person is described as guilty, self-deprecating, doubtful, ruminative, obsessive, passive, depressed, and anxious. Research at various settings reported by Leary (1957) identified a substantial proportion of self-effacing–masochistic personalities within clinical samples and comparatively lower percentages in normal populations (e.g., 13% of 537 psychiatric clinic admissions; 14% of 133 university clinic patients; 22% of 49 individual psychotherapy patients; 11% of 28 hospitalized psychotic patients; 2% of 415 college undergraduates; 2% of 121 middle-class, female weight-disorder patients; 0% of 39 university male graduate students; 2% of 52 male stockade prisoners; and 0% of 39 officers in military service).

Subsequent research has verified the self-effacing–masochistic interpersonal style, although it has been given somewhat different descriptions and titles. Lorr, Bishop, and McNair (1965) found an abasement dimension across a variety of samples, appearing by itself or within a larger cluster defined by inhibited, submissive, and abasive interpersonal styles. In Wiggins' (1979) revision of the interpersonal circumplex, the self-effacing–masochistic style was subsumed within a broader "lazy (failure)–submissive (weakness)" dimension. The eight adjectives from Wiggins' (1979) Interpersonal Adjective Scale for the submissive (weakness) vector are self-doubting, self-effacing, timid, meek, unbold, unaggressive, forceless, and unauthoritative. Kiesler's (1983) revision of the circumplex again included a vector that involved SDPD traits. The "unassured" vector at a mild level of pathology was characterized as "self-doubting or dependent" and at the more severe level as "abasive and helpless."

The SDPD is also similar to the self-handicapping disorder described by Berglas (1985). Self-handicappers protect their self-esteem by finding or creating impediments that make good performance unlikely or by withdrawing effort so as to invite probable failure. The basis for and similarities to SDPD of maladaptive self-handicapping behavior patterns are discussed by Dr. Berglas in Chapter 11 of this text and are therefore not covered here.

Psychiatry

Schneider (1958) included a "depressive psychopath" in his influential taxonomy of personality disorders. It is a diagnosis that is quite similar to the masochistic character as described by Reich (1933/1976) and Horney (1939, 1935/1967) and the psychoanalytic concept of a depressive character (Bemporad, 1985; Chodoff, 1972). "The basic common characteristic of depressives is the constant pessimism or at any rate their very skeptical view of life, which they seem to reject yet at the same time seem to love in a rather dismal way" (Schneider, 1958, p. 79). Schneider described these depressive psychopaths as deploring the past and fearing the future. They are distracted by daily worries, hypochondriacal fears, and doubts over life itself. Their lives are replete with unhappy experiences and crises. "Suffering is taken as a mark of quality and there is a tendency to establish an aristocracy of discomfort" (p. 80).

Beck's (Sacco & Beck, 1985) cognitive model of depression proposes that individuals who are prone to depression have acquired a psychological predisposition toward depression through early experiences that shape the development of cognitive schemas in a negative, self-referential manner. The person thinks of himself or herself as unworthy, incapable, and undesirable, to expect failure, rejection, and dissatisfaction, and to perceive most experiences as confirming these negative expectations. Beck incorporated within his cognitive model the analytic concept of masochism (Simons, 1987), including the tendency "to interpret the lack of complete success as failure; to have self-doubts even when successful; to magnify . . . personal defects; to react to criticism with self-debasement; and to expect rejection" (Beck, 1967, p. 178).

The DSM-III-R Criteria Set for SDPD

There was some consideration to include a masochistic–depressive personality disorder diagnosis in DSM-III, but there was not enough time to give it adequate review, and preference at that time was to classify chronically abasive, self-critical, depressive, and pessimistic behavior as an affective disorder (Frances, 1980). Since the appearance of DSM-III the recommendations have continued (Frances & Cooper, 1981; Gunderson, 1983; Kernberg, 1984; Simons, 1983). Therefore, the Work Group to Revise DSM-III Advisory Committee on Personality Disorders formulated a draft proposal (Work Group, 1985).

The proposal, however, generated considerable and heated controversy, including volatile committee meetings, protest demonstrations, threats of legal action (Rosewater, 1986), and vituperative commentaries in local and national media (Coalition Against Misdiagnosis, 1986). One such committee meeting was held in November of 1985 and was attended by members of the advisory committee and opponents to the diagnosis to discuss the various issues (Widiger, 1987). The name of the disorder was then changed to "self-defeating personality disorder" to distinguish the diagnosis from the early psychoanalytic theory, two exclusion criteria were added to rule out depression and situational reactions to abusive relationships, and individual items were revised in response to concerns regarding potential gender biases and overlap with depression and other personality disorders (Work Group, 1986). The work group recommended to the APA Board of Trustees that the SDPD diagnosis be included in DSM-III-R, but it was placed instead within an appendix. Table 1 presents a summary of the final criteria that appeared in DSM-III-R.

The controversy, however, has not abated. The Council of Representatives of the APA provided a formal statement at the August, 1986, national meeting opposing SDPD inclusion, even within an appendix, and urged its members not to use it (D'Ercole, 1987). The APA has also been considering the development of an alternative diagnostic taxonomy (Landers, 1986, 1987). Various other groups have in addition continued to express opposition (Caplan, 1987; Coalition Against Misdiagnosis, 1986; Rosewater, 1987a; Walker, 1987a).

TABLE 1. DSM-III-R Criteria for Self-Defeating Personality Disorder[a]

A. A pervasive pattern of self-defeating behavior, beginning by early adulthood and present in a variety of contexts, as indicated by at least five of the following:

1. Chooses people and situations that lead to disappointment, failure, or mistreatment even when better options are clearly available.
2. Rejects or renders ineffective the attempts of others to help.
3. Following positive personal events responds with depression, guilt, or a behavior that produces pain.
4. Incites angry or rejecting responses from others and then feels hurt, defeated, or humiliated.
5. Rejects opportunities for pleasure, or is reluctant to acknowledge enjoying himself or herself (despite having adequate social skills and the capacity for pleasure).
6. Fails to accomplish tasks crucial to his or her personal objectives despite demonstrated ability to do so.
7. Is uninterested in or rejects people who consistently treat him or her well (e.g., is unattracted to caring sexual partners).
8. Engages in excessive self-sacrifice that is unsolicited by the intended recipients of the sacrifice.

B. The behaviors in A do not occur exclusively in response to, or in anticipation of, being physically, sexually, or psychological abused.

C. The behaviors in A do not occur only when the person is depressed.

[a]Reprinted with permission from the *Diagnostic and Statistical Manual of Mental Disorders, Third Edition, Revised.* Copyright 1987 American Psychiatric Association.

CRITIQUES

The principal arguments against the inclusion of the SDPD into the DSM are the following: (1) it is a sex-biased diagnosis that will be harmful to women (Brown, 1986a, 1987; Caplan, 1987; Walker, 1986, 1987a, 1987b; Rosewater, 1986, 1987a, 1987b); (2) the behavior pattern is more properly diagnosed as an affective disorder rather than a personality disorder (Akiskal, 1983; Liebowitz, 1987); and (3) it is not distinct enough from current personality disorder diagnoses to provide any unique, additional information (Vaillant & Perry, 1985). We summarize each of these arguments in turn.

Sex Bias

A major concern with respect to the SDPD diagnosis is that it may be biased against women. Kaplan (1983) argued that the DSM-III histrionic and dependent personality disorders were biased against women. She suggested that stereotypically feminine behavior had been codified in DSM-III as pathological, due to masculine biases regarding what behaviors are unhealthy. For example, many of the criteria for the histrionic personality disorder describe exaggerated, stereotypical feminine traits (e.g., emotionality and concern with physical appearance), and from a masculine perspective that considers these traits as less desirable there may be a tendency to label them as reflecting dysfunction or dyscontrol. Kaplan (1983) therefore suggested that "behaving in a feminine stereotyped manner alone will earn a DSM-III diagnosis" (p. 791). Williams and Spitzer (1983) responded in part by indicating that a differential sex prevalence does not necessarily suggest a sex bias. However, there are also data to indicate that clinicians overdiagnose histrionic symptoms and traits in women (Chodoff, 1982; Lazare, Klerman, & Armor, 1966; Presly & Walton, 1973; Warner, 1978), and the complementary stereotypical assumptions and biases that might result in an overdiagnosis of antisocial or compulsive personality disorder in men may not have as many negative consequences or pejorative connotations (Kaplan, 1983).

Similar concerns have been raised with respect to the SDPD. Brown (1986a, 1986b), for example, argued that "women are more likely to be diagnosed with it simply by virtue of compliance with norms of femininity" (p. 5). Some of the items do describe tendencies toward self-sacrifice and devotion that are seen more often in women (Eagly & Crowley, 1986), and when observed outside of the context of a psychiatric setting they may be esteemed and revered. But when interpreted in the context of a psychiatric evaluation, a woman's helping behavior may be diagnosed as reflecting a self-defeating personality disorder (Brown, 1986b).

Women have been subject to considerable discrimination, much of it in the form of subtle and accepted social conventions and assumptions. Early psychoanalytic theory was influenced by sex biases that were prevalent within the culture at that time (Caplan, 1984). For example, suffering and pain is an integral part of some normal biological functions in women (e.g., childbirth and the menstrual cycle), and this was interpreted by Freud (1924/1961) as being consistent with inherent masochistic tendencies. Deutsch (1944) was a strong advocate of this theory—"Women. . . are masochistic and seek pain and suffering" (p. 241). Self-sacrifice, devotion to a husband, and even charitable service could be misdiagnosed in women as masochism. "The willingness to serve a cause or a human being with love and abnegation may be a reflection of feminine masochism" (Deutsch,1944, p. 273). There has been considerable progress in overcoming sex-role stereotyping and discriminatory sexist practices, but biases clearly remain. The suggestion to give formal recognition to a diagnosis titled "masochism" raises the spectre of encouraging a return to archaic sex biases.

The bias would be particularly harmful to women within abusive relationships (Brown, 1987; Rosewater, 1987b). It may seem inexplicable to some clinicians why a woman would stay with or return to a man who beats her. It may be convenient to simply diagnose her with an SDPD, implying that she desires or seeks the pain and suffering. Trait variables are often confused with situational variables when explaining the behavior of others (Mischel, 1984), and many victims of abusive relationships could be misdiagnosed as suffering from an SDPD (Symonds, 1979).

Snell, Rosenwald, and Robey (1964), for example, assessed 12 families in which the wife had recently charged the husband with assault and battery. In each case the marriage was the wife's first, the average duration of marriage was over 13 years, and the physical abuse had occurred throughout the years of marriage. The husbands were stable in employment but abused alcohol and were described as passive, indecisive, and sexually inadequate. The wives were described as efficient, hardworking, and aggressive, assuming all responsibilities for the finances and caretaking. However, this competence, which in many cases may have been in response to the husband's negligence, was perhaps denigrated in the characterization of her as "aggressive, efficient, masculine, and sexually frigid" (Snell *et al.*, 1964, p. 111). Her control of the family and finances was described as "castrating," and his violent behavior gave her "masochistic gratification" and helped "to deal with the guilt arising from the intense hostility expressed in her controlling, castrating behavior" (Snell *et al.*, 1964, p. 111). The battering was not simply a result of his sadistic, aggressive dyscontrol but was a way of "filling masochistic needs of the wife and to be necessary for the wife's (and the couple's) equilibrium" (Snell *et al.*, 1964, p. 110).

The masochistic label also provides a rationalization for social agencies to neglect economic, social, and environmental contributions to victimization (Brown, 1986a). Failure to overcome overwhelming social and economic forces that impede efforts to help repeatedly victimized women may be blamed on a lack of motivation to change. "A great many of the psychologic problems that social agencies have to deal with in their women clients are based on such masochistic ties" (Deutsch, 1944, p. 276). If she is to blame for the failure to change, if she in fact unconsciously wishes to be abused, then why attempt the thankless and pointless task of intervening at the community, legal, or economic level? The woman may then be victimized not only by her lover, but also by a mental health agency.

Walker (1984, 1987a) argues that personality variables are not a principal reason for women entering or remaining within abusive relationships. She suggests instead that the self-defeating behavior pattern is situationally rather than trait determined. She describes the typical abusive relationship as involving an initial phase of increasing tension and friction, a second phase of violent abuse, and a third phase of apologetic remorse, contrition, kindness, affection, and promises to reform. "This third phase provides the positive reinforcement for remaining in the relationship" (Walker, 1984, p. 96). An effort to leave is severely punished by immediate and escalated abuse. Walker suggests that women who are especially likely to remain are those who possess traditional attitudes with respect to sex roles (e.g., that women should be passive, submissive, acquiescent, and tolerant) and have a history of victimization during childhood. The interaction of sex-role socialization and early victimization result in a learned helplessness behavior pattern (Peterson & Seligman, 1983) that contributes to an inability to resist adult victimization (Walker & Browne, 1985).

Brown (1987) suggests that a more appropriate diagnosis for victims of abuse is an "abuse or oppression artifact disorder" that would include not only victims of sex abuse but also victims of physical abuse, cultural racism, and hostages. This diagnosis would direct the clinician toward the environmental source for the dysfunction (i.e., oppression) rather than implying an intrapsychic pathology. Walker (1987b) similarly suggests delaying all personality disorder diagnoses for at least 6 months to be certain that the behavior pattern is not better conceptualized as an extended posttraumatic stress disorder. Rosewater (1987b) questions whether any personality disorder diagnosis should ever be given, because they tend to discourage optimism regarding the effectiveness of treatment and imply that victims are to be blamed for their victimization.

Affective Disorder

DSM-II included a diagnosis of "cyclothymic personality," but a variety of studies indicated that this behavior pattern was genetically associated with bipolar affective disorder, often responded with hypomanic episodes to tricyclic antidepressants, and responded therapeutically to lithium, suggesting that it was best characterized as a subaffective or mild variant of bipolar affective disorder (Akiskal *et al.*, 1977). Cyclothymia was therefore classified as an affective disorder in DSM-III (Frances, 1980). Similarly, chronic pessimism, rejection of opportunities for pleasure, rejection of efforts to help, self-criticism, guilt, disinterest in caring partners, and failure to complete tasks may all be seen in patients suffering from depression, and SDPD may then be a subaffective or mild variant of chronic depression (Akiskal, 1983). The SDPD diagnosis may then even be detrimental to clinical practice by encouraging a continued reliance on psychosocial interventions and a failure to try more effective pharmacological interventions (Liebowitz, 1987).

It is likely that many of the persons who meet the criteria for SDPD will be depressed, and it will often be very difficult to determine whether personality traits or an affective disorder is the primary basis for the behavior pattern. A similar problem has plagued Beck's (1967) cognitive theory for the etiology of depression. It is not always clear if the pessimistic cognitive style is the result or the cause of the somatic and behavioral features of depression. The "depressogenic cognitive triad" consists of the tendency to perceive the self as defective, worthless, or undesirable, the world as harsh and offering only failure and punishment, and the future as involving continued suffering and deprivation. The cognitive triad is seen in persons suffering from depression, it contributes to the escalation and maintenance of depression, and therapy that focuses on cognitive restructuring is often more effective in ameliorating depression than pharmacological interventions (Sacco & Beck, 1985). But the cognitive triad typically remits along with the depressed mood, and longitudinal studies have not been very successful in identifying persons who are predisposed to depression on the basis of the cognitive style (Silverman, Silverman, & Eardley, 1984).

Other Personality Disorders

A criticism of the DSM-III taxonomy of personality disorders was the considerable degree of overlap among them. Most of the patients who meet the criteria for one personality disorder also meet the criteria for another, contributing to numerous multiple diagnoses (Widiger & Frances, 1985). The substantial degree of overlap suggests that there may be considerable redundancy.

Vaillant and Perry (1985) were skeptical regarding the value of including SDPD in DSM-III-R because it is so similar to the dependent and passive–aggressive personality disorders and may not provide any additional or unique information. Tolerance of an abusive spouse was in fact included in the DSM-III criteria for dependent personality disorder, a behavior that is now considered to reflect masochistic, self-defeating traits. Persons with self-defeating behavior patterns are likely to display DSM-III-R dependent personality traits, such as being fearful of being alone, helpless when relationships end, unable to make everyday decisions without excessive advice, unable to initiate projects, easily hurt by criticism, and acquiescent to others in making important life decisions (APA, 1987).

Earlier formulations of masochistic personality also contained dependent and passive–aggressive traits. The masochists of Reich (1933/1976) and Horney (1939) were described as being annoying, provocative, complaining, and indirectly hostile (i.e., passive–aggressive). Millon's (1981) formulation of the negativistic personality syndrome was an integration of prior formulations of the masochistic and passive–aggressive personality disorders. Millon (1986) has since separated the negativistic syndrome into self-defeating and passive–aggressive subtypes, but this reformulation was to some extent in anticipation of the revision of DSM-III.

DISCUSSION

The arguments against the inclusion of SDPD in DSM-III-R are substantial. We now discuss relevant empirical data with respect to each of them.

Sex Bias

In response to the concern regarding sex bias, some have suggested that SDPD will be just as common among men as among women (Asch, 1986; Simons, 1987). Kass *et al.* (1986) assessed the prevalence of a preliminary set of 10 "masochistic" personality traits in a sample of 59 ongoing psychotherapy cases of 15 psychiatrists and residents. Of the sample, 64% were female, and 14% were considered to be masochistic by the clinicians employing their own criteria (75% of these were female). The correlation between the presence (versus absence) of the sum of the 10 masochistic traits and the sex of the patient was not statistically significant ($r = .15$). It should be noted, however, that the clinicians providing the ratings were largely aware of the purpose of the study (i.e., to assess the prevalence and validity of the criteria set).

J. Reich (1987) obtained a prevalence rate of 18% in a randomly selected sample of 82 outpatients diagnosed by the Personality Diagnostic Questionnaire (PDQ; Hyler, Rieder, Spitzer, & Williams, 1982), a self-report inventory that contains 11 items to assess masochism that were based on a preliminary draft of the DSM-III-R SDPD criteria set. Only 58% of the 15 masochistic subjects were female, a rate not significantly different from the overall prevalence of females in the outpatient sample. A qualification to this finding, however, is that the PDQ may not be the optimal or most valid instrument for assessing SDPD (Widiger & Frances, 1987b). J. Reich, Noyes, & Troughton (1986) reported that there was little agreement between the PDQ and two other instruments with respect to the diagnosis of DSM-III personality disorders.

In a subsequent study with a much broader sample of 367 outpatients, Kass (1987) found that at least 13% of the subjects would be diagnosed as masochistic (employing a subsequent revision of the draft criteria for DSM-III-R). A significantly higher proportion of females scored positive on five of the nine items (i.e., remains in exploitative or abusive relationship; believes that she almost always sacrifices her own interests; rejects help, gifts, or favors so as not to be a burden; responds to positive events by feeling undeserving or worrying excessively; and thinks only about her own worst features).

It is likely that SDPD will be diagnosed in women much more frequently than in men (APA, 1987). This differential sex prevalence, however, is inherently inconclusive. It can be the result of sex bias or etiological factors that affect females more frequently or more severely than males (Williams & Spitzer, 1983). There are also personality disorders that occur more frequently in men (e.g., antisocial and obsessive–compulsive; Kass, Spitzer, & Williams, 1983; J. Reich, 1987), and this is unlikely to result primarily from sex biases against male patients. Whether differential prevalence is the result of sex bias requires additional information beyond differential prevalence.

Fuller and Blashfield (in press) assessed sex bias in the diagnosis of masochistic personality by providing 150 clinicians with 15 case histories, 5 of which involved masochistic patients drawn from a variety of sources (e.g., one case was Sacher-Masoch, for whom the sexual disorder was originally named). Three of the cases were prototypic examples and two were not prototypic. Sex was varied across case histories. The accuracy in diagnosing masochistic personality disorders did not vary across sex. Subjects were no more likely to diagnose masochistic personality in females than in males for both prototypic and unclear cases (however, the rate of masochistic diagnosis was so low in the nonprototypic cases for both sexes that sex comparisons may be inappropriate).

The findings of Fuller and Blashfield (in press) suggest that clinicians may not be biased in their diagnosis of SDPD. However, this still does not refute the hypothesis that the criteria are biased. The argument of Brown (1986a), Rosewater (1987a), and Walker (1987a) is that the criteria describe stereotypical femininity from a biased masculine perspective and that normal women who are self-sacrificing, devoted to a spouse, and adaptively responding to an abusive situation will be misdiagnosed as suffering from SDPD. Determining that similarly described males are also diagnosed as self-defeating does not refute the argument that the criteria are themselves biased. Clinicians may apply the criteria in a fair manner, but if the criteria are biased then they will be impelled to overdiagnose SDPD in women.

The hypothesis that the criteria select normal women rather than women with maladaptive personality traits requires construct validation studies that assess the extent to which the criteria select persons who have a history, current covariates, and/or future course consistent with the construct of a personality disorder. One example of particular importance is the extent to which the criteria will adequately distinguish between women who are responding to situational variables within an abuse relationship from those who remain or return because of maladaptive personality traits.

Rosewater (1987a) compared Minnesota Multiphasic Personality Inventory (MMPI) scale elevations of 106 women who were currently within an abusive relationship to 12 women who had previously been abused. The formerly battered women had lowered elevations but a similar profile pattern. This might suggest that the traits remained stable despite the termination of battering, but Rosewater also reported significant correlations between the frequency of battering, degree of violence, and various subscale elevations. Rosewater suggested that these results indicated that the apparent personality traits were a response to rather than a cause of the victimization.

Rosewater's (1987a) results do indicate that self-report inventory measurement of traits are sensitive to situational and state factors. J. Reich *et al.* (1986, 1987) similarly found that state anxiety and state depression substantially affected self-report inventory measurement of emotional strength, dependency, and extraversion. However, the inventories used in these studies, including the MMPI, are known to be quite sensitive to state factors, and they may not be optimal for measuring maladaptive personality traits (Widiger & Frances, 1987b). J. Reich *et al.* (1986) also found that the Lazare *et al.* (1966) measure of obsessional, hysterical, and oral traits were resistant to state factors, and it is possible that the PDQ (Hyler *et al.*, 1982) or the Millon Clinical Multiaxial Inventory (Millon, 1983) would provide more stable measurement of the personality traits of battered women.

In addition, the validity of the SDPD does not imply that all or even most battered women have maladaptive personality traits. Walker and Browne (1985) report that personality trait variables typically fail to differentiate between battered women and other women in clinical treatment. But it is likely that only a small proportion of abused women have SDPD traits. The diagnosis is not intended to be the sole or even the major explanation for victimization. Walker's (1984) own research indicates that her three-phase cycle of violence in abusive relationships also fails to be comprehensive. Tension building and loving contrition were evident in only 65% and 58%, respectively, of 384 cases of battered women.

Snyder and Fruchtman (1981) identified four distinct patterns of abuse in a sample of 119 women from a battered women's shelter. One pattern was consistent with a personality disorder model. The women in this group were characterized by an extensive history of violence in their family of origin. All of them reported extensive parental neglect and physical abuse on at least a monthly basis. Physical violence pervaded their adult relationships. Twenty-seven percent had been abused by their spouses even prior to marriage, and nearly half reported additional abuse as adults by persons other than their current boyfriend. These women were also much more likely than other battered women to accept only a short-term separation from their spouse, with 60% eventually leaving the shelter and returning to their assailants. Snyder and Fruchtman (1981) concluded that these "women have grown to expect violence and accept it as part of their lives" (pp. 883–884). The fact that they represented only a small minority of battered women (9%) indicates that they are unlikely to be evident in studies comparing undifferentiated samples of battered women.

Walker's (1984) results have also failed to support the hypothesis that battered women are characterized by rigid, conservative, and traditional sex-role attitudes. Her results have indicated that battered women view themselves as much more liberal (feminist) in their sex-role attitudes than comparison groups of women, consistent with the findings of Rosenbaum and O'Leary (1981). These findings are surprising and difficult to understand. They may be an artifact of the time in which the data were collected. The battered women in both studies were currently in treatment (e.g., battered women shelters), and 70% of the subjects in Walker's (1984) study were separated from the assailant. Their self-descriptions may then have been influenced by the treatment agencies that supported and encouraged efforts to end the abuse, to separate from the spouse, to terminate the relationship, and perhaps even to prosecute. Their self-description may not be an accurate retrospective assessment of their attitudes during the years in which they accepted and/or tolerated the abuse.

Walker (1987a) concluded that her research indicated that "no causative relationship was found between events in childhood and those factors originating in an adult abusive relationship" (p. 184). However, her findings demonstrated a relationship between childhood and adulthood victimization. Her research does tend to refute the early psychoanalytic model (that the masochistic woman seeks or enjoys pain and suffering), but it is consistent with other trait models. Some victims of spouse abuse do appear to have a self-defeating behavior pattern, as described in DSM-III-R, that is associated with a childhood history of victimization.

Some researchers have found battered women to be no more likely than American women in general to have experienced domestic violence in childhood (Okun, 1986). However, Browne and Finkelor (1986), in a review of the research on childhood victimization, particularly sex abuse, concluded that a history of victimization in childhood was associated with long-term, maladaptive behavior patterns. Women who were victimized as children were "more likely to manifest depression, self-destructive behavior, anxiety, feelings of isolation and stigma, poor self-esteem, a tendency towards revictimization, and substance abuse" (p. 72). For example, Russell (1986) surveyed 930 women in a random sample of the San Francisco community. Of childhood incest victims, 82% were later victims of a serious sexual assault as an adult, 68% were later raped by nonrelatives, and 62% were raped by their husbands (compared to the rates of 48%, 38%, and 21%, respectively, in the nonvictimized group).

The learned helplessness model offered by Walker (1984) to explain these findings is consistent with a personality disorder model (Shainess, 1979; Simons, 1987). Repeated episodes of childhood victimization contribute to the development of a passive resignation to victimization. The person may not seek pain and suffering, but she or he may develop a tolerance for abuse when it occurs and a self-definition as a victim, a belief that she or he is a person to whom victimization is an expected, natural occurrence. These traits would contribute to a vulnerability to revictimization.

Gold (1986) verified the learned helplessness hypothesis in a study of 103 adult women who were victimized as children. Victims were more likely than nonvictims to "attribute bad events to global factors and to internal, stable, global factors; to blame their character and behavior for bad events; and to attribute good events to external factors" (p. 473). This attributional style may predispose them to self-blame, low self-esteem, a diminishment of the importance of positive events, a failure to avoid victimization, a failure to accept opportunities for pleasure, a tendency to choose or enter situations that lead to disappointment or failure even though other opportunities are available, a failure to accomplish tasks crucial to self-improvement, and other traits characteristic of an SDPD.

Affective Disorders

The argument that the self-defeating behavior pattern represents an affective rather than a personality disorder is in part an argument concerning the relative importance of state (affective) versus trait (personality) factors and the relative importance of biological (affective) versus psychosocial (personality) variables. Each of these issues is discussed.

State versus Trait

Self-defeating behavior will at times be due to a depressive state rather than self-defeating traits. It is for this reason that DSM-III-R includes the exclusion criterion that the behavior pattern does not occur only when the person is depressed (see Table 1). Peterson and Seligman (1984), in their review of the learned helplessness research, concluded that the data do suggest that the helpless explanatory style precedes and is a predisposition to depression and is not simply a result of depression. However, there are no studies on the longitudinal comorbidity of SDPD and depression.

The distinction between states and traits, however, is to some extent arbitrary (Allen & Potkay, 1981, 1983). A state is a person's reaction at a given point in time, while a trait is the tendency to react in a particular manner. A state is the single, discrete occurrence (readily observable), whereas a trait is a disposition or an inferred property indicated by repeated or regular responses to similar situations (Fridhandler, 1986). Personality traits are then the disposition or tendency to respond with a particular state to certain situations (Levy, 1983). The depressed mood of a patient is both a state (depressed affect) and trait (manifestation of the disposition to become depressed). Self-defeating persons are characterized in part by the tendency to become easily depressed. They are likely to be depressed much of the time. "When susceptibilities to specific moods are chronic, they are traits of character" (Ryle, 1949, p. 96). It is then to some extent inaccurate to say that low self-esteem, pessimism, or passivity are a result of depression rather than a self-defeating personality disorder. Self-defeating persons are predisposed to become depressed in response to minor setbacks and even in response to success and good fortune. Determining that self-defeating traits covary with depressed mood does not negate the diagnosis of SDPD.

Biological versus Psychosocial Variables

It has also been suggested that many cases of chronic pessimism, self-blame, self-criticism, and guilt involve an affective disorder and are therefore more likely to be responsive to pharmacological interventions. Akiskal (1983) provides a set of indicators to differentiate characterologically based depression from a subaffective dysthymia. Both disorders involve an insidious onset in childhood or adolescence and follow a protracted course throughout life. However, subaffective dysthymia typically involves a continuous or intermittent course (versus only intermittent); Schneiderian depressive features (versus dependent, histrionic, or sociopathic traits); melancholic manifestations during syndromal depression (e.g., psychomotor inertia, hypersomnia, anhedonia, and diurnal variation); habitual introversion; unremarkable developmental history (versus childhood parental loss or broken homes); family history of unipolar or bipolar affective disorders (versus both parents with personality disorders or alcoholism); shortened latency to the first onset of rapid eye movement sleep; and brief, hypomanic responses to pharmacological interventions. Akiskal has found that chronic and mild depressives with these features tend to be more responsive to tricyclic antidepressants and/or lithium.

It should be noted, however, that the "characterological depressives" constituted the majority of Akiskal's (1983) chronic and mild depressives. In addition, although his indicators are helpful in identifying a particular drug-responsive subgroup, it should not be assumed that the identification of biogenetic covariates and drug responsivity imply an affective rather than a personality disorder, while psychosocial covariates and psychotherapy responsivity imply a personality disorder (Gunderson & Pollack, 1985; Widiger & Frances, 1987a). Some personality disorders, particularly the antisocial and schizotypal, have been shown to have a biogenetic predisposition (Siever, Klar, & Coccaro, 1985), and there is no reason to assume that personality traits are unresponsive to pharmacological interventions. Similarly, it is readily apparent that many affective disorders (including chronic dysthymia) result from psychosocial variables and are responsive to psychosocial interventions (Sacco & Beck, 1985).

Other Personality Disorders

Initial studies do suggest that there may be a substantial overlap of SDPD with the dependent personality disorder and perhaps the passive–aggressive. J. Reich (1987) found that over 70% of 15 persons diagnosed with SDPD by the PDQ also met the criteria for dependent personality disorder as assessed by the PDQ (76%), the Millon Clinical Multiaxial Inventory (82%),and a semistructured interview (73%). At least 50% of the SDPD subjects also met criteria for the borderline and avoidant personality disorders on two of the three diagnostic instruments. J. Reich (1987) concluded that the data do not indicate that the SDPD diagnosis can predict validating criteria beyond what is already predicted by the dependent, borderline, and avoidant personality disorders.

Kass replicated across two studies that most of the individual items from the SDPD criteria (preliminary drafts) were more highly correlated with clinical ratings of masochism (Kass *et al.*, 1986) or with the presence of the other SDPD items (Kass, 1987) than with the ratings for any other personality disorder (Kass *et al.*, 1986) or with the presence of an aggregate collection of items from other personality disorders (Kass, 1987). However, in both studies the clinicians who provided the SDPD ratings also provided the ratings for the other personality disorders, and most were aware of the purpose of the study. The internal consistency data will likely be poorer when independent ratings are obtained.

The self-defeating, the dependent, and, to a lesser extent, the passive–aggressive personality traits are likely to occur in the same person. All three personality disorders share a passive, submissive interpersonal style. However, in those cases in which they are distinguished, the differentiation may be useful clinically. The meaning, purpose, or reason for the submission will often be different for each personality disorder. It may be useful clinically to distinguish between a self-deprecating, abasive submissiveness (SDPD), a docile, ingenuous submissiveness (dependent), and a hostile, resistant submissiveness (passive–aggressive).

A similar argument was made for the inclusion of the avoidant personality disorder in DSM-III. Although the avoidant and schizoid personality disorders are both characterized by social withdrawal, the reasons for the withdrawal are very different (i.e., social anxiety and shyness versus anhedonia and indifference, respectively), and they have substantially different implications for treatment (Frances, 1980; Frances & Widiger, in press; Liebowitz, Stone, & Turkat, 1986). The inclusion of the avoidant personality disorder in DSM-III appears to have been an appropriate and beneficial decision (Widiger, Trull, & Frances, 1987), and the same may prove true for the self-defeating personality disorder.

CONCLUSIONS

A major reason for including the SDPD in DSM-III-R was to broaden clinical perspective by facilitating the recognition of personality factors in the etiology and treatment of persons who repeatedly fail at tasks they have the ability to perform, repeatedly place themselves within abusive and destructive situations and respond helplessly, and repeatedly fail to take advantage of alternatives when they are clearly available. Prior to DSM-III-R, self-defeating behavior patterns would be diagnosed primarily, if not solely, as an affective disorder. The advantage of a multiaxial system of diagnosis is that it allows a consideration of the contribution of a variety of factors to a particular dysfunction.

The absence of an adequate system for diagnosing social-interpersonal relationship patterns is problematic for a fully comprehensive assessment. The concern that relationship factors will be ignored is understandable. The DSM-III-R diagnoses favor organismic pathology (Spitzer & Williams, 1985) and do not adequately consider social system variables. Until an adequate method is available for classifying relationship factors, their recognition will be hindered.

Determining the relative importance of trait and situational variables is especially problematic because they are often interactive and are not mutually exclusive. A personality disposition is the tendency to display a particular behavior pattern when certain conditions are met (Levy, 1983; Widiger & Trull, 1987). The conditional factors are often situational. A claustrophobic person is predisposed to act fearfully when in an elevator but not when in a field; an extraverted person has the disposition to be flirtatious at parties but not at a funeral; and a self-defeating person is predisposed to respond to victimization with a resigned, self-blaming helplessness, but the helpless passivity may be less evident when the person is not being victimized. Persons without the dispositions do not respond to the particular situations in a similar fashion. Personality disorders are distinguished from other dispositional concepts (such as phobias) by being substantially more chronic and pervasive in expression (Frances & Widiger, 1986), but it is not inconsistent with the concept of a personality disorder for the behavior to be relatively less evident in situations that do not support or perhaps even suppress the behavior pattern.

The DSM-III-R diagnoses are meant to be descriptive, not explanatory (APA, 1987; Spitzer & Williams, 1985). Historically, the term *masochism* has been associated with an early psychoanalytic theory that hypothesized an unconscious association of pleasure and pain. However, the behavior pattern described by the SDPD diagnosis may also be explained by an underlying cognitive style (Sacco & Beck, 1985), a learned helplessness (Peterson & Seligman, 1983), a subaffective disorder (Akiskal, 1983), guilt and narcissistic conflicts (Asch, 1986; Bemporad, 1985), self-esteem conflicts (Berglas, 1985), and/or sociocultural sex-role indoctrination (Walker, 1984). A personality disorder diagnosis does not necessarily imply a psychodynamic etiology. It simply describes a particular chronic and pervasive maladaptive behavior pattern, the etiology for which is often uncertain.

The diagnosis of SDPD does have the potential for misuse, particularly for female victims of abusive relationships (Caplan, 1987; Rosewater, 1987b; Walker, 1987a). This does not justify ignoring the presence and contribution of personality traits to inadequate responses to victimization, but it does indicate the need to be particularly cautious and sensitive. The prevalence of victimization is much higher than has been assumed, and clinic patients may be reluctant to reveal their victimization (Jacobson & Richardson, 1987; Rosewater, 1987a; Walker, 1987a). In addition, a disorder that involves an exaggeration of stereotypical sex-role behavior is prone to sex-biased misdiagnosis. There are personality disorders that occur more frequently in men, but the threshold for diagnosing the disorders that occur more frequently in women may be lower and may contain more pejorative connotations and negative sociopolitical consequences.

The need for empirical data is evident. The benefits in description, prediction, and treatment, relative to the costs of misdiagnosis, should be assessed empirically. Does the diagnosis of SDPD provide any unique information that is not already provided by other personality disorder diagnoses? Is it misused in the treatment of abused women? Are the diagnostic criteria biased against women? Should it be classified as an affective or perhaps a posttraumatic stress disorder? The literature we reviewed addressed these issues, but the answers we suggested are only tentative and are based on limited data.

REFERENCES

Akiskal, H. (1983). Dysthymic disorder: Psychopathology of proposed chronic depressive subtypes. *American Journal of Psychiatry, 140,* 11–20.

Akiskal, H., Djenderedjian, A., Rosenthal, R., & Khani, M. (1977). Cyclothymic disorder: Validating criteria for inclusion in the bipolar affective group. *American Journal of Psychiatry, 134,* 1227–1233.

Allen, B., & Potkay, C. (1981). On the arbitrary distinction between states and traits. *Journal of Personality and Social Psychology, 41,* 916–928.

Allen, B., & Potkay, C. (1983). Just as arbitrary as ever: Comments on Zuckerman's rejoinder. *Journal of Personality and Social Psychology, 44,* 1087–1089.

American Psychiatric Association. (1987). *Diagnostic and statistical manual of mental disorders* (3rd ed., rev.). Washington, DC: Author.

Asch, S. (1986). The masochistic personality. In R. Michels & J. Cavenar (Eds.), *Psychiatry* (rev. ed., Chap. 27, pp. 1–13). Philadelphia: Lippincott.

Beck, A. (1967). *Depression: Clinical, experimental, and theoretical aspects.* New York: Harper & Row.

Bemporad, J. (1985). Long-term analytic treatment of depression. In E. Beckham & W. Leber (Eds.), *Handbook of depression* (pp. 82–99). Homewood, IL: Dorsey.

Berglas, S. (1985). Self-handicapping and self-handicappers: A cognitive/attributional model of interpersonal self-protective behavior. *Perspectives in Personality, 1,* 235–270.

Brown, L. (1986a, August). Diagnosis and the zeitgeist: The politics of masochism in the DSM-III-R. In R. Garfinkel (Chair), *Politics of diagnosis: Feminist psychology and the*

DSM-III-R. Symposium conducted at the 94th Annual Convention of the American Psychological Association, Washington, DC.

Brown, L. (1986b). Gender-role analysis: A neglected component of psychological assessment. *Psychotherapy, 23*, 243–248.

Brown, L. (1987, August). Toward a new conceptual paradigm for the Axis II diagnosis. In J. Worell (Chair), *DSM-III*. Symposium conducted at the 95th Annual Convention of the American Psychological Association, New York.

Browne, A., & Finkelhor, D. (1986). Impact of child sexual abuse. A review of the research. *Psychological Bulletin, 99*, 66–77.

Caplan, P. (1984). The myth of women's masochism. *American Psychologist, 39*, 130–139.

Caplan, P. (1987). The psychiatric association's failure to meet its own standards. The dangers of self-defeating personality disorder as a category. *Journal of Personality Disorder, 1*, 178–182.

Chodoff, P. (1972). The depressive personality: A critical review. *Archives of General Psychiatry, 27*, 666–673.

Chodoff, P. (1982). Hysteria and women. *American Journal of Psychiatry, 139*, 545–551.

Coalition Against Misdiagnosis. (1986). *Information packet: The DSM-III-R diagnoses*. Seattle, WA: Author.

D'Ercole, A. (1987). The DSM-III-R: An outrage. *The Community Psychologist, 20*, 34.

Deutsch, H. (1944). *The psychology of women* (Vol. 1). New York: Grune & Stratton.

Eagly, A., & Crowley, M. (1986). Gender and helping behavior: A meta-analytic review of the social psychological literature. *Psychological Bulletin, 100*, 283–308.

Frances, A. (1980). The DSM-III personality disorders: A commentary. *American Journal of Psychiatry, 137*, 1050–1054.

Frances, A., & Cooper, A. (1981). Descriptive and dynamic psychiatry: A perspective on DSM-III. *American Journal of Psychiatry, 138*, 1198–1202.

Frances, A., & Widiger, T. (1986). The classification of personality disorders: An overview of problems and solutions. In A. Frances & R. Hales (Eds.), *Psychiatry update: American Psychiatric Association annual review* (Vol. 5, pp. 240–257). Washington, DC: American Psychiatric Press.

Frances, A., & Widiger, T. (in press). Personality disorders. In J. Greist, J. Jefferson, & R. Spitzer (Eds.). *Treatment of mental disorders* (rev. ed., pp.). New York: Oxford University Press.

Freedman, M., Leary, T., Ossorio, A., & Coffey, H. (1951). The interpersonal dimension of personality. *Journal of Personality, 20*, 143–161.

Freud, S. (1961). The economic problem of masochism. In J. Strachey (Ed.), *The standard edition of the complete psychological works of Sigmund Freud* (Vol. 19, pp. 157–174). London: Hogarth Press. (Original work published 1924)

Fridhandler, B. (1986). Conceptual note on state, trait, and the state–trait distinction. *Journal of Personality and Social Psychology, 50*, 169–174.

Fuller, A., & Blashfield, R. (in press). Masochistic personality disorder and sex bias. *Journal of Nervous and Mental Disease*.

Gold, E. (1986). Long-term effects of sexual victimization in childhood: An attributional approach. *Journal of Consulting and Clinical Psychology, 54*, 471–475.

Gunderson, J. (1983). DSM-III diagnosis of personality disorders. In J. Frosch (Ed.), *Current perspectives on personality disorders* (pp. 20–39). Washington, DC: American Psychiatric Press.

Gunderson, J., & Pollack, W. (1985). Conceptual risks of the Axis I-II division. In H. Klar & L. Siever (Eds.), *Biologic response styles. Clinical implications* (pp. 82–95). Washington, DC: American Psychiatric Press.

Horney, K. (1939). *New ways in psychoanalysis*. New York: Norton.

Horney, K. (1967). The problem of feminine masochism. In H. Kelman (Ed.), *Feminine psychology* (pp. 214–233). New York: Norton. (Original work published 1935)

Hyler, S., Rieder, R., Spitzer, R., & Williams, J. (1982). *The personality diagnostic questionnaire (PDQ)*. New York: New York State Psychiatric Institute.

Jackson, D. (1974). *Personality research form manual*. Goshen, NY: Research Psychologists Press.

Jacobson, A., & Richardson, B. (1986). Assault experiences of 100 psychiatric inpatients: Evidence of the need for routine inquiry. *American Journal of Psychiatry, 144,* 908–913.

Kaplan, M. (1983). A woman's view of DSM-III. *American Psychologist, 38,* 786–792.

Kass, F. (1987). Self-defeating personality disorder: An empirical study. *Journal of Personality Disorders, 1,* 168–173.

Kass, F., MacKinnon, R., & Spitzer, R. (1986). Masochistic personality: An empirical study. *American Journal of Psychiatry, 143,* 216–218.

Kass, F., Spitzer, R., & Williams, J. (1983). An empirical study of the issue of sex bias in the diagnostic criteria of DSM-III Axis II personality disorders. *American Psychologist, 38,* 799–801.

Kernberg, O. (1984). *Severe personality disorders*. New Haven, CT: Yale University Press.

Krafft-Ebing, R. (1950). *Psychopathia sexualis: A medico-forensic study*. New York: Pioneer Publications. (Original work published 1901)

Kiesler, D. (1983). The 1982 interpersonal circle: A taxonomy for complementarity in human transactions. *Psychological Review, 90,* 185–214.

Landers, S. (1986, November). DSM by APA? *APA Monitor,* p. 7.

Landers, S. (1987, nality disorders. *American Psychologist, 38,* 799–801.

Kernberg, O. (1984). *Severe personality disorders*. New Haven, CT: Yale University Press.

Krafft-Ebing, R. (1950). *Psychopathia sexualis: A medico-forensic study*. New York: Pioneer Publications. (Original work published 1901)

Kiesler, D. (1983). The 1982 interpersonal circle: A taxonomy for complementarity in human transactions. *Psychological Review, 90,* 185–214.

Landers, S. (1986, November). DSM by APA? *APA Monitor,* p. 7.

Landers, S. (1987, February). Debated DSM-III categories now official. Psychology moves ahead on plans for own manual. *APA Monitor,* p. 24.

Lazare, A., Klerman, G., & Armor, D. (1966). Oral, obsessive, and hysterical personality patterns. Archives of General Psychiatry, 14, 624–630.

Leary, T. (1957). *Interpersonal diagnosis of personality*. New York: Ronald Press.

Levy, L. (1983). Trait approaches. In M. Hersen, A. Kazdin, & A. Bellack (Eds.), *The clinical psychology handbook* (pp. 123–142). New York: Pergamon Press.

Liebowitz, M. (1987). Commentary on the criteria for self-defeating personality disorder. *Journal of Personality Disorders, 1,* 197–199.

Liebowitz, M., Stone, M., & Turkat, I. (1986). Treatment of personality disorders. In A. Frances & R. Hales (Eds.), *Psychiatry update: American Psychiatric Association annual review* (Vol. 5, pp. 356–393). Washington, DC: American Psychiatric Press.

Lorr, M., Bishop, P., & McNair, D. (1965). Interpersonal types among psychiatric patients. *Journal of Abnormal Psychology, 70,* 468–472.

Millon, T. (1981). *Disorders of personality. DSM-III: Axis II*. New York: Wiley.

Millon, T. (1983). *Millon clinical multiaxial inventory manual* (3rd ed.). Minneapolis, MN: National Computer Services.

Millon, T. (1986). Personality prototypes and their diagnostic criteria. In T. Millon & G. Klerman (Eds.), *Contemporary directions in psychopathology. Toward the DSM-IV* (pp. 671–712). New York: Guilford Press.

Mischel, W. (1984). Convergences and challenges in the search for consistency. *American Psychologist, 34,* 351–364.

Murray, H. (1938). *Explorations in personality*. New York: Oxford University Press.

Okun, L. (1986). *Woman abuse: Facts replacing myths*. New York: State University of New York Press.

Peterson, C., & Seligman, M. (1983). Learned helplessness and victimization. *Journal of Social Issues, 39*, 103–116.

Peterson, C., & Seligman, M. (1984). Causal explanations as a risk factor for depression: Theory and evidence. *Psychological Bulletin, 91*, 347–374.

Presly, A., & Walton, J. (1973). Dimensions of abnormal personality. *British Journal of Psychiatry, 122*, 269–276.

Reich, J. (1987). Prevalence of DSM-III-R self-defeating (masochistic) personality disorder in normal and outpatient populations. *Journal of Nervous and Mental Disease, 175*, 52–54.

Reich, J., Noyes, R., & Coryell, W., & O'Gorman, T. (1986). The effect of state anxiety on personality measurement. *American Journal of Psychiatry, 143*, 760–763.

Reich, J., Noyes, J., Hirschfeld, R., Coryell, W., & O'Gorman, T. (1987). State and personality in depressed and panic patients. *American Journal of Psychiatry, 144*, 181–187.

Reich, J., Noyes, R., & Troughton, E. (1986, March). *Lack of agreement between instruments assessing DSM-III personality disorders*. Paper presented at the Conference on the Millon Clinical Inventories, Miami, FL.

Reich, W. (1976). *Character analysis* (3rd ed.). New York: Pocket. (Original work published 1933)

Rosenbaum, A., & O'Leary, K. (1981). Marital violence: Characteristics of abusive couples. *Journal of Consulting and Clinical Psychology, 49*, 63–71.

Rosewater, L. (1986). The DSM-III-R: Ethical and legal implications for feminist therapists. In R. Garfinkel (Chair), *Politics of diagnosis: Feminist psychology and the DSM-III-R*. Symposium conducted at the 94th Annual Convention of the American Psychological Association, Washington, DC.

Rosewater, L. (1987a). A critical analysis of the proposed self-defeating personality disorder. *Journal of Personality Disorders, 1*, 190–195.

Rosewater, L. (1987b, August). Personality disorders: The dinosaur of the DSM? In J. Worell (Chair), *DSM-III*. Symposium conducted at the 95th Annual Convention of the American Psychological Association, New York.

Russell, D. (1986). *The secret trauma: Incest in the lives of girls and women*. New York: Basic Books.

Ryle, G. (1949). *The concept of mind*. London: Hutchison.

Sacco, W., & Beck, A. (1985). Cognitive therapy of depression. In E. Beckham & W. Leber (Eds.), *Handbook of depression* (pp. 3–38), Homewood, IL: Dorsey.

Schneider, K. (1958). *Psychopathic personalities*. Springfield, IL: Charles C. Thomas.

Shainess, N. (1979). Vulnerability to violence: Masochism as process. *American Journal of Psychotherapy, 33*, 174–188.

Siever, L., Klar, H., & Coccaro, E. (1985). Psychobiologic substrates of personality. In H. Klar & L. Siever (Eds.), *Biologic response styles: Clinical implications* (pp. 37–66). Washington, DC: American Psychiatric Press.

Silverman, J. S., Silverman, J. A., & Eardley, D. (1984). Do maladaptive attitudes cause depression? *Archives of General Psychiatry, 41*, 28–30.

Simons, R. (1983, May). *Applicability of DSM-III to psychiatric education*. Paper presented to the American Psychiatric Association's Committee to Evaluate DSM-III, Washington, DC.

Simons, R. (1987). Self-defeating and sadistic personality disorders: Needed additions to the diagnostic nomenclature. *Journal of Personality Disorders, 1*, 161–167.

Snell, J., Rosenwald, R., & Robey, A. (1964). The wifebeater's wife. A study of family interaction. *Archives of General Psychiatry, 11,* 107–112.

Snyder, D., & Fruchtman, L. (1981). Differential patterns of wife abuse: A data-based typology. *Journal of Consulting and Clinical Psychology, 49,* 878–885.

Spitzer, R., & Williams, J. (1985). Classification of mental disorders. In H. Kaplan & B. Sadock (Eds.), *Comprehensive textbook of psychiatry/IV* (4th ed., Vol. 1, pp. 592–613). Baltimore, MD: Williams & Wilkins.

Symonds, A. (1979). Violence against women—the myth of masochism. *American Journal of Psychotherapy, 33,* 161–173.

Vaillant, G., & Perry, J. (1985). Personality disorders. In H. Kaplan & B. Sadock (Eds.), *Comprehensive textbook of psychiatry/IV* (4th ed., Vol. 1, pp. 958–986). Baltimore, MD: Williams & Wilkins.

Walker, L. (1984). *The battered woman syndrome.* New York: Springer.

Walker, L. (1986, August). Diagnosis and politics: Abuse disorders. In R. Garfinkel (Chair), *Politics of diagnosis: Feminist psychology and the DSM-III-R.* Symposium conducted at the 94th Annual Convention of the American Psychological Association, Washington, DC.

Walker, L. (1987a). Inadequacies of the masochistic personality disorder diagnosis for women. *Journal of Personality Disorders, 1,* 183–189.

Walker, L. (1987b, August). Is victimization evidence of deviancy? In J. Worell (Chair), *DSM-III.* Symposium conducted at the 95th Annual Convention of the American Psychological Association, New York.

Walker, L., & Browne, A. (1985). Gender and victimization by intimates. *Journal of Personality, 53,* 178–195.

Warner, R. (1978). The diagnosis of antisocial and hysterical personality disorders. *Journal of Nervous and Mental Disease, 166,* 839–845.

Widiger, T. (1987). The self-defeating personality disorder. Introduction. *Journal of Personality Disorders, 1,* 157–160.

Widiger, T., & Frances, A. (1985). The DSM-III personality disorders. Perspectives from psychology. *Archives of General Psychiatry, 42,* 615–623.

Widiger, T., & Frances, A. (1987a, May). Comorbidity of personality and Axis I disorders. In J. Mezzich (Chair), *Comorbidity: Diagnostic and treatment implications.* Symposium conducted at the 140th Annual Meeting of the American Psychiatric Association, Chicago, Illinois.

Widiger, T., & Frances, A. (1987b). Interviews and inventories for the measurement of personality disorders. *Clinical Psychology Review, 7,* 49–75.

Widiger, T., & Trull, T. (1987). Behavioral indicators, hypothetical constructs, and personality disorders. *Journal of Personality Disorders, 1,* 82–87.

Widiger, T., Trull, T., & Frances, A. (1987, May). Controversies about avoidant personality disorder. In H. Klar (Chair), *Current controversies in personality disorders.* Symposium conducted at the 140th Annual Meeting of the American Psychiatric Association, Chicago, Illinois.

Wiggins, J. (1979). A psychological taxonomy of trait-descriptive terms: The interpersonal domain. *Journal of Personality and Social Psychology, 37,* 395–412.

Williams, J., & Spitzer, R. (1983). The issue of sex bias in DSM-III. A critique of "A woman's view of DSM-III" by Marcie Kaplan. *American Psychologist, 38,* 793–798.

Work Group to Revise DSM-III. (1985). *DSM-III-R in development.* Washington, DC: American Psychiatric Association.

Work Group to Revise DSM-III. (1986). *DSM-III in development: Second draft.* Washington, DC: American Psychiatric Association.

CHAPTER 13

THE PARADOX OF THE SELF

A PSYCHODYNAMIC AND SOCIAL-COGNITIVE INTEGRATION

TIMOTHY J. STRAUMAN

INTRODUCTION

Can theories of the self help explain the apparent paradox of self-defeating behavior? Under what conditions will an individual behave in contradictory and self-defeating ways? What features or processes of the self lead to ill-advised decisions and actions? Can a theory of the self provide alternatives for therapeutic interventions to halt and prevent self-defeating behavior patterns?

To this author's knowledge, the present volume is the first major effort to bring together the most promising clinical and experimental approaches to self-defeating behavior. With the recent controversy surrounding the proposal for a psychiatric diagnosis of a *masochistic* or *self-defeating personality disorder*, the necessity for a comprehensive understanding of the phenomenon has become increasingly clear (Kass, MacKinnon, & Spitzer, 1986). Unfortunately, the need for interventions to alleviate self-defeating behavior patterns has greatly outstripped the extent of our knowledge regarding such behaviors (Asch, 1985; Caston, 1984; Reich, 1987). The paradox presented by the masochistic individual—who persists in behaviors that are followed contingently by seemingly aversive consequences—strains the adequacy of traditional approaches to abnormal behavior (Brown & Cunningham, 1981). Above all, the enigma of

TIMOTHY J. STRAUMAN • Department of Psychology, University of Wisconsin-Madison, Madison, Wisconsin 53706.

self-defeating behavior illustrates the need for clarification and refinement of the concept of the *self,* with all its philosophical and metatheoretical significance.

Why an integrative review in a publication devoted to experimental findings and practical implications? As the chapters in this volume attest, the evolution of knowledge about the self is at a decisive point. Without a solid grasp of the issues, and the theories that have sought to address them, further progress will become increasingly difficult. This chapter is based on the premise that continued development of self theory and research, particularly in the context of self-defeating behavior, will come from an *integration* of approaches rather than a continuation of isolated research programs.

This chapter attempts to deal with some of the complex issues underlying the nature of the self, particularly the influence of self-representations on behavior. The two fields of inquiry that most frequently utilize the self as an explanatory construct, social-cognitive and psychodynamic psychology, will be surveyed in an effort to determine the state of the art in self theory and research. Naturally, such an inclusive topic defies efforts at summarization. It can be argued, for example, that any theory in which the individual's experience or knowledge of his or her own identity plays a significant role is a self theory (Allport, 1955). To make the task manageable, we will concentrate on those theories that have made explicit efforts to address self issues and have at least been indirectly applied to the understanding of self-defeating behaviors.

As even a cursory glance at current journals will reveal, psychologists have only begun to fully address the intricacies of the self (e.g., Suls & Greenwald, 1983; Markus & Wurf, 1987). Despite the diversity of approaches, however, some vital issues have been identified that an integrated model of the self and its role in self-defeating behaviors must address. Following discussion of several such issues, the outlines of a new and as yet largely untested approach to self-representations is described. The model is presented primarily for its (presumed) heuristic value, in recognition of the unique opportunity that the present volume offers. The reader will hopefully find it useful in appraising the empirical and clinical literatures contained in other chapters and perhaps even as a rough guide to further study of the paradox of the self.

PSYCHODYNAMIC APPROACHES: MASOCHISM AND THE THREE HARSH MASTERS

Psychologists who do not identify themselves as psychodynamically oriented are likely to think of psychodynamic psychology as a homogeneous entity. The distinctions among major dynamic theories are of interest here because of their implications for the self. I will present the most influential psychodynamic approaches to self phenomena, highlighting their similarities and differences. Given that a lack of experimental support for these models is a long-standing criticism of the entire field (e.g., Mischel, 1973), my commentary focuses instead on how each model might facilitate our understanding of self-defeating behavior.

Early Psychodynamic Theories

The basic premise of psychodynamic models of personality, that is, that observed behaviors are indirect (and symbolic) manifestations of underlying (and presumably unconscious) processes, is a logical starting point for unraveling the paradox of the self. Freud himself (1920/1966) was of the opinion that most neuroses could be characterized as syndromes of self-defeating behavior, since they represented unsatisfactory resolutions to chronic intrapsychic conflict and crippled the individual's ability to love and work. Early psychoanalytic writings presented cases in which self-perpetuating cycles of maladaptive behaviors had been maintained for months or years (Fenichel, 1945). The dynamic formulation of neurosis stated that when conflicts arising from unconscious id impulses were not successfully repressed, they inevitably found expression as symptoms which bore a symbolic resemblance to the underlying conflict (Freud, 1915a, 1915b, 1915c). The necessity for the person to avoid becoming aware of unacceptable wishes (typically of a sexual nature) led to a compromise defensive process whereby the impulses achieved partial gratification in a form sufficiently different from their original nature. The integrity of the *conscious* experience of self (in Freud's terms, the conscious portion of the ego; see Freud, 1923/1961) was said to be maintained at the expense of the individual's psychological health.

A major thorn in Freud's instinct-based motivational model of the psyche was the problem of masochism—the fact that under certain circumstances the "pleasure principle" seemed to defer to directly or indirectly self-destructive tendencies, thus contradicting the primary source of drives (Freud, 1924). Attempts to apply the analytic formulation to masochistic behavior brought apparent contradiction, since it seemed paradoxical that a feared pain might be avoided or denied by actually suffering pain. However, despite the problems for Freud's metapsychology, the clinical theory of psychoanalysis suggested that such a paradox was possible when one of several conditions was fulfilled (Fenichel, 1945, pp. 358–359): (1) deeply ingrained learning experiences where pain and sexual pleasure were connected, so that suffering became the prerequisite for sexual pleasure; (2) masochistic activities that took the form of a "sacrifice," a price paid in advance to "appease the gods" at a relatively lesser cost; (3) fighting anxiety by a playful anticipatory action of what is feared, even if the playfulness reverts to aggression with time; and (4) regression to oral-receptive passive behaviors.

Subsequently, Freud revised his theory of the instincts, postulating two primordial "qualities in the mind" as the motivational basis for conflict and behavior. These two forces were a *self-destructive* quality, the "death instinct" (which can be turned against the outside world and thus become a "destructive instinct") and an *object-seeking* quality, striving for expression of sexual and affectional drives in the form of a person to be loved (Freud, 1920/1966, Chap. 21). While the death instinct concept has been justifiably criticized on both phenomenological and theoretical grounds (Rapaport & Gill, 1959), the notion of aggression-based or survival-based motives has met with general agreement in psychodynamic circles. More importantly, what Freud observed in the psychoneurotic syndromes of his day—recurrent patterns of self-defeating resolutions to intrapsychic conflicts—remains of importance to clinicians. The well-known characterization of the ego as subject to "three harsh masters"—id, superego, and external reality (Freud, 1923/1961, p. 46)—carried the implication that symptoms and pathological behaviors are likely to represent maladaptive coping strategies.

While from the start Freud espoused the view that symptoms were a form of defense against underlying impulses (Freud, 1894/1950), it was his student Adler who suggested a more direct link between symptoms and pathological behaviors. Adler (e.g., 1917/1966) introduced the notion of self-protective or safeguarding effects of symptoms in both normal and clinical populations. Whereas Freud conceived of symptoms as unconsciously evoked compromise formations that protected against awareness of unacceptable wishes, Adler also regarded them as excuses for past and future failures that threatened self-esteem. Adler's notion ultimately influenced the dynamic conceptualization of defense mechanisms, which came to be understood more generally as cognitive strategies used to reduce anxiety caused by threatening situations (internal as well as external) with which the individual cannot otherwise adequately cope (Ellenberger, 1970, Chap. 8). In this regard, Adler's view that symptoms could serve self-protective purposes was similar to the defense mechanism of rationalization (A. Freud, 1948), as well as to the currently popular concept of self-handicapping (see Chapter 11, this volume).

The Interpersonal Perspective

H. S. Sullivan's clinical and theoretical writings (e.g., Sullivan, 1953, 1956) contain a number of ideas that are remarkably similar to concepts currently espoused by self researchers in social-cognitive psychology. Sullivan's unique contribution was his hypothesis that the self is an interpersonal as well as intrapsychic phenomenon. His concept of the *personified self* (Sullivan, 1954/1970) is analogous to recent models of the self-schema (Pratkanis & Greenwald, 1985). Sullivan postulated the existence of a *self-system*, an organization within the total personality that was derived from the influences of significant others on the individual's overt and implicit sense of well-being. The personified self is the segment of the overall self-system of which the individual is aware. It includes what the person esteems and disparages about himself or herself as well as his or her characteristic *security operations* (defensive–coping strategies; Sullivan, 1954/1970, pp. 168–169). These security operations were said to function through such cognitive mechanisms as denial or distortion of the interpersonal significance of one's behavior. In this approach, personification implies that people will tend to develop biases or expectations in perceiving their own behaviors as well as the actions of familiar others. These biases resemble stereotypes in person perception (Snyder, Tanke, & Berscheid, 1977) in their overinclusiveness, their tendency to confirm desired outcomes, and their potential for misrepresentation of the meanings of behaviors.

Sullivan postulated that the most common way people bias or distort their perceptions and interpretations of interpersonal events is through the process of *selective attention* (and its converse, selective inattention) (Safran, 1984b). The selective attention strategy plays a critical defensive role by enabling the individual to avoid recognizing the self-incriminating implications of his or her behaviors. In turn, a frequent concomitant of selective attention is an excessive degree of certainty that social information is being processed and interpreted in a relatively objective fashion (Darley & Gross, 1983), providing a further security barrier (as well as a further impairment of reality testing in the area under scrutiny). Anxiety was a central explanatory construct in Sullivan's writings, designating any type of emotional distress related to an impending loss of self-esteem. Anxiety was seen as threatening self-esteem and making clear perception and interpretation of the social world more difficult. The individual comes to rely on self-deceiving interpretive strategies that provide an artificial sense of personal integrity at the cost of perpetuating maladaptive cognitive and behavioral patterns.

Object Relations and Self Psychology

In contrast to Freud and the orthodox analytic tradition, more recent psychodynamic theorists have emphasized both the "conflict-free" realm of ego functions (those capacities that are not derivatives of id impulses; see Hartmann, 1951) and the role of pre-Oedipal influences on personality formation. This shift has resulted in a more complex view of the self. That is, self-representation is seen as initially undifferentiated and gradually organizing around two basic "poles" or issues: the self–nonself distinction and early impressions of good versus bad (Schweber, 1979). Such a characterization of the self as a primordial psychological organization suggests that self-representations will necessarily involve memories of images and feelings from the earliest years of life.

The concept of the *object* in psychodynamic thinking has come to play a central role in theories of personality and psychopathology. The concept refers to an internal representation of some motivationally significant other (Jacobsen, 1964). This definition implies a distinctive scope and character for object relations models of the self. First, it is *the object as configured intrapsychically* that forms the basis for early experiences rather than the actual behaviors of the other person. This postulate is especially striking given object relations theorists' emphasis on infantile and early childhood substrates of adult personality (Mahler, Pine, & Bergman, 1975). Second, the object is a partial, incomplete, and primitive representation of the other person, so that the interaction between the self and the object (played out in an intrapsychic arena) involves two partially formed entities with limited capacities for integrating good and bad features (Mahler & Furer, 1968). Third, since the self is hypothesized to develop in part by incorporating (in an elementary sense) or identifying with (at a more sophisticated level) objects, early object relations can influence both the permanent character of the self and the rigidity or flexibility of its functioning (Winnicott, 1971).

The primary contribution of object relations theory to an understanding of self-defeating behavior lies in the postulate that in certain vulnerable individuals the "core" of the self remains a primitive objectlike entity rather than a rational, integrated, and complex structure demonstrating consistent reality-testing and judgment (Jacobsen, 1964). Developmental difficulties may hinder the self–other differentiation process, limiting the individual's capacity to comprehend and relate to objects with both good and bad qualities. Such difficulties can render the individual vulnerable to chronic life patterns that recapitulate the unsuccessful struggle with early objects (Basch, 1977; Jacobsen, 1959). The resulting behavior patterns are self-defeating in that the persisting crisis in early object relations cannot be resolved through repeated unconscious reenactments. The adult can become trapped in a self-destructive relationship where the major issue is symbolic of the undiscovered early-life conflicts (Wallerstein, 1983; Winnicott, 1960). Winnicott's notion of true and false selves embodies the overall contribution of object relations theory to an understanding of self-defeating behavior. The false-self system, a "shell" of misinterpreted and conflicted self-experiences, is postulated to result from unsuccessful and unintegrated early object relations that necessitated the creation in later life of a protective external identity.

Beginning with the observations of Knight (1953), who suggested that many neurotic individuals actually suffered from more fundamental ego defects, the concept of the *borderline personality disorder* has gained popularity. The best-known formulation of the dynamics of borderline pathology is that of Kernberg (e.g., 1980). Kernberg designated borderline personality disorder as "a group of psychopathological constellations which have in common a rather specific and remarkably stable form of pathological ego structure" (p. 3). Certain emotional and behavioral characteristics lead to a presumptive diagnosis of borderline pathology, including diffuse, chronic anxiety, "polysymptomatic" neurosis, perverse sexual trends, primitive character structure, and tendencies to addictions and poor impulse control. In the tradition of object relations theory, borderline pathology is presumed to represent a structural derivative of pathological early object relationships (Masterson, 1975), resulting in a syndrome of generalized ego weakness. The most frequent manifestations of defective ego functioning include intolerance for anxiety, a scarcity of well-developed channels for sublimation of instinctual drives, and the lack of a stable, well-integrated experience of self (Kernberg, 1980). The primitive defense mechanisms upon which borderline-level personalities rely result in a fundamental inability to perceive self and others as integrated beings with both favorable and unfavorable qualities. Such defenses also appear frequently in narcissistic and depressive-masochistic character structures, in which apparently mature cognitive and interpersonal skills coexist alongside primitive intolerance for ambiguity and anxiety. Persons with borderline personality organizations become mired in cyclical, self-defeating lives dominated by affective lability, aggressive and self-destructive tendencies, and vulnerability to periodic shallow psychotic episodes (Gunderson & Kolb, 1978).

In another offshoot of the traditional psychoanalytic model, Kohut (1971, 1977) has devised a theory of pathological narcissism that focuses on the early development and pathology of the self. This model postulates a special class of primitive internalized object, the *selfobject*, which is said to be "experienced as part of the self" (Kohut, 1971, p. 55). The appearance of selfobjects represents a normal aspect of psychological maturation. The infant's expectation of control over the selfobject is assumed to be approximately equal to its expectation of control over body parts. There are two kinds of selfobject proposed within Kohut's self psychology: *mirroring* (objects that respond to and confirm the child's innate sense of vigor and greatness) and *idealized parent* (objects the child can admire and merge with to gain a sense of calmness). The appearance of selfobjects is viewed as a necessary precondition for the formation of the self. The emergent self ultimately involves three major constituents: a pole striving for power and success, a pole that contains basic idealized goals, and an intermediate range of skills and talents that are activated by the tension between ambitions and ideals (Kohut, 1977).

Depending on the quality of internal relations between self and selfobjects during infancy and early childhood, the self will emerge either as a firm, healthy structure or as a more or less damaged one. Therefore, the self present during adolescence and adulthood can possess varying degrees of coherence, from cohesion to fragmentation; varying degrees of vitality, from vigor to enfeeblement; and varying degrees of functional harmony, from order to chaos (Kohut, 1971). Significant failures to achieve cohesion, vigor, or harmony (or a loss of these qualities after they have been tentatively established) result in chronic distress and the lack of a purposive, satisfying, goal-directed lifestyle (Stolorow & Lachman, 1980).

The self-psychology characterization of pathological narcissistic transferences in analytic therapy (e.g., Basch, 1981) suggests an alternative genesis for self-defeating lifestyles—as a function of *deficits* rather than conflicts (Lichtenberg, 1983). In the idealizing transference, for example, the client is seen as seeking an omnipotent figure to provide a soothing influence; in a mirroring transference, the client instead is viewed as desiring that the other affirm his or her own sense of greatness or omnipotence. Both are interpersonal styles that predispose to problematic relationships and difficulties in achievement-related contexts. The therapeutic interventions necessary to interrupt such patterns (Kohut, 1977) require a secure client–therapist relationship in which the transferences (often alternating) can emerge and be safely explored. Ideally, a self-psychology treatment can help to correct deficits in self-formative experiences and eliminate the need for a pathological lifestyle (Wolf, 1980).

EVALUATION OF PSYCHODYNAMIC MODELS OF THE SELF

The psychodynamic perspective has never been fully integrated into the mainstream of American psychology, which tends to value empirical methodology over clinical inference. The customary disinterest of psychodynamic clinicians toward experimental verification of theories and concepts only serves to solidify boundaries and stereotypes that hamper a mutual exchange of ideas. The result is the unfortunate circumstance that these descriptively rich and complex models still lack conventional operationalization of key variables and critical processes. Even the rather courageous experimentalist desiring to test such models will discover little in the way of specific instructions as to where to "find" self structures and processes (Erdelyi & Goldberg, 1979). While psychodynamic thinkers often bemoan the inaccuracies of experimental renderings of their concepts, they may be partially responsible through neglecting sources of knowledge supplementary to therapy sessions (Holt, 1984).

Nonetheless, psychodynamic theories appear to have several valuable insights into the causes of self-defeating behaviors with potential for clinical and research application. First, the theories emphasize events and memories from the earliest years of life as having a pervasive impact on behaviors up through adulthood. This focus on development provides a much needed complement to other approaches that concentrate on the "mature" self. Hypothetical early-life deficits or conflicts are legitimate explanatory constructs of possible value for predicting maladaptive behaviors. To the extent that infancy research (as an example) can substantiate the inferences of dynamic developmental models, and to the extent that direct, meaningful connections can be demonstrated between problems in the emergence of self and eventual self-defeating behavior, the models could greatly enhance our clinical armamentarium.

Second, another traditional focus of dynamic theorists—the combination of personal, idiosyncratic *contents* and general developmental *processes*—could greatly enhance self research. Investigators might benefit from a modified idiographic approach to assessment of self-representations that allows each subject to reveal his or her particular experience of a hypothetically universal stage of development (e.g., Higgins & King, 1981; Kelly, 1955). The alternative seems to be a "forced-choice" style that runs the risk of overlooking possible associations between self processes and self-defeating behavior. Interview techniques (e.g., Sullivan, 1954/1970), assessment strategies (Kelly, 1955), and analogous self-report procedures are an essential part of a comprehensive approach to understanding self-representations.

The most challenging (yet potentially most valuable) feature of psychodynamic self theories is the assumption that the development and maintenance of the self is *motivated* from its inception. The reality of what the self means to the survival and adaptation of the individual is acknowledged, in contrast to the current research climate favoring "nonmotivational explanations for social-cognitive phenomena" (Markus & Zajonc, 1985, pp. 139–140). The presumption of motivational processes as both raison d'etre and modus operandi for the self means that investigators need to consider the possibility that the self may not be identical to other cognitive processes and structures. The apparent irrationality of self-defeating lifestyles seems less impenetrable through the motivational perspective of psychodynamic self theory.

Nonetheless, these models require some caveats as well. While it would be presumptuous to reject outright the clinical evidence in support of psychodynamic models, more precision and clarity are needed in conceptualizing *how* early self-formative experiences influence adult behavior. Despite occasional attempts to translate psychodynamic principles into contemporary experimental and cognitive concepts (e.g., DeBeaugrande, 1984), it may still be premature to move from clinical to laboratory settings. Given the current emphasis in cognitive social psychology on finding nonmotivational explanations for why some knowledge structures are more influential than others (Wyer & Srull, 1981), similar attention must be paid among dynamic theorists to alternative explanations in their own work.

SOCIAL-COGNITIVE APPROACHES: SOME LIKE IT COLD

In general, psychodynamic perspectives on the self share a set of basic assumptions. Social-cognitive models represent a more heterogeneous collection of hypotheses varying in scope and specificity. Nevertheless, recent reviews of social-cognitive research on the self (Higgins & Bargh, 1987; Markus & Wurf, 1987) have identified two premises shared by most investigators in the field. First, it is typically accepted that the self *mediates* between the environment and behavior and is not simply a reflection or epiphenomenon of how the individual behaves. The self is viewed as actively organizing behaviors, as interpreting and responding to contextual cues, and as capable of complex regulatory processes (Gergen, 1971; Markus & Wurf, 1987). For instance, Schlenker (1985) and others have summarized the evidence suggesting that the self plays a unique role in the organization and interpretation of social behavior. In the last 15 years, empirical findings regarding self variables have finally begun to support the theories postulating a "dynamic" role for the self (Epstein, 1983; Markus, 1983).

Second, many social-cognitive self researchers have appropriated information-processing concepts into their models (Kihlstrom & Cantor, 1984). These notions provide useful analogies for such hypothesized self functions as response selection, environmental monitoring, behavior-standard discrepancy reduction, and controlled allocation of attentional resources (Greenwald & Pratkanis, 1984). Though it has been argued that exclusive reliance on a "cold" computer as the central metaphor for social cognition may result in less-than-optimal understanding of the "hot," emotional aspects of interpersonal phenomena (Sorrentino & Higgins, 1986), the usefulness of the information processing perspective for self research is clear.

Few social-cognitive models have focused explicitly on paradoxical and self-defeating behaviors. The best-known of these theories, self-handicapping and learned helplessness, are reviewed in other chapters (see Chapters 10 and 11). Almost any theory involving hypothetical self processes can (at least in principle) make predictions regarding self-frustrating behaviors. Therefore, this review is confined to explicit theoretical statements about the self and data that bear on such predictions.

THEORIES OF SELF-INCONSISTENCY

Cognitive dissonance theory (Festinger, 1957) appears to have generated more research than any other single contribution in the field of self-perception (McGuire, 1966). The theory postulates that a person experiences discomfort or tension when two cognitions are psychologically inconsistent. Dissonance was originally viewed as a *drive state* that, when aroused, elicited actions intended to return the individual to a lower level of arousal (Brehm & Cohen, 1962). Several major research paradigms (e.g., insufficient reward, insufficient punishment, justification of effort) emerged from dissonance studies as investigators sought to demonstrate that dissonance was (or was not) an important determinant of self-perception and behavior.

While criticisms of dissonance theory and research have abounded (see Brown, 1965 for a review), the most frequent has been that there are major limitations to both its applicability and its capacity to rule out alternative explanations of dissonance-type phenomena (Bem, 1965, 1967; Snyder & Ebbesen, 1972). What seems to have survived intact is a general assumption that *inconsistency* between two important, concurrently held beliefs creates motivation to alleviate the inconsistency. By extension, dissonance-type phenomena should be observed in association with self-beliefs as well.

One of the most fertile areas of self research concerns the knowledge structures or sets of beliefs individuals possess about themselves (Kihlstrom & Cantor, 1984). These beliefs are postulated by some theorists to actually constitute the self (Epstein, 1980). Recent models have suggested that cognitive representations of self-beliefs are stored in the form of propositions (e.g., Bower & Gilligan, 1979); others characterize the self as an organization of traits, attributes, or memories of behavioral instances (e.g., Carver & Scheier, 1981; T. B. Rogers, 1981). The extensive literature on the self as a "schema" or a collection of schemas (Greenwald & Pratkanis, 1984) also bases its predictions on the assumption that the self-schema influences social and self-perception through processes such as stimulus categorization and interpretation (Higgins, Strauman, & Klein, 1986).

Models of self-beliefs and self-consistency have included both the person's own responses and the responses of others toward him or her as cues (e.g., Gergen, 1971; Lecky, 1961). Aronson (1960) proposed a version of dissonance theory that emphasized self-beliefs as the major locus of inconsistency. The theory proposed that when people behave in a manner that is inconsistent with their self-concept, they tend to experience discomfort (see also Adler, 1964; Allport, 1955; Freud, 1923/1961; James, 1890/1948; C. R. Rogers, 1959, 1961). The classic dissonance studies—wherein, for example, a person believing himself or herself to be basically honest persuades another person to participate in an exceedingly boring task—did not directly address self-defeating behaviors. Nonetheless, dissonance research is potentially applicable to the common situation in which self-defeating patterns are maintained in order to avoid the persistent realization of self-inconsistency. These models need a more detailed analysis of the phenomena underlying recognition of self-paradox in order to be directly applicable to self-defeating behavior.

Many other researchers have proposed that people need consistency among their self-perceived attributes to form and maintain the self-concept (e.g., Allport, 1955; Epstein, 1973; Lecky, 1961; C. R. Rogers, 1961). Whether due to external feedback or through self-observation, incompatibility among self-beliefs is postulated to carry significant motivational and affective consequences. It should be noted that despite (or perhaps because of) the adoption of information-processing concepts, few investigators have been able to elaborate a clear mechanism in which contrary self-beliefs are—or are not—recognized by the individual or make specific predictions for the consequences that result.

Gergen (1971) has pointed out that the question of self-consistency involves several qualifications. For example, dissonance theory predicts that discomfort (and the motivation to reduce the discomfort) only occurs when the person is cognizant of the inconsistency. Several alternatives follow from this prediction:

1. Can self-inconsistency lead to significant motivational and/or affective consequences *without* the individual's explicit awareness? Both psychodynamic (e.g., Sullivan, 1956) and cognitive (Erdelyi & Goldberg, 1979) analyses of repression have proposed that it is generally unlikely that people can or would attend fully to significant self-inconsistency.
2. What mediating factors (e.g., individual differences, learning history, life goals) increase the likelihood that self-inconsistency will remain unrecognized? One intuitive possibility is *repression-sensitization* (Byrne, 1964), an individual difference variable for the tendency to avoid and repress (or approach) anxiety-provoking stimuli. To my knowledge, none of these factors have as yet been definitively linked to self-defeating behaviors.
3. What are the implications (for the self as well as for clinical intervention) of chronic nonawareness of self-inconsistency? Are the factors maintaining the nonawareness gradually "introjected" into the self-relevant knowledge structures, becoming an essential aspect of self-representation (e.g., Blatt, 1974)? If so, one would anticipate a particularly rigid and inflexible pattern of self-perception resulting that would make behavior change difficult.

The theory of self-awareness (Duval & Wicklund, 1972; Wicklund, 1975, 1978) was one of the first to include motivational concepts in tandem with a focus on cognitive representations of the self. The theory postulates a motivational state resulting from the combination of a within-self discrepancy and self-focused attention (Wicklund & Hormuth, 1981). Once the self-aware individual has focused on a salient and sizeable discrepancy, the motivated state will induce that person to act in order to extricate himself or herself from the inconsistency. There are two routes by which this can be achieved: (1) by eliminating self-focus through avoiding the provocative stimuli and/or seeking distractions and (2) by dealing with the discrepancy through efforts to reduce it or to behave in accordance with personal standards. Both the explicit motivational aspects of the model and the possibility of deliberate *avoidance* of self-focus suggests that self-awareness theory has value in understanding self-paradoxical behavior. Wicklund has more recently proposed a theory of symbolic self-completion (e.g., Wicklund & Gollwitzer, 1982) in which individuals who are committed to self-definition, but have not achieved it completely, experience a psychological tension that motivates completion strategies. The strategies adopted presumably might favor consistency over accuracy, even to the extent that a self-defeating lifestyle is tolerated for its own sake (Wicklund, 1986).

Higgins and his colleagues have proposed a model of the relations between the self and affect based on self-discrepancy theory (Higgins, 1987). The theory seeks to explain how different types of discrepancies between self-representations are systematically related to motivational states as well as different kinds of emotional vulnerabilities. The model postules that a discrepancy between the *actual* self-state (the self-concept, or the representations of the attributes an individual believes that someone feels he or she actually possesses) and the *ideal* self-state (the representation of an individual's beliefs about his or her own or a significant other's hopes, wishes, or aspirations for the person: "the person I would ideally like to be") will tend to induce the negative motivational state of the absence of positive outcomes, which is associated with dejection-related emotions. In contrast, a discrepancy between the actual self-state and the *ought* self-state (the representation of an individual's beliefs about his or her own or a significant other's views of the individual's duties or obligations: "the person I ought to be") will tend to induce the negative motivational state of the anticipated presence of negative outcomes, which is associated with agitation-related emotions. The ideal and ought self-representations represent self-directive standards or self-guides.

Laboratory studies using both undergraduate and clinical samples (Higgins, Bond, Klein, & Strauman, 1986; Strauman & Higgins, 1987; Strauman, 1989) have provided strong evidence for self-discrepancies as cognitive structures. Mismatches or inconsistencies between the actual self and the self-guides were shown to possess characteristics of cognitive structures. First, the data indicated that both chronic and momentary accessibility of the mismatches (i.e., the likelihood that the mismatch structure would be utilized in interpreting the immediate social context; see Higgins & King, 1981) was related to the magnitude and quality of subjects' emotional responses. Second, it was demonstrated that activating either part of the mismatch (i.e., either the actual-self attribute or the self-guide attribute) could induce an emotional response, suggesting that the two attributes were structurally linked. Most importantly, covert contextual activation of subjects' mismatches induced specific momentary emotional syndromes even though subjects were not aware that the activation had occurred.

This model has yet to be directly applied to instances of self-defeating behavior. Nonetheless, preliminary investigations have suggested an intriguing application for self-discrepancy theory. It was observed (Van Hook & Higgins, 1988) that inconsistencies among an individual's self-guides (e.g., between ideal and ought self-representations) were associated with identity confusion and certain maladaptive personality styles. Incompatibility between two motivationally significant self-guides (e.g., I *ideally* would like to be an assertive, career-oriented woman; my parents feel that it is my *obligation* to be traditional and submissive) represents the negative psychological situation of double approach–avoidance conflict. In such a situation there may be no adaptive responses available to the individual. As a result, heightened defensiveness (e.g., prominent "hysterical" personality traits) and uncertainty regarding identity and goals may result in self-defeating behavior patterns (Horney, 1946).

Cybernetic Models of Self-Regulation

An increasing number of social-cognitive theories of the self have appropriated cybernetic or systems-theory principles (e.g., Miller, Galanter, & Pribram, 1960). The general approach is to postulate a cybernetic or self-regulatory *cycle*, including the monitoring of behavior, a decision or judgment about the sufficiency and outcome of the behavior, and evaluation of the repercussions for the self (e.g., Kanfer, 1970).

Carver (1979) proposed a cybernetic model of self-attention processes based on information-processing notions. As with self-awareness theory, this model assumes that self-directed attention leads to an analysis of self-related information (which corresponds experientially with increased awareness of some salient aspect of the self-concept or identity). If a relevant standard is currently active within the system, a "matching-to-standard" operation takes place with either positive or negative implications for resultant behavior. Carver (1979) postulated that positive self-to-standard matching would not lead to difficulties for the self, but a negative matching would lead to behavioral withdrawal or some attempt to reduce the discrepancy. As an effort to capture the essence of self-consistency in a "pure" information-processing model, Carver's model has not included motivational constructs or direct predictions to psychopathology. Still, he and others suggest that self-defeating behavior can be understood using the cybernetic principles embodied in the model.

Carver & Scheier (1981, 1982) also posited that the self-structure is elaborated into an interconnected hierarchy of control systems at progressively higher levels of abstraction. Therefore, they characterize both conscious control of behavior and unconscious (automatic) processing of information within the same scheme. Different levels of control can operate at cross purposes, with the result that the individual either experiences or behaves as though he or she experiences inconsistency between the processing goals of each system (e.g., inconsistency among self-relevant standards). This model awaits a definitive verification of its predictions regarding self-defeating behavior. Nonetheless, it implies that self-paradox can be understood as a function of incongruity among self-standards utilized in cycles of self-evaluative information processing. As with the other models reviewed, the role of cybernetic self-regulation in self-defeating behavior patterns remains to be clearly delineated.

Self-Efficacy

The principle that expectancies can determine an individual's choice of goals and goal-seeking behaviors has played an important role in social-cognitive self research. The major theoretical statement of the role of expectations of abilities to control behavior and reach desired end states is that of Bandura (e.g., 1977, 1982, 1986). The term *self-efficacy* refers both to an understanding of the self's importance in the regulation of behavior and (in a more specific usage) to the individual's perception of her or his ability to accomplish a particular task. According to Bandura's model, perceptions of self-efficacy are determined by both stable (e.g., previous operant and observational learning) and variable (e.g., situational constraints) factors. Moreover, the person's beliefs regarding efficacy in a certain domain have been shown to be related to choice of goal-seeking behavior, to the degree of persistence in laboratory tasks, to the degree of effort marshalled in such tasks, and to the contents of cognition during and immediately after efficacy-related behaviors (Bandura, 1977; Bandura, Reese, & Adams, 1982).

Critiques of the self-efficacy approach have focused on theoretical issues rather than empirical findings. While the model has been useful in understanding clinical phenomena such as performance anxiety and phobias (Bandura, Taylor, Williams, Mefford, & Barchas, 1985), the theory lacks a compelling rationale for predicting the range of affects and behaviors observed when a person's efficacy beliefs do not meet his or her expectations of task demands. Individual differences in vulnerability to anxious versus dysphoric affect (Beidel, Turner & Dancu, 1986; Strauman & Higgins, 1987), or tendencies to react with helplessness and withdrawal (Abramson, Seligman, & Teasdale, 1978) versus antisocial or acting-out behaviors (Horney, 1946), may mediate the relationship between self-efficacy and self-defeating behavior. Second, expectancy can be confounded with other variables, including ability and willingness to behave in a certain way (Kirsch, 1985). Such variables operate independent of expectancy and performance and are highly influenced by external factors (e.g., environmental contingencies) and internal factors (e.g., intrinsic motivation and beliefs about control; Deci, 1975). These critiques imply that a more circumscribed set of conditions in which efficacy considerations predominate need to be delineated in order for the model to be of greater value in conceptualizing self-paradox.

EVALUATION OF SOCIAL-COGNITIVE MODELS OF THE SELF

It would be illogical to fault social-cognitive models of the self because they lacked validation in clinical samples. Such was not their original purpose; further, the same critique could be levelled at some psychodynamic models. It is also the case that the diversity of approaches taken by social-cognitive researchers results in the comparison of apples to oranges by reviewers. Instead, I will attempt an overall evaluation by returning to the original question: what do these models tell us about the self that can be of value in understanding and alleviating self-defeating behaviors?

It seems generally accepted (e.g., Greenwald & Pratkanis, 1984; Strauman & Higgins, 1987; Markus & Sentis, 1982) that the self is a *unique* cognitive structure. Recent models have started with the assumption that the characteristics of self-representations had important information-processing consequences. Surprisingly, though, some authors (Higgins & Bargh, 1987; Klein & Kihlstrom, 1986) have suggested that many of the hypothetical characteristics are still awaiting verification, so that much may still be conjecture. Should it be assumed, for example, that *all* memory structures associated with the self possess a uniform set of characteristics (either in terms of content or motivational valence)? Given the complexity of each person's psychological history and the sheer volume of disconfirming information to which people are typically exposed, it may be reasonable to explore the possibility that some self-representations are more resistant to change than others (Rappaport, 1951). How can we determine the circumstances in which consistency models will be useful in predicting self-paradoxical behavior?

In addition, while classic cognitive-developmental theories (e.g., Piaget, 1937/1969; Werner & Kaplan, 1963) postulate that schemas develop in order to facilitate social information processing and self-evaluation, under some circumstances self processes can inhibit accurate self-evaluations as well (Safran, 1984a, 1984b). What are the conditions under which the accuracy of self-perception and self-evaluation is decreased (e.g., Bennett & Holmes, 1975)? Comprehensive approaches to the questions of when and how the self facilitates or inhibits social information processing will certainly improve the applicability of social-cognitive data to self-defeating behavior.

Finally, perhaps the most telling aspect of social-cognitive self research is its near-exclusive focus on the "grown-up-ness" of self-representations. A naive reader might be led to conclude that the self emerges concurrently with one's first experiences in introductory psychology courses. Developmental theorists (e.g., Fischer, 1980; Harter, 1975, 1986) postulate that mental representations of the self differ in content and function depending on the circumstances that led to their formation. Models of the self should be held accountable for the extraordinary range of possible self-representations, even among college sophomores.

The characteristic adult-centeredness of the social cognition approach cuts across both content and process issues.* It seems to be a truism that the contents of self-beliefs vary from age to age (Higgins & Parsons, 1983). Yet, the eventual fate of "obsolete" self-beliefs—and their corresponding memory structures—remains largely a mystery. With the remarkable changes in the child's ability to deal with more complex and symbolic material with increasing maturity, some researchers appear to be as dazzled as their subjects into overlooking the manner in which newfound cognitive sophistication must itself be assimilated or accommodated into the overall personality.

UNRESOLVED ISSUES IN THE PARADOX OF THE SELF

Despite the extensive literature dealing with the self, it appears that self theory is far from unified. A summary of the models presented does not readily offer a precise characterization of the structure, process, genesis, or motivational nature of the self. Only in the most general sense can we speak of a "self" capable of opposing the individual's customary self-evaluative or regulatory mandates. At best, it seems the self can only be considered a frame of reference or a set of general assumptions.

As Gergen and Gergen (1982) have pointed out, there are so many issues associated with self theories that almost no two are alike in their specific focus. It

*There are some notable recent exceptions to this trend, however. For example, see the special issue of *Social Cognition* (1986, Volume 4, Number 2) concerning cognitive-developmental models in social cognition research.

would not be unreasonable to surmise that as much as anything else, psychologists' faith in the reality of the self has kept it alive as a viable topic of research (Markus & Wurf, 1987). Faced with the dilemma of self-defeating behaviors, self literatures have surprisingly little of direct relevance to lend.

We require a comprehensive theory of the self that can make self-defeating behavior understandable, predict its occurrence, and provide therapeutic strategies. I contend that an integration of the two perspectives highlighted in this review is necessary to progress toward such a theory. Several authors have already described the need for integration. Gergen (1971), in summarizing the major issues in self research, suggested that a theory of the self needed to incorporate experiential, cognitive, and motivational components while addressing both process and structural considerations. Epstein (e.g., 1983) has called for a multilevel model of self and identity that incorporates the principles of cognitive development, psychodynamics, and reinforcement theory. Kelly (1955), though rejecting drive-based and reinforcement conceptions of personality, sought to encompass the idiosyncratic contents of personal knowledge structures within a model that anticipated much of the self-inconsistency and cognitive therapy literatures.

In appraising potential starting points for such an ambitious enterprise as a social-cognitive–psychodynamic integration, my own sense is that developmental studies may provide a reasonable basis for a synthesis. There is a considerable body of observation to support the initial hypothesis that *social interaction and cognitive maturation combine to lead the individual through a process of self-differentiation* via increasing complexity of self-representations. I will begin by reviewing the observations that support this hypothesis, and then suggest several elaborations that form the basis for a theory of self-representations.

The evidence in support of a social-maturational perspective on the self is extensive. Beginning with the work of Piaget (e.g., 1937/1969) and Werner (1948/1957; Werner & Kaplan, 1963), many theorists have adopted a cognitive-developmental framework as the basis for the emergence of the self. Harter (1983) described how children progress in their understandings (and representations) of the attributes of self and others. Fischer (1980), Montemayor and Eisen (1977), and Ruble and Rholes (1981) have likewise documented the progressive development and differentiation of self-states as an interactive function of cognitive maturation and diverse social experiences. The self as a cognitive phenomenon reflects a combination of increasingly complex structural aspects (e.g., constructs that encompass increasingly abstract and symbolic rather than literal material) and experientially related contents.

Psychodynamic theorists have also focused on the development of self-representations. However, rather than emphasizing the cognitive contents of self-states, these authors have assigned primary importance to the affective qualities of representations (Beres & Joseph, 1970). Wolff (1967) proposed that while Piaget assumed an equal intensity for all actions (regardless of the state of the organism) in his developmental model, psychodynamic theories typically assume a hierarchy of motivations in which some actions (and their representations) are more important than others (Shapiro, 1965). Some psychodynamic writers (e.g., Mahler & Furer, 1968) have postulated a developmental sequence in which successive levels of object representation reflect the interaction of such factors as the quality of interpersonal relationships, the success of internalization processes, and the degree of differentiation of major intrapsychic structures (Blatt, 1974; Sandler & Rosenblatt, 1962). Object representations can include crude images of an object immediately present (and associated feelings of gratification) as well as symbolic evocations of absent figures (and associated negative affects). As Blatt (1974) wrote, earlier forms of object representation, as *cognitive-affective* entities, are based primarily on action sequences associated with needs and gratification. Intermediate forms are generally constructed from perceptual features, while later representations are primarily symbolic and conceptual.

As mentioned, psychodynamic theorists assert that early mental contents do not "phase out" but remain an active part of the individual's expanding self-system. These models assume that self-representations (i.e., contents and motives) that were significant at an earlier point in development often retain their significance through subsequent stages. If a developmental task is satisfactorily addressed, then representations associated with task-related experiences should gradually take a secondary role in self-evaluation and behavior. Ideally, such a successful coping process will result in increased differentiation and integration of self- and object representations. However, an unresolved task is predicted to persist as an active motivational influence, on the basis of the representational structure(s) involved. In the absence of a successful resolution, the associated representations should exert a disproportionate influence on self-evaluation and behavior even at a later stage when most representations would involve language rather than action patterns or more primitive forms of encoding.

Given this set of assumptions, behavior patterns resulting from primitive, relatively undifferentiated self-representations are likely to diverge from behaviors associated with more mature, integrated self-representations because of the extensive differences in content and motive (Rapaport, 1951). Additionally, the primitive representations should be difficult for the individual to consciously experience and acknowledge, since (1) they are likely to be encoded differently than the majority of the individual's accessible representations and (2) awareness would necessitate a potentially distressing self-inconsistency (Erdelyi, 1987).

This preliminary consolidation of social-cognitive and psychodynamic conceptions of self-representations leads to a second general hypothesis, that *self-defeating behavior stems from inconsistency or conflict among different aspects of the individual's self-representations* (see Shapiro, 1965). The inconsistency remains largely out of the individual's awareness (for reasons outlined above), so that the maladaptive pattern persists despite its harmful effects. There is not sufficient space to address even the more direct implications of this rather sweeping hypothesis. Instead, the remainder of the chapter outlines reasons for cautious optimism that the two approaches to the self can achieve a profitable alliance. I will present a preliminary model of self-representations that incorporates both perspectives and then suggest how the proposed model might benefit our understanding of the paradox of the self.

TOWARD AN INTEGRATED THEORY OF SELF-REPRESENTATIONS

The apparent dissimilarity of self theories proposed by social-cognitive researchers and those proposed by psychodynamic theorists stems largely from differences in subject populations and research methods rather than from truly opposing views of self processes. Social-cognitive investigators typically have used undergraduates and other nonpsychiatric populations and focus on relatively accessible self-beliefs. Psychodynamic writers tend to study troubled individuals and prefer to focus on aspects of the self that are not as readily accessible. But the basic functions attributed to the self—reality testing, self-evaluation, and behavioral regulation—can be clearly identified in both sets of literatures.

If both groups are focusing on the same phenomenon (albeit from different viewpoints and at different life stages), how are their approaches to be integrated? To begin, I suggest that it is not the case that the perspectives are contradictory because social-cognitive models emphasize "mature" cognition and motivation while psychodynamic models emphasize what Rapaport and Gill (1959) refer to as the *genetic* perspective (i.e., the causal primacy of early over subsequent experience). If there is anything on which the two approaches clearly agree it is that the self-concept is *multifaceted* rather than unidimensional (Higgins & Bargh, 1987). The problem of consolidating the two perspectives requires us to conceptualize the self as an entity flexible enough to incorporate diverse "data bases" of memories and motives and yet permanent enough to account for long-term stability (Epstein, 1983; Pratkanis & Greenwald, 1985).

It appears reasonable to postulate that in cognitive terms the self is a loose conglomerate of representations rather than a unified structure (Higgins & Bargh, 1987). The "contents" of the representations would most likely comprise experiences and motives, united in their historical self-relevance but varying in their psychological age, cognitive accessibility, and emotional valence. This conception of the self suggests that what the different manifestations of self have in common is that at some point in the individual's development, each representation was closely associated with significant experiences, motives, or goals. Thus, the criterion for inclusion into the self is historical self-relevance (i.e., the representation must have had sufficient motivational significance that it "mattered" at the time at which it was stored).

Why should numerous elements comprise the self? This question can be addressed on the basis of existing knowledge regarding cognitive development. Simply put, the answer would be that self-differentiation proceeds on the basis of the characteristics of the organism at that point (i.e., currently accessible memories and currently active motives and goals for behavior). Self-representations are generated on the basis of both accessible material from memory and information derived from interpretation and appraisal of present events (Higgins, Strauman, & Klein, 1986). New representations would emerge in content areas where a sufficient degree of attention was directed, including behaviors relevant to currently active goals. (This would be true for both self-consistent and self-defeating goals.) Completely novel manifestations of the self would be unlikely, since they would have to overcome the strong "top-down" influence of existing memory structures as well as the "bottom-up" influence of perceptual input from the events to which attention was previously directed (Bargh, 1984). More likely to emerge from the interaction between the individual and the social context would be modifications and transformations of existing, salient representations.

The hypothetical sequence of events resulting in the formation of a single self-representation would also be unlikely to lead to a tightly organized network of the sort typically postulated in cognitive research. Different self-representations would involve different types of information in different encoding formats, situated according to developmentally distinct themes (Erdelyi & Goldberg, 1979). Thus, the content and motivational significance of the material at the time it became permanently stored would determine the extent to which a representation becomes a central or outlying node in the overall configuration. Once stored, each self-feature would vary in accessibility as a function of such factors as frequency and recency of activation as well as motivational significance (Higgins & King, 1981).

How would one be able to verify that a particular mental representation was part of this loosely organized self? Based on priming techniques used in cognitive psychology (e.g., Bargh, 1982; Srull & Wyer, 1979), one might seek to activate the construct using a variant of *contextual priming*. If the activation resulting from priming the particular representation then spread to other representations, evidence for an associative network of self-representations would be obtained (see Strauman & Higgins, 1987, for an example of this strategy). To achieve such activation, it might be necessary to know the *encoding context* for the representations, that is, the major events, motives, goals, and beliefs that were salient for the individual at the time.

Can such a general model of self-representations account for both self-perceived consistency of identity and behavior *and* the process of change over time? An important assumption here is that representations that had become part of the organization would remain so even if successive experiences did not frequently activate them. The "substrate" of the self, that is, the reservoir of available representations, would remain essentially constant; any transformation in the links or arrangement of the organization would be slow and would require sustained variation in both contextual and personal factors. The assumptions outlined above suggest that as long as a particular representation or group of features was associated with an "active" motive or goal, they would be unlikely to be modified (Blatt, 1974; Fast, 1985). Assimilation and accommodation would generally occur when a representation was no longer of prime motivational significance.

What *would* be expected to change, however, would be both the extent of the individual's knowledge resources and the "critical mass" of highly accessible representations that comprised the "working" self at any point in time. There could be points of evolution in the self at which qualitative changes in the overall structure (i.e., in encoding format, network of associative links, and/or retrieval strategy) would occur (as in the cognitive phenomenon of "chunking," where the individual acquires the ability to manipulate larger, more meaningful units of information). A possible example of such change would be the gradual shift in object representation toward abstract and symbolic contents (Blatt, 1974).

One application of this principle can be found in the writings of Mahler (e.g., Mahler, Pine, & Bergman, 1975) and the object relations theorists. When a child emerges from the separation–individuation phase, he or she does not begin anew with a "clean slate" of memories. The vestiges of recent and remote significant events remain (in the form of highly significant memories) even though a newer and more advanced degree of self-experience has emerged. For the child whose struggles with separation were relatively brief and painless, the self organization would be expected to have been impacted only moderately by the course of events. For another child, whose battle for individuation was more tumultuous, the self organization would be more substantially modified and would remain so through subsequent development. The latter child would be expected to be more easily influenced by later events and situations involving themes of individuation and independence to the extent that (1) he or she continued to possess unresolved issues stemming from these developmental tasks, and (2) subsequent events activated the representations derived from the original developmental crisis.

As investigators of autobiographical memory have noted (e.g., Kihlstrom, 1981), recall of early childhood events is initially difficult because both the encoding context and the encoding scheme are substantially different from the context and cognitive organization years later at recall. Such memory studies typically deal with relatively innocuous memories rather than traumatic or negative ones. As we have seen, psychodynamic clinicians use the general presumption that memories associated with intense experiences still exist as a substrate within the self and can have deleterious effects *without reaching awareness* in the adult's experience. It is not being suggested here that this assumption be accepted in the absence of empirical validation. Rather, the point is that the hypothesis of a loosely organized self composed of individual representations varying in both content and motivational qualities may provide a more comprehensive framework for studying self-paradox.

How could this approach contribute to our understanding of the etiology and persistence of self-defeating behavior patterns? Two extensions of the basic assumptions may be useful here. The first concerns differences among the motives associated with self-representations formed at different points in the life span. There appear to be two major classes of motivation involved in the differentiation of the self. The first group consists of *survival-related* motives (e.g. Bowlby, 1969, 1973; Freud, 1917), which provide the impetus for such essential processes as refinement of reality testing, maturation of cognitive capacities, and the progression of interpersonal skills beginning with language. Survival is understood here to represent the fundamental goal-context for psychological processes, insofar as they facilitate survival and maturation within a specific range of functioning (Bowlby, 1969, p. 46–47). Psychological maturation, as from a functionalist perspective (e.g., James, 1890/1948), is presumed to aid the organism's struggle to survive, and specific early behavior patterns are presumed to have a basis in the survival motive. In addition, several major psychodynamic theorists have emphasized survival-related motivation as the basis for the establishment of a self structure or system (Hartmann, 1951; Rapaport, 1951; Sullivan, 1956). Survival motives are usually viewed as having relatively direct links to physiological systems responsible for reflexive behaviors (fight or flight) and emotional reactions (separation anxiety, depressive withdrawal). As we mature, however, survival motives become less paramount; rather, the derivatives of survival motives, including self-representations, come to the fore as "secondary" incentives for behavior.

The other major class of motivations has been described by both social-cognitive and psychodynamic theories: motives to *maintain consistency* within the self and particularly among currently active or accessible representations. Psychodynamic (Freud, 1923/1961; Sullivan, 1953), phenomenological (C. R. Rogers, 1961), and social-cognitive (Duval & Wicklund, 1972; Higgins, 1987) models of self processes all specify the maintenance of consistency among self-beliefs and experiences as a fundamental motivation in areas such as self-evaluation and interpersonal relations. In general, consistency motivation emerges later in the developmental process.

The second addition to the model is based on the earlier assertion that self-representations involve both a content and an emotional–motivational valence. Studies of such phenomena as mood-state-dependent memory (Bower & Gilligan, 1979), autobiographical memory (Kihlstrom, 1981), and category-based affective responses (Fiske & Pavelchak, 1986) all demonstrate that under certain circumstances cognitive elements possess *both* an experientially derived content and an emotional or motivational impetus. In the language of this proposal, salient motives accompanying self-experience would be encoded and stored as part of the representation. Therefore, the associative links among individual self-features would involve a loose networking of both content and motivation, and activation can spread across individual representations by means of either feature.

The present model suggests a particular understanding of the paradox of self-defeating behavior. The complexity of the adult self is such that complete consistency among all of an individual's most salient and important self-representations is no longer possible (Guidano, 1987). In all probability there would exist inconsistent or conflicting potential interpretations of a given behavior (Sullivan, 1956). At this point in psychological development, further elaborations of the self would highlight the need to maintain consistency among more highly accessible self-features more so than the survival motives that may have originally been associated with important self-representations. The persistence of the original motives (as would result from a major unresolved developmental crisis) would eventually become dysfunctional, that is, the behaviors associated with the more primitive motives would be likely to contradict those associated with more mature consistency motives (Horney, 1946).

The model predicts that at least two kinds of incompatibility among self-representations (and associated self-frustrating patterns of behavior) can occur within the complex self-organization. The first, *content inconsistency*, would occur whenever two concurrently accessible self-representations were incompatible in terms of the meaning or connotation of the feature. This type of self-conflict has been described by social-cognitive research (for a review, see Higgins, 1987) as well as cognitive-behavioral clinicians (e.g., Beck, Rush, Shaw, & Emery, 1979; Ellis, 1962). In general, self-content inconsistency would have two characteristics: (1) it would generally involve moderately or highly accessible self-features and (2) therefore, it would tend to involve developmentally mature rather than infantile or childhood representations. These characteristics also suggest that self-content inconsistency would be associated with specific instances of self-defeating behavior, due to the increased content specificity of mature representations (Piaget, 1968). Self-handicapping behaviors provide an example of self-defeating patterns resulting from content inconsistency. The individual who uses self-handicapping to ease the burden of possible failure at an interpersonal task is engaging in a relatively high-level cognitive process with the goal of avoiding self-content inconsistency.

The second type of self-incompatibility is *motivational inconsistency*. This incompatibility involves the concurrent activation of self-representations that differ in their motivational impetus, for example, when one self-feature involves a survival-class motive (for instance, "I must do what my parents say or they will withdraw their love") while a concurrently active self-feature involves a consistency motive (for instance, "it is important for me to be independent of my parents while my friends are around"). The divergent character of the two classes of motivation inspires some intriguing predictions for this type of conflict. First, since survival motives tend to dominate psychological development early in life while consistency motives come to the fore at a later point, this class of conflict will generally involve two elements that differ substantially in age of acquisition. Second, a person's (or a therapist's) attempts to resolve self-motivational conflict will be incomplete unless these differences in motive as well as age of origin are recognized. Third, in a more speculative vein, since survival-based representations are hypothetically linked to the biological response mechanisms from which they developed (Bowlby, 1969), one could postulate that more severe, somatically based manifestations of psychopathology (and associated maladaptive behaviors) might involve self-motivational inconsistency. Fourth, following similar reasoning, those individuals whose inherited biological characteristics included excessive reactivity in a survival-related response mechanism would be likely to manifest heightened sensitivity to conflict involving survival-motive self-representations. These hypotheses remain to be tested, of course, but they are presented to illustrate the potential value of integrative approaches to self phenomena.

CONCLUSION

It is easier to point out limitations (and inconsistencies) in existing models than to generate new and better ones. The impressive accumulation of clinical observation and empirical studies addressing the causes and cures of self-defeating behavior is not to be dismissed lightly or underestimated. Psychologists who wear the hats of both therapist and researcher have an intuitive appreciation of the complexity and capacity for paradox inherent in the self. All the models reviewed represent substantial contributions to our knowledge, and many have already demonstrated their value in the eyes of clinicians (and, hopefully the individuals who seek their help). And yet, the challenge to the field remains enormous—to come to terms with what might be the most enigmatic and most deeply personal of all topics in psychology. The curiosity and persistence of self researchers provides ample encouragement that our investigations are not simply another instance of self-defeating efforts. It is hoped that the observations presented in this chapter serve as a small contribution to a field on the verge of unprecedented opportunity for a new integration of perspectives on the self.

ACKNOWLEDGMENTS

I would like to thank Rebecca Curtis for her invaluable comments on an earlier version of this chapter.

REFERENCES

Abramson, L. Y., Seligman, M. E. P., & Teasdale, J. D. (1978). Learned helplessness in humans: Critique and reformulation. *Journal of Abnormal Psychology, 87*, 49–74.

Adler, A. (1964). *Problems of neurosis*. New York: Harper & Row. (Original publication 1917)

Allport, G. (1955). *Becoming: Basic considerations for a psychology of personality*. New Haven: Yale University Press.

Aronson, E. (1969). The theory of cognitive dissonance: A current perspective. *Advances in experimental social psychology, 4*, 1–34.

Asch, S. S. (1985). Depression, masochism and biology. *Hillside Journal of Clinical Psychiatry, 7*(1), 34–53.

Bandura, A. (1977). Self-efficacy: Toward a unifying theory of behavioral change. *Psychological Review, 84*, 191–215.

Bandura, A. (1982). Self-efficacy mechanism in human agency. *American Psychologist, 37*, 122–147.

Bandura, A. (1986). *Social foundations of thought and action: A social cognitive theory*. Englewood Cliffs, NJ: Prentice-Hall.

Bandura, A., Reese, L., & Adams, N. E. (1982). Microanalysis of action and fear arousal as a function of differentiated levels of perceived self-efficacy. *Journal of Personality and Social Psychology, 43*, 5–21.

Bandura, A., Taylor, C. B., Williams, S. L., Mefford, I. N., & Barchas, J. D. (1985). Catecholamine secretion as a function of perceived coping self-efficacy. *Journal of Consulting and Clinical Psychology, 53*, 406–414.

Bargh, J. A. (1982). Attention and automaticity in the processing of self-relevant information. *Journal of Personality and Social Psychology, 43*, 5–21.

Bargh, J. A. (1984). Automatic and conscious processing of social information. In R. S. Wyer & T. K. Srull (Eds.), *Handbook of social cognition* (Vol. 3, pp. 1–43). Hillsdale, NJ: Erlbaum.

Basch, M. (1977). Developmental psychology and explanatory theory in psychoanalysis. *Annals of Psychoanalysis, 5*, 229–263.

Basch, M. (1981). Self object disorders and psychoanalytic theory: A historical perspective. *Journal of the American Psychoanalytic Association, 29*, 337–351.
Beck, A. T., Rush, A. J., Shaw, B., & Emery, G. (1979). *Cognitive therapy of depression*. New York: Guilford Press.
Beidel, D. C., Turner, S. M., & Dancu, C. V. (1985). Physiological, cognitive, and behavioral aspects of social anxiety. *Behaviour Research and Therapy, 23*, 109–117.
Bem, D. (1965). An experimental analysis of self-persuasion. *Journal of Experimental Social Psychology, 1*, 199–218.
Bem, D. (1967). Self-perception: An alternative interpretation of cognitive dissonance phenomena. *Psychological Review, 74*, 183–200.
Bennett, D. H., & Holmes, D. (1975). Influence of denial (situational redefinition) and projection on anxiety associated with threat to self-esteem. *Journal of Personality and Social Psychology, 32*, 915–921.
Beres, D., & Joseph, E. D. (1970). The concept of mental representation in psychoanalysis. *International Journal of Psychoanalysis, 51*, 1–9.
Blatt, S. J. (1974). Levels of object representation in anaclitic and introjective depression. *Psychoanalytic Study of the Child, 29*, 107–157.
Bower, G. H., & Gilligan, S. G. (1979). Remembering information related to one's self. *Journal of Research in Personality, 13*, 420–432.
Bowlby, J. (1969). *Attachment*. New York: Basic Books.
Bowlby, J. (1973). *Separation*. New York: Basic Books.
Brehm, J., & Cohen, A. (1962). *Explorations in cognitive dissonance*. New York: Wiley.
Brown, J. S., & Cunningham, C. L. (1981). The paradox of persisting self-punitive behavior. *Neuroscience and Biobehavioral Review, 5*(3), 343–354.
Brown, R. (1965). *Social psychology*. New York: Free Press.
Byrne, D. (1964). Repression-sensitization as a dimension of personality. In B. Maher (Ed.), *Progress in experimental personality research* (Vol. 1, pp. 57–79). New York: Academic Press.
Carver, C. S. (1979). A cybernetic model of self-attention processes. *Journal of Personality and Social Psychology, 37*, 1251–1280.
Carver, C. S., & Scheier, M. F. (1981). *Attention and self-regulation: A control theory approach to human behavior*. New York: Springer-Verlag.
Carver, C. S., & Scheier, M. F. (1982). Control theory: A useful conceptual framework for personality, social, clinical, and health psychology. *Psychological Bulletin, 92*, 111–135.
Caston, J. (1984). The relation between masochism and depression. *Journal of the American Psychoanalytic Association, 32*(3), 603–614.
Darley, J. M., & Gross, P. H. (1983). A hypothesis-confirming bias in labeling effects. *Journal of Personality and Social Psychology, 44*, 20–33.
DeBeaugrande, R. (1984). Freudian psychoanalysis and information processing: Notes on a future synthesis. *Psychoanalysis and Contemporary Thought, 7*(2), 147–194.
Deci, E. L. (1975). *Intrinsic motivation*. New York: Plenum.
Duval, S., & Wicklund, R. A. (1972). *A theory of objective self-awareness*. New York: Academic Press.
Ellenberger, H. (1970). *The discovery of the unconscious: The history and evolution of dynamic psychiatry*. New York: Basic Books.
Ellis, A. (1962). *Reason and emotion in psychotherapy*. New York: Lyle Stuart.
Epstein, S. (1973). The self-concept revisited, or a theory of a theory. *American Psychologist, 28*, 404–416.
Epstein, S. (1980). The self-concept: A review and a proposal of an integrated theory of personality. In E. Staub (Ed.), *Personality: Basic issues and current research*. Englewood Cliffs, NJ: Prentice-Hall.

Epstein, S. (1983). The unconscious, the preconscious, and the self-concept. In J. Suls & A. G. Greenwald (Eds.), *Psychological perspectives on the self* (Vol. 2), pp. 110–139). Hillsdale, NJ: Erlbaum.

Erdelyi, M. H. (1987). Repression, reconstruction and defense: History and integration of the psychoanalytic and experimental frameworks. In J. Singer (Ed.), *Repression: Defense mechanism and personality style*. Chicago: University of Chicago Press.

Erdelyi, M. H., & Goldberg, B. (1979). Let's not sweep repression under the rug: Toward a cognitive psychology of repression. In J. Kihlstrom & F. Evans (Eds.), *Functional disorders of memory*. Hillsdale, NJ: Erlbaum.

Fast, I. (1985). *Event theory: A Piaget–Freud integration*. Hillsdale, NJ: Erlbaum.

Fenichel, O. (1945). *The psychoanalytic theory of neurosis*. New York: Norton.

Festinger, L. (1957). *A theory of cognitive dissonance*. Evanston, IL: Row, Peterson.

Fischer, K. W. (1980). A theory of cognitive development: The control and construction of hierarchies of skills. *Psychological Review, 87*, 477–531.

Fiske, S. T., & Pavelchak, M. A. (1986). Category-based versus piecemeal-based affective responses: Developments in schema-triggered affect. In R. Sorrentino & E. T. Higgins (Eds.), *Handbook of motivation and cognition: Foundations of social behavior* (pp. 167–203). New York: Guilford Press.

Freud, A. (1948). *The ego and the mechanisms of defense*. London: Hogarth Press.

Freud, S. (1950). The defense neuropsychoses. In J. Strachey (Ed.), *The standard edition of the complete psychological works of Sigmund Freud* (Vol. 3, pp. 43–86). London: Hogarth Press.

Freud, S. (1915a). Instincts and their vicissitudes. Reprinted in P. Reiff (Ed.), *Freud: General psychological theory* (pp. 83–103). New York: Collier.

Freud, S. (1915b). Repression. Reprinted in P. Reiff (Ed.), *Freud: General psychological theory* (pp. 104–115). New York: Collier.

Freud, S. (1915c). The unconscious. Reprinted in P. Reiff (Ed.), *Freud: General psychological theory* (pp. 116–150). New York: Collier.

Freud, S. (1917). Mourning and melancholia. Reprinted in P. Reiff (Ed.), *Freud: General psychological theory* (pp. 164–179). New York: Collier.

Freud, S. (1924). The economic problem in masochism. Reprinted in P. Reiff (Ed.), *Freud: General psychological theory* (pp. 190–201). New York: Collier.

Freud, S. (1961). The ego and the id. In J. Strachey (Ed. and Trans.), *The standard edition of the complete psychological works of Sigmund Freud* (Vol. 19, pp. 3–66). London: Hogarth Press. (Original publication 1923)

Freud, S. (1966). Introductory lectures on psychoanalysis. In J. Strachey (Ed. and Trans.), *The standard edition of the complete psychological works of Sigmund Freud* (Vols. 15–16). London: Hogarth Press. (Original publication 1920)

Gergen, K. J. (1971). *The concept of self*. New York: Holt, Rinehart & Winston.

Gergen, K. J., & Gergen, M. M. (1988). Narrative and the self as relationship. *Advances in Experimental Social Psychology, 21*, 17–56.

Greenwald, A. G., & Pratkanis, A. R. (1984). The self. In R. S. Wyer & T. K. Srull (Eds.), *Handbook of social cognition* (Vol. 3, pp. 129–178). Hillsdale, NJ: Erlbaum.

Guidano, V. F. (1987). *Complexity of the self: A developmental approach to psychopathology and therapy*. New York: Guilford Press.

Gunderson, J. G., & Kolb, J. E. (1978). Discriminating features of borderline patients. *American Journal of Psychiatry, 132*, 1–10.

Harter, S. (1975). Developmental perspectives on the self-system. In P. H. Mussen (Ed.), *Handbook of child psychology* (4th ed., pp. 275–385). New York: Plenum.

Harter, S. (1983). The development of the self-system. In M. Hetherington (Ed.), *Handbook of child psychology: Social and personality development* (Vol. 4, pp. 275–385). New York: Wiley.

Harter, S. (1986). Cognitive-developmental processes in the integration of concepts about emotions and the self. *Social Cognition, 4*, 119–151.

Hartmann, H. (1951). Ego psychology and the problem of adaptation. In D. Rapaport (Ed.), *Organization and pathology of thought* (pp. 362–398). New York: Columbia University Press.

Higgins, E. T. (1987). Self-discrepancy: A theory relating self and affect. *Psychological Review, 94*(3), 319–340.

Higgins, E. T., & Bargh, J. A. (1987). Social cognition and social perception. *Annual Review of Psychology, 38*, 369–425.

Higgins, E. T., Bond, R., Klein, R., & Strauman, T. (1986). Self-discrepancies and emotional vulnerability: How magnitude, type and accessibility of discrepancy influence affect. *Journal of Personality and Social Psychology, 51*(1), 5–15.

Higgins, E. T., & King, G. (1981). Accessibility of social constructs: Information processing consequences of individual and contextual variability. In N. Cantor & J. Kihlstrom (Eds.), *Personality, cognition, and social interaction* (pp. 69–121). Hillsdale, NJ: Erlbaum.

Higgins, E. T., & Parsons, J. E. (1983). Social cognition and the social life of the child: Stages as subcultures. In E. T. Higgins, D. N. Ruble, & W. W. Hartup (Eds.), *Social cognition and social development: A socio-cultural perspective* (pp. 15–62). New York: Cambridge University Press.

Higgins, E. T., Strauman, T. J., & Klein, R. (1986). Standards and the process of self-evaluation: Multiple affects from multiple stages. In R. Sorrentino & E. T. Higgins (Eds.), *Handbook of motivation and cognition: Foundations of social behavior* (pp. 23–63). New York: Guilford Press.

Holt, R. R. (1984, August). *The current status of psychoanalytic theory*. Paper presented at the annual meeting of the American Psychological Association, Toronto.

Horney, K. (1946). *Our inner conflicts: A constructive theory of neurosis*. London: Routledge & Kegan Paul.

Jacobsen, E. (1959). *Psychotic conflict and reality*. London: Hogarth Press.

Jacobsen, E. (1964). *The self and the object world*. New York: International Universities Press.

James, W. (1948). *Psychology*. New York: World. (Original work published 1890)

Kanfer, F. H. (1970). Self-regulation: Research, issues, and speculations. In C. Neuringer & J. Michael (Eds.), *Behavior modification in clinical psychology* (pp. 101–129). New York: Appleton-Century-Krofts.

Kass, F., MacKinnon, R. A., & Spitzer, R. L. (1986). Masochistic personality: An empirical study. *American Journal of Psychiatry, 143*(2), 216–218.

Kelly, G. A. (1955). *The psychology of personal constructs*. New York: Norton.

Kernberg, O. (1980). *Borderline conditions and pathological narcissism*. Northvale, NJ: Aronson.

Kihlstrom, J. F. (1981). On personality and memory. In N. Cantor & J. F. Kihlstrom (Eds.), *Personality, cognition, and social interaction* (pp. 123–149). Hillsdale, NJ: Erlbaum.

Kihlstrom, J. F., & Cantor, N. (1984). Mental representations of the self. *Advances in Experimental Social Psychology, 17*, 1–47.

Kirsch, I. (1985). Self-efficacy and expectancy: Old wine with new labels. *Journal of Personality and Social Psychology, 49*, 824–830.

Klein, S. B., & Kihlstrom, J. F. (1986). Elaboration, organization, and the self-reference effect in memory. *Journal of Experimental Psychology: General, 115*, 26–38.

Knight, R. P. (1953). Borderline states. *Bulletin of the Menninger Clinic, 17*, 1–12.

Kohut, H. (1971). *The analysis of the self*. New York: International Universities Press.

Kohut, H. (1977). *The restoration of the self*. New York: International Universities Press.

Lecky, P. (1961). *Self-consistency: A theory of personality*. New York: Shoe String Press.
Lichtenberg, J. (1983). An application of the self psychological viewpoint to psychoanalytic technique. In J. Lichtenberg & S. Kaplan (Eds.), *Reflections on self psychology* (pp. 220–256). Hillsdale, NJ: Erlbaum.
Mahler, M., & Furer, M. (1968). *On human symbiosis and the vicissitudes of individuation*. New York: International Universities Press.
Mahler, M., Pine, F., & Bergman, D. (1975). *The psychological birth of the human infant*. New York: Norton.
Markus, H. (1983). Self-knowledge: An expanded view. *Journal of Personality, 51*, 543–565.
Markus, H., & Sentis, K. (1982). The self in social information processing. In J. Suls (Ed.), *Psychological perspectives on the self*. (pp. 41–70). Hillsdale, NJ: Erlbaum.
Markus, H., & Wurf, E. (1987). The dynamic self-concept: A social psychological perspective. *Annual Review of Psychology, 38*, 299–337.
Markus, H., & Zajonc, R. B. (1985). The cognitive perspective in social psychology. In G. Lindzey & E. Aronson (Eds.), *The handbook of social psychology, Third edition* (Vol. .1, pp. 137–230). New York: Random House.
Masterson, J. F. (1975). The borderline syndrome. The role of the mother in the genesis and psychic structure of the borderline personality. *International Journal of Psychoanalysis, 56*, 163–177.
McGuire, W. J. (1966). Attitudes and opinions. *Annual Review of Psychology, 17*, 475–514.
Miller, G. A., Galanter, E., & Pribram, K. H. (1960). *Plans and the structure of behavior*. New York: Holt, Rinehart & Winston.
Mischel, W. (1973). On the empirical dilemmas of psychodynamic approaches. *Journal of Abnormal Psychology, 82*, 335–344.
Montemayor, R., & Eisen, M. (1977). The development of self-conceptions from childhood to adolescence. *Developmental Psychology, 13*, 314–319.
Piaget, J. (1968). *On the development of memory and identity*. Barre, MA: Clark University Press.
Piaget, J. (1969). *The construction of reality in the child*. New York: Basic Books. (Original publication 1937)
Pratkanis, A. R., & Greenwald, A. G. (1985). How shall the self be conceived? *Journal of the Theory of Social Behaviour, 15*, 311–330.
Rapaport, D. (1951). Toward a theory of thinking. In D. Rapaport (Ed.), *Organization and pathology of thought* (pp. 689–730). New York: Columbia University Press.
Rapaport, D., & Gill, M. M. (1959). The points of view and assumptions of metapsychology. *International Journal of Psychoanalysis, 40*, 153–162.
Reich, J. (1987). Prevalence of DSM-III-R self-defeating (masochistic) personality disorder in normal and outpatient populations. *Journal of Nervous and Mental Disorders, 175*(1), 52–54.
Rogers, C. R. (1959). A theory of therapy, personality, and interpersonal relationships, as developed in the client-centered framework. In S. Koch (Ed.), *Psychology: A study of a science: Volume 3. Formulations of the person and the social context* (pp. 72–114). New York: McGraw-Hill.
Rogers, C. R. (1961). *On becoming a person*. Boston: Houghton Mifflin.
Rogers, T. B. (1981). A model of the self as an aspect of the human information processing system. In N. Cantor & J. Kihlstrom (Eds.), *Personality, cognition, and social interaction* (pp. 193–214). Hillsdale, NJ: Erlbaum.
Ruble, D., & Rholes, W. (1981). The development of children's perceptions and attributions about their social world. In J. Harvey, W. Ickes, & R. Kidd (Eds.), *New directions in attribution research* (Vol. 3) Hillsdale, NJ: Erlbaum.
Safran, J. D. (1984a). Some implications of Sullivan's interpersonal theory for cognitive

therapy. In M. A. Reda & M. J. Mahoney (Eds.), *Cognitive psychotherapies: Recent developments in theory, research and practice* (pp. 92–127). New York: Plenum.

Safran, J. D. (1984b). Assessing the cognitive-interpersonal cycle. *Cognitive Therapy and Research, 8*(4), 333–348.

Sandler, J., & Rosenblatt, B. (1962). The concept of the representational world. *Psychoanalytic Study of the Child, 17*, 128–145.

Schlenker, B. R. (1985). Identity and self-identification. In B. R. Schlenker (Ed.), *The self and social life* (pp. 114–156). New York: McGraw-Hill.

Schweber, E. (1979). On the 'self' within the matrix of analytic theory—Some clinical reflections and reconsiderations. *International Journal of Psychoanalysis, 60*, 467–479.

Shapiro, D. (1965). *Neurotic styles*. New York: Basic Books.

Snyder, M., & Ebbesen, E. B. (1972). Dissonance awareness: A test of dissonance theory versus self-perception theory. *Journal of Experimental Social Psychology, 8*, 502–517.

Snyder, M., Tanke, E. D., & Berscheid, E. Social perception and interpersonal behavior: On the self-fulfilling nature of social stereotypes. *Journal of Personality and Social Psychology, 35*, 656–666.

Sorrentino, R. M., & Higgins, E. T. (1986). Motivation and cognition: Warming up to synergism. In R. Sorrentino & E. T. Higgins (Eds.), *Handbook of motivation and cognition: Foundations of social behavior* (pp. 3–19). New York: Guilford Press.

Srull, T. K., & Wyer, R. S. (1979). The role of category accessibility in the interpretation of information about persons: Some determinants and implications. *Journal of Personality and Social Psychology, 37*, 1660–1672.

Stolorow, R., & Lachmann, F. (1980). *Psychoanalysis of development arrests*. New York: International Universities Press.

Strauman, T. J. (1989). Self-discrepancies in clinical depression and social phobia: Cognitive structures that underlie emotional disorders? *Journal of Abnormal Psychology, 98*, 14–22.

Strauman, T. J., & Higgins, E. T. (1987). Automatic activation of self-discrepancies and emotional syndromes: When cognitive structures influence affect. *Journal of Personality and Social Psychology, 53*, 1004–1014.

Sullivan, H. S. (1953). *The interpersonal theory of psychiatry*. New York: Norton.

Sullivan, H. S. (1956). *Clinical studies in psychiatry*. New York: Norton.

Sullivan, H. S. (1970). *The psychiatric interview*. New York: Norton. (Original publication 1954)

Suls, J., & Greenwald, A. G. (Eds.). (1983). *Psychological perspectives on the self* (Vol. 2). Hillsdale, NJ: Erlbaum.

Van Hook, E., & Higgins, E. T. (1988). Self-related problems beyond the self-concept: Motivational consequences of discrepant self-guides. *Journal of Personality and Social Psychology, 55*(4), 625–633.

Wallerstein, R. S. (1983). Self psychology and "classical" psychoanalytic psychology—The nature of their relationship: A review and overview. In J. Lichtenberg & S. Kaplan (Eds.), *Reflections on self psychology* (pp. 16–52). Hillsdale, NJ: Erlbaum.

Werner, H. (1957). *Comparative psychology of mental development*. New York: International Universities Press. (Original publication 1948)

Werner, H., & Kaplan, B. (1963). *Symbol formation*. New York: Wiley.

Wicklund, R. A. (1975). Objective self-awareness. *Advances in Experimental Social Psychology, 8*, 1–45.

Wicklund, R. A. (1978). Objective self-awareness. In L. Berkowitz (Ed.), *Cognitive theories in social psychology* (pp. 233–275). New York: Academic Press.

Wicklund, R. A. (1986). Orientation to the environment versus preoccupation with human

potential. In R. Sorrentino & E. T. Higgins (Eds.), *Handbook of motivation and cognition: Foundations of social behavior* (pp. 64–95). New York: Guilford Press.
Wicklund, R. A., & Gollwitzer, P. M. (1982). *Symbolic self-completion*. Hillsdale, NJ: Erlbaum.
Wicklund, R. A., & Hormuth, S. E. (1981). On the functions of the self: A reply to Hull & Levy. *Journal of Personality and Social Psychology, 40*(6), 1029–1037.
Winnicott, D. (1960). The theory of the parent–infant relationship. *International Journal of Psychoanalysis, 41*, 585–595.
Winnicott, D. (1971). *Therapeutic consultations in child psychiatry*. London: Hogarth Press.
Wolf, E. (1980). On the developmental line of selfobject relations. In A. Goldberg (Ed.), *Advances in self psychology* (pp. 210–243). New York: International Universities Press.
Wolff, P. H. (1967). Cognitive considerations for a psychoanalytic theory of language acquisition. *Psychological Issues, 18/19*, 299–343.
Wyer, R. S., & Srull, T. K. (1981). Category accessibility: Some theoretical and empirical issues concerning the processing of social stimulus information. In E. T. Higgins, C. P. Herman, & M. P. Zanna (Eds.), *Social cognition: The Ontario symposium* (pp. 161–197). Hillsdale, NJ: Erlbaum.

Part IV

CONCLUSIONS

CHAPTER 14

INTEGRATION

CONDITIONS UNDER WHICH SELF-DEFEATING AND SELF-ENHANCING BEHAVIORS DEVELOP

REBECCA CURTIS

The chapters in this volume have provided an overview of the ways in which self-defeating behaviors are learned and maintained. The authors have examined some of the ways in which beliefs about self and others, whether adaptive or maladaptive, are confirmed and disconfirmed in new situations.

The purpose of this final chapter is to (1) review the major unifying themes of the various contributions; (2) present a model of the development and maintenance of self-defeating behaviors that includes (a) the objective conditions of reinforcement which lead to self-defeating behaviors, (b) the interpersonal realizations of these contingencies, and (c) the intrapsychic beliefs which arise with these experiences; and (3) suggest implications for changing such behaviors.

REVIEW OF THE THEMES THAT EMERGE IN THESE CHAPTERS

Although the formation of self-beliefs was beyond the scope of this volume, it is assumed that these beliefs are derived from a variety of life experiences, including observations, statements made by others, and by inferences about the causes of events. The chapters in this volume on belief perseverance, self-fulfilling prophecies, and perspectives on the self demonstrate some of the ways

REBECCA CURTIS • Department of Psychology, Adelphi University, Garden City, New York 11530.

in which negative and erroneous self-beliefs as well as discrepancies between beliefs about actual and ideal selves can lead to self-defeating behaviors.

The work on belief perseverance indicates that beliefs about oneself and others become part of a broader view of the world as people develop explanations about the causes of events and "social theories." What emerges from the initial chapter by Slusher and Anderson on belief perseverance and remains a theme throughout the volume is how unshakable many beliefs are once they have become established (cf. Greenwald, 1980; Nisbett & Ross, 1980). Thus, the early experiences in life and expectations derived from relationships with significant others (cf. Weiss & Sampson, 1986) affect subsequent interactions. These expectations also lead to the avoidance of many potentially beneficial types of interactions. These expectations may have been developed at a preverbal or at a later stage of maturation.

Hilton, Darley, and Fleming (Chapter 3) point out that, as perceivers, we may be able to correct our biases if our major goal in an interaction is to assess the other person accurately. This is probably rarely our goal, however. Even when accurate projection is the major goal of interaction, as when a man or woman is deliberately assessing another's qualifications as a potential spouse, it is unlikely that our behaviors will remain unaffected by the belief-relevant cues we glean from clothes, physical attractiveness, style of speech, and other early pieces of information unless we have a standard set of interview questions or say almost nothing at all except to repeat the themes presented by the other person, as many psychoanalysts do in the initial sessions of therapy.

The work on belief perseverance and expectancy confirmation elucidates the processes which, for nearly a century, psychoanalysts have referred to in the therapy situation as "transference." Analysts have claimed that people bring into this relatively neutral situation beliefs about others and about relationships which lead to a distortion in their perception of the analyst. In their everyday life experiences, their distorted beliefs have led to behaviors which have confirmed their expectancies. For example, if the person has anticipated being disliked by others, the person has acted in a manner which has led this expectation to come true with greater frequency than would have been the case if the person held the expectation of being liked (Curtis & Miller, 1986). The analyst attempts to intervene in the expectancy confirmation process and to point out the individual's particular self-defeating expectations and behaviors. The object relations school of psychoanalysis has described the process by which people repeat ways of relating that were developed with important figures earlier in life, but it has not used the term *belief perseverance* or explicitly referred to the *research* on self-fulfilling prophecies.

The chapters which follow those on belief perseverance and self-fulfilling prophecies begin to elucidate the difficulties which arise from negative or erroneous beliefs about the self and others. For example, poor performance expectations lead to a lack of effort, but overly optimistic expectations lead to wasted effort in impossible situations. In the research dealing with excuses, self-handicapping, and making things harder for yourself, we see the extent to which people protect their beliefs. Why is it so important for people to *not* realize that they are, at times, somewhat less competent or likeable than they had originally believed? Would this reality reduce our illusion of control? Or are we avoiding reexperiencing early painful fears of being humiliated, unloved, abandoned, or psychologically fragmented, as the analytic community has hypothesized?

Excuse making, self-handicapping, and success avoidance are all behaviors which help individuals maintain consistent self-views. Although, as discussed by Higgins and C. R. Snyder (Chapter 5) and M. L. Snyder and Frankel (Chapter 6), it is not difficult to understand why people are motivated to maintain positive views of themselves, it is more difficult to comprehend why people would wish to maintain more negative views of themselves than reality suggests. Strauman (Chapter 13) points out that the importance of maintaining consistency in one's self-view, even if it is negative at times, has been the focus of much of the social psychological research.

Canavan (Chapter 7) and Curtis (Chapter 8) present the view that particular types of strivings for positive self-views and psychological independence may have led to anxiety on the part of a parent or caretaker. The chapter by Curtis moves from the concern with maintaining views consistent with one's self-image to concerns with maintaining a cohesive self-theory altogether. Here the suggestion is made that the individual who engages in self-punishment may feel, "If I am not a victim, then I am nothing." Thus, the individual feels threatened with something worse than information which is inconsistent with the self-view or inconsistent with a favorable self-view: The individual is threatened with a fragmented self-theory which cannot make sense of the various aspects of experience. Epstein (1980) has argued that the need to maintain a self-theory is separate from, and even at times in conflict with, the need to enhance one's self-view. He points out that a person's theory about himself or herself must be maintained so that the person can fulfill other vital functions in a satisfactory manner.

Thus, the behaviors described in the volume up to this point provide ways of avoiding information, events, thoughts, feelings, or impulses that would threaten the self-theory. Janoff-Bulman and Thomas (Chapter 9) described what happens when disastrous events which are unambiguous and irrefutably inconsistent with self and world views occur. The processes which take place may be parallel to those which take place when other types of less objectively catastrophic events occur. When they are assimilated accurately, they result in revisions in the self-system. When the new thoughts are too anxiety provoking to be assimilated, Janoff-Bulman and Thomas tell us that they continue to intrude upon the individual in upsetting ways. Sullivan (1953), in his discussion of the process of dissociation, has previously described what happens when events and feelings are so anxiety provoking that people do not allow themselves to be aware of them and thus fail to integrate the new material into their self-systems. The posttraumatic stress reaction of intrusive thoughts in normal individuals is similar to the process described by Sullivan and others in obsessive disorders. The major difference is that in obsessive disorders, the obsessive behavior occurs in the absence of an unambiguous environmental trauma which the person can identify as the stressor. As Canavan and Curtis point out, when people are not aware of the nature of the anxiety-provoking stimulus, they repeatedly avoid success and self-punish in situations in which it no longer serves a purpose. Curtis notes that if people can discriminate the difference between a relationship in which self-punishment is reinforcing from other relationships in which it is not reinforcing, the self-punishing behavior will extinguish. Unfortunately, negative beliefs about others and expectancy confirmation effects frequently make the new, different relationships similar to past ones, when they need not have been.

The other major adverse reaction to victimization, which Janoff-Bulman and Thomas describe, is characterological self-blame. Peterson and Bossio (Chapter 10) elaborate upon this reaction to uncontrollable aversive events and describe the depression which ensues from this type of response. They make the point that the term *learned helplessness* should be applied to situations in which there has been a pattern of random or noncontingent reinforcement or punishment, not situations in which dependency and passivity have been reinforced.

The question then arises as to whether the types of behavior associated with chronic and excessive excuse making, self-handicapping, success avoidance, and self-punishment constitute a personality disorder which is distinct from depression, dependency, and narcissism. Widiger and Frances (Chapter 12) address this issue. Certainly some people who repeatedly engage in self-defeating behaviors will be depressed and, if so, should benefit from the best available treatment for depression. Other people who engage in these behaviors, however, may not exhibit the symptoms associated with depression, such as anhedonia and feeling sad, or fit the descriptions of dependent, narcissistic, or passive–aggressive personalities. Thus, there may be personalities whose chronic behaviors are described by the self-protective and secondary gain characteristics differentiated by Berglas and for whom no other existing diagnostic category is appropriate. Because all pathological behaviors are in a general sense self-defeating, the term *self-handicapping personality disorder*, originally suggested by Berglas (1985), might have sounded less ubiquitous. For those readers who are not familiar with the American Psychiatric Association's *Diagnostic and Statistical Manual of Mental Disorders* (1980, 1987), the specific behaviors being labeled "self-defeating" by the diagnosticians are clearly different from other behaviors previously referred to as neurotic, which includes (1) anxiety disorders, such as obsessive–compulsive disorders, phobic disorders, and panic attacks, and (2) the somatoform and dissociative disorders, such as amnesia and multiple personality.

For years, clinicians have observed a type of personality, previously called "masochistic," which does not fit other diagnostic categories. The label "self-defeating personality" might aid therapists in focusing upon aspects of the personality which will lead the person to self-handicap before or after successes have been obtained. These tendencies may be overlooked if the person is given another diagnosis. At the moment, there are many people whose behaviors fit the criteria for more than one personality disorder (borderline and narcissistic, for example). Therefore, at present, the problem with overlap should not be an eliminating factor. Hopefully, in the future, more exclusive diagnostic criteria will be determined for all the disorders.

Strauman (Chapter 13) differentiates the research in social psychology regarding attempts to maintain beliefs which are consistent with one's self-theory from theory in clinical psychology which describes the more severe problems emanating from a lack of a cohesive self-theory. The social psychological research thus deals primarily with behaviors related to self-esteem protection that fall within the old "neurotic" category. The recent clinical writings have dealt with behaviors related to the self-protection of more seriously disturbed persons who are considered to be narcissistic (Kohut, 1971, 1977) or borderline (Kernberg, 1975, 1984) in their basic personality development, though not psychotic. These people have no cohesive self-theory or world theory and thus either become concerned with the way they appear, in the case of the narcissistic personalities, or respond to momentary impulses, in the case of the borderline personalities. This lack of a cohesive belief system leads to the malaise and nihilism described by Bloom (1987), Lasch (1979), and other social theorists.

CONDITIONS UNDER WHICH SELF-DEFEATING BEHAVIORS OCCUR

A wide range of self-defeating behaviors have been described in this volume. It is now important to attempt to understand the conditions which lead to the different types of self-defeating behaviors.

An examination of these behaviors reveals, not surprisingly, the importance of the role of two general factors in their development: (1) the lack of a clear history of sufficient, positive, contingent reinforcement for self-actualizing behaviors, which in turn results in the experience of poor outcomes or the expectation of poor or unpleasant outcomes; and (2) the frequent co-occurrence of maladaptive beliefs about the self and the world, leading to additional behavioral patterns consistent with the maladaptive belief system. Consistent with psychodynamic, behavioral, and social-cognitive theories, the greater the role of punishment in the learning of the original behavioral pattern, the greater the anxiety and the greater the defensive avoidance of potentially corrective experiences will be. In terms of the integrative model being presented here, to the extent that a person anticipates unpleasant outcomes or an inability to cope effectively with potentially aversive events, the person will be unlikely to engage in self-actualizing behaviors or the behavior necessary to appropriately regulate the maladaptive views of the self and of the world. The person need not be aware of what is being avoided. The role of fear and anxiety in perpetuating maladaptive, defensive behaviors is widely accepted and has been noted by theorists as diverse as Bandura (1977) and Sullivan (1953), among many others.

What, then, are the particular histories of reinforcement, experienced or anticipated unpleasant events, and maladaptive belief systems which have been

*For any reader unfamiliar with reinforcement theories, it is understood that both positive and negative reinforcers increase the probability of a response.

identified as precursors to the different types of self-defeating behaviors described in the various chapters? The work on achievement behavior (see Chapter 4 by Feather) has shown that the greatest persistence at tasks occurs when the expectations and value of success are high and the fear of failure (anxiety) is relatively low. Indeed, Kuhl (1982) has argued that those high in achievement motivation are those with high expectations. In the case of poor achievement, there is a history of a lack of contingent positive reinforcement for success or self-efficacious behaviors and/or a history of contingent punishment for failure. When a person has low expectations for success, appropriately challenging tasks are avoided, and anxiety may interfere with optimum performance on any tasks which are not believed to be easy. Although Feather also discusses the pathology of high expectations, these erroneous expectations can be corrected through failure experiences, unless such failures are "excused" in the manner described by Higgins and C. R. Snyder because taking responsibility for them is too aversive. Feather discusses persistence in terms of achievement on tasks, but the same principles should apply to interpersonal relationships.

The work on self-handicapping grew out of laboratory research regarding situations of noncontingent reinforcement. In these types of self-defeating behaviors, the individual's self-view, at least the conscious self-view, is unrealistically high. Unconsciously, the person may perceive that future outcomes are uncontrollable, and aversive consequences are likely to be anticipated if the self-view is lowered to a more realistic level. In real life, noncontingent reinforcement may have been given by a parent for whom recognition of the child's failures was particularly anxiety provoking.

The work on fear of success reveals histories of contingent punishment for particular types of successes and self-enhancing behaviors. The individual's self-view is unrealistically low, and self-enhancing behaviors led to anxiety in the child by threatening the parent's sense of well-being. The work on choosing to suffer reveals a history of negative reinforcement for self-punitive behaviors and unrealistically low expectations of self and others. In both cases, the child sacrifices personal fulfillment in order to protect the parent's sense of well-being. The child then brings the expectation of the necessity of sacrificing personal fulfillment into new relationships.

Feelings of helplessness and depression come from a history of noncontingent punishment leading to a generalized and pervasive expectation of unpleasant outcomes in the future. Again, the expectations regarding self and others are unrealistically poor. M. L. Snyder and Frankel (Chapter 6) also argue that depressed people may engage in further self-defeating behaviors in order to prevent the possibility of the poor self-view becoming even worse. Peterson and Bossio (Chapter 10) point out that the type of helplessness they are describing is different from that derived from a history of positive reinforcement for passivity, self-derogation, and dependency.

Thus, in summary, the experimental literatures in the most objective sense demonstrate the following past histories which may lead to the expectation of poor, unpleasant, or unpredictable future outcomes (see Table 1): positive reinforcement of self-defeating behaviors, negative reinforcement of self-defeating

TABLE 1. Conditions under which Self-Defeating and Self-Enhancing Behaviors Develop

	Reinforcement				Punishment		
	Contingent		Noncontingent	None	Contingent		Noncontingent
Positive	Positive	Negative	Positive				
For self-enhancing behaviors	For self-defeating behaviors				For successes	For failures	
Self-enhancing behaviors	Passive dependent behaviors	Choosing to suffer	Self-handicapping, making things harder	Low achievement	Success-avoidance	Failure-avoidance	Depression

behaviors (through relief from more aversive states), lack of positive reinforcement of self-enhancing behaviors, contingent punishment for failure to engage in self-enhancing behaviors, contingent punishment for self-enhancing behaviors, noncontingent punishment of behaviors, and noncontingent reinforcement of behaviors. From our knowledge of learning theory, we can assume that poor or negative expectations can also be learned vicariously through the observation of others.

The negative expectations highlighted in many of these chapters, or the "favorable but fragile" expectations apparent in some of them, stand in contrast to the positive but secure expectations (even if somewhat unrealistic) held by people who are not self-defeating. The reader is referred to the work on the positivity bias of normal, nondepressed people (Pyszczynski, Holt, & Greenberg, 1987; Taylor & Brown, 1988) and to the work on the illusion of control (Langer, 1975, 1978; Langer & Roth, 1975) for a further discussion of positive but erroneous belief systems. When expectations are "positive but secure," in contrast to "favorable but fragile," self-handicapping is less likely to occur.

Baumeister and Scher (1988) have recently delineated three categories of self-defeating behaviors among normal individuals, taken from laboratory research in social psychology. The first category is that of "primary self-destruction," in which people foresee and desire harm to themselves. Baumeister and Scher find no clear evidence of this type of intentional self-destructiveness among normal (nonclinical) individuals. The second category, which they call "tradeoffs," involves behaviors which lead to short-term benefits but result in long-term, foreseeable costs. The third category, "counterproductive strategies," is one of unforeseen and undeserved consequences in which people make choices which defeat their goals or lead to risk of harm. They find considerable evidence for the latter two types of behaviors in normal individuals. The current exploration of self-defeating behaviors suggests that the precursors to these behaviors in real-life situations are experiences which lead to poor, unpleasant, or uncertain expectations regarding future outcomes, the failure of self-regulatory mechanisms to change these expectations when aversive consequences have interfered with "discrepancy production" behaviors (Bandura, in press), and further choices which confirm the original expectations of negative or uncertain outcomes. To the extent that anxiety was lacking in the formation of the original beliefs, the expectations will be disconfirmed and the theories modified in the manner discussed by Hilton, Darley, and Fleming (Chapter 3) and by Slusher and Anderson (Chapter 2). The processes which lead to expectancy-confirming and -disconfirming behaviors are discussed further in the following section.

AN OUTLINE FOR AN INTEGRATED MODEL OF SELF-DEFEATING BEHAVIORS

The literatures presented in this volume provide us with an overview of how self-defeating behaviors develop and persist, including: (1) a delineation of their histories of reinforcement, (2) knowledge of the social variables and interpersonal processes by which objective reinforcing and punishment stimuli take on human meaning, and (3) an understanding of the intrapsychic representations of self and others composing the implicit (sometimes explicit) theories of interpersonal reality and causality by which people organize their lives. The integrated model suggested here is presented in Figure 1. According to this model, behaviors, affects, and beliefs are developed through the reinforcements and punishments delivered by actual experiences with other people, the culture, and environmental circumstances. Many self-defeating behaviors are explained by this reinforcement process alone.

In other instances, however, people imagine particular outcomes which they desire to obtain. In these instances, the roles of symbolism and fantasy, that is, mental processes, become particularly important. People formulate goals as suggested in the early theories of learning of Tolman (1932) and Hull (1943), in functional theories of social behavior (Merton, 1949), and in the manner elaborated upon by Bandura (1986) and by Jones and Thibaut (1958) for interpersonal situations. The latter two theories are described briefly in the present volume by Feather and by Hilton, Darley, and Fleming. When the outcomes (reinforcement–punishment ratios) people obtain differ from the outcomes they desire, they attempt to reduce the discrepancy they perceive by acting to change their outcomes—if the outcomes they have obtained differ from the outcomes they had expected (see Figure 1), or if the outcomes they expect to obtain differ from the outcomes they desire. Thus, the consistency-related motives discussed by Strauman (Chapter 13) begin to affect behavior. People hold expectations about outcomes, as Bandura (1977) has discussed, and about themselves, others, and relationships, as Epstein (1980), self-psychologists (Kohut, 1977), object relation theorists (see Greenberg & Mitchell, 1983), and others have pointed out. In short, people hold theories of social reality and of social causality. Expectations are one type of belief which are held consciously or unconsciously. People incorporate their expectations into their social and self-theories.

To the extent that people have received contingent, positive reinforcement for self-enhancing behaviors, they will engage in increased efforts to obtain the goal desired, as Feather (Chapter 4) has described. If the increased effort does not result in an outcome closer to the one expected, people will need to consider changing their expectations. People will then engage in expectancy-disconfirming behaviors, similar to what Bandura (in press) has called discrepancy-production behaviors, in order to test their theories of self and of social reality.

Although they risk obtaining poorer outcomes as a consequence of their new behaviors and new hypotheses about themselves and others, they may obtain better outcomes as a consequence of their new behaviors and new expectations. Thus, they may create a different self. By taking risks they may obtain the outcomes they desire or outcomes closer to the ones desired. This view is consistent with Wachtel's (1987) theory that the tolerance of anxiety is central to engaging in effective behaviors.

To the extent that people have experienced punishment, negative, and/or noncontingent reinforcement—or in the language of other theories, to the extent

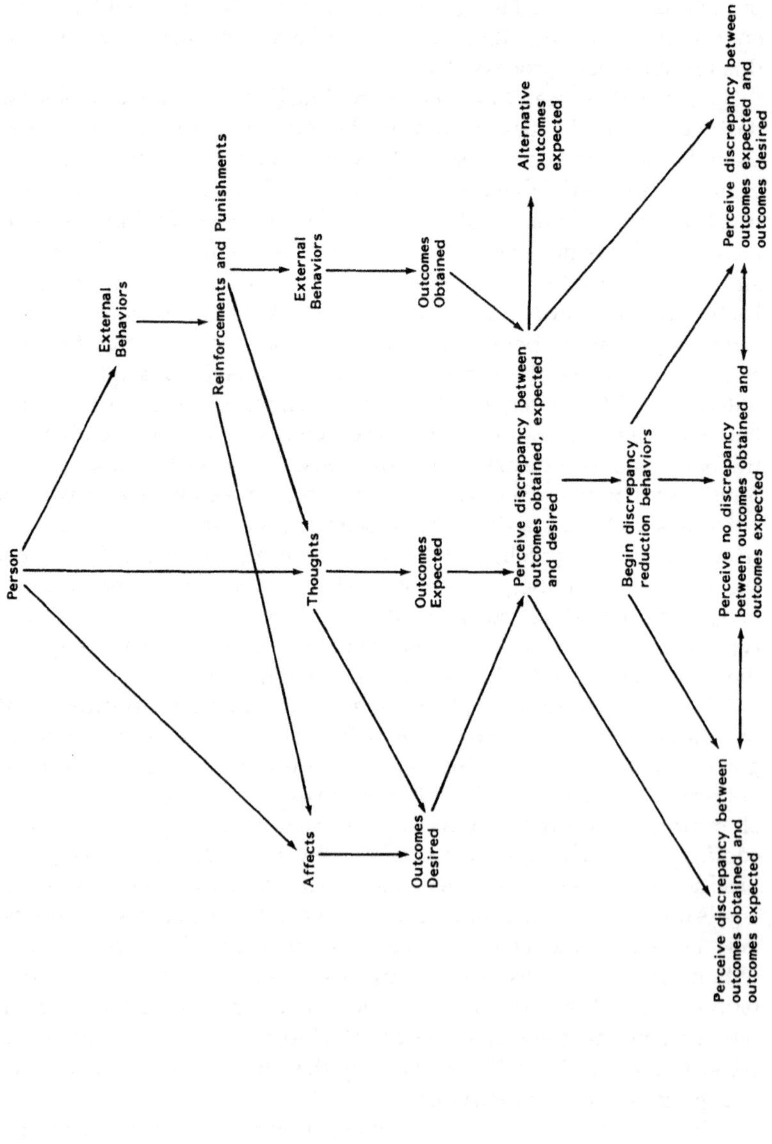
Person
External Behaviors
Reinforcements and Punishments
External Behaviors
Thoughts
Affects
Outcomes Obtained
Outcomes Expected
Outcomes Desired
Alternative outcomes expected
Perceive discrepancy between outcomes obtained, expected and desired
Begin discrepancy reduction behaviors
Perceive discrepancy between outcomes expected and outcomes desired
Perceive no discrepancy between outcomes obtained and outcomes expected
Perceive discrepancy between outcomes obtained and outcomes expected

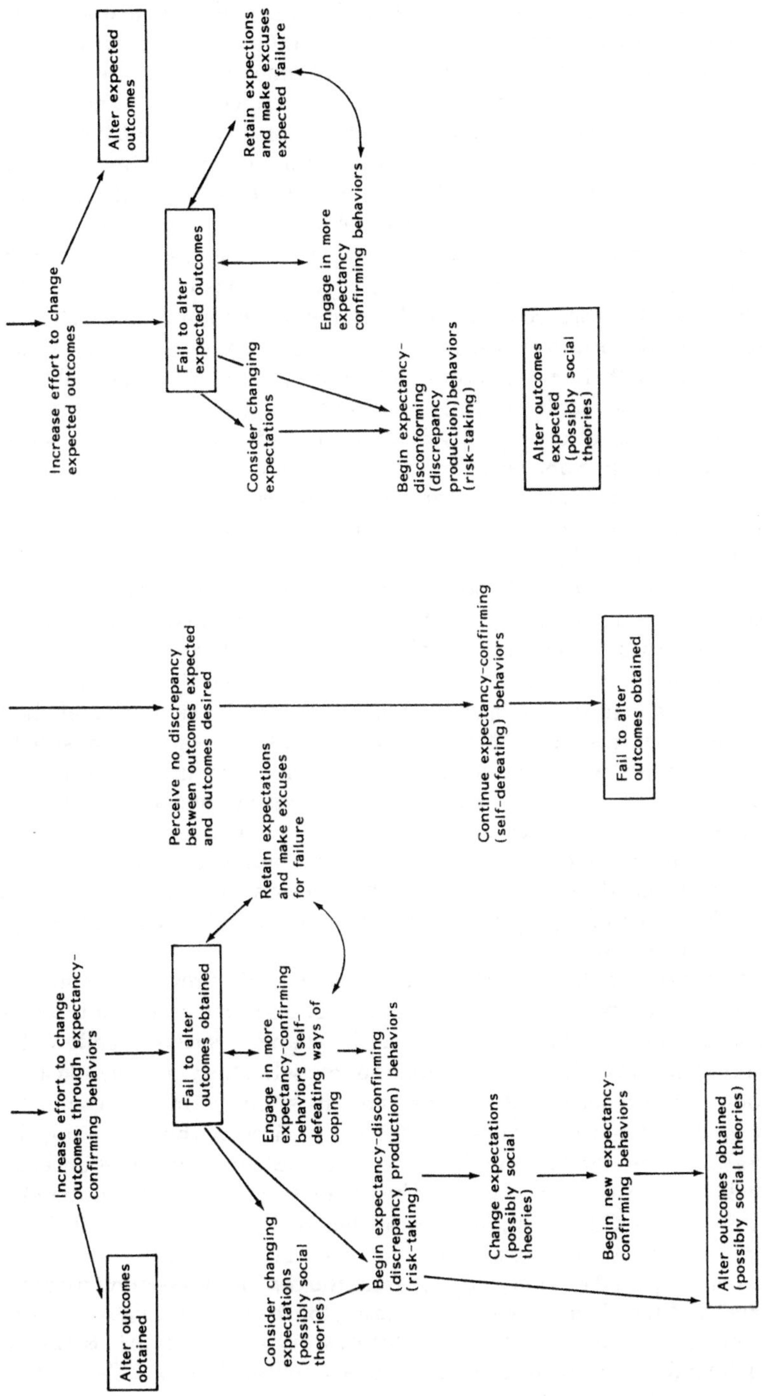

FIGURE 1. Integrated model of the development and maintenance of self-defeating and self-enhancing behaviors.

that they have experienced anxiety—people will be more likely to fear engaging in the behaviors which were punished and continue to engage in the self-defeating style of behaviors described in this volume. This assertion is supported by the data demonstrating that a high-level of arousal leads to facilitation of performance of dominant (or well-learned) behaviors (Zajonc, 1965; Zajonc & Sales, 1966). People fear that the expectation of obtaining the desired outcome may have to be abandoned or altered. They fear the loss associated with acknowledging that the desired outcomes are not attainable, or that the rewards are attainable but at a greater cost than anticipated. The increase in the discrepancy between the desired outcomes and the expected ones is aversive. People thus fear lowering their expectations and possibly abandoning their self- and social theories. In Bandura's terms, they hold low efficacy expectations. When people fear changing their expectations, and possibly their self- and social theories, they cope with the fear by making excuses as to why the expected outcome was not obtained. Fearful of engaging in expectancy-disconfirming behaviors, they engage in the expectancy-confirming behaviors discussed in the various chapters on self-defeating behaviors throughout this volume. The expectations remain intact, but the outcomes obtained continue to differ from the outcomes desired. The erroneous beliefs persist, and the self-defeating behaviors perpetuate the original self- and social theories of poor or negative expectations. People believe that behaviors leading to alternative outcomes may exist, but they do not know either what these behaviors are or how to perform them.

When the outcomes people expect to obtain differ from the outcomes they desire, they act in a manner similar to that described previously to change their anticipated outcomes (instead of their actual outcomes). The reader familiar with psychoanalytic theory will note the similarity of the concepts of the expected negative outcome and the desired outcome in the present model with the concepts of fear and wish in the Freudian model. As in that model, people need not be able to label the expected outcomes and desired outcomes verbally; that is, they may not be explicitly aware of the outcomes they are imagining. Obviously, the self-defeating ways of coping and excuse making are similar to psychoanalytic ideas about defenses.

The advantages of the current model are that it: (1) provides a cohesive model for integrating behavioral, social-cognitive, and psychodynamic views known of behaviors, cognitions, affects, and the change process; (2) allows for verbalizations of intrapsychic representations of the self, other, and relationships of behaviors and outcomes that are amenable to scientific research; and (3) allows for goal-directed behaviors (drives, motivation) without making the "goals" essential to understanding many behaviors. Statements about expectations and beliefs, such as those articulated by Millon (1983), Luborsky (Luborsky, 1977; Luborsky, Crits-Christoph, Walster & Mellon, 1986), and Ellis (1987) are amenable to research in interpersonal situations in the laboratory.

The model proposed obviously draws from the contributions of many other psychological and sociological models, including those of self-regulatory theory (Carver & Scheier, 1981; Miller, Galanter, & Pribram, 1960; Pyszczynski & Greenberg, 1987), field theory (Lewin, 1936), functional analysis (Merton, 1949), attention and curiosity (Berlyne, 1960), dissonance (Cooper & Fazio, 1984; Festinger,

1957), social schemas (Markus, 1977), hypothesis testing (Bruner, Goodnow, & Austin, 1956; Levine, 1966), approach–avoidance conflicts (Dollard & Miller 1950), equity theory (Adams, 1965; Walster, Walster, & Berscheid, 1978), and cognitive psychotherapy (Raimy, 1975). The present model is obviously overly simplistic and relies heavily upon the work of the various contributors in this volume and other theorists for many of the details.

The model presented does not require that the expectations people hold be conscious ones. Thus, the model holds for animals to the extent that they perceive relationships in the environment. When the expectations people hold, however, and/or the outcomes people desire are associated with their fundamental self and social theories, these belief systems must be recognized as important variables affecting subsequent behavior. These belief systems in humans have a life of their own which, for many people, is the essence of their "humanity." Although the role of mental processes, especially of cognitions, has been emphasized in presentation of this model, the reader will note that the role of affect is crucial in each phase of the process. The perception of a discrepancy between outcomes obtained and outcomes expected or desired is experienced as affective arousal. Fear or anxiety decreases the possibility of engaging in discrepancy-production behaviors.

The model proposed should also hold for groups of people as well as for individuals, although other variables may need to be considered. Groups also experience reinforcements and punishments, develop shared belief systems, and perpetuate self-defeating expectations by failing to solicit feedback from other groups (Janis, 1972) and by failing to engage in "discrepancy-production" behaviors. Groups, as well as individuals, fail to engage in expectancy-disconfirming behaviors for fear of negative consequences generalized inappropriately from earlier experiences in the life of the group.

APPLICATIONS OF THE INTEGRATED MODEL

Some clinical illustrations should help to clarify the model of self-defeating behaviors being proposed. Three types of examples are described. In the first type, the self-defeating behavior need not involve expectations or the person's self-theory. In the second type, the self-defeating behavior involves expectations associated with the self- and social theories, but not with the individual's fundamental world view. In the third example, the individual's self- and social theories are involved, but also the individual's answers to the basic human question, "How should I live?"

Many examples of self-defeating behaviors can be found which do not involve expectations or self-theories. Think, for instance, of a man who eats too much. He would like to be thin and trim (his desired outcome), but he is fat (his obtained outcome). It is not necessary to know whether he expects to be thin or fat. His reinforcement history and the biological consequences explain his eating behavior. As a boy his mother gave him food whenever he felt unhappy. The food was a reinforcer, and he learned to eat whenever he had a problem.

An example of this type of self-defeating behavior in an interpersonal situation is also provided. Consider a young man who brags too much. His group of high school friends liked it when he bragged. He continues the behavior into adulthood but does not obtain the goal he desires of being extremely well liked. Although he may hold erroneous expectations about the consequences of his actions, his behavior can be explained by his reinforcement history alone—he was reinforced for bragging and so the bragging continues. There is no need to examine his expectations. Once he is told that the behavior is annoying to several people now, he stops the excessive bragging.

The second type of example requires examining the person's expectations leading to behaviors which have not themselves been previously reinforced. A woman has experienced several relationships with men which have terminated in conflict. This woman was abandoned by her father at a young age. The woman is now afraid her current husband is also going to leave her. She is hostile and at times overwhelmed by somatic complaints, to the extent of crying for hours in bed about headaches and other ailments for which physicians can find no cause. Her hostility and somatic complaints alienate her husband to the point that he is beginning to think of leaving her. His mentioning this possibility increases her somatic complaints and her hostility. These behaviors can be explained better by her expectancy that she will be abandoned than by the history of the reinforcement of these behaviors.

The woman's desired outcome is a good relationship with her husband, her obtained outcome is a poor relationship, and her expected outcome is to be abandoned. Once her expected outcome and the source of the erroneous belief are articulated, her expectancy-confirming behaviors (somatic complaints and hostility) can be identified. Then she can begin to try other ways of interacting, all the while believing that they will likely be a waste of effort. At this stage she is only considering a change in expectations. If the new behaviors are successful in creating a renewed commitment from her husband, she may then change her expectations about being abandoned. Her frustration and stress, leading to increased hostility and somatic complaints, will then continue to decrease.

Another example of the type of self-defeating behaviors which requires examination of the belief system is that of a young man who desires to have friends and relationships. He has never had a friend, expects never to have one, and is so lonely and hopeless about ever not being lonely that he attempts suicide and is hospitalized. His obtained outcome has been consistent with his expected outcome, and he has engaged in self-defeating expectancy-confirming behaviors. His therapist challenges the expectation of never having any friends and convinces the young man to speak to others. Yet when he attempts to speak to others, he becomes so anxious that he must leave the room. He and his therapist explore what he fears. At this point it becomes clear that another expected negative outcome is that if he becomes involved in a relationship, he will hurt the other person, as his abusive father hurt him. This belief, he states, leads him to leave the room when he becomes anxious. He believes it is better to hurt himself than to hurt others. This belief system generates behaviors which can be better explained by knowing this belief than by examining the patient's recollection of his reinforcement history. The therapist persuades the man to reconsider his expectation that he will be hurtful, to stay in the room with another person, and to continue speaking. The man does so and gets angry (an expectancy-confirmation) but does not become physically abusive (an expectancy-disconfirmation). Over time he is able to change his behaviors and his former expectation that he will hurt others if he is involved with them.

Although the self- and social theories needed to be changed in the preceding type of example, in order to change their behavior, the people did not need to change their fundamental world views about how people should behave and treat one another. Many times, however, people do face dilemmas involving their fundamental world views, as was discussed by Curtis (Chapter 8). In the example which follows, the woman must change her fundamental beliefs about how people should live.

The third example is a young woman who is very unhappy. Her father has told her that if she ever gets married, he will die. She believes that what he says is true. The young woman has several desired outcomes. She wishes to be a good person, to be happy, and to get married and have her father live. Her expected outcomes are to get married and have her father die or to be a "good" person, but unhappy. She believes that good people don't hurt other people and certainly don't kill their own fathers. She perceives her choice, as did Hamlet and Eveline (see Chapter 8 by Curtis), as one of hurting herself or hurting another. Thus she has stayed home and achieved her desired outcome of being a good person, but she has failed to obtain her goal of getting married and of being happy. Once an attractive, outgoing young woman, her behaviors change. She no longer takes care of her appearance, she is poorly groomed, becomes overweight, and remains very quiet around others. These new behaviors are most easily explained by examining her beliefs about her father and about being a good person. Fortunately, her friends challenge her belief that good people sacrifice their lives for their parents' pathology. She explores with them other beliefs about the responsibility of people for their own lives and the responsibilities of parents and children. She is then able to change her appearance and her behavior, to eventually make plans to get married, to feel like a good person, be happy, and work out arrangements for her father to live nearby.

IMPLICATIONS FOR CHANGE

A model of self-defeating behaviors has been presented which differentiates self-defeating behaviors which are developed with important implications for a person's beliefs about the self and the world from those which are learned without such implications. To the extent that the behaviors were learned without important ramifications for the belief system, they should be modifiable through behavioral and cognitive change techniques.

These change techniques may also be effective when beliefs about the self and the world have developed, to the extent that the beliefs are (1) a consequence of a lack of positive reinforcement, or (2) a consequence of noncontingent reinforcement without a strong fear of an unpleasant outcome in the future. In these cases the erroneous self-view should be able to be modified by positive experiences, new information, and encouragement of experiences which will lead to feedback inconsistent with the erroneous self-perceptions. Thus, the cognitive, cybernetic models of the self provide an adequate understanding of how the self-view and self-defeating behaviors may be changed, unless punishment has played a significant role in the development of the self-view and the learning of the inappropriate behaviors.

When punishment of appropriate self-regulatory behaviors has occurred, self-views and self-defeating behaviors will be less amenable to simple cognitive and behavioral change techniques to the extent the person is unaware of the nature of the original threatening stimulus and to the extent that the person is unaware of the nature of the self-defeating response. This likely will be the case when the threatening stimulus has not been labeled verbally and/or when the individual's response has been encoded nonverbally, that is, when the original experience is encoded affectively or through sensory processes. Bucci (1982; Bucci & Freedman, 1978) has differentiated people who have encoded emotionally charged experiences with vivid, concrete images from those who have encoded emotionally charged experiences in a more vague manner. Without specific verbal labels or images, the person may be anxious, but the therapist will not know exactly what threat to discuss or to present in a relaxed setting (see Curtis & Elkin, 1987). This situation may have been brought about by a parent frequently praising a child's accomplishments but becoming anxious, as Canavan and Curtis point out, when a child engages in particular types of independent or creative behaviors. Once aware of the parent's anxiety, the original threat may still exist, as in the third type of clinical illustration presented above. For example, the parent's psychological health may still deteriorate if the individual engages in the self-efficacious behaviors. The greater the magnitude and probability of the current threat, the more difficult it will be to change the self-defeating behavior after the threat and response have been correctly identified.

When the person's fundamental belief system must be changed, the change process must begin by the assessment of the nature of these beliefs, must proceed by confrontation about their maladaptive effects, and must provide a secure situation for the time during which there may be no cohesive view of reality and for the development of a new belief system. The process of becoming aware of the nature of the threatening stimuli, recognizing the broader "personal meaning systems," and engaging in further cognitive elaboration has been identified in the extensive research by Rice and Greenberg (1984) and by Weiss and Sampson (1986) regarding the psychotherapy process.

When people attempt to overcome self-defeating behaviors outside the therapy process, they must question their self-theory by soliciting feedback from others about their behaviors, personalities, life choices, and abilities, and they must engage in activities which provide diagnostic information about their abilities and their limitations. People must solicit negative information and risk failure in order to engage in more effective behaviors.

CONCLUSIONS

A model of self-defeating behaviors has been articulated which incorporates the understandings drawn from social, cognitive-behavioral, and analytic traditions within psychology. The model obviously does not attempt to be novel or innovative but, instead, emphasizes the role of the self-theories and world views that people bring into new interactions. Specific self-defeating behaviors and beliefs frequently can be changed through the application of cognitive and behavior modification techniques, but changing self-defeating behaviors many times requires addressing the fundamental belief systems of individuals and the meanings they make of their existence.

ACKNOWLEDGMENTS

The author wishes to thank C. R. Snyder, Michael Leippe, Steven Berglas, and Paul Wachtel for their helpful comments on an earlier draft of this chapter.

REFERENCES

Adams, J. S. (1965). Inequity in social exchange. In L. Berkowitz (Ed.), *Advances in experimental social psychology* (Vol. 2, pp. 267–299). New York: Academic Press.

American Psychiatric Association. (1980). *Diagnostic and statistical manual of mental disorders* (3rd ed.). Washington, DC: Author.

American Psychiatric Association. (1987). *Diagnostic and statistical manual of mental disorders* (3rd ed. rev.). Washington, DC: Author.

Bandura, A. (1977). Self-efficacy: Toward a unifying theory of behavioral change. *Psychological Review, 84*, 191–215.

Bandura, A. (1986). *Social foundations of thought and action*. Englewood Cliffs, NJ: Prentice-Hall.

Bandura, A. (in press). Self-regulation of motivation and action through goal systems. In G. Hamilton, B. H. Bowen, & N. A. Fryda (Eds.), *Cognition, motivation and affect: A cognitive science view* (pp. 1–25). Dordrecht: Martinus Nijholl.

Baumeister, R. F., & Scher, S. J. (1988). Self-defeating behavior patterns among normal individuals. *Psychological Bulletin, 104*, 3–22.

Berglas, S. (1985). Self-handicapping and self-handicappers: A cognitive/attributional model of interpersonal self-protective behavior. In R. Hogan & H. Jones (Eds.), *Perspectives in personality* (Vol. 1, pp. 235–270). Greenwich, CT: JAI Press.

Berlyne, D. E. (1960). *Conflict, arousal, and curiosity*. New York: McGraw-Hill.

Bloom, A. (1987). *The closing of the American mind*. New York: Simon & Schuster.

Bruner, J. S., Goodnow, J. J., & Austin, G. A. (1956). *A study of thinking*. New York: Wiley.

Bucci, W. (1982). Vocalization of painful affection. *Journal of Communication Disorders, 15*, 415–440.

Bucci, W., & Freedman, A. (1978). Language and hand: The dimension of referential competence. *Journal of Personality, 46*, 594–622.

Carver, C. S., & Scheier, M. F. (1981). *Attention and self-regulation*. New York: Springer-Verlag.

Cooper, O., & Fazio, R. H. (1984). A new look at dissonance theory. In L. Berkowitz (Ed.), *Advances in experimental social psychology* (Vol. 17, pp. 229–266). New York: Academic Press.

Curtis, R., & Elkin, R. (1987, August). *The perseverance of erroneous beliefs: Differential effects of event imagination, emotional responding and causal reasoning*. Paper presented at the annual meeting of the American Psychological Association, New York.
Curtis, R., & Miller, K. (1986). Believing another likes or dislikes you: Behaviors making the beliefs come true. *Journal of Personality and Social Psychology, 51*, 284–290.
Dollard, J., & Miller, N. E. (1950). *Personality and psychotherapy*. New York: McGraw-Hill.
Ellis, A. (1987). The impossibility of achieving consistently good mental health. *American Psychologist, 42*, 364–375.
Epstein, S. (1980). The self-concept: A review and the proposal of an integrated theory of personality. In E. Staub (Ed.), *Personality: Basic aspects and current research* (pp. 81–132). Englewood Cliffs, NJ: Prentice-Hall.
Festinger, L. (1957). *A theory of cognitive dissonance*. Stanford, CA: Stanford University Press.
Goldfried, M. R., & Robins, C. (1983). Self-schemas, cognitive bias, and the processing of therapeutic experiences. In P. C. Kendall (Ed.), *Advances in cognitive-behavioral research and therapy* (Vol. 2, pp. 33–80). New York: Academic Press.
Greenberg, J. R., & Mitchell, S. A. (1983). *Object relations in psychoanalytic theory*. Cambridge, MA: Harvard University Press.
Greenwald, A. G. (1980). The totalitarian ego: Fabrication and revision of personal history. *American Psychologist, 35*, 603–618.
Hull, C. L. (1943). *Principles of behavior*. New York: Appleton-Century-Crofts.
Janis, I. L. (1972). *Victims of groupthink*. Boston: Houghton Mifflin.
Jones, E. E., & Thibaut, J. (1958). Interaction goals as bases of inference in interpersonal perception. In R. Tagiuci & L. Petrillo (Eds.), *Person perception and interpersonal behavior*. Stanford, CA: Stanford University Press.
Kernberg, O. (1975). *Borderline conditions and pathological narcissism*. New York: Jason Aronson.
Kernberg, O. (1984). *Severe-personality disorders: Psychotherapeutic strategies*. New Haven: Yale University Press.
Kohut, H. (1971). *The analysis of the self*. New York: International Universities Press.
Kohut, H. (1977). *The restoration of the self*. New York: International Universities Press.
Kuhl, J. (1982). The expectancy-value approach within the theory of social motivation: Elaborations, extensions, critique. In N. T. Feather (Ed.), *Expectations and actions: Expectancy-value models in psychology* (pp. 125–160). Hillsdale, NJ: Erlbaum.
Langer, E. J. (1975). The illusion of control. *Journal of Personality and Social Psychology, 32*, 311–328.
Langer, E. J. (1978). The psychology of chance. *Journal for the Theory of Social Behavior, 7*, 185–207.
Langer, E. J., & Roth, J. (1975). Heads I win, tails it's chance: The illusion of control as a function of the sequence of outcomes in a purely chance task. *Journal of Personality and Social Psychology, 32*, 951–955.
Lasch, C. (1979). *The culture of narcissism: American life in an age of diminishing expectations*. New York: Warner Books.
Levine, M. (1966). Hypothesis behavior by humans during discrimination learning. *Journal of Experimental Psychology, 71*, 331–338.
Lewin, K. (1936). *Principles of topological psychology*. New York: McGraw-Hill.
Luborsky, L. (1977). Measuring a pervasic psychic structure in psychotherapy: The core conflictual relationship theme. In N. Freedman & S. Grand (Eds.), *Communicative structures and psychic structures* (pp. 367–395). New York: Plenum.
Luborsky, L., Crits-Christoph, P., & Mellon, J. (1986). Advent of directive measures of the transference concept. *Journal of Consulting and Clinical Psychology, 54*, 39–47.

Markus, H. (1977). Self-schemata and processing information about the self. *Journal of Personality and Social Psychology, 35*, 63–78.

Merton, R. K. (1949). *Social theory and social structure*. New York: Free Press.

Miller, G. A., Galanter, E., & Pribram, K. H. (1960). *Plans and the structure of behavior*. New York: Holt, Rinehart & Winston.

Millon, T. (1983). *Millon Clinical Multiaxial Inventory Manual* (3rd ed.). Minneapolis, MN: National Computer Systems.

Nisbett, R., & Ross, L. (1980). *Human inference: Strategies and shortcomings of social judgement*. Englewood Cliffs, NJ: Prentice-Hall.

Pyszczynski, T., & Greenberg, J. (1987). Self-regulatory perseveration and the depressive self-focusing style: A self-awareness theory of reactive depression. *Psychological Bulletin, 102*, 122–138.

Pyszczynski, T., Holt, K., & Greenberg, J. (1987). Depression, self-focused attention and expectancies for positive and negative future life events for self and others. *Journal of Personality and Social Psychology, 52*, 994–1001.

Raimy, V. (1975). *Misunderstandings of the self: Cognitive psychotherapy and the misconception hypothesis.* San Francisco: Jossey-Bass Publishers.

Rice, L. N., & Greenberg, L. S. (1984). *Patterns of change: Intensive analysis of psychotherapy process*. New York, NY: Guilford Press.

Sullivan, H. S. (1953). *The interpersonal theory of psychiatry*. New York: Norton.

Taylor, S. E., & Brown, J. O. (1988). Illusion and well-being: A social psychological perspective on mental health. *Psychological Bulletin, 103*, 193–210.

Tolman, E. C. (1932). *Purposive behavior in animals and man*. New York: Appleton-Century-Crofts.

Wachtel, P. L. (1987). *Action and insight*. New York: Guilford Publications.

Walster, E., Walster, G. W., & Berscheid, E. (1978). *Equity: Theory and research*. Boston: Allyn & Bacon.

Weiss, J., & Sampson, H. (1986). *The psychoanalytic process: Theory, clinical observation, and empirical research*. New York: Guilford Publications.

Zajonc, R. B. (1965). Social facilitation. *Science. 149*, 269–274.

Zajonc, R. B., & Sales, S. (1966). Social facilitation of dominant subordinant responses. *Journal of Experimental Social Psychology, 2*, 160–168.

AUTHOR INDEX

SUBJECT INDEX

GPSR Compliance

The European Union's (EU) General Product Safety Regulation (GPSR) is a set of rules that requires consumer products to be safe and our obligations to ensure this.

If you have any concerns about our products, you can contact us on ProductSafety@springernature.com

In case Publisher is established outside the EU, the EU authorized representative is:

Springer Nature Customer Service Center GmbH
Europaplatz 3
69115 Heidelberg, Germany

Batch number: 10844655

Printed by Printforce, the Netherlands